Semantic Structures

Current Studies in Linguistics
Samuel Jay Keyser, general editor

Semantic Structures

Ray Jackendoff

Nov/3/1991.

The MIT Press
Cambridge, Massachusetts
London, England

This book was set in Palatino by Asco Trade Typesetting Ltd., Hong Kong, and printed and bound by The Halliday Lithograph in the United States of America.

Library of Congress Cataloging-in-Publication Data

Jackendoff, Ray S.
  Semantic structures / Ray Jackendoff.
      p.   cm.—(Current studies in linguistics; 18)
  Includes bibliographical references. ⸙
  ISBN 0-262-10043-6
  1. Semantics. 2. Generative grammar. 3. Grammar, Comparative and general—Syntax.
I. Title. II. Series: Current studies in linguistics series; 18.
  P325.5.G45J3   1990
  401'.43—dc20   89-78192
                                                                         CIP

For Noam, on whose shoulders it has
been a privilege to stand

Contents

Series Foreword

We are pleased to present this book as the eighteenth volume in the series Current Studies in Linguistics.

As we have defined it, the series will offer book-length studies in linguistics and neighboring fields that further the exploration of man's ability to manipulate symbols. It will pursue the same editorial goals as its companion journal, *Linguistic Inquiry*, and will complement it by providing a format for in-depth studies beyond the scope of the professional article.

By publishing such studies, we hope the series will answer a need for intensive and detailed research that sheds new light on current theoretical issues and provides a new dimension for their resolution. Toward this end it will present books dealing with the widest range of languages and addressing the widest range of theoretical topics. From time to time and with the same ends in view, the series will include collections of significant articles covering single and selected subject areas and works primarily for use as textbooks.

Like *Linguistic Inquiry*, Current Studies in Linguistics will seek to present work of theoretical interest and excellence.

Samuel Jay Keyser

Acknowledgments

I am grateful to the many people who have offered their ears and their commentary to this material in its nascent stages. I especially wish to thank my students at Brandeis University over the past five or six years, and the students in my 1987 course at the University of Arizona. I have received important comments on various portions of the work from Dwight Bolinger, Noam Chomsky, Joe Emonds, Jerry Fodor, Jim Higginbotham, Barbara Landau, John Macnamara, Alec Marantz, Donna Jo Napoli, Jean-Roger Vergnaud, Wendy Wilkins, Edwin Williams, Maria-Luisa Zubizarreta, my Arizona colleagues Peter Culicover, Ann Farmer, David Lebeaux, Adrienne Lehrer, and Dick Oehrle, and particularly my Brandeis colleagues Jane Grimshaw, Joan Maling, Alan Prince, and Moira Yip. Jay Keyser, Beth Levin, Urpo Nikanne, and Malka Rappaport read major portions of the manuscript; their comments made the final revisions both necessary and useful. I should also acknowledge the important influences on my work of three other manuscripts whose progress I have followed while writing this: Jane Grimshaw's *Argument Structure*, Steve Pinker's *Learnability and Cognition: The Acquisition of Argument Structure*, and Jill Carrier and Janet Randall's *From Conceptual Structure to Syntax*. Finally, as usual, I apologize in advance for slighting all the work out there that I should have cited but didn't.

Other versions of parts of this work have appeared elsewhere:

Chapter 1
"What Is a Concept, That a Person Can Grasp It?" *Mind and Language* 4.1/2 (1989)
Section 1.5
"X-Bar Semantics," in *Berkeley Linguistics Society: Proceedings of the Thirteenth Annual Meeting* (1987)
Chapters 2–4, section 7.1
"The Status of Thematic Relations in Linguistic Theory," *Linguistic Inquiry* 18.3 (1987)
Section 6.1
"Distributive Location," *Sophia Linguistica* 20/21 (1986)

Sections 8.1, 10.1, 10.2
"Babe Ruth Homered His Way into the Hearts of America," in *Syntax and Semantics*, vol. 24 (1990)
Chapters 8–10
"Adjuncts," ms., Brandeis University (1987)

This research was supported in part by NSF grants IST 84-20073 and IRI 88-08286 to Brandeis University.

And, after all, there is Elise to thank for ongoing sanity.

Introduction

The closing words of Chomsky's monograph *Syntactic Structures* are these:

> ...one result of the formal study of grammatical structure is that a syntactic framework is brought to light which can support semantic analysis. Description of meaning can profitably refer to this underlying syntactic framework, although systematic semantic considerations are apparently not helpful in determining it in the first place. The notion of "structural meaning" as opposed to "lexical meaning", however, appears to be quite suspect, and it is questionable that the grammatical devices available in language are used consistently enough so that meaning can be assigned to them directly. Nevertheless, we do find many important correlations, quite naturally, between syntactic structure and meaning; or, to put it differently, we find that the grammatical devices are used quite systematically. These correlations could form part of the subject matter for a more general theory of language concerned with syntax and semantics and their points of connection. (Chomsky 1957, 108)

To develop the "more general theory" that Chomsky envisions, one must confront two basic problems, which might be called the Problem of Meaning and the Problem of Correspondence. The Problem of Meaning is to characterize the phenomena that a theory of meaning is to account for, and to develop a formal treatment of semantic intuitions. In particular, a formal theory of meaning must be expressive enough to account for the distinctions of meaning made by language users, and for the semantic relations—including inference—that speakers can draw among words, phrases, and sentences. It must also provide the basis on which speakers relate words, phrases, and sentences to their understanding of the nonlinguistic world, so that they can make judgments of reference and truth.

The Problem of Correspondence is to characterize the relationship between the formal treatment of meaning and the formal structure of syntax. These two problems are clearly not entirely separate. One's choice of semantic formalism has an immediate effect on possible solutions to the Problem of Correspondence. Other things being equal, we should rate more highly a solution to the Problem of Meaning that permits a more perspicuous solution to the Problem of Correspondence. On the other hand, one cannot work out a theory of meaning solely for the purpose of simplifying the Problem of Correspondence: there are many other boundary conditions that must simultaneously be satisfied.

The present study is an exploration of the interaction between these two problems. Much of my research over the past fifteen years has been concerned with laying the foundations of a theory of meaning called Conceptual Semantics, using first principles parallel to those that motivate generative syntax and phonology. *Semantics and Cognition* (*S&C*) and *Consciousness and the Computational Mind* (*C&CM*) situate the study of meaning in an overall psychological framework, integrating it not only with linguistic theory but also with the theories of perception, cognition, and conscious experience. However, for reasons of space and emphasis, these works did not expand the coverage of linguistic phenomena much beyond the analyses I had published in the early and middle 1970s. The time is now ripe to turn back to language and work out the consequences of Conceptual Semantics for a richer range of lexical items and syntactic constructions.

The book is organized into three parts. Part I begins with a précis of the relevant arguments in *S&C* and *C&CM*, setting out the basic parameters of the formalization of meaning and some general results. It then works out some fundamental aspects of the treatment of argument structure and thematic roles, in particular the present theory's counterpart of the θ-Criterion. It also deals with issues of lexical structure, including how the various syntactic frames in which a lexical item occurs are correlated with alternative meanings.

Part II is concerned with the Problem of Meaning—specifically, with extending the range of semantic fields encompassed by the Conceptual Semantics formalism. These chapters cover a miscellany of topics, chosen partly for their own intrinsic interest, and partly for their utility in dealing with phenomena to be addressed in part III, but also as illustration of the methodology by which one decides among alternative formalizations of meaning within the framework. It is shown that a number of new fields are profitably analyzed by adding features to existing conceptual primitives, rather than by introducing altogether new primitives. More significantly, it develops that meaning, like phonological structure, is organized into independent but interacting *tiers*, each of which contributes a different class of conceptual distinctions to meaning as a whole.

Part III deals with the Problem of Correspondence. The first three chapters address a wide range of adjunct constructions in English. The overall effect is to disrupt the rather tidy view of the syntax-semantics correspondence worked out in *S&C* and reviewed in part I: alongside the canonical relations of syntactic to semantic arguments that are mediated by the head of a phrase, there prove to be numerous other strategies in the language for syntactically encoding thematic roles. In compensation for this additional complexity, though, it turns out to be possible to drastically simplify the argument structure specified by lexical items and to work out very general principles for the linking of complements to semantic argument positions; this is the topic of the final chapter.

In the passage quoted above, Chomsky rejects the assumption that syntax is totally determined by the structure of meaning, an assumption that underlies such otherwise divergent approaches as Montague Grammar and Langacker's (1986) Cognitive Grammar. To a certain extent, this assumption has also permeated contemporary Government-Binding (GB) Theory: despite a rather rudimentary conception of the semantic theory behind theta-roles, great reliance is increasingly placed on the θ-Criterion and the Projection Principle of Chomsky (1981)—and even Baker's (1988) more stringent Uniformity of Theta Assignment Hypothesis—for determining analyses of syntactic structure. With the more substantial understanding of semantic structure achieved here, we can better assess the extent to which the semantics determines or constrains the syntax. We also find areas where semantics rather naturally takes over some of the work normally attributed to syntax. The upshot is that the view taken by Chomsky in *Syntactic Structures* is in some ways closer to the truth than that in, say, *Aspects of the Theory of Syntax*: some parts of the semantics map fairly nicely into syntax—though still with all sorts of marked exceptions—but other parts of the semantics receive comparatively unsystematic syntactic realization. Thus a better articulation of semantic theory and its connections to syntax has significant repercussions for the autonomy of syntax.

Because this approach to the syntax-semantics connection is somewhat novel, certain very general questions arise frequently. Here are some of the more common ones.

"Aren't you introducing a lot of new machinery? How do you know it won't proliferate, unconstrained?"

I offer two lines of reply. First, there just are a lot of parts to meaning. Consider that perhaps a hundred thousand lexical items, each with a distinct meaning, must be projected into the five syntactic categories N, V, A, P, and Adv. I think it is therefore reasonable to expect a much richer formal system for semantics than for syntax.

Second, I consider the state of development of this theory to be comparable to the state of generative syntax in the early 1960s, say the time of Lees's *Grammar of English Nominalizations* and Klima's "Negation in English." As in that period in syntax, the emphasis at the moment is on descriptive power—tackling a wide range of phenomena, being able to state alternative solutions with some precision, and finding criteria to decide among them. In the case of generative syntax, it was only through some years of experience in applying the formal machinery to a broad range of constructions that the issues bearing on the proper way of constraining the theory began to emerge. I believe that similar experience in semantic description is necessary before we can fully apprehend the right directions to pursue in constraining the theory. So, although I keep issues of explanation constantly in mind, they are for the moment somewhat secondary to formulating an interesting description of the phenomena. One can hope, however, that having the experience of syntax and phonology as a guide will help speed the process of finding the right questions to ask.

"How do you know your putative semantic primitives really are primitive? Mightn't there be an infinite regress?"

Again, there are two lines of reply. Of course we don't know in advance if we have reached bottom. However, every time a further decomposition emerges for elements previously thought to be primitive, it reveals further layers of generalization and explanation. For example, my previous work treated the notion of causation as a semantically primitive function CAUSE. Chapter 7, however, shows that this function decomposes into a pair of more primitive functions, each of which carries a number of features. In turn, these functions and features prove to run through broad swaths of the language, precisely as one would want in an explanatory theory.

Recall also the experience from everyone's favorite hard science, physics. The discovery of the periodic table of elements was one kind of decomposition of substances into primitives; but the atoms then turned out to decompose further into a nucleus and electrons, the nucleus decomposed into protons and neutrons, the protons and neutrons decomposed into quarks, and the quarks themselves are sets of features (spin, color, charm, etc.). Do the physicists worry about never hitting bottom? I don't know, but it doesn't stop them from trying to achieve further explanation.

"I'm a syntactician. Why should I get involved with all these strange semantic solutions? Besides, suppose the problems we're working on turn out to be purely syntactic after all—won't I have wasted my time?"

My reply to this is simple: You are perfectly free to pursue science according to your own taste. My feeling though, is that this strategy essentially amounts to looking for a lost coin under the streetlamp, because that's where we can see. The strategy I'm adopting here is to build more lamps.

PART I
Basic Machinery

Chapter 1
Overview of Conceptual Semantics

1.1 E-Concepts and I-Concepts

This study is concerned with the form of knowledge that ordinary language calls *concepts, thoughts,* or *ideas* and with how such knowledge is expressed in the syntax of natural language. As the investigation of conceptual knowledge is to be grounded in first principles parallel to those for generative syntactic and phonological theory, I would like to begin by making explicit these first principles and the extent of the parallelism.

There is a fundamental tension in the ordinary language term *concept*. On one hand, it is something out there in the world: "the Newtonian concept of mass" is something that is spoken of as though it exists independently of who actually knows or grasps it. Likewise, "grasping a concept" evokes comparison to grasping a physical object, except that one does it with one's mind instead of one's hand. On the other hand, a concept is spoken of as an entity within one's head, a private entity, a product of the imagination that can be conveyed to others only by means of language, gesture, drawing, or some other imperfect means of communication.

Precisely the same tension has been discussed by Chomsky (1986) with respect to the term *language*. He differentiates the two poles as *E-language* —external language, the language seen as external artifact—versus *I-language*—internal language, the language as a body of internally encoded information.[1] I will adopt Chomsky's terminology and speak of E-concepts versus I-concepts.

For Chomsky's purpose—the characterization of the mental resources that make possible human knowledge of language—the notion of I-language rather than E-language is the appropriate focus of inquiry. Chomsky argues this point at length in Chomsky 1986, and he has in fact been quite explicit on this point at least since Chomsky 1965. The new terminology only helps make clearer an old and forceful point.

However, the choice of I-language as the focus of Chomsky's linguistic theory does not rest on a priori argumentation alone. It rests primarily on the suitability of this notion to support scientific investigation into the issues that flow from the overarching goals of the inquiry. To the extent that generative linguistics has indeed been successful in increasing our understanding of the human language capacity, the choice of I-language as the object of inquiry has been vindicated. (And notice that disagreement, even violent disagreement, among its practitioners does not diminish the fact that progress has been made. It stands to reason that, at any particular moment, the most time and energy are being spent at the frontiers of understanding, not in the areas that have been settled. Any linguist will acknowledge that the frontiers have expanded considerably over the past three decades.)

an extension of Chomsky's goals.

My purpose—the characterization of the mental resources that make possible human knowledge and experience of the world—is conceived as an extension of Chomsky's goals. Accordingly, an important boundary condition on my enterprise is that it be in all respects compatible with the world view of generative linguistics. In particular, it is crucial to choose I-concepts rather than E-concepts as the focus for a compatible theory of knowledge.

1.2 First Principles of I-Conceptual Knowledge

syntax and creativity of language.

The fundamental motivation behind generative syntax is of course the creativity of language—the fact that speakers of a language can understand and create an indefinitely large number of sentences that they have never heard before. It follows from this observation that a speaker's repertoire of syntactic structures cannot be characterized just as a finite list of sentences. Nor, of course, can it be characterized as an infinite set of possible sentences of the language, because it must be instantiated in a finite (albeit large) brain. Rather, a speaker's potential repertoire of syntactic

syntactic structures.

structures must be mentally encoded in terms of a finite set of primitives and a finite set of principles of combination that collectively describe (or generate) the class of possible sentences. In speaking or understanding a sentence, then, a language user is taken to be creating or invoking a mental information structure, the syntactic structure of the sentence, which is organized in conformance with the principles of syntactic structure.

grammar of sentential concepts.

Parallel arguments obtain for I-concepts, in two different ways. First, a language user presumably is not gratuitously producing and parsing syntactic structures for their own sake: a syntactic structure encodes an I-concept (or a "thought"). On the basis of this concept, the language user can perform any number of tasks, for instance checking the sentence's consistency with other linguistic or extralinguistic knowledge, performing inferences, formulating a response, or translating the sentence into another language. Corresponding to the indefinitely large variety of syntactic structures, then, there must be an indefinitely large variety of concepts that can be invoked in the production and comprehension of sentences. It follows that the repertoire of I-concepts expressed by sentences cannot be mentally encoded as a list, but must be characterized in terms of a finite set of mental primitives and a finite set of principles of mental combination that collectively describe the set of possible I-concepts expressed by sentences. For convenience, I will refer to these two sets together as the *grammar of sentential concepts*.

It is widely assumed, and I will take for granted, that the basic units out of which a sentential concept is constructed are the concepts expressed by the words in the sentence, that is, *lexical* concepts. It is easy to see that lexical I-concepts too are subject to the argument from creativity. For instance, consider the concept expressed by the word *dog*. Someone who knows this concept, upon encountering an indefinitely large variety of objects, will be able to judge whether or not they are dogs. Thus the concept cannot be encoded as a list of the dogs one has previously encountered; nor, because the brain is finite, can it be a list of all dogs there ever have been and will be, or of all possible dogs. Rather, it must be some sort of finite schema that can be compared with the mental representations of arbitrary new objects to produce a judgment of conformance or nonconformance.

Two immediate qualifications. First, there may well be objects for which people's judgments disagree. This does not entail that there is no concept *dog* or that people do not know the meaning of the word. Rather, since our concern is with people's internalized schemas, we simply conclude that people may have schemas for *dog* that differ in various details, and that these differences too may bear examination.

Second, there may be novel objects such that one cannot judge clearly whether they are dogs or not. ("It's sort of a dog and sort of a wolf.") Again, this does not necessarily challenge the idea that one has an internalized schema. Rather, from such examples we conclude that there is a potential degree of indeterminacy either in the lexical concept itself, or in the procedure for comparing it with mental representations of novel objects, or in both. Such indeterminacies are in fact rampant in lexical concepts; section 1.7 will discuss the characteristics of conceptual knowledge that give rise to them.

To sum up so far: paralleling the argument from creativity to the necessity for principles or rules in syntactic knowledge, we have argued (1) that sentential concepts cannot be listed but must be mentally generated on the basis of a finite set of primitives and principles of combination; (2) that lexical concepts cannot of a list of instances but must consist of finite schemas that can be creatively compared (i.e. in rule-governed fashion) to novel inputs.

The second major issue in the foundation of syntactic theory flows from the problem of acquisition: how can a child acquire the rules of syntax on the basis of the fragmentary evidence available? In particular, how does the child induce *rules* from *instances* of well-formed sentences? This question is rendered especially pointed by the fact that the community of generative linguists, with all their collective intelligence, have not been able to fully determine the syntactic rules of English in over thirty years of research, supported by centuries of traditional grammatical description; yet of course every normal child exposed to English masters the grammar by the age of ten or so. This apparent paradox of language acquisition motivates the central hypothesis of generative linguistics: that children come to the task of language learning equipped with an innate Universal Grammar that narrowly restricts the options available for the grammar they are trying to acquire. The driving issue in generative linguistics, then, is to determine the form of Universal Grammar, consonant both with the variety of human languages and also with their learnability.

The parallel argument can be made for the logical problem of concept acquisition, in both the sentential and lexical domains. For the former case, consider that the language learner must acquire not only the principles for constructing syntactically well-formed sentences but also the principles for constructing the corresponding sentential concepts. Like the rules of syntax, these principles must be acquired on the basis of some combination of linguistic experience, nonlinguistic experience, and innate constraints on possible principles. As in syntax, then, an important part of our task is to determine what aspects of the grammar of sentential concepts are learned and what aspects are innate; the innate parts must be sufficiently rich to make it possible to acquire the rest.

Turning to lexical concepts, consider that one is capable of acquiring during one's life an indefinitely large number of concepts, each of them on the basis of rather fragmentary evidence. (What evidence might be involved in learning the concepts expressed by such words as *bevel, prosaic, phonology, justice,* or *belief*?) Again, since lexical concepts must be encoded as unconscious schemas rather than lists of instances (and in the case of the words above it is not even clear what *could* be presented as instances), lexical concept acquisition too presents a problem parallel to the acquisition of syntax. As in syntax, we adopt the hypothesis that one's stock of lexical concepts is constructed from an innate basis of possible concepts, modulated by the contribution of linguistic and nonlinguistic experience.

But now the argument from creativity applies in a new way. If there is an indefinitely large stock of possible lexical concepts, and the innate basis for acquiring them must be encoded in a finite brain, we are forced to conclude that the innate basis must consist of a set of generative principles —a group of primitives and principles of combination that collectively determine the set of lexical concepts. This implies in turn that most if not all lexical concepts are composite, that is, that they can be decomposed in terms of the primitives and principles of combination of the innate "grammar of lexical concepts." Learning a lexical concept, then, is to be thought *[learning c of a lexical concept.]* of as constructing a composite expression within the grammar of lexical concepts, associating it with phonological and syntactic structures, and storing them together in long-term memory as a usable unit. (This contrasts sharply with Jerry Fodor's view that lexical concepts are cognitively primitive monads linked with each other by meaning postulates. The Appendix to this chapter compares the two positions.)

Given the parallelism in first principles, I therefore believe that the central *[parallelism of syntax and semantics.]* issue of the theory of conceptual knowledge ought to parallel that of the theory of syntax: What are the innate units and principles of organization that make human lexical and sentential concepts both possible in all their variety and also learnable on the basis of some realistic combination of linguistic and nonlinguistic experience?[2]

1.3 Three Models for the Description of Meaning

The preceding section has used the expression *concept* operationally to *[concept. an operational definition]* mean essentially "a mental representation that can serve as the meaning of a linguistic expression." In the present framework, then, the act of understanding a sentence S—recovering its meaning—is to be regarded as placing S in correspondence with a mentally encoded concept C, which has internal structure derivable from the syntactic structure and lexical items of S. On the basis of C, one can draw inferences, that is, construct further *[✳]* concepts that are logical entailments of C. One can also compare C with *[evaluation of the meaning of C sentence.]* other concepts retrieved from memory ("Do I know this already?"; "Is this consistent with what I believe?") and with conceptual structures derived from sensory modalities ("Is this what's going on?"; "Is that what I should be looking for?"). That is, the meaning of the sentence can be evaluated with respect to what one believes and perceives.

The idea that a meaning is a sort of mental representation is, of course, not universally accepted. Perhaps the most prestigious tradition in the study of meaning grows out of Frege's "On Sense and Reference" (1892), where he very carefully disassociates the "sense" of an expression—what he takes to be an objective, publicly available entity—from the "ideas" that users of the expression carry in their heads, which are subjective and variable. Frege's notion of "sense" underpins the approach to meaning in *truth-conditional semantics* (including model-theoretic semantics and Situation Semantics as subcases). This is seen clearly, for instance, in the following quotation from David Lewis's foundational paper "General Semantics."

> I distinguish two topics: first, the description of possible languages or grammars as abstract semantic systems whereby symbols are associated with aspects of the world; and second, the description of the

psychological and sociological facts whereby a particular one of these abstract semantic systems is the one used by a person or population. Only confusion comes of mixing these two topics. This paper deals almost entirely with the first (Lewis 1972, 170)

It is hard to find a clearer statement that the purposes of truth-conditional semantics are different from those of generative linguistics. To be sure, both generative grammar and truth-conditional semantics treat language as a formal system. But they differ radically in the goals they wish to accomplish through such treatment. The avowed purpose of truth-conditional semantics is to explicate Truth, a relation between language and reality, independent of language users. In turn, truth-conditions can be treated as speaker-independent only if both reality *and* the language that describes it are speaker-independent as well. Hence a truth-conditional semantics in the Tarskian or Davidsonian sense requires a theory of E-language, of language as an abstract artifact extrinsic to speakers.

As stressed in section 1.1, the purpose of generative grammar has always been to explicate I-language, the principles internalized by speakers that constitute knowledge of a language. A typical statement of generative linguistic theory, say "Sentence S is grammatical in Language L because of Principle P," is taken to be shorthand for a psychological claim, roughly "Speakers of Language L treat Sentence S as grammatical because their knowledge of Language L includes Principle P," subject to the usual caveats about attentional and processing limitations. A compatible theory of meaning must therefore concern the principles internalized in speakers that permit them to understand sentences, draw inferences, and make judgments of truth: it must be a theory of I-semantics, not E-semantics. Within a theory of I-semantics, a statement in the Tarskian vein like "Sentence S in Language L is true if and only if condition C is met" is taken as shorthand for something like "Speakers of Language L treat Sentence S as true if and only if their construal of the world meets Condition C," and it is subject to similar caveats about attentional and processing limitations. This is the basis of the approach of *Conceptual Semantics,* in which a level of mental representation called *conceptual structure* is seen as the form in which speakers encode their construal of the world.

It is sometimes proposed that there is no inherent conflict between the two approaches to semantics. One is about the way the world *is,* and the other is about the way we *grasp* the world. They might lead to altogether different insights—hopefully complementary ones. I see nothing wrong with this conclusion in principle. The difficulty, however, is one of terminological imperialism, as exemplified by Lewis's (1972) widely quoted slogan to the effect that the study of "Mentalese"—in effect I-semantics—isn't *really* semantics. Along with this goes the implication that what the I-semanticist and the psychologist are doing isn't really *anything* worth doing. For my part, I don't care what the enterprise is called; but notice that relativistic physics *is* a way of doing physics, not some curious nonenterprise, and it does share most of the basic terminology of Newtonian physics despite a radical conceptual restructuring. Such, I suggest, is the case in the contrast of E-semantics and I-semantics.

It is also sometimes suggested that my characterization of model-theoretic semantics as a type of E-semantics is unfair. In principle, model-theoretic semantics is neutral between E-semantics and I-semantics; even if the approach was developed with E-semantics in mind, we are always free to choose a model that conforms to psychological constraints and thereby to produce a model-theoretic I-semantics. Again I agree—in principle. But to my knowledge, all model-theoretic semantics, other than a few exceptions such as the work of Bach (1986a) and Verkuyl (1989), has in practice been E-semantics. And, of course, the project of determining a psychologically defensible model theory is pretty much equivalent to the enterprise of Conceptual Semantics, that is, finding out how human beings actually encode their construal of the world. So again, I don't want to make heavy weather of the terminology. If some readers are more comfortable thinking of Conceptual Semantics as a very particular and eccentric brand of model-theoretic semantics, I have no objection. It is the *psychological* claim, not the name of the theory, that is crucial. (See chapters 2, 3, and 5 of Jackendoff 1983 (henceforth *S&C*) and chapter 7 of Jackendoff 1987a (henceforth *C&CM*), for amplification of these points, in particular for discussion of Lewis's frequently cited attack on the study of "Mentalese.")

It is next necessary to differentiate Conceptual Semantics from Fodor's (1975) *"Language of Thought" Hypothesis.* On the face of it Fodor's position seems closer to mine: his purpose is to understand the character of mind. Unlike the model theorists, he is committed to a combinatorial mental representation in terms of which language users make inferences and formulate responses. Moreover, Fodor stresses that the performance of these tasks must be explained purely by virtue of the form of the representations. There can be no appeal to what the representations "mean." His argument is that the buck has to stop somewhere: if one is to characterize the brain as a computational device, driven by the syntax of internal representations, an appeal to meaning in the outside world amounts to an invocation of magic.

So far Fodor's story is altogether compatible with Conceptual Semantics. But now it splits in two directions. On one hand, Fodor argues (1980) for "methodological solipsism"—the idea that the only causal determinants of behavior (including inference) are the formal properties of internal representations. This is again consistent with Conceptual Semantics, in which rules of inference do not reach out from conceptual structures to the "world" but are rather confined to examining conceptual structures themselves.

However, another thread in Fodor's work (seen especially in Fodor 1987) is his insistence on "Intentional Realism," the idea that the mental representations over which these computations take place still *do* have further semantic content—that they are representations of propositions with real-world reference and truth-value. This view allegedly makes contact with Chomsky's notion of Universal Grammar in the following way:

> It is, however, important to the Neocartesian [i.e. Chomskian] story that what is innately represented should constitute a bona fide object of propositional attitudes.... Now, the notion of computation is intrinsically connected to such semantical concepts as implication, confirmation, and logical consequence. Specifically, a computation is a transformation of representations which respects these sorts of semantic relations.... So, Chomsky's account of language learning is the story of how innate endowment and perceptual experience interact *in virtue of their respective contents* [Fodor's italics]. (Fodor 1983, 4–5)

I find this a serious misconstrual of generative grammar. Look at the representations of, say, phonology. It makes little sense to think of the rules of phonology as propositional; for instance it is strange to say that English speakers know the proposition, *true in the world independent of speakers of English,* that in English syllable-initial voiceless consonants aspirate before stress. This amounts to an appeal to the properties of E-language. In generative phonology as it is conducted by its practitioners, the rule of aspiration is a principle of internal computation, not a fact about the world. "Such semantical concepts as implication, confirmation, and logical consequence" seem curiously irrelevant. In short, the notion of computation need not have anything to do with "respecting semantic relations," at least in the domains of phonology and syntax.

If one has hesitations about this argument with respect to phonology, we may also consider a slightly more exotic cognitive domain, the understanding of music. As shown in Lerdahl and Jackendoff 1983, the factors that make a piece of music cohere for a listener into something beyond a mere sequence of notes involve complex internal computations over abstract mental representations of the piece. Fodor's insistence on respecting semantic relations seems totally out of place here. These abstract structures are part of mental life, but one would hardly want to make a metaphysical claim about there being something "real" in the world that constitutes the "propositional content" of these representations.

The question at issue, then, is whether conceptual structure is somehow different from phonology, syntax, and music—whether, when we enter the domain of meaning, the rules of the game should be changed, so that propositional content rather than computational form ought to be the focus of inquiry. Fodor's position, as I understand it, is that the generalizations (or laws) of psychology are intentional (that is, concern the propositional content of representations), but that the mechanisms that instantiate these generalizations are merely formal computations that have no access to propositional content. The fact that these computations preserve semantic properties comes from the fact that the formal structures mirror the structure of the content in detail. In fact, Fodor argues for the combinatorial character of mental representations precisely on the grounds that they must mimic what he takes to be the undeniable combinatoriality of propositional content. Put in present terms, his position is that we *grasp* the world the way we do precisely because that is the way the world *is*. (This argument is perhaps clearest in the Appendix to Fodor 1987.) What Fodor appears to require, then, is a marriage between the Realism of truth-conditional semantics and the mentalism of generative grammar—that is, a unified theory of E-semantics and I-semantics, mediated by the relation of intentionality, which even to Fodor is mysterious.[3]

Conceptual Semantics, on the other hand, is concerned most directly with the form of the internal mental representations that constitute conceptual structure and with the formal relations between this level and other levels of representation. The theory of conceptual structure is thus taken to be entirely parallel to the theory of syntactic or phonological structure. The computation of inference, like for instance the computation of rhyme in phonology, is a matter internal to the organism.

But for Fodor, as for the model theorists, such an inquiry does not count as semantics: he requires a theory of semantics to include a Realist account of truth-conditions and inference. Once again, I don't care too much about terminology. I would rather that the enterprise be judged on its merits than dismissed because it doesn't address issues that someone calls the True Issues of Semantics. If one prefers to call the enterprise logical or conceptual syntax, or the "Syntax of Thought" Hypothesis, that's fine with me.[4] We should be clear, though, that it is in principle as different from "straight" syntax (the grammar of NPs, VPs, etc.) as straight syntax is from phonology.

How do the two approaches differ empirically? The difference is that Fodor insists that all combinatorial properties of I-concepts must be mirrored in Reality, while a theory of pure I-semantics is not necessarily subject to that constraint. As will be seen throughout this study, there are many structural properties of Conceptual Semantics that make little sense as properties of Reality, but a great deal of sense as properties of mind. I will therefore conclude that Fodor's insistence on Intentional Realism is misguided for the purpose of doing scientific psychology.

(Note that this conclusion is not inconsistent with Fodor's observation, seconded by Dennett (1987), that Intentional Realism is an extremely useful stance for dealing with people in ordinary life. But "folk physics" is a good stance for ordinary life, too. That does not make it a productive constraint for doing scientific physics. So why get mired in "folk psychology" when studying the mind?)

To conclude this section, I should mention the relation of Conceptual Semantics to a program of research called *Cognitive Grammar* or *Cognitive Semantics* (e.g. Fauconnier 1984; Langacker 1986; Herskovits 1986; Lakoff 1987). This work, like Conceptual Semantics, is concerned with the mental representation of the world and its relation to language. It shares with Conceptual Semantics a concern with the encoding of spatial concepts and their extension to other conceptual fields (see section 1.6). Some work in this tradition, especially that of Talmy (1980, 1983, 1985), has provided important insights and analyses to the present framework. Conceptual Semantics differs from Cognitive Grammar, however, in that (1) it is committed to an autonomous level of syntactic representation rather than to its abandonment; (2) it is committed to rigorous formalism, insofar as possible, on the grounds that formal treatment is the best way of rendering a theory testable; (3) it makes contact with relevant results in perceptual psychology rather than leaving such relationships tacit; (4) it is committed to exploring issues of learnability and hence to the possibility of a strong innate formal basis for concept acquisition.

1.4 Organization of the Grammar

For concreteness, I will assume an overall organization of the mental information structure involved in language as diagrammed in (1).

(1)

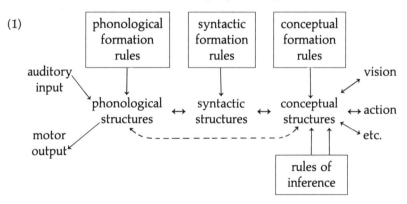

This organization includes three autonomous levels of structure: phonological, syntactic, and conceptual. Each of these has its own characteristic primitives and principles of combination and its own organization into subcomponents, such as segmental phonology, intonation contour, and metrical grid in phonology, and D-Structure, S-Structure, Phonetic Form (PF), and Logical Form (LF) (or counterparts in other theories) in syntax. Each of the levels is described by a set of *formation rules* that generates the well-formed structures of the level.

The grammar also contains sets of *correspondence rules* that link the levels. The correspondence of phonological structure to syntactic structure is specified by one such set. This is, for instance, the locus of "readjustment rules" such as cliticization and the resegmentation of sentences like (2). Notice that the labels of categories in the syntactic structure are chosen from the syntactic vocabulary, whereas those in the phonological structure are phonological in character.

(2) a. *Syntactic structure*

  [$_S$ This is [$_{NP}$ the cat [$_S$ that ate [$_{NP}$ the rat [$_S$ that ate the cheese]]]]]

  b. *Phonological structure*

  [$_{IntPhr}$ This is the cat] [$_{IntPhr}$ that ate the rat] [$_{IntPhr}$ that ate the cheese]

An explicit theory of the syntax-phonology correspondence appears in Selkirk 1984; see also Gee and Grosjean 1983 and *C&CM*, section 5.7 and appendix A.

The correspondence of syntactic and conceptual structures is specified by what used to be called "projection rules" (Katz and Fodor 1963), which determine the relation of syntactic structure to meaning. In addition, if there are aspects of meaning that are determined directly by phonological structure without syntactic intervention, these can be captured by a third set of correspondence rules, indicated by the dashed line in (1). (A candidate for such a phenomenon is the interpretation of intonation in English, which is governed by phonological rather than syntactic domains.)

Figure (1) also includes correspondence rules between the linguistic levels and nonlinguistic domains. On one end, there must be a mapping from the acoustic analysis provided by the auditory system into phonological structure; this mapping is the subject matter of acoustic phonetics. There must also be a mapping from phonological structure into motor commands to the vocal tract, the domain of articulatory phonetics. On the other end, there must be mappings between conceptual structure and other forms of mental representation that encode, for instance, the output of the visual faculty and the input to the formulation of action. One such representation will be mentioned briefly in section 1.7.1.

Since conceptual structure is the domain of mental representation over which inference can be defined, figure (1) also includes a component called *rules of inference*, which maps conceptual structures into conceptual structures. I include in this component not only rules of logical inference but also rules of invited inference, pragmatics, and heuristics: whatever differences there may be among these categories of rules, they are all defined over the same level of mental representation. That is, there is no proprietary level of "semantic representation" at which only logical properties of sentences are encoded, with other "pragmatic" properties reserved for a different level. (This is argued in detail in *S&C*, chapters 5 and 6.)

It should be pointed out that, under the view being laid out here, the level of conceptual structure is not completely language-dependent, since it serves as an interface between linguistic information and information germane to other capacities such as vision and action. I assume, on grounds of evolutionary conservatism, that nonlinguistic organisms—both higher animals and babies—also possess a level of conceptual structure in their mental repertoire, perhaps not as rich as ours, but formally similar in many respects. The difference between us and the beasts is that we have evolved a capacity to process syntactic and phonological structures, as well as the mappings from them to conceptual structure and to the auditory and motor peripheries. These mappings are what permit us a relatively overt realization of conceptual structure—language—that is unavailable to other organisms.

Figure (1) as it stands contains no explicit lexical component. Where is the lexicon in this picture? Under the standard view of the lexicon, a lexical item establishes a correspondence between well-formed fragments of phonological, syntactic, and conceptual structure; that is, the lexicon is a part of the correspondence rule component. Similarly, rules of morphology in general may have phonological parts (how an affix is pronounced, how it affects stress, and so on), syntactic parts (what lexical category an affix is attached to and the lexical category of the resultant), and conceptual parts (what kinds of meanings the affix can be applied to and the meaning of the resultant). Thus we can regard each component in figure (1) as divided into lexical principles (those that apply within words) and extralexical principles (those that apply to domains larger than the word level). However, the basic alphabet of primitives and principles of combination is shared by the two subcomponents. For instance, Selkirk (1982) has argued that the syntactic part of morphology, or word formation, consists essentially of an extension of the principles of X-bar syntax down below the word level. Similarly, in phonology, the lexical and extralexical principles of stress assignment, though different in details, deal in exactly the same kinds of formal entities.

In parallel fashion, we can ask about the relation between the grammar of sentential concepts and the grammar of lexical concepts, both of which are subsumed under the rubric "conceptual formation rules" in figure (1). Gruber (1965), *S&C*, and indeed the generative semanticists (McCawley

1968a, Postal 1970; Lakoff 1971) argue that the semantic combinations that can be expressed through syntactic phrases can in many cases also be incorporated into lexical conceptual structures. For instance, to the extent that *two times* paraphrases *twice*, or *cause to die* paraphrases *kill*, or *break violently* paraphrases *smash*, or *give away in exchange for money* paraphrases *sell*, the extralexical conceptual structures expressed by the paraphrases must be reproduced internal to unitary lexical items.[5] That is, the grammars of sentential concepts and of lexical concepts interpenetrate in much the same way as do the grammars of, say, sentential and lexical stress: they share many of the same primitives and principles of combination, even if they differ in details. In short, the division of the overall grammar into three independent levels linked by correspondence rules is crosscut by a subsidiary division of each component into lexical versus extralexical principles.

A final remark on (1) might be in order. One remnant of the Katz-Postal (1964) Hypothesis has survived into the lore of contemporary generative grammar: the idea that the creative capacity of the language is invested in the syntax, and that phonology and semantics are "interpretive" components that derive their respective structures from some level or another of syntactic structure. (This is seen clearly in the usual construal of GB Theory, for instance, where PF and LF are taken to be derived from S-Structure and further components map these into phonology and "meaning" respectively.) The organization proposed in (1), by contrast, eliminates this syntactocentrism. It treats the three levels as equally "creative"; none is derived from the others. Rather, they are autonomous structures, placed in correspondence with each other by further independent rule components. This is clearly the correct approach to the syntax-phonology correspondence, given the autonomous phonological grids, planes, and so forth of modern phonological theory. The usual "interpretive" approach can be seen in this light as a historical relic of *SPE* (Chomsky and Halle 1968), where phonological form looked essentially like a more detailed syntactic surface structure. I suggest that the same is true of the syntax-semantics correspondence. As long as there was no independent characterization of conceptual structure, one could only "derive" semantics from syntax by "projection rules." However, with the introduction of an autonomous generative component that characterizes conceptual form, and particularly if conceptual form is not language-dependent, the relation comes properly to be seen as a correspondence rather than a derivation.

1.5 Intuitions about Lexical Relations

The rest of this chapter lays out in a preliminary way some of the basic parameters of conceptual structure. One of the first problems we encounter is, What counts as a lexical item? At one extreme, it is fairly clear that we want to count genuinely homonymous items such as the river *bank* and the savings *bank* as separate lexical items. At the other extreme, it is fairly clear that words that differ only in inflectional suffix, such as *dog* and *dogs*, should count as alternate forms of the same lexical item. In between are a host of different cases that are not so clear. Here are a few.

A sort of case we will be heavily concerned with in this study involves uses of a verb in different syntactic frames. Examples appear in (3)–(6).

(3) a. The window broke.
    b. Bill broke the window.

(4) a. Harry climbed the mountain.
    b. Harry climbed down the mountain.

(5) a. Sue believes that Joe likes her.
    b. Sue believes Joe to like her.
    c. Sue believes in the dictatorship of the proletariat.

(6) a. Max looked at the insects.
    b. Max looked for the insects.
    c. Max looked smart.
    d. It looks at though we'd better leave.

Each of these requires its own story. The action described in (3a) is also described in (3b), but the latter contains an extra element, namely Bill's bringing that action about. Thus there is a systematic relation between the two sentences, and we would want to say that the two uses of *break* are therefore related, though possibly not identical. In (4), the first example involves Harry going *up* the mountain, while the second patently does not. Yet we have the sense that the verbs *climb* are still not unrelated. In (5), the first two sentences are virtually synonymous, so it seems clear that these two syntactic frames use (essentially) the same lexical item *believe*. However, what about (5c)? Does this frame use the same word, a different word, or "sort of" the same word? Similarly, in (6), what is the relation, if any, among the different uses of *look*? In (6a), the insects are there under Max's gaze; in (6b), Max is gazing about in search of insects; in (6c), Max is if anything under someone else's gaze and being judged by that person; in (6d), the notion of gaze is largely gone but the notion of judgment remains. Of these four uses, (6a) and (6b) seem relatively close but not identical, (6c) and (6d) seem relatively close but not identical, and the two pairs seem in turn more distantly related to each other, if at all. The formal theory of lexical concepts must permit us to capture and explain these intuitions.

One question we should be asking is how many different uses of a lexical item have to be listed in the lexicon at all. One case in which we probably do not want to make any lexical distinction is in the uses of a verb with or without optional place and time phrases, as in (7).

(7) a. Harry bought a yoyo in Chicago.
         Harry bought a yoyo.
     b. The clock ran down on Tuesday.
         The clock ran down.

For a more radical case, consider the uses of *ham sandwich* and *Ollie North* in (8).

(8) a. [One waitress says to another:]
         The ham sandwich over in the corner wants some more coffee.
         (after Nunberg 1979)
     b. The candidate Ollie Northed her interview.
         (after Clark and Clark 1979)

It is clear, I assume, that the lexicon of English does not include a use of *ham sandwich* that denotes a person, nor does it include a transitive verb *to Ollie North*. Rather, sentences such as (8a, b) manage to be comprehensible by virtue of very general "rules of construal" or "rules of pragmatics." Such rules permit an NP that normally denotes X to denote instead an individual (in (8a)) or an action (in (8b)) that is contextually or characteristically associated with X. Since these principles apply so widely, it would be stupid to insist that their outputs be listed as potential lexical meanings, or to use (8) as evidence that *ham sandwich* and *Ollie North* lack a fixed meaning.

Notice that there *are* lexical items that *do* freeze the output of such principles, for example exocentric compounds like *big top, redhead, yellow-jacket*. These do not denote just anything with a big top, red head, or yellow jacket; one must learn that they denote a circus tent, a person, and a bee respectively. By contrast, one doesn't have to learn anything special about ham sandwiches to understand (8a), or anything beyond the salient properties of Colonel North to understand (8b). Similarly, one does not have to learn anything about the word denoting a physical object to know that it can be used to denote a picture, model, or other representation of that object. For this reason, I will not regard such extensions of meaning as part of the lexicon. (Section 10.6 will suggest how such "rules of construal" might fit into the more standard principles of phrasal interpretation.)

Examples (3)–(8) are intended only as preliminary illustrations of the problem of lexical relatedness. Part of my procedure here will be to go through many different lexical alternations, asking (1) what formal relation obtains among different uses, (2) whether that relation can be expressed as a general principle of construal, so that one term of the relation does not have to be listed at all in the lexicon, or (3) barring that, how the relation can be expressed lexically so as to minimize the difference among the uses in question. In the worst case, we can always fall back on mere homonymy (the two *bank*'s). But in the interests of making the learner's job easier, a formal lexical relation is preferable: learning one use then makes it easier to learn the other.

1.6 X-Bar Semantics

The title of this section obviously alludes to X-bar syntax, the aspect of the Extended Standard Theory and its descendants that concerns the nature of syntactic categories. Chomsky's original paper on the topic, "Remarks on Nominalization" (1970), was written in reaction to a series of arguments (e.g. Postal 1966a; Ross 1969; Lakoff 1971) that since two syntactic categories (say Adj and V) share certain properties, one must be transformationally derived from the other. Chomsky argued that it is impossible to state a transformational derivation with any generality and that the sharing of properties should instead be expressed by decomposing syntactic categories into a feature system—just as properties shared among phonological segments of a language are expressed in terms of distinctive features. While this program of research still cannot be considered complete, the points of similarity among syntactic categories that form the underpinnings of X-bar theory are undeniable. This section will sketch three major subsystems within conceptual structure, showing that cross-categorial feature decompositions with an "X-bar" flavor play an important role in the characterization of I-concepts.

1.6.1 Ontological Categories and Argument Structure

S&C, chapters 3, 4, and 9, proposes a basic organization for conceptual structure. Instead of a division of formal entities into such familiar logical types as constants, variables, predicates, and quantifiers, each of which has nothing in common with the others, it is argued that the essential units of conceptual structure are *conceptual constituents*, each of which belongs to one of a small set of major ontological categories (or conceptual "parts of speech") such as Thing, Event, State, Action, Place, Path, Property, and Amount. These are obviously all quite different in the kind of reference they pick out, but formally (algebraically) they have a great deal in common. Here are six points of similarity.

1. Each major syntactic constituent of a sentence (excluding contentless constituents such as epenthetic *it* and *there*) maps into a conceptual constituent in the meaning of the sentence. For example, in *John ran toward the house*, *John* and *the house* correspond to Thing-constituents, the PP *toward the house* corresponds to a Path-constituent, and the entire sentence corresponds to an Event-constituent.

Note that this correspondence is stated very carefully. As will be seen presently, the converse of this correlation does not hold: not every conceptual constituent in the meaning of a sentence corresponds to a syntactic constituent, because (for one thing) many conceptual constituents of a sentence's meaning are completely contained within lexical items. In addition, note that the matching is by *constituents*, not by *categories*, because the mapping between conceptual and syntactic categories is many-to-many. For instance, an NP can express a Thing (e.g. *the dog*), an Event (*the war*), or a Property (*redness*); a PP can express a Place (*in the house*), a Path (*to the kitchen*), or, idiomatically in English, a Property (*in luck*); and an S can express a State (*Bill is here*) or an Event (*Bill ran away*). These realizations are subject to markedness conditions: in the unmarked case, NP expresses Thing, S or VP expresses Action, and so on.[6]

2. Each conceptual category supports the encoding of units not only on the basis of linguistic input but also on the basis of the visual (or other sensory) environment. For example, (9a) points out a Thing in the environment; (9b) points out a Place; (9c) accompanies the demonstration of an Action; (9d) accompanies the demonstration of a Distance, independent of the object whose length it is.

(9) a. *That* is a robin.
   b. *There* is your hat.
   c. Can you do *this*?
   d. The fish was *this* long.

3. Many of the categories support a type-token distinction. For example, just as there are many individual tokens of the Thing-type expressed by *a hat*, there may be many tokens of the Event-type expressed by *John ate his hat*, and there may be many different individual Place-tokens of the Place-type expressed by *over your head*. (Properties and Amounts, however, do not so clearly differentiate tokens and types.)

4. Many of the categories support quantification:

(10) a. Every dinosaur had a brain.   (Things)
    b. Everything you can do, I can do better.   (Actions)
    c. Anyplace you can go, I can go too.   (Places)

5. Each conceptual category has some realizations in which it is decomposed into a function-argument structure; each argument is in turn a conceptual constituent of some major category. The standard notion of "predicate" is a special case of this, where the superordinate category is a State or Event. For instance, in (11a), which expresses a State, the arguments are *John* (Thing) and *tall* (Property); in (11b), also a State, both arguments are Things; and in (11c), an Event, the arguments are *John* (Thing) and ⟨*PRO*⟩ *to leave* (Event or Action).[7]

(11) a. John is tall.
    b. John loves Mary.
    c. John tried to leave.

But a Thing also may have a Thing as argument, as in (12a) or (12b); a Path may have a Thing as argument, as in (13a), or a Place, as in (13b); and a Property may have a Thing, as in (14a), or an Event/Action, as in (14b).

(12) a. father of the bride
    b. president of the republic

(13) a. to the house
    b. from under the table

(14) a. afraid of Harry
    b. ready to leave

6. The conceptual structure of a lexical item is an entity with zero or more open argument places. The meanings of the syntactic complements of the lexical item fill in the values of the item's argument places in the meaning of the sentence. For instance, the verb *be* in (11a) expresses a State-function whose arguments are found in the subject and predicate adjective position; *love* in (11b) expresses a State-function whose arguments are found in subject and object positions; *try* in (11c) expresses an Event-function whose arguments are the subject and the complement clause; *father* and *president* in (12) express Thing-functions whose arguments are in the NP complement; *from* in (13b) expresses a Path-function whose argument is a complement PP; *afraid* in (14a) expresses a Property-function whose argument is the complement NP.

These observations, though slightly tedious, should convey the general picture behind X-bar semantics: none of the major conceptual categories can be insightfully reduced to the others, but they share important formal properties. Thus, parallel to the basic formation rules of X-bar syntax in (15), a basic formation rule for conceptual categories can be stated along the lines in (16).

(15) XP → Spec — X′
    X′ → X — Comp
    X → [±N, ±V]

(16) [Entity] →
$$\begin{bmatrix} \text{Event/Thing/Place/} \ldots \\ \text{Token/Type} \\ F\left(\langle \text{Entity}_1, \langle \text{Entity}_2, \langle \text{Entity}_3 \rangle \rangle \rangle\right) \end{bmatrix}$$

(16) decomposes each conceptual constituent into three basic feature complexes, one of which, the argument structure feature, allows for recursion of conceptual structure and hence an infinite class of possible concepts.

In addition, observation 1 above—the fact that major syntactic phrases correspond to major conceptual constituents—can be formalized as a general correspondence rule of the form (17); and observation 6—the basic correspondence of syntactic and conceptual argument structure—can be formalized as a general correspondence rule of the form (18). (XP stands for any major syntactic constituent; X^0 stands for any lexical item whose complements are (optionally) YP and ZP.)

(17) XP corresponds to [Entity].

(18) $\begin{bmatrix} X^0 \\ \underline{\quad} \langle YP \langle ZP \rangle \rangle \end{bmatrix}$ corresponds to $\begin{bmatrix} \text{Entity} \\ F(\langle E_1 \rangle, \langle E_2, \langle E_3 \rangle \rangle) \end{bmatrix}$
where YP corresponds to E_2, ZP corresponds to E_3, and the subject (if there is one) corresponds to E_1.

The examples given for observations 1–6 show that the syntactic category and the value of the conceptual *n*-ary feature Thing/Event/Place...are irrelevant to the general form of these rules. The algebra of conceptual structure and its relation to syntax is best stated cross-categorially.

1.6.2 Organization of Semantic Fields

A second cross-categorial property of conceptual structure forms a central concern of the "localistic" theory of Gruber (1965) and others. The basic insight of this theory is that the formalism for encoding concepts of spatial location and motion, suitably abstracted, can be generalized to many other semantic fields. The standard evidence for this claim is the fact that many verbs and prepositions appear in two or more semantic fields, forming intuitively related paradigms. (19) illustrates some basic cases.

(19) a. *Spatial location and motion*
   i. The bird went from the ground to the tree.
   ii. The bird is in the tree.
   iii. Harry kept the bird in the cage.

   b. *Possession*
   i. The inheritance went to Philip.
   ii. The money is Philip's.
   iii. Susan kept the money.

   c. *Ascription of properties*
   i. The light went/changed from green to red.
      Harry went from elated to depressed.
   ii. The light is red.
      Harry is depressed.
   iii. Sam kept the crowd happy.

d. *Scheduling of activities*
  i. The meeting was changed from Tuesday to Monday.
  ii. The meeting is on Monday.
  iii. Let's keep the trip on Saturday.

Each of these sets contains a verb *go* or *change* (connected with the prepositions *from* and/or *to*), the verb *be*, and the verb *keep*. The *go*-sentences each express a change of some sort, and their respective terminal states are described by the corresponding *be*-sentences. The *keep*-sentences all denote the causation of a state that endures over a period of time. One has the sense, then, that this variety of uses is not accidental.

On the other hand, the generalization of lexical items across semantic fields is by no means totally free. Each word is quite particular about what fields it appears in. For instance, *go* cannot be substituted for *change* in (19d), and *change* cannot be substituted for *go* in (19a). *Travel* occurs as a verb of change only in the spatial field; *donate* only in possessional; *become* only in ascriptional; and *schedule* only in scheduling.

Gruber's Thematic Relations Hypothesis, as adapted in Jackendoff 1972, 1976 and in *S&C*, chapter 10, accounts for the paradigms in (19) by claiming that they are each realizations of the basic conceptual functions given in (20). (The ontological category variable is notated as a subscript on the brackets; nothing except convenience hangs on this notational choice as opposed to that in (16).)

(20) a. $[_{\text{Event}} \text{GO} ([\quad], [_{\text{Path}} \begin{smallmatrix} \text{FROM} ([\quad]) \\ \text{TO} ([\quad]) \end{smallmatrix}])]$

   b. $[_{\text{State}} \text{BE} ([\quad], [_{\text{Place}} \quad])]$

   c. $[_{\text{Event}} \text{STAY} ([\quad], [_{\text{Place}} \quad])]$

The paradigms are distinguished from one another by a *semantic field feature* that designates the field in which the Event or State is defined. In the cited works, the field feature is notated as a subscript on the function: $\text{GO}_{\text{Spatial}}$ (or, more often, simply GO) versus GO_{Poss} versus GO_{Ident} (using Gruber's term *Identificational*) versus GO_{Temp}. Again, not much hangs on this particular notation. The point is that at this grain of analysis the four semantic fields have parallel conceptual structure. They differ only in what counts as an entity being in a Place. In the spatial field, a Thing is located spatially; in possessional, a Thing belongs to someone; in ascriptional, a Thing has a property; in scheduling, an Event is located in a time period.

This notation captures the lexical parallelisms in (19) neatly. The different uses of the words *go, change, be, keep, from,* and *to* in (19) are distinguished only by the semantic field feature, despite the radically different sorts of real-world events and states they pick out. However, the precise values of the field feature that a particular verb or preposition may carry is a lexical fact that must be learned. Thus *be* and *keep* are unrestricted; *go* is marked for spatial, possessional, or ascriptional; and *change* is marked for ascriptional or scheduling. On the other hand, *travel, donate, become,* and *schedule* are listed with only a single value of the field feature. Similarly, *from* and *to* are unrestricted, but *across* is only spatial and *during* is only temporal.

Recall that in each paradigm in (19), the *be*-sentence expresses the end-state of the *go*-sentence. This can be captured in the informally stated inference rule (21), which is independent of semantic field.

(21) At the termination of $[_{\text{Event}}$ GO $([X], [_{\text{Path}}$ TO $([Y])])]$,
   it is the case that $[_{\text{State}}$ BE $([X], [_{\text{Place}}$ AT $([Y])])]$.

A variety of such inference rules appear, in slightly different formalism, in Jackendoff 1976. In particular, it is shown that many so-called implicative properties of verbs follow from generalized forms of inference rules developed to account for verbs of spatial motion and location. As a result, inferential properties such as "factive," "implicative," and "semifactive" need not be stated as arbitrary meaning postulates. This is just the sort of explanatory power one wants from a theory of lexical decomposition into conceptual features.

Each semantic field has its own particular inference patterns as well. For instance, in the spatial field, one fundamental principle stipulates that an object cannot be in two disjoint places at once. From this principle plus rule (21), it follows that an object that travels from one place to another is not still in its original position. However, in the field of information transfer, this inference does not hold. If Bill transfers information to Harry, by (21) we can infer that Harry ends up having the information. But since information, unlike objects, can be in more than one place at a time, Bill still may have the information too. Hence rule (21) generalizes from the spatial field to information transfer, but the principle of exclusive location does not. Thus inference rules as well as lexical entries benefit from a featural decomposition of concepts: the Thematic Relations Hypothesis and the use of the semantic field feature permit us to generalize just those aspects that are general, while retaining necessary distinctions.[8]

1.6.3 Aggregation and Boundedness

The phenomena discussed so far in this section involve areas where the syntactic category system and the conceptual category system match up fairly well. In a way, the relation between the two systems serves as a partial explication of the categorial and functional properties of syntax: syntax presumably evolved as a means to express conceptual structure, so it is natural to expect that some of the structural properties of concepts would be mirrored in the organization of syntax.

On the other hand, there are other aspects of conceptual structure that display a strong "X-bar" character but are not expressed in so regular a fashion in syntax (at least in English). One such aspect (discussed in Vendler 1957; Verkuyl 1972, 1989; Mourelatos 1981; Dowty 1979; Hinrichs 1985; Bach 1986b; Talmy 1978; Link 1983; Platzack 1979; and Declerck 1979, among others) can be illustrated by the examples in (22).

(22) $\begin{cases} \text{For hours,} \\ \text{Until noon,} \end{cases}$

    a. Bill slept.
    b. the light flashed.   (repetition only)
    c. lights flashed.
    d. *Bill ate the hot dog.
    e. Bill ate hot dogs.
    f. *Bill ate some hot dogs.
    g. Bill was eating the hot dog.
    h. ?Bill ran into the house.   (repetition only)
    i. people ran into the house.
    j. ?some people ran into the house.   (repetition only)
    k. Bill ran toward the house.
    l. Bill ran into houses.
    m. Bill ran into some houses.   (repetition only)
    n. Bill ran down the road.
    o. *Bill ran 5 miles down the road.   (OK only on the reading where 5 miles down the road is where Bill was, not on the reading where 5 miles down the road is how far he got.)

The question raised by these examples is why prefixing *for hours* or *until noon* should have such effects: sometimes it leaves a sentence acceptable, sometimes it renders it ungrammatical, and sometimes it adds a sense of repetition. The essential insight is that *for hours* places a measure on an otherwise temporally unbounded process, and that *until noon* places a temporal boundary on an otherwise temporally unbounded process. *Bill slept*, for instance, inherently expresses an unbounded process, so it can be felicitously prefixed with these expressions. On the other hand, *Bill ate the hot dog* expresses a temporally bounded event, so it cannot be further measured or bounded.

In turn, there are two ways in which a sentence can be interpreted as a temporally unbounded process. One is for the sentence to inherently express a temporally unbounded process, as is the case in (22a,c,g,i,k,l,n). We will return to these cases shortly. The other is for the sentence to be interpreted as an indefinite repetition of an inherently bounded process, as in (22b,h,j,m). (*Bill ate the hot dog*, like *Bill died*, is bounded but unrepeatable, so it cannot be interpreted in this fashion.) This sense of repetition has no syntactic reflex in English. However, some languages such as Hungarian and Finnish have an iterative aspect that does express it; this aspect must be used in the counterparts of (22b,h,j,m).

How should this sense of iteration be encoded in conceptual structure? It would appear most natural to conceive of it as an operator which maps a conceptual constituent that encodes a single Event into a conceptual constituent that encodes a repeated sequence of individual Events of the same type. Brief consideration suggests that in fact this operator has exactly the same semantic value as the plural marker, which maps a conceptual constituent that encodes an individual Thing into a conceptual constituent that encodes a collection of Things of the same type. That is, this operator is not formulated specifically in terms of Events, but rather should be applicable in X-bar fashion to any conceptual entity that admits of individuation. The fact that this operator does not receive consistent expression across syntactic categories should not obscure the essential semantic generalization. However, it is a place in the grammar (at least in most languages) where the syntax and the semantics are not parallel in organization.

Returning to the inherently unbounded cases, it has often been observed that the bounded/unbounded (event/process, telic/atelic) distinction is strongly parallel to the count/mass distinction in NPs. An important criterion for the count/mass distinction has to do with the description of parts of an entity. For instance, a part of *an apple* (count) cannot itself be described as *an apple*; but any part of a body of *water* (mass) can itself be described as *water* (unless the part gets too small with respect to its molecular structure). This same criterion applies to the event/process distinction: a part of *John ate the sandwich* (event) cannot itself be described as *John ate the sandwich*. By contrast, any part of *John ran toward the house* (process) can itself be described as *John ran toward the house* (unless the part gets smaller than a single stride). These similarities suggest that conceptual structure should encode this distinction cross-categorially too, so that the relevant inference rules do not care whether they are dealing with Things versus Substances or Events versus Processes.

It has also often been observed that plurals behave in many respects like mass nouns and that repeated events behave like processes. (Talmy suggests the term *medium* to encompass them both.) The difference is only that plural nouns and repeated events fix the "grain size" in terms of the singular individuals making up the unbounded medium, so that decomposition of the medium into parts is not as arbitrary as it is with substances and processes. Thus the structure of the desired feature system is organized as in (23).

(23)

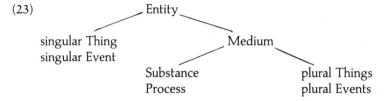

singular Thing
singular Event

Medium

Substance
Process

plural Things
plural Events

That is, the features that distinguish Things from Events are orthogonal to the features differentiating individuals from media, and within media, homogeneous media from aggregates of individuals.

The examples in (22) provide evidence that Paths also participate in the system shown in (23). For instance, *to the house* is a bounded Path; no subparts of it except those including the terminus can be described as *to the house*. By contrast, *toward the house* and *down the road* are unbounded Paths, any part of which can also be described as *toward the house* or *down the road*. *Into houses* describes multiple bounded Paths, one per house. Thus the cross-categorial feature system in (23) extends to yet another major ontological category.

What factors are involved in determining whether a sentence expresses an Event or a Process? The examples in (22) illustrate a wider range of factors than are cited in any single piece of work in the literature I am familiar with. These factors include the following:

1. Choice of verb ((22a) vs. (22b))
2. Choice of aspect ((22d) vs. (22g))
3. Choice of singular or bare plural in the subject ((22h) vs. (22i)), in the object ((22d) vs. (22e)), and in the object of a preposition ((22h) vs. (22l))
4. Choice of determiner in the subject ((22i) vs. (22j)), in the object ((22e) vs. (22f)), and in the object of a preposition ((22l) vs. (22m))
5. Choice of preposition ((22h) vs. (22k))
6. Choice of prepositional specifier ((22n) vs. (22o))

How all these factors enter into the choice of boundedness or unboundedness for a sentence is not altogether clear. The general shape of the solution would seem to take the form of an algebraic system that combines the values of the features for any conceptual function and its arguments to derive a value for the entity as a whole. This system, operating recursively up through the conceptual embeddings, will eventually take into account the values for each of the parts of the sentence. (Many of the authors cited above propose fragments of such a system, but none develops it in the full generality required by the range of examples in (22).) It is tempting to speculate that such a system is at the root of a deeper account of the scope of quantification—an explanation of why an operator on a single NP in a sentence can extend its effects over the entire sentence.

To sum up the discussion of (22): these examples show that (1) there is
a common feature system that deals with boundedness and individuation,
cutting across Things, Events, and Paths; (2) the system is expressed by a
heterogeneous collection of syntactic factors, including lexical choice, aspect, determiner, and perhaps case (e.g. the use of partitive in some languages to express unboundedness); and (3) there is a set of algebraic
principles over conceptual structure that correlates the values of the features in all parts of the sentence with the features of the sentence as a
whole.

Here is an example that illustrates some of the explanatory power
achieved through the system of features in (22): the meaning of the word
end. For a first approximation, an *end* is a 0-dimensional boundary of an
entity conceived of as 1-dimensional. So, for the simplest case, the end of
a line is a point. A beam is conceived of (as in Marr 1982) as a long axis
elaborated by a cross section. The end of a beam is a point bounding the
long axis, elaborated by the same cross section; this makes it 2-dimensional.
A table can be said to have an end just in case it can be seen as having a
long axis (e.g. it is rectangular or oval but not square or circular); the end
is then just the boundary of the long axis elaborated by the short axis.
However, in the expected X-bar fashion, we can speak of the end of a week
(a point bounding a 1-dimensional period of time) and the end of a talk (a
0-dimensional State bounding an Event that extends over time).

However, there is an apparent difficulty in this account of *end*. If the end
of a talk is a point in time, how can one felicitously say "I am now giving
the end of my talk" or "I am now finishing my talk"? The progressive
aspect in these sentences implies the existence of a process taking place
over time and therefore seems to attribute a temporal extent to the end.

An answer is provided by looking at the treatment of the boundaries of
Things. Consider what is meant by *Bill cut off the end of the ribbon*. Bill
cannot have cut off the geometrical boundary of the ribbon. Rather, the
sense of this sentence shows that the notion of end permits an optional
elaboration: the end may consist of a part of the object it bounds, extending from the actual boundary into the object some small distance ϵ.

There are other boundary words that *obligatorily* include this sort of
elaboration. For instance, a *crust* is a 2-dimensional boundary of a 3-
dimensional volume, elaborated by extending it some distance ϵ into the
volume. *Border* carrier a stronger implication of such elaboration than does
edge: consider that the *border of the rug* is liable to include a pattern in the
body of the rug, while the *edge of the rug* is more liable to include only the
binding.

The claim, then, is that *end* includes such an elaboration as an optional
part of its meaning. Going back to the case of Events, I can therefore
felicitously say "I am now giving the end of my talk" or "I am now

finishing my talk" if I am within the region that extends backward the permissible distance ϵ from the actual cessation of speech. In other words, the featural machinery of dimensionality and boundaries, with which we characterize Things and the regions of space they occupy, extends to Events as well. That's why the word *end* is so natural in either context. The main difference in the systems is that Things have a maximum dimensionality of 3, while Events have a maximum dimensionality of only 1, so that certain distinctions in the Thing system are leveled out or unavailable in the Event system. Only in a theory of conceptual structure that permits this sort of cross-categorial generalization can even the existence of a word like *end* be explained, much less the peculiarities of its use in so many different contexts—and the fact that these peculiarities are evidently learnable. (This subsystem of conceptual structure will be treated in detail in Jackendoff, in preparation.)

A general conclusion emerges from these three brief case studies. Beneath the surface complexity of natural language concepts lies a highly abstract formal algebraic system that lays out the major parameters of thought. The distinctions in this system are quite sharp and do not appear to be based on experience. Rather, I would claim, they are the machinery available to the human mind to channel the ways in which all experience can be mentally encoded—elements of the Universal Grammar for conceptual structure.

Significantly, the primitives of this system cannot appear in isolation. Rather, they are like phonological features or the quarks of particle physics: they can only be observed in combination, built up into conceptual constituents, and their existence must be inferred from their effects on language and cognition as a whole. This result militates against Fodor's Intentional Realism, in that one should not expect constant counterparts in reality for every aspect of the conceptual system.

1.7 Where Traditional Features Fail

One of the abiding reasons for skepticism about feature-based semantics, even among those who believe in semantic decomposition, is that simple categorical features are clearly inadequate to the full task of conceptual description. These suspicions have been voiced since the earliest days of semantics in generative grammar (Bolinger 1965; Weinreich 1966) and continue to the present day (e.g. Lakoff 1987). This section will briefly mention some of the problems and the forms of enrichment proposed within Conceptual Semantics to deal with them.

1.7.1 Spatial Structure of Objects

The first problem has to do with specifying the shapes of objects. For instance, consider the lexical entries for *duck* and *goose*. Both of these presumably carry features to the effect that they are animate, nonhuman categories of Things, that they are types of birds, perhaps types of waterfowl. But what comes next? How are they distinguished from one another? One possible factor, which clearly enters into learning the words in the first place, is how ducks and geese *look*, and how they differ in appearance. But to encode this difference in binary features, say [±long neck], is patently ridiculous. Similarly, how is a *chair* to be distinguished from a *stool*? Do they differ in a feature [±has-a-back]? What sort of feature is this? It is surely not a primitive. But, if composite, how far down does one have to go to reach primitives—if one can at all? To put a ± sign and a pair of brackets around any old expression doesn't make it into a legitimate conceptual feature.

This problem is addressed in *C&CM*, chapter 10, in the context of the connection between the linguistic and visual faculties. In order for an organism to accomplish visual identification and categorization, independent of language, there must be a form of visual representation that encodes geometric and topological properties of physical objects. The most plausible proposal I have encountered for such a representation is the *3D model structure* of Marr 1982 (perhaps with enrichments such as those proposed in Biederman 1987). This structure can be interfaced with conceptual structure via a set of correspondence rules, as suggested in figure (1). This correspondence effects a translation of visual information into linguistic format, enabling us to talk about what we see.

Marr's approach is interesting because of the way it goes beyond a simple template theory of visual recognition. The 3D model is much more than a "statue in the head." It is an articulated structure that encodes the decomposition of objects into parts, the geometric systems of spatial axes around which objects are organized, and the relations among the parts. Within this framework, it is possible to represent not just single objects in single positions, but ranges of sizes, ranges of angles of attachment of parts, and ranges of detail from coarse- to fine-grained. Thus it is admirably suited to encoding just those geometric aspects of an object's appearance that are an embarrassment to any reasonable feature system.

C&CM suggests, therefore, that the lexical entry for a physical object word includes a 3D model representation in addition to its phonological, syntactic, and conceptual structures. The 3D model in fact plays the role sometimes assigned to an "image of a stereotypical instance," except that it is much more highly structured along the lines suggested by Marr and includes parameters of variation among instances. The distinctions between *duck* and *goose* and between *chair* and *stool*, then, can appear in the 3D model instead of conceptual structure. We thereby eliminate the need for a plethora of objectionable conceptual features in favor of a geometric representation with entirely different primitives and principles of combination.

objection *C&M* shows that this natural division of labor is of benefit not only to the theory of the lexicon but also to the theory of visual categorization; I will not repeat the arguments here.

I should however add that the use of the 3D model need not pertain just to objects and the nouns that denote them. Marr and Vaina (1982) propose a natural extension of the 3D model to encode action patterns such as throwing and saluting. This can be used to address a parallel problem in the verbal system: how is one to distinguish, say, *running* from *jogging* from *loping*, or *throwing* from *tossing* from *lobbing*? If the lexical entries for these verbs contain a 3D model representation of the action in question, no distinction at all need be made in conceptual structure. The first set of verbs will all simply be treated in conceptual structure as verbs of locomotion, the second set as verbs of propulsion. Thus again we are relieved of the need for otiose feature analyses of such fine-scale distinctions.

An important boundary condition on this analysis is that conceptual structure is the necessary conduit between 3D model information and syntactic information. This means that any semantic distinction that makes a *syntactic* difference must be encoded in conceptual structure. Differences that appear only in 3D model structure can by hypothesis have no syntactic effects. For example, *run, jog,* and *lope* are syntactically parallel, as are *throw, toss,* and *lob.* Thus the members of each set can be identical in conceptual structure and differ only in the associated 3D model. But since the two sets differ syntactically, it follows that their conceptual structures must differ as well. That is, 3D model differences, although crucial in distinguishing word meanings, are invisible to syntax.

1.7.2 Focal Values in a Continuous Domain

A second area in which a simple feature analysis fails concerns domains with a continuous rather than a discrete range of values. Consider the domain expressed by temperature words (*hot, warm, tepid, cool, cold,* etc.) or the domain of color words. One cannot decompose *hot* or *red* exhaustively into discrete features that distinguish them from *cold* and *yellow* respectively. The proper analysis seems to be that these words have a semantic field feature (Temperature or Color) that picks out a "cognitive space" consisting of a continuous range of values. In the case of Temperature, the space is essentially linear; in the case of Color, it is the familiar 3D color solid (Miller and Johnson-Laird 1976). For a first approximation, each temperature or color word picks out a point in its space, which serves as a focal value for the word.

According to this analysis, a percept can be categorized in terms of its relative distance from available focal values. So, for example, a percept whose value in color space is close to focal red is easily categorized as red; a percept whose value lies midway between focal red and focal orange is categorized with less certainty and with more contextual dependence. Thus color categorization is a result of the interaction between the intrinsic structure of the color space—including physiologically determined salient values—and the number and position of color values for which the language has words (Berlin and Kay 1969).

Refinements can be imagined in the structure of such spaces. For example, the field of temperature has both positive and negative directions, so one can ask either *How hot?* or *How cold?* By contrast, the field of size words has only a positive direction from the zero point, so that *How big?* asks a neutral question about size but *How small?* is intended in relation to some contextually understood small standard. I will not pursue such refinements here. The point is that the introduction of continuous "cognitive spaces" in which words pick out focal values is an important enrichment of the expressive power of conceptual structure beyond simple categorical feature systems.

1.7.3 Preference Rule Systems

A different challenge to feature systems arises in the treatment of so-called cluster concepts. Consider the following examples:

(24) a.   Bill climbed (up) the mountain.
     b.   Bill climbed down the mountain.
     c.   The snake climbed (up) the tree.
     d.   ?*The snake climbed down the tree.

Climbing appears to involve two independent conceptual conditions: (1) an individual is traveling upward; and (2) the individual is moving with characteristic effortful grasping motions, for which a convenient term is *clambering*. On the most likely interpretation of (24a), both these conditions are met. However, (24b) violates the first condition, and, since snakes can't clamber, (24c) violates the second. If *both* conditions are violated, as in (24d), the action cannot at all be characterized as climbing. Thus neither of the two conditions is necessary, but either is sufficient.

However, the meaning of *climb* is not just the disjunction of these two conditions. That would be in effect equivalent to saying that there are two unrelated senses of the word. If this were the correct analysis, we would have the intuition that (24a) is as ambiguous as *Bill went down to the bank.* But in fact it is not. Rather, (24a), which satisfies both conditions at once, is more "stereotypical" climbing. Actions that satisfy only one of the conditions, such as (24b,c), are somewhat more marginal but still perfectly legitimate instances of climbing. In other words, the two conditions combine in the meaning of a single lexical item *climb*, but not according to a standard Boolean conjunction or disjunction. *S&C*, chapter 8, calls a set of conditions combined in this way a *preference rule system*, and the conditions in the set *preference rules* or *preference conditions*.[9]

A similar paradigm can be displayed for the verb *see*:

(25) a.   Bill saw Harry.
     b.   Bill saw a vision of dancing devils.
     c.   Bill saw the sign, but he didn't notice it at the time.
     d.   *Bill saw a vision of dancing devils, but he didn't notice it at the time.

The two preference conditions for *x sees y* are roughly that (1) x's gaze makes contact with y, and (2) x has a visual experience of y. Stereotypical seeing (i.e. veridical seeing) satisfies both these conditions: x makes visual contact with some object and thereby has a visual experience of it. (25b) violates condition (1) and (25c) violates condition (2), yet both felicitously use the word *see*. But if both are violated at once as in (25d), the sentence is extremely odd. Again, we don't want to say that there are two homonymous verbs *see* and hence that (25a) is ambiguous. The solution is to claim that these two conditions form a preference rule system, in which stereotypical seeing satisfies both conditions and less central cases satisfy only one—but either one.[10]

Similar phenomena arise in the lexical entries for nouns that denote functional categories: form and function often are combined in a preference rule system. For instance, a stereotypical *chair* has a stereotypical form (specified by a 3D model) and a standard function (roughly "portable thing for one person to sit on"). Objects with the proper function but the wrong form—say beanbag chairs—are more marginal instances of the category; and so are objects that have the right form but cannot fulfill the function— say chairs made of newspaper or giant chairs. An object that violates both conditions—say a pile of crumpled newspaper—is by no stretch of imagination a chair. This is precisely the behavior we saw in *climb* and *see*.

A further aspect of preference rule systems is that when one lacks information about the satisfaction of the conditions, they are invariably assumed to be satisfied as *default values*. Thus the reason (24a) and (25a) are interpreted as stereotypical climbing and seeing is that the sentences give no information to the contrary. It is only in the (b) and (c) sentences, which do give information to the contrary, that a condition is relinquished.

The examples of preference rule systems given here have all involved only a pair of conditions. Systems with a larger number of conditions are likely to exist but are harder to ferret out and articulate without detailed analysis. On the other hand, a preference rule system with only one condition degenerates to a standard default value. More generally, preference rule systems are capable of accounting for "family resemblance" categories such as Wittgenstein's (1953) well-known example *game*, for

Rosch's (1978) "prototypes," and for other cases in which systems of necessary and sufficient conditions have failed because all putative conditions have counterexamples, but not all at once.

Still more broadly, *S&C* shows that preference rule systems are an appropriate formalism for a vast range of psychological phenomena, from low-level visual and phonetic perception to high-level operations such as conscious decision-making. The formalism was in fact developed originally to deal with phenomena of musical cognition (Lerdahl and Jackendoff 1983) and was anticipated by the Gestalt psychologists in their study of visual perception (Wertheimer 1923). There seems every reason, then, to believe that preference rule systems are a pervasive element of mental computation; we should therefore have no hesitation in adopting them as a legitimate element of conceptual structure. (See *S&C*, chapters 7 and 8, for extended discussion of preference rule systems, including comparison with systems of necessary and sufficient conditions, prototype theory, and fuzzy set theory.)

To sum up, this section has suggested three ways in which the decomposition of lexical concepts goes beyond simple categorial feature oppositions. These mechanisms conspire to make word meanings far richer than classical categories. Each of them creates a continuum between stereotypical and marginal instances, and each can create fuzziness or vagueness at category boundaries. Moreover, each of them can be motivated on more general cognitive grounds, so we are not multiplying artifices just to save the theory of lexical decomposition. And indeed, they appear collectively to go a long way toward making a suitably expressive theory of word meaning attainable.

1.8 Appendix: Lexical Composition versus Meaning Postulates

Section 1.2 argued from the creativity of lexical concept formation to the position that lexical conceptual structures must be compositional—that one has an innate "Universal Grammar of concepts" that enables one to construct new lexical concepts as needed. An important aspect of Fodor's work on the Language of Thought Hypothesis has been to deny lexical compositionality. Not that Fodor has offered any alternative of lexical concepts that deals with any of the problems discussed in the last two sections; indeed, his arguments are almost exclusively negative. Nevertheless, for completeness I had better address his concerns.

Fodor's first set of arguments (Fodor 1970; Fodor et al. 1980) builds on the virtual impossibility of giving precise definitions for most words. If definitions are impossible, Fodor argues, there is no reason to believe that words have internal structure. But in fact, all this observation shows is that if there are principles of lexical conceptual composition, they are not entirely identical with the principles of phrasal conceptual composition. If the principles are not identical, it will often be impossible to build up an expression of conceptual structure phrasally that completely duplicates a lexical concept. In particular, it appears that the nondiscrete elements discussed in section 1.7 play a role only in lexical semantics and never appear as a result of phrasal combination. Hence phrasal expansions of these aspects of lexical meaning cannot be constructed. Yet they are indubitably compositional. So this argument of Fodor's does not go through; it is founded on a false assumption that lexical and phrasal compositions are completely uniform.

The second set of arguments concerns processing. Fodor's supposition is that if lexical concepts are composite, a more complex word ought to induce a greater processing load and/or take more time to access or process than a less complex word. Finding no experimental evidence for such effects (Fodor, Fodor, and Garrett 1975), Fodor concludes again that lexical items cannot have compositional structure.[11] I see no reason to accept the premise of this argument. As is well known, the acquisition of motor concepts (such as playing a scale on the piano) *speeds up* performance over sequential performance of the constituent parts. Nevertheless, such motor concepts must still be compositional, since the same complex motor patterns must be invoked. It stands to reason, then, that acquisition of a lexical concept might also speed up processing over a syntactically complex paraphrase, without in any way reducing conceptual complexity: a lexical item is "chunked," whereas a phrasal equivalent is not.

Because Fodor can find no system of lexical composition that satisfies his criteria of intentionality and of decomposition into necessary and sufficient conditions (both of which are abandoned in Conceptual Semantics), he decides that the enterprise is impossible and that lexical concepts must in fact be mentally encoded as indissoluble monads. He recognizes two difficulties in this position, having to do with inference and acquisition, and he offers answers. I will take these up in turn.

The first issue is how inference can be driven by lexical concepts with no internal structure. If one is dealing with inferences such as

(P & Q) → P,

as Fodor does in most of his discussion, there is little problem, assuming principles of standard logic. But for inferences that involve nonlogical lexical items, such as *John forced Harry to leave* → *Harry left* or *Sue approached the house* → *Sue got closer to the house*, there can be no general principles. Rather, each lexical item must be accompanied by its own specific meaning postulates that determine the entailments of sentences it occurs in. This is the solution Fodor advocates, though he does not propose how it is to be accomplished except perhaps in the most trivial of cases, such as *Rover is a dog* → *Rover is an animal*.

The trouble with such an approach, even if it can succeed observationally, is that it denies the possibility of generalizing among the inferential properties of different lexical items. Each item is a world unto itself. Thus, for instance, consider the entailment relationship between the members of causative-noncausative pairs such as those in (26).

(26) a. x killed y → y died
      b. x lifted y → y rose
      c. x gave z to y → y received z
      d. x persuaded y that P → y came to believe that P

In a meaning postulate theory, these inferences are totally unrelated. Intuitively, though, they are all instances of a schema stated roughly as (27), where E is an Event.

(27) x cause E to occur → E occur

In order to invoke a general schema like (27), the left-hand verbs in (26) must have meaning postulates like (28), in which the bracketed expressions are Events.

(28) a. x kill y → x cause [y die]
      b. x lift y → x cause [y rise]
      c. x give z to y → x cause [y receive z]
      d. x persuade y that P → x cause [y come to believe that P]

But this is a notational variant of the analysis of causative in a lexical decomposition theory: it claims that there is an element *cause* that (1) is mentioned in the analysis (here, the lexical meaning postulates) of many lexical items and (2) gives access to more general-purpose rules of inference.

I suggest that, for fans of meaning postulates, lexical decomposition can be regarded systematically in this light: each element in a lexical decomposition can be regarded as that item's access to more general-purpose rules of inference. The problem of lexical decomposition, then, is to find a vocabulary for decomposition that permits the linguistically significant generalizations of inference patterns to be captured formally in terms of schemas like (27) and rule (21). (See Jackendoff 1976 for a range of such rules of inference.)

I conclude therefore that a meaning postulate approach to inference either misses all generalizations across inferential properties of lexical items or else is essentially equivalent to a decomposition theory. Thus Fodor has correctly identified a problem for his approach but has proposed a nonsolution.

Innateness ¶ The second difficulty Fodor sees for noncompositional lexical concepts is how one could possibly acquire them. In any computational theory, "learning" can consist only of creating novel combinations of primitives already innately available. This is one of the fundamental arguments of Fodor (1975), and one that I accept unconditionally. However, since for Fodor all lexical concepts are primitive, they cannot be learned as combinations of more primitive vocabulary. It follows that all lexical concepts must be innate, including such exotica as *telephone, spumoni, funicular,* and *soffit,* a conclusion that strains credulity but that Fodor evidently embraces.

Notice how Fodor's position is different from saying that all lexical concepts must be within the innate expressive power of the grammar of conceptual structure, as advocated here. The difference is that in the present approach it is the *potential* of an infinite number of lexical concepts that is inherent in the grammar of conceptual structure—just as the potential for the syntactic structures of all human languages is inherent in Universal Grammar. Lexical acquisition then requires constructing a particular lexical concept and associating it with a syntactic and phonological structure.

Fodor notes of course that not every speaker has a phonological realization of every lexical concept. Since his notion of "realization" cannot include learning, he advocates that somehow the attachment of an innate lexical concept to a phonological structure is "triggered" by relevant experience, perhaps by analogy with the way parameter settings in syntax are said to be triggered. However, the analogy is less than convincing. The setting of syntactic parameters is determined within a highly articulated theory of syntactic structure, where there is a limited number of choices for the setting. The supposed triggering of lexical concepts takes place in a domain where there is by hypothesis *no* relevant structure, and where the choices are grossly underdetermined. As far as I know, then, Fodor has offered no account of lexical concept realization other than a suggestive name. By contrast, real studies of language acquisition have benefited from decompositional theories of lexical concepts (e.g. Landau and Gleitman 1985; Pinker 1989), so the decomposition theory has empirical results on its side in this area as well.

An especially unpleasant consequence of Fodor's position is that, given the finiteness of the brain, there can be only a finite number of possible lexical concepts. This seems highly implausible, since one can coin new names for arbitrary new types of objects and actions ("This is a glarf; now watch me snarf it"), and we have no sense that we will someday run out of names for things. More pointedly, the number of potential category concepts is at least as large as the number of concepts for individuals (tokens), since for every individual X one can form a category of "things just like X" and give it a monomorphemic name. It is hard to believe that nature has equipped us with an ability to recognize individual things in the world that is limited to a finite number. So far as I know, Fodor has not addressed this objection. (See *S&C*, section 5.2, for a stronger version of this argument.)

From these considerations I conclude that Fodor's theory of lexical concepts cannot deal at all with the creativity of concept formation and with concept acquisition. Nor can any other theory that relies on monadic predicates linked by meaning postulates. By contrast, a compositional theory in principle offers solutions parallel to those for the creativity and acquisition of syntax.

Chapter 2
Argument Structure and Thematic Roles

Chapter 1 sketched some of the conceptual categories and functions developed in *S&C* and showed how they correspond to syntactic constituents. This chapter will develop systematically the way in which the lexical conceptual structure of a head is combined with its arguments and modifiers to form a phrasal conceptual structure.

2.1 Basic Function-Argument Structures

Following the analysis of *S&C*, section 1.6.1 proposed that the innate formation rules for conceptual structure include a repertoire of major conceptual categories, the "semantic parts of speech." These categories include such entities as Thing (or Object), Event, State, Action, Place, Path, Property, and Amount. Each of these can be elaborated into a function-argument organization of the general form given in schema (1.16).[1] Within the constraints of this schema, each category permits a variety of more specific elaborations, which can be stated as specialized formation rules. Some of the most important ones for the spatial domain appear in (1).

(1) a. [PLACE] → [$_{\text{Place}}$ PLACE-FUNCTION ([THING])]

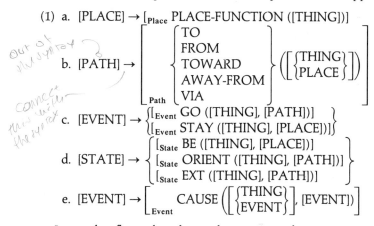

> b. [PATH] → $\left[_{\text{Path}} \left\{\begin{array}{l} \text{TO} \\ \text{FROM} \\ \text{TOWARD} \\ \text{AWAY-FROM} \\ \text{VIA} \end{array}\right\} \left(\left[\left\{\begin{array}{l}\text{THING}\\\text{PLACE}\end{array}\right\}\right]\right)\right]$

> c. [EVENT] → $\left\{\begin{array}{l}[_{\text{Event}} \text{ GO ([THING], [PATH])}] \\ [_{\text{Event}} \text{ STAY ([THING], [PLACE])}]\end{array}\right\}$

> d. [STATE] → $\left\{\begin{array}{l}[_{\text{State}} \text{ BE ([THING], [PLACE])}] \\ [_{\text{State}} \text{ ORIENT ([THING], [PATH])}] \\ [_{\text{State}} \text{ EXT ([THING], [PATH])}]\end{array}\right\}$

> e. [EVENT] → $\left[_{\text{Event}} \text{ CAUSE} \left(\left[\left\{\begin{array}{l}\text{THING}\\\text{EVENT}\end{array}\right\}\right], \text{[EVENT]}\right)\right]$

Let me briefly explain these rules. (1a) says that a conceptual constituent belonging to the category Place can be elaborated as a Place-function plus an argument that belongs to the category Thing. The argument serves as a spatial reference point, in terms of which the Place-function defines a region. For example, in the expression *under the table*, *the table* designates a reference object, and *under* expresses a Place-function that maps the table into the region beneath it. (1b) similarly elaborates a Path, or trajectory, as one of five functions that map a reference Thing or Place into a related trajectory. An example of a Path with a reference Thing is *to the house*; an example of a Path with a reference Place is *from under the table*, where the trajectory begins at the Place "under the table."

(1c) says that a constituent of the category Event can be elaborated as either of the two Event-functions GO or STAY, each of which takes two arguments. The arguments of GO, which denotes motion along a path, are the Thing in motion and the Path it traverses. This structure is seen most transparently in a sentence like *Bill went to New York*. The arguments of STAY, which denotes stasis over a period of time, are the Thing standing still and its location, as seen in *Bill stayed in the kitchen*, for instance. (1d) gives three State-functions. The first, BE, is used for specifying the location of objects (*The dog is in the park*), the second, ORIENT, for specifying the orientation of objects (*The sign points toward New York*), and the third, EXT, for the spatial extension of linear objects along a path (*The road goes from New York to San Francisco*). Finally, (1e) elaborates an Event as the Event-function CAUSE plus two arguments. The first argument, if a Thing, is Agent; if an Event, is Cause. The second argument, an Event, is the Effect. (See *S&C*, chapter 9, for more detailed discussion.)

In *S&C*, the functions in (1) are treated as conceptual primitives. However, one has the suspicion that STAY is likely composite, perhaps some sort of durational form of BE. EXT is clearly related to GO, since most of the verbs of extension (*reach, extend,* and *go* itself) can also be used as verbs of motion. (The notation used for EXT in my previous work was GO_{Ext}, suggesting but not formalizing the parallelism.) CAUSE too turns out to be composite rather than primitive, as will be seen in chapter 7. Finally, Jackendoff (in preparation) will show that various Place- and Path-functions have feature decompositions as well. Thus the decomposition in (1) may be regarded as roughly parallel to the stage in chemistry in which one has identified the elements of the periodic table but has not yet probed the internal structure of the atom: there is significant decomposition down to a certain level, but one should not regard it necessarily as complete.

The fundamental principle of correspondence between syntax and conceptual structure was stated in section 1.6.1: Every content-bearing major phrasal constituent of a sentence (S, NP, AP, PP, etc.) corresponds to a conceptual constituent of some major conceptual category. It was also observed there that within this general correspondence rule, there are again more specialized principles, partly language-specific, concerning which syntactic category can express which conceptual category. For instance, an NP can express almost any conceptual category; a PP can express a Place, a Path, and, in English, a Property; an S can express an Event or a State.

The relation of syntactic and conceptual argument structure was schematized in rule (1.18). An example like (2) provides a good first illustration.

(2) a. *Syntactic structure*

   $[_S[_{NP}$ John] $[_{VP}$ ran $[_{PP}$ into $[_{NP}$ the room]]]]

   b. *Conceptual structure*

   $[_{Event}$ GO $([_{Thing}$ JOHN], $[_{Path}$ TO $([_{Place}$ IN $([_{Thing}$ ROOM])])])]$

The sentence corresponds to the entire Event in conceptual structure. The verb corresponds to the Event-function GO, that is, this is a sentence expressing motion. The subject of the sentence corresponds to the first argument of GO, and the PP corresponds to the second argument. This second argument is itself composite: the Path-function TO takes a Place as its argument, and the Place in turn decomposes into the Place-function IN and a Thing argument expressed by the object of the preposition.

In order to see how (2b) is put together from its parts, let us examine the lexical entries for the two words *into* and *run*, using the formalism of S&C.[2]

(3) a.
$$\begin{bmatrix} \text{into} \\ \text{P} \\ \underline{\quad} \text{NP}_j \\ [_{Path} \text{ TO } ([_{Place} \text{ IN } ([_{Thing} \quad]_j)])] \end{bmatrix}$$

b.
$$\begin{bmatrix} \text{run} \\ \text{V} \\ \underline{\quad} \langle \text{PP}_j \rangle \\ [_{Event} \text{ GO } ([_{Thing} \quad]_i, [_{Path} \quad]_j)] \end{bmatrix}$$

Into subcategorizes for an NP object, which is coindexed with the open argument position—the reference object—in conceptual structure. *Run*, which expresses a GO-function, requires two arguments: the Thing in motion and the Path that specifies the trajectory of motion. The first is indexed *i*, which we will take by convention to indicate subject position or "external argument" in the sense of Williams (1984). The second argument is filled in with the reading of the postverbal PP, with which it is coindexed in the subcategorization feature. If no PP is syntactically present, the Path is simply unspecified: *John ran* means in part "John traversed some (unspecified) trajectory." In other words, the well-formedness conditions on conceptual structure require the Path argument to be present in conceptual structure even if it is not expressed syntactically; it is an "implicit argument."

A similar conceptual structure can be expressed in different syntactic form, for example by a sentence like (4).

(4) John entered the room.

The lexical entry of the verb is given in (5).

$$(5) \quad \begin{bmatrix} \text{enter} \\ \text{V} \\ \underline{\quad\quad} \langle NP_j \rangle \\ [_{\text{Event}} \text{ GO } ([_{\text{Thing}} \quad]_i, [_{\text{Path}} \text{ TO } ([_{\text{Place}} \text{ IN } ([_{\text{Thing}} \quad]_j)])])] \end{bmatrix}$$

Enter incorporates into its meaning the Path- and Place-functions expressed separately by the preposition *into* in (3a). As a result, the second argument is a Thing rather than a Path and must be expressed by an NP-complement. Notice further that the intransitive version, *John entered*, means not just "John traversed some path" but "John went into something." That is, the sense of *into* appears even when the second argument is implicit.[3]

These examples show the elementary properties of the mapping between syntactic and conceptual arguments. Words in general need not correspond to complete conceptual constituents—they correspond to constituents with open argument places. The argument places in turn may be embedded two or more functions down into the conceptual constituent, as seen in (3a) and (5); the only stipulation on arguments is that they themselves be full constituents. (This is codified as the "Lexical Variable Principle" in *S&C*, section 9.5.)

2.2 The Status of Thematic Roles

From this elementary exposition of function-argument structure, we can already begin to understand the status of thematic (θ-)roles within the present theory. This is crucial because of the centrality of θ-roles and θ-marking in GB Theory and of parallel notions in other syntactic theories (see Wilkins 1988a for a broad sampling). Given the importance of thematic roles, it is worth becoming very clear about what they really are, so that they have an independent life of their own. We must be sure we are not invoking them as a thinly disguised wild card to meet the exigencies of syntax.

The fundamental point, from which all else proceeds, is that *thematic roles are part of the level of conceptual structure, not part of syntax*. Recall Gruber's (1965) intuitive definition of Theme: the object in motion or being located. This can be structurally defined as the first argument of the functions in (lc, d). Source, "the object from which motion proceeds," appears structurally as the argument of the Path-function FROM. Note that Source is *not* a direct argument of the Event-function but is embedded within a Path-constituent. Similarly, Goal, "the object to which motion proceeds," is the argument of the Path-function TO.[4] Agent is the first argument of the Event-function CAUSE. Experiencer presumably is an argument of an as yet unexplored State-function having to do with mental states (see section 7.5 for one possibility). In other words, thematic roles are nothing but particular structural configurations in conceptual structure; the names for them are just convenient memonics for particularly prominent configurations.[5]

In support of this claim, notice that there are many kinds of arguments for which there is no traditional name. Consider the object of the verb *pass*, as in *John passed the house*. This sentence means essentially "John went *by* the house." *By* is an elaboration of the Path-function VIA—roughly VIA NEAR; this function is incorporated into the transitive verb *pass*, just as TO IN is incorporated into *enter*. The direct object of transitive *pass* thus is understood as the argument of this Path-function; it is neither Source nor Goal nor Theme in the usual sense. (Section 4.2 treats *pass* in more detail.)

Similarly, consider the direct objects of *jump* (*John jumped the gorge*), *approach* (*John approached Harry*), and *pierce* (*The arrow pierced the target*). These verbs incorporate OVER/ACROSS, TOWARD, and THROUGH (or VIA IN), respectively. Although there is no standard name for the thematic roles of these direct objects, their conceptual roles are perfectly well defined and fall out of the general account of Path-functions.

A slightly different case arises with the transitive use of the verb *climb*. In *John climbed the mountain*, it is not the mountain that is Goal, but the top of the mountain. That is, transitive *climb* embeds its NP argument in a structure something like

$$[_{\text{Path}} \text{ TO } ([_{\text{Place}} \text{ TOP-OF } ([_{\text{Thing}} \quad]_j)])].$$

There is a Goal, both intuitively and formally, but it is a location on the Thing denoted by the direct object—not the Thing itself. Again, we do not want to have to invent a new thematic role for the object of *climb*; treating thematic roles as structural positions in conceptual configurations eliminates any such need.

My claim, therefore, is that the terms *Theme, Agent,* and so on, are not primitives of semantic theory. Rather, they are relational notions defined structurally over conceptual structure, with a status precisely comparable to that of the notions Subject and Object in many syntactic theories (e.g. Standard Theory, Extended Standard Theory, GB Theory, but not Lexical-Functional Grammar (LFG) and Relational Grammar). In particular, they are not marked as annotations to D-Structure (GB Theory) or to predicate argument structure (LFG; see Bresnan 1982d, 293). Nor are they specified at a special level of representation such as Stowell's (1981) "θ-grid," Williams's (1984, 640) "argument structure," or Culicover and Wilkins's

1986) "R-structure." In another approach, Higginbotham (1985, 555) speaks of the "thematic grid" of the lexical item *see*, but gives it just the content $\langle 1, 2, E \rangle$, that is, a first and second argument plus an "event argument." Such a level is actually devoid of thematic content in the original sense of thematic roles; it is just a syntactic indexing device. Grimshaw's (1987, 1990) level of argument structure consists of a hierarchichically arranged set of indices to thematic roles; here again the structure is devoid of semantic content.

The present approach to the syntax-semantics correspondence gives a principled account of the intuitions behind these various approaches to argument structure. Using the notation shown in (3) and (5), a list of a verb's arguments can be constructed simply by extracting the indices from the verb's lexical conceptual structure; the thematic role connected with each index is determined by the structural position of the index in the overall conceptual structure. In theories such as Williams's that divide arguments into internal and external arguments, i is the external argument. Higginbotham's "event argument," which licenses existential quantification and modification over the Event as a whole, is represented in the present notation by the bracketing $[_{Event} \quad]$ that surrounds the verb's lexical conceptual structure. The hierarchy of θ-roles in Grimshaw's theory is, for a first approximation, provided by the relative depth of embedding of the indices in conceptual structure (see chapter 11 for amplification). In short, "argument structure" can be thought of as an abbreviation for the part of conceptual structure that is "visible" to the syntax.

Why is this important? It has to do with the independent motivation of thematic analyses. If there is going to be any way to determine the thematic roles in a sentence, it has to begin with semantic intuitions like those that motivated Gruber. To deal with unclear cases, these intuitions must be regimented into a format that permits independent semantic constraints. An annotation of syntax or a list of θ-roles in the sentence permits no such independent constraints. By contrast, the present account embeds the theory of thematic roles in a rich system governed by its own combinatorial properties, such as those illustrated in (1).

In addition, an important way of differentiating thematic roles is to see how they behave in rules of inference. Each kind of argument position plays a distinct role in rules of inference, which are stated over full conceptual structures, not over a list of thematic roles. Recall inference rule (1.21), which says, informally, that at the end of an Event of going to some place, one is at that place. This inference depends on the total conceptual configuration; it does not hold if either of the functions in the Event is changed—for instance if TO is changed to TOWARD, as in *Bill ran toward the house*, or if GO is changed to ORIENT, as in *Bill pointed to the house*.

An important test of a putative generalization of thematic roles to a new case, then, is to see whether the rules of inference generalize properly. In the present context, the point is that one cannot state inference rules over a mere list of thematic roles in a sentence, since a list of thematic roles does not express an assertion. On the other hand, if thematic roles are regarded as structural relations in conceptual structure, as proposed here, the inferential possibilities grow directly out of the structure in which the θ-role-bearing NPs are embedded.

Still, it certainly turns out that only limited aspects of conceptual structure interact with syntax. This might be seen as motivation for an independent level of θ-structure that encodes only a subset of conceptual information. But there is an alternative account that requires no extra level of representation: one can incorporate the constraints directly into the correspondence rule component. For example, various syntactic processes make use of the singular–plural distinction, but none (so far as I know) ever make use of the red/orange distinction. One could account for this either (1) by claiming that there is a level of argument structure that encodes plurality but not color, or else (2) by claiming that the correspondence rules between semantics and syntax can refer only to plurality but not color. As far as I can see without detailed examples, the constraints on the theory and the need for stipulation are exactly the same in either case, and the latter treatment makes do with one fewer level of representation.

To sum up, thematic relations are *not* like case-markers, that is, a system of diacritics. Rather, they are a system of structural relations. The constraints on their number and type follow from whatever constraints exist on the range of conceptual functions necessary to express the meanings of verbs and prepositions.

Three quick consequences follow from this conclusion. First, there is no θ-role of *subject* (as appears in Baker 1988, for example, and as alluded to, perhaps in a moment of terminological inattention, by Chomsky (1981, 148, note 113)). *Subject* is a syntactic relation, not a conceptual one, and syntactic subjects can hold a variety of different thematic roles.

Second, not only NPs receive thematic roles. For instance, *green* is a Goal in (6a), and *PRO shut up* is a Goal in (6b).

(6) a. The light changed from red to green.
    b. Bill talked Harry into shutting up.

From the latter case we see also that *proposition* is not the thematic role for a subordinate clause, as suggested by Bresnan (1982d, 293). *Proposition* may be a conceptual category like Thing and Event, expressed most frequently by an S. But if there is such a conceptual category, it can occur in various thematic roles, just as Things can.

Third, there cannot be a "default" thematic role in the sense that there is a "default" or "neutral" case Objective in Fillmore's (1968) Case Grammar —a thematic role that an NP is assigned when it has nothing else. Rather, an NP must correspond to a specific argument position in conceptual structure and therefore must have a specific thematic role. Some treatments have taken Theme or Patient to be such a default role—if one can't think of anything else to call an NP, call it Theme or Patient (and the two terms have sometimes been treated as interchangeable). However, Theme has a specific structural definition, following Gruber, and Patient (traditionally the "object affected by the action") is not a role in Gruber's system. Thus neither can serve as a default case. We will take up a treatment of Patients in chapter 7; meanwhile, the claim here is that every putative thematic role assignment must be justified on the grounds of its place in conceptual structure. The notion of a default conceptual role is incoherent.

2.3 Argument Fusion and Selectional Restrictions

Having laid out the basic position of Conceptual Semantics on the status of thematic roles, I want next to be more specific about the combinatorial rules that develop the conceptual structure of a sentence from its parts. Let us consider again how the lexical entries in (3) are used to build up the conceptual structure (2b). For a first approximation, the general principle involved might be (7), a refinement of the preliminary rule (1.18).

(7) *Argument Substitution* (version 1)

To form the conceptual structure for a syntactic phrase XP headed by a lexical item H:

a. For each indexed constituent C in H's lexical conceptual structure (LCS), substitute the conceptual structure of that phrase YP that satisfies the coindexed position in H's subcategorization feature.

b. If H is a verb, substitute the conceptual structure of the subject for the constituent indexed *i* (the external argument) in H's LCS.

(7) applies in (2a) three times: part (a) substitutes the reading of *the room* for the variable in the LCS of *into*; it also substitutes the reading of *into the room* for the Path-variable in the LCS of *run*; part (b) substitutes the reading of *John* for the Thing-variable in the LCS of *run*.

(7) as it stands assumes that all linkings between argument positions and syntactic positions are stipulated in the head's lexical entry. Yet clearly there are regularities of linking, for example the fact that Agents invariably appear in subject position. One can imagine various ways to express such regularities and thereby to leave predictable indices out of lexical entries. One way would be to express predictable correspondences by means of special cases within (7), for example "For the first argument of CAUSE,

substitute the reading of the subject." Another alternative would be to preserve the form of (7) but fill in predictable coindexing within lexical entries by redundancy rules, for example "Assign to the first argument of CAUSE the index *i*." Although this issue is crucial, I defer discussing it until chapter 11, after a number of potential obstacles are cleared out of the way. In the interests of not juggling too many balls at once, I will retain lexically stipulated coindexing until then.

A more immediate issue concerns the adequacy of the term *substitute* in (7). As stated, (7) permits the reading of any NP in a subcategorized position to be substituted for the coindexed variable in the verb's LCS. So, for example, it would apply to (8a) to give a reading (8b).

(8) a. Sincerity entered the room.

b. [$_{Event}$ GO ([$_{Property}$ SINCERITY], [$_{Path}$ TO ([$_{Place}$ IN ([$_{Thing}$ ROOM])])])]

The trouble with (8), among other things, is that the Theme is of an incorrect conceptual category: a Property cannot be the Theme of spatial motion. This restriction is already present in the lexical entry (5) for *enter*, where the position indexed *i* is specified as a Thing. (7), however, does not attend to such specification: it just dumbly substitutes the reading of the subject, whatever its category, for the requisite variable.

An immediate remedy would be to revise (7) to (9) (changes in italics).

(9) *Argument Substitution* (version 2)

To form the conceptual structure for a syntactic phrase XP headed by a lexical item H:

a. For each indexed constituent C in H's LCS, substitute the conceptual structure of that phrase YP that satisfies the coindexed position in H's subcategorization feature, *if its conceptual category matches that of C.*

b. If H is a verb, substitute the conceptual structure of the subject for the constituent C indexed *i* in H's LCS, *if its conceptual category matches that of C.*

Given this extra condition, the subject of (8a) would fail to be substituted into the appropriate argument position and hence the sentence could not receive a well-formed reading.

However, the problem with (8) is actually symptomatic of a broader problem, that of how to stipulate selectional restrictions. Selectional restrictions are general semantic restrictions on arguments, which may go into much more detail than merely the conceptual category. Three typical examples are the object of *drink*, which must be a liquid, the direct object of *pay*, which must be an amount of money, and the subject of German *fressen* ("eat"), which is predicated only of animals. In each of these cases, the selectional restriction is part of the verb's lexical entry, but it does not follow in any obvious way from the action predicated by the verb. One can pour a powder down one's throat, but one cannot *drink* a powder; one can give someone five cats in exchange for a book, but one cannot *pay* someone five cats for a book; and while a girl can eat, *Das Mädchen frisst* can only be meant facetiously.

Selectional restrictions evidently are constructed out of a subvocabulary of conceptual structures. That is, the set of possible selectional restrictions is chosen from primitives and principles of combination present in conceptual structure, including not only major conceptual category but also distinctions such as solid versus liquid, human versus animal, and so on. Thus the appropriate linguistic level for stating them is conceptual structure and not syntax or a putative level of argument structure.

Chomsky (1965, 110–111) suggests that selectional restrictions be formally treated as conditions on lexical insertion—essentially, that a verb cannot be inserted into a sentence if its arguments violate its selectional restrictions. Rule (9) is stated in this spirit. However, if we are interested in accounting for the *interpretations* of sentences as well as their *grammaticality*, Chomsky's formalization is not enough. For instance, it tells us only that the sentences in (10) are grammatical; it does not tell us that *it* in (10a) is understood to be a liquid, that *a lot* in (10b) is understood to be a lot of money, or that *sie* in (10c) is understood to be a female animal.

(10) a. Harry drank it.
      b. Bill paid Harry a lot.
      c. Sie frisst.

This fact is noticed by Weinreich (1966), who points out that anomalies caused by selectional restriction violations and the construal of proforms in the context of selectional restrictions ought to be recognized as reflections of the same phenomenon.

The proper treatment of selectional restrictions is suggested by further cases, where an argument is not even syntactically expressed:

(11) a. Harry drank (again).
      b. Bill paid.

Here Harry is still understood to have ingested a liquid and Bill to have given away some amount of money. From this we see that in fact *selectional restrictions are just explicit information that the verb supplies about its arguments.* If an argument is unexpressed, the information is supplied entirely by the verb. If an argument is expressed by an NP, the verb supplements the NP's reading with material of its own. If the NP argument is a proform, the verb's selectional features are added to the interpretation of the proform; if the NP is content-bearing, the selectional features are still added, though in some cases they will be redundant. (They are not always redundant: in *Hans frisst*, we know that Hans is an animal.) Finally, a selectional restriction violation occurs if the features supplied by the verb conflict with those of the NP argument.

In short, a selectional restriction should not be regarded as a contextual condition on the insertion of a verb. Rather, it is part of the verb's meaning and should be fully integrated into the verb's argument structure.

To capture this theoretical intuition in the present framework, we can treat a selectional restriction simply as ordinary conceptual structure that happens to occur within an indexed conceptual constituent. So, for example, *drink* will have a lexical entry like (12). (I will assume it means "cause a liquid to go into one's mouth," obviously an oversimplification, but sufficient for the present point.)

(12)
$$\begin{bmatrix} \text{drink} \\ \text{V} \\ \underline{\quad\quad} \ \langle NP_j \rangle \\ [_{\text{Event}} \ \text{CAUSE} \ ([_{\text{Thing}} \quad]_i, [_{\text{Event}} \ \text{GO} \ ([_{\text{Thing}} \ \text{LIQUID}]_j, \\ \quad\quad [_{\text{Path}} \ \text{TO} \ ([_{\text{Place}} \ \text{IN} \ ([_{\text{Thing}} \ \text{MOUTH OF} \ ([_{\text{Thing}} \quad]_i)])])])]) \end{bmatrix}$$

In this entry, the selectional restriction on the direct object appears as the conceptual information LIQUID within the constituent indexed j.

In order to make use of this information, we cannot simply substitute the reading of the direct object NP for the constituent indexed j. Rather, it is evidently necessary to regard the reading of an NP argument as somehow *fused* or *merged* with the semantic information already present in the constituent. I will not try to characterize such an operation of fusion formally, but intuitively its effect is clear: a conceptual constituent C resulting from the fusion of constituents C_1 and C_2 contains all the information of C_1 and C_2, and redundant information is deleted. If C_1 and C_2 contain incompatible information, the fusion of C_1 and C_2 is anomalous. This will occur, for example, if the offending features are sisters in a taxonomy of mutually exclusive possibilities, such as Thing/Property/Place/Event/etc. or solid/liquid/gas.

Under this view, we should replace Argument Substitution with a rule of Argument Fusion:[6]

(13) *Argument Fusion*

To form the conceptual structure for a syntactic phrase XP headed by a lexical item H:

a. Into each indexed constituent in H's LCS, fuse the conceptual structure of that phrase YP that satisfies the coindexed position in H's subcategorization feature.

b. If H is a verb, fuse the conceptual structure of the subject into the constituent indexed i in H's LCS.

In *Harry drank the wine*, Argument Fusion combines the reading of *wine* with the constituent [$_\text{Thing}$ LIQUID]$_j$; the redundant feature LIQUID is deleted. In *Harry drank it*, the result of fusion is the reading "contextually specific liquid," the former part coming from the pronoun and the latter from the verb. In *Harry drank*, there is no NP to be fused with the *j*-indexed constituent, so the reading is merely "liquid" and otherwise unspecified. In *Harry drank the powder*, fusion combines *powder*, carrying the feature SOLID, with LIQUID, the selectional restriction, producing a clash. In *Harry drank sincerity*, the clash is on the major category feature: the verb supplies the feature Thing but *sincerity* supplies the feature Property. Thus Argument Fusion deals with all the observed phenomena concerning selectional restrictions—including the use of selectional restrictions to make sure that the major conceptual category of an argument matches that stipulated by the verb.

According to this account, selectional restrictions on arguments are of exactly the same form as stipulation of totally incorporated arguments such as the Theme in (14a) and the Goal in (14b).

(14) a. Harry buttered the bread.
b. Joe pocketed the money.

The verbs in (14) have the conceptual structures in (15).

(15) a. [$_\text{Event}$ CAUSE ([$_\text{Thing}$]$_i$, [$_\text{Event}$ GO ([$_\text{Thing}$ BUTTER], [$_\text{Path}$ TO ([$_\text{Place}$ ON ([$_\text{Thing}$]$_j$)])])])]
b. [$_\text{Event}$ CAUSE ([$_\text{Thing}$]$_i$, [$_\text{Event}$ GO ([$_\text{Thing}$]$_j$, [$_\text{Path}$ TO ([$_\text{Place}$ IN ([$_\text{Thing}$ POCKET])])])])]

In (15a), the Theme bears no index and thus is not connected to a subcategorized position. Hence it is totally filled in with information from the verb and understood as "nonspecific butter." In (15b), the Path bears no index and thus receives its interpretation "into a pocket" entirely from the verb.

Comparing (15a) with (12), we notice that the similarities and differences between *butter* and *drink* fall out directly from the notation adopted here. There is no need to interpose a level of argument structure to encode them. Both are verbs that mean "cause something to go someplace." They differ semantically in what further information they stipulate about the Theme and the Path; they differ syntactically only in that *butter* is obligatorily transitive and *drink* is optionally transitive. From the present point of view, though, their most striking difference is in the syntactic-semantic correspondence they stipulate. The direct object of *butter* is the Goal, and the Theme is completely specified by the verb. By contrast, the direct object of *drink* is the Theme, and the Path is (almost) completely specified by the verb.

The point of this comparison is that the specification of conceptual structure within arguments of the verb—part of the verb's meaning—can be regarded as in large part orthogonal to the positions of indices on arguments—the way the verb links its arguments to syntactic structure. If a constituent of the verb's meaning is indexed, its semantic features appear as a selectional restriction; if a constituent is unindexed, its features appear as the content of an implicit argument. Thus the notion of selectional restriction can be dropped altogether from linguistic theory except as a convenient name for the effects of Argument Fusion.[7]

We have now established the basic machinery for relating arguments in conceptual structure to arguments in syntax. Each lexical item in the sentence specifies how its conceptual arguments are linked to syntactic positions in the phrase it heads. The rule of Argument Fusion uses this lexical information to integrate the readings of syntactic complements and subjects with indexed argument positions in the conceptual structure of the head.

Along the way, the theory has provided an explication of various important theoretical terms. *Thematic role* or *θ-role* is now a term for an argument position in conceptual structure; the particular *θ-roles* such as Agent and Theme now are particular structural positions, with conceptual content. *θ-marking* now amounts to establishing a correspondence between syntactic and conceptual arguments of a verb, as formalized by the coindexing conventions. *Selectional restrictions* are now formalized as conceptual information that a head supplies within an indexed conceptual constituent. *Argument structure* consists of the set of indices that relate the syntactic and conceptual arguments of a head. An *implicit argument* is a conceptual argument that is not expressed syntactically. This integration of the theory is possible only because argument structure is worked out in terms of a full representation of conceptual structure rather than as a set of diacritics that annotate the syntax or as a highly impoverished set of indices. I take this to be a virtue of the present approach.

2.4 Restrictive Modification

So far we have discussed only elaborations of conceptual structure that involve function-argument organization. However, there is at least one other kind of conceptual elaboration: the use of one constituent as a *modifier* of another. The prototypical case of modification is an AP modifier of an NP, but modification occurs with a wide range of modifying and modified categories. I will notate modification by placing the conceptual structure of the modifier within the brackets of the conceptual structure for the head, as illustrated in (16).

(16) a. red hat   (AP modifier of NP)

$$\begin{bmatrix} \text{HAT} \\ _{\text{Thing}} [_{\text{Property}} \text{ RED}] \end{bmatrix}$$

b. house in the woods   (PP modifier of NP)

$$\begin{bmatrix} \text{HOUSE} \\ _{\text{Thing}} [_{\text{Place}} \text{ IN } ([_{\text{Thing}} \text{ WOODS}])] \end{bmatrix}$$

c. John went home quickly.   (AdvP modifier of VP)

$$\begin{bmatrix} \text{GO } ([_{\text{Thing}} \text{ JOHN}], [_{\text{Path}} \text{ TO } ([_{\text{Place}} \text{ HOME}])]) \\ _{\text{Event}} [_{\text{Property/Manner}} \text{ QUICK}] \end{bmatrix}$$

d. John went home at 6:00.   (PP modifier of VP)

$$\begin{bmatrix} \text{GO } ([_{\text{Thing}} \text{ JOHN}], [_{\text{Path}} \text{ TO } ([_{\text{Place}} \text{ HOME}])]) \\ _{\text{Event}} [_{\text{Place}} \text{ AT}_{\text{Temp}} ([_{\text{Time}} \text{ 6:00}])] \end{bmatrix}$$

e. high on the hill   (AP modifier of PP)

$$\begin{bmatrix} \text{ON } ([_{\text{Thing}} \text{ HILL}]) \\ _{\text{Place}} [_{\text{Property}} \text{ HIGH}] \end{bmatrix}$$

f. [pp here [pp in the house]]   (PP modifier of PP)

$$\begin{bmatrix} \text{HERE} \\ _{\text{Place}} [_{\text{Place}} \text{ IN } ([_{\text{Thing}} \text{ HOUSE}])] \end{bmatrix}$$

The overall schema for such expansions is given in (17). It parallels the general schema (1.16) for function-argument structure.

(17) *Restrictive modification schema*

$$[\text{Entity}_1] \rightarrow \begin{bmatrix} X \\ [\text{Entity}_2] \end{bmatrix}$$

(17) obviously must be constrained with respect to the possible combinations of ontological categories in head and modifier. For instance, I find it hard to imagine a Thing or an Event modifying a Manner—though this may just reflect my lack of imagination. However, the examples in (16) (and others in *S&C*, pages 70–71) show that restrictive modification displays strong X-bar character, just like function-argument structure.[8]

In order to integrate the readings of restrictive modifiers into the readings of the phrases they modify, we must add a rule alongside Argument Fusion in the correspondence rule component. Let us assume for simplicity that all restrictive modifiers of a phrase XP are daughters of X" within XP, that is, one syntactic level higher than subcategorized phrases. (More complicated configurations will affect the rule in obvious but for present purposes irrelevant ways.)

(18) *Restrictive Modifier Rule*
If YP is daughter of X" in XP,
and the conceptual structure of YP is [C$_y$],
then the conceptual structure of XP is of the form

$$\begin{bmatrix} \dots \\ [C_y] \end{bmatrix}.$$

Let us use (18) to derive the conceptual structure in (16d) for the sentence *John went home at 6:00*. The head of the phrase is *go*, whose lexical entry is (19).

$$(19) \quad \begin{bmatrix} \text{go} \\ V \\ \underline{\qquad} \; PP_j \\ [_{Event} \; GO \; ([_{Thing} \quad]_i, [_{Path} \quad]_j)] \end{bmatrix}$$

By Argument Fusion, the readings of *John* and *home* are fused with that of *go* to form (20), the function-argument structure for the sentence.

(20) $[_{Event} \; GO \; ([_{Thing} \; JOHN], [_{Path} \; TO \; ([_{Place} \; HOME])])]$

The conceptual structure of the PP *at 6:00* is constructed similarly by Argument Fusion:

(21) $[_{Place} \; AT_{Temp} \; ([_{Time} \; 6:00])]$

Next, the PP is a daughter of V'' (by assumption), so the Restrictive Modifier Rule applies. It specifies that the reading of *John went home at 6:00* is (22).

$$(22) \quad \begin{bmatrix} \cdots \\ [_{Place} \; AT_{Temp} \; ([_{Time} \; 6:00])] \end{bmatrix}$$

Since the reading of the sentence must be consistent with both (20) and (22), it has to be (23), the fusion of the two.

(23) $(= (16d))$
$$\begin{bmatrix} \qquad GO \; ([_{Thing} \; JOHN], [_{Path} \; TO \; ([_{Place} \; HOME])]) \\ _{Event} \; [_{Place} \; AT_{Temp} \; ([_{Time} \; 6:00])] \end{bmatrix}$$

Overall, then, the system works like this so far: If YP within XP is subcategorized by the head H or is a subject, its place in the conceptual structure of XP is determined by H, and its reading is integrated into the sentence by Argument Fusion. On the other hand, if YP is neither subcategorized by H nor a subject, it does not participate in Argument Fusion and must be integrated into the reading of XP by other means. The Restrictive Modifier Rule is the simplest of such means; we will encounter others in part III.

A final comment on restrictive modification: in the case of multiply specified Paths it is often hard to distinguish head from modifier. I will therefore adopt the notation illustrated in (24).

(24) from the house to the barn
$$\begin{bmatrix} \qquad FROM \; ([_{Thing} \; HOUSE]) \\ _{Path} \; TO \; ([_{Thing} \; BARN]) \end{bmatrix}$$

It is not clear to me whether this is of theoretical significance or just a notational convenience.

Speaking of notational convenience, it should already be apparent that the formal notation for conceptual structure rapidly becomes cumbersome when we start to write more complex expressions. As an effort to spare us all from typographical overload, I will freely omit many self-evident parentheses and category labels from here on.

Chapter 3
Multiple Thematic Roles for a Single NP

3.1 The Status of the θ-Criterion

In the light of the theory of thematic roles developed in the previous chapter, let us examine the θ-Criterion, which says, in our terms, (1) that each subcategorized NP (plus the subject) corresponds to exactly one argument position in conceptual structure, and (2) that each open argument position in conceptual structure is expressed by exactly one NP.[1] Given the centrality of the θ-Criterion to GB Theory, and the existence of parallel notions in other theories (such as biuniqueness in LFG), it is worth asking whether it can bear the theoretical weight it has been required to carry. Here is a variety of examples that collectively suggest that the θ-Criterion must be weakened.

3.1.1 Cases Where an NP Has More Than One θ-Role
In sentences with transaction verbs such as *buy, sell, exchange,* and *trade,* there are two actions going on at once. For instance, *buy* involves at least the components (1a) and (1b).

(1) X buy Y from Z
    a. Y changes possession from Z to X
    b. money changes possession from X to Z

Thus X and Z have two semantic roles apiece. We cannot save the θ-Criterion by just saying that the roles in the countertransfer (1b) do not count: it is precisely the presence of the countertransfer that distinguishes *buy* from *obtain.*

Moreover, the presence of a countertransfer may be reflected in syntax. Notice what happens when we append *for $5* to both *buy* and *obtain*:

(2) a. X bought Y from Z for $5.
    b. X obtained Y from Z for $5.

Both of these sentences express a countertransfer whose Theme is *$5.* *Obtain* permits a countertransfer to be indicated by a *for*-phrase, in which case X and Z take on the requisite extra roles. On the other hand, *buy* always entails a countertransfer, which *may* be expressed in part by the *for*-phrase. So the countertransfer does have syntactic effects. (See chapter 9 for a more thorough treatment.)

Another verb with multiple θ-roles on each NP is *chase* (a classic example whose treatment goes back to Weinreich 1966 and Katz 1972). For an action to count as chasing, at least three conditions must be satisfied:

(3) X chase Y
  a. Y in motion
  b. X moves toward (or along path of) Y
  c. X intends to go to (or catch) Y

If Y is standing still, X isn't chasing Y (though (3a) is conceivably a preference rule rather than a necessary condition for *chase*). Similarly, if X isn't moving toward Y, X isn't chasing Y, whatever Y's motions and X's intentions; and if X doesn't intend to go to (or catch) Y, X is at best *following* Y, not chasing Y. Thus X has two essential roles and Y three. Is there any reason to call one of these *the* θ-role of X or Y? Perhaps, but it requires some motivation.

3.1.2 Cases Where Multiple NPs Hold a Single θ-Role

Conversely, there are other cases where two NPs in the sentence seem to have the same θ-role. Here are three (pointed out by Gruber (1965, section 7.3) and by Richard Carter in talks at MIT, fall 1984):

(4) a. The box has books in it.
  b. Bill brought/carried some books with him.
  c. The list includes my name on it.

In (4a), *the box* and *it* do not appear to have distinct θ-roles; notice the apparent synonymy with *there are books in the box*, where this participant in the state is expressed only once. Notice also that it is impossible to question the object of the preposition (**What does the box have books in?*), as would be expected, given that it is necessarily coreferential with the subject. The object of the preposition is also curious in that it cannot be a reflexive (**The box has books in itself*), even though for all the usual structural reasons it ought to be (Wilkins (1988b) proposes an analysis on which I am not prepared to make a judgment at this point).

Similar considerations apply to (4b, c), where *with him* and *on it* do not seem to add any information. They can be omitted without loss, and cannot be questioned (**Who did Bill bring some books with?*; **What does the list include my name on?*). No other NP can be substituted in (4b) (**Bill brought some books with Harry*), and only NPs that express some location within the list can be substituted in (4c) (*The list includes my name on its/the* *first page*). Again the reflexive is unaccountably ruled out (***Bill brought some books with himself*).

In each of these cases, then, two different NPs in the sentence appear to satisfy the same θ-role. We thus have counterexamples to both parts of the θ-Criterion.

Why is this important? The θ-Criterion is normally based on the view of θ-roles as annotations to syntactic structure; in fact, many linguists write of θ-marking and case-marking as though these are comparable phenomena —see, for example, Dowty 1988. My purpose in presenting these examples is to show that the θ-Criterion as generally understood is not so obviously correct and that the view of θ-roles that it presupposes is itself problematic. The correspondence between syntax and θ-roles must be stated in somewhat less rigid terms, in particular admitting the real richness of thematic roles. The rest of this chapter will recast in more adequate terms the insight that the θ-Criterion attempts to express.

3.2 Argument Binding

As stated so far, the rule of Argument Fusion (2.13) does not stipulate that the coindexing of syntactic and conceptual arguments is biunique. That is, there is nothing to prevent two indexed positions in conceptual structure from bearing the same index and hence being filled with the same information from syntax. This is one way in which we could imagine a single NP coming to receive multiple θ-roles, as seen in (1) and (3). Similarly, there is nothing to prevent two *syntactic* positions from bearing the same index and hence being mapped into the very same θ-role, as seen in (4).

Let us concentrate on the former case. Under this view, the lexical entry of *buy* would look something like (5). In the LCS of (5), the countertransfer (changing hands of money) is treated as an argument of a modifying function EXCH ("in exchange for"). The Theme of the countertransfer, [MONEY], is a completely incorporated argument, just like the incorporated argument [BUTTER] in the verb *butter*. (This analysis is justified in section 9.3; for now, nothing much hangs on its precise details.)

(5)
$$
\begin{bmatrix}
\text{buy} \\
\text{V} \\
\underline{\quad\quad} \ \text{NP}_j \langle \text{from NP}_k \rangle \\
\begin{bmatrix}
\text{GO}_{\text{Poss}} \ ([\quad]_j, \begin{bmatrix} \text{FROM} [\quad]_k \\ \text{TO} [\quad]_i \end{bmatrix}) \\
[\text{EXCH} [\text{GO}_{\text{Poss}} \ ([\text{MONEY}], \begin{bmatrix} \text{FROM} [\quad]_i \\ \text{TO} [\quad]_k \end{bmatrix})]]
\end{bmatrix}
\end{bmatrix}
$$

In this representation, the multiple roles arise from the fact that the external argument and the object of *from* are each coindexed to two positions in the

LCS. As a result, Argument Fusion fills in the readings of each of these NPs in two places. For example, *Bill bought the book from Sue* will end up with the conceptual structure (6).

$$(6) \quad \begin{bmatrix} GO_{Poss} ([BOOK], \begin{bmatrix} FROM\ [SUE] \\ TO\ [BILL] \end{bmatrix}) \\ [EXCH\ [GO_{Poss}\ ([MONEY], \begin{bmatrix} FROM\ [BILL] \\ TO\ [SUE] \end{bmatrix})]] \end{bmatrix}$$

Now consider a sentence in which the *from*-phrase is absent:

(7) Bill bought the book.

As in cases we have discussed previously (e.g. *enter*), the implicit argument does not just disappear from the conceptual structure of (7): for Bill to have bought the book, he has to have gotten it from someone and have given money to someone.

This however raises a difficulty for the LCS in (5): it does not indicate that when the *from*-phrase is absent, the Source of the main transfer and the Goal of the countertransfer are still necessarily the same unmentioned character. Bill could be getting the book from one person and giving money to another.

Similarly, in the passive (8), the external argument has become implicit (by mechanisms to be suggested in section 4.3).

(8) The book was bought from Sue.

Here both the Goal of the main transfer and the Source of the counter-transfer are unfilled. Yet it is clear again that these two roles are performed by the same individual.

Looking a little more deeply, there is in fact a problem even with the idea of fusing the reading of an NP into two distinct conceptual positions, as would be required by the theory so far. Consider a case like (9).

(9) Bill bought a book from a funny old man.

If the reading of *a funny old man* is fused into both positions marked k in (5), there is nothing that says the two positions are the same funny old man.

The solution to these problems is to devise a way of stipulating co-reference among arguments—whether they are expressed syntactically or not. One could take the indices i and k shared by the positions in (5) as expressing such a stipulation. However, it becomes useful for future purposes to make a strict separation between two kinds of coindexing: (1) coindexing that links a syntactic constituent to a conceptual constituent—the type we have used so far; and (2) coindexing that stipulates that two or more thematic roles are satisfied by the same individual—the type we need to solve these problems with the lexical entry of *buy*.

There are many possible notations for this latter type of coindexing; here is one. Let us define an asymmetrical relation of *argument binding*, which obtains between a *binding argument* (or *binder*) and one or more *bound arguments* (or *bindees*). Each complex of binder and bindees represents a unified character in conceptual structure, and a character's properties comprise the fusion of properties inherited from all binding and bound positions in the complex. A binding argument will be notated by a Greek superscript; its bindees will be notated by a Greek letter within the square brackets. Using this notation, (6) might be rewritten as (10).

$$(10) \begin{bmatrix} \text{GO}_{\text{Poss}} \, ([\text{BOOK}], \begin{bmatrix} \text{FROM } [\text{SUE}]^\alpha \\ \text{TO } [\text{BILL}]^\beta \end{bmatrix}) \\ [\text{EXCH } [\text{GO}_{\text{Poss}} \, ([\text{MONEY}], \begin{bmatrix} \text{FROM } [\beta] \\ \text{TO } [\alpha] \end{bmatrix})]] \end{bmatrix}$$

[handwritten annotation: binder / bindee]

This avoids the repetition of the conceptual material represented by SUE and BILL; at the same time it explicitly represents the unity of the characters carrying out the multiple roles.

This relation of argument binding can be incorporated directly into the lexical entry of *buy*. Instead of (5), then, we will have (11).

$$(11) \begin{bmatrix} \text{buy} \\ \text{V} \\ \underline{\qquad} \text{NP}_j \langle \text{from NP}_k \rangle \\ \begin{bmatrix} \text{GO}_{\text{Poss}} \, ([\quad]_{j'} \begin{bmatrix} \text{FROM } [\quad]^\alpha_k \\ \text{TO } [\quad]^\beta_i \end{bmatrix}) \\ [\text{EXCH } [\text{GO}_{\text{Poss}} \, ([\text{MONEY}], \begin{bmatrix} \text{FROM } [\beta] \\ \text{TO } [\alpha] \end{bmatrix})]] \end{bmatrix} \end{bmatrix}$$

[handwritten annotation: (i, j, k) concern what in the syntax goes to what in conceptual structure. (α, β, γ) are the relation between conceptual structure.]

The distinction between the two types of coindexing is explicit in the notation. Roman alphabet subscripts stipulate correspondence between syntactic and conceptual positions; Greek letters stipulate binding between conceptual positions. The Roman letters thus play no role internal to conceptual structure, but the binding structures do, as seen in (10).

Notice how argument binding in (11) solves the problems raised above. There are now only one i and one k in the lexical entry; the other roles of these characters are just bound arguments. Thus, if the *from*-phrase is absent, the Source of the main transfer is implicit, as before; but whoever it is, conceptual structure is still explicit that it is the same character as the Goal of the countertransfer. Similarly, if the subject is absent, for instance in the passive, conceptual structure is still explicit that the Goal of the main transfer and the Source of the countertransfer are the same individual. Finally, in (9), the indefinite *a funny old man* is fused into only one position, the Goal of the main transfer; the other role is bound to this one. Hence there is no possibility that the indefiniteness of the phrase leads to the postulation of two distinct characters.[2]

Adopting this enrichment of conceptual structure enables us to formulate almost trivially a more adequate version of what the θ-Criterion is intended to express:

(12) *Linking Condition* (Neo-θ-Criterion) $(i, \jmath)$

Each index linking syntactic and conceptual structure in a lexical entry must appear only once in the entry's LCS. All other θ-roles that the coindexed NP holds must be expressed by arguments bound to the indexed conceptual constituent.[3]

[handwritten margin note: same index/ carry the same information.]

This has the formal effect desired for the sake of the syntax: each syntactic argument is linked uniquely with a conceptual argument. At the same time, the possibility of an NP having multiple θ-roles is explicitly acknowledged and provided for. Furthermore, argument binding makes it possible for an implicit argument to have multiple roles as well, as is necessary for the cases discussed above.

There remains the issue of which of a bound complex of θ-roles is the unique indexed constituent and binder, and which are the bound arguments. In (11), I have somewhat arbitrarily put the indexed constituents in the main transfer, though formally they could reside equally well in the countertransfer. The intuition behind this choice is fairly clear: the part of the meaning that links most directly to syntax ought to be the main function rather than a modifier. More specifically, there is a relation of "dominance" among multiple θ-roles in a bound complex, such that a θ-role in the main function dominates one in a modifier; the *dominant θ-role* is the one that is linked to a syntactic position. A more thorough account of the choice will appear in chapter 11, where we take up general principles of linking.

3.3 On So-Called Syntactic Binding

It has been customary in the literature to notate coreference between NPs by means of subscripts in syntactic structure. In GB Theory, these subscripts are taken to be part of syntactic structure: they are marked by the binding theory, which applies at LF. We are now faced with an apparent duplication of descriptive machinery, since argument binding also marks coreference, but entirely within conceptual structure. Can this duplication be eliminated?

We have just seen that the need for argument binding is most highly motivated precisely when there is no NP to express the roles in question. Hence syntactic binding does not lend itself to being extended to these further cases. The question thus arises whether argument binding might take over the work traditionally ascribed to syntactic binding, so that binding can be treated as a unified mechanism.[4] I will provide some arguments in this section and the next that this is the proper approach.

Note first, as a point of plausibility, that coreference is fundamentally a semantic notion. Whatever notation is introduced into syntax, conceptual structure still needs some sort of formal machinery to indicate that two conceptual constituents are intended to describe the same individual—this is part of *meaning*. If syntax too contains a coindexing notation that encodes coreference or anaphoric dependence, then the correspondence rule component must contain a principle that maps syntactic coindexing into the formal features that encode coreference in conceptual structure. Thus, attempting to encode binding in conceptual structure instead of in syntax is just working out machinery that is necessary in any event, while reducing the expressive power of syntax.

The idea behind this approach, then, is that the relation between an anaphor and its antecedent is not to be treated as a coindexation in syntactic structure. Rather, the anaphor is linked to a bound argument in conceptual structure, and its antecedent is linked to its binder. In other words, within the present theory, the standard notation (13a) is to be considered an abbreviation for the formal treatment (13b).[5]

(13) a. *GB Theory notation*

$$NP_i \text{ binds } \begin{bmatrix} NP \\ anaphor \end{bmatrix}_i$$

b. *Conceptual Semantics formalism*

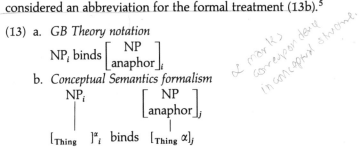

It would be too much to expect at this point to recast the entire GB binding theory in these terms. However, let me propose some suggestions as to how one would proceed.

A good entry into the problem is provided by the interplay between argument binding and syntactic binding in an example like the verb *dress*. This verb appears in four subcategorization frames, with both direct object and PP-complement optional:

(14) Bill dressed (Harry) (in a new suit).

What is of interest here is the effect of omitting the direct object. In previous cases such as *drink* and *enter*, the conceptual constituents indexed *j* became implicit arguments, with readings "nonspecific liquid" and "nonspecific enclosure" respectively. But intransitive *dress* does not mean "dress someone"—it means "dress oneself"; that is, the character being dressed becomes a bound argument instead of an implicit argument.

(15a) is a lexical entry for the transitive form of *dress*; (15b) is an entry for the intransitive form. The formal relation between these entries will be expressed in section 4.2.[6]

(15) a.
$$\begin{bmatrix} \text{dress} \\ \text{V} \\ \underline{\hspace{1cm}} \text{ NP}_j \langle \text{PP}_k \rangle \\ \text{[CAUSE ([\ \ ]}_i, \text{ [GO ([\ \ ]}_j, \text{ [TO [IN [CLOTHING]]}_k])])] \end{bmatrix}$$

b.
$$\begin{bmatrix} \text{dress} \\ \text{V} \\ \underline{\hspace{1cm}} \langle \text{PP}_k \rangle \\ \text{[CAUSE ([\ \ ]}^\alpha_i, \text{ [GO ([}\alpha], \text{ [TO [IN [CLOTHING]]}_k])])] \end{bmatrix}$$

Note that this alternation is lexically specific. The verb *clothe* is minimally different from *dress* in requiring the presence of the direct object:

(16) a.   Bill clothed Harry (in a new suit).
     b.   *Bill clothed in a new suit.

Thus one cannot appeal to any obvious general convention to account for the behavior of *dress*.

Now consider the conceptual structure of *Bill dressed himself*. This is for all intents and purposes synonymous with *Bill dressed*. How does this come about? Suppose that the conceptual structure of *himself* is just the feature MALE plus a variable ξ that must be satisfied by a binding index. Since *himself* is the direct object, Argument Fusion will substitute this variable into the position indexed j in (15a), yielding structure (17).

(17) [CAUSE ([BILL], [GO ($\begin{bmatrix} \text{MALE} \\ \xi \end{bmatrix}$, [TO [IN [CLOTHING]]])])]

What is missing in this representation, of course, is the assignment of a value of ξ, in particular the value α. A rule is necessary to establish this assignment. The general form of the rule will be (18).

(18)   *Binding principles*
Bind a conceptual constituent consisting of a variable ξ to a conceptual constituent superscripted α under the following conditions:

        [List of conditions]

The conditions in (18) will be the present theory's counterpart to the GB binding theory, stating under what conditions binding can and cannot be applied. Whatever the content of the conditions, the effect of applying rule (18) to (17) will be to change ξ to α, resulting in a representation identical to that of *Bill dressed*. In turn, this indirectly establishes the coreference of the NP *himself* with the NP *Bill*; that is, the linking and binding relations are as shown in (13b).

Since the configuration in (13b) includes both syntactic and conceptual structure, it may be expected that the conditions in the binding principles (18) may involve structural configurations in both. Thus an approach of this sort begins to make more sense of conditions on reflexivization that seem to involve the θ-roles as well as the structural positions of the NPs in question. Such conditions appear to be implicated in cases such as these, first noticed by Postal (1971):

(19) a.   Bill talked to Mary about herself.
     b. ?*Bill talked about Mary to herself.

(20) a.   ?Bill showed Mary herself (in the mirror).
     b. *Bill showed Mary to herself (in the mirror).

In Jackendoff 1972 these cases were analyzed in terms of a Thematic Hierarchy Condition on the interpretation of reflexives: roughly, a reflexive must be lower on an ordered list of θ-roles than its antecedent. In terms of a purely syntactic theory of anaphora, this seems a rather arbitrary stipulation. But in the present approach, the θ-roles of the NPs are as accessible to the binding principles as their syntactic positions; moreover, the thematic hierarchy may itself emerge as a configurational condition in conceptual structure, parallel to the syntactic conditions on binding such as c-command. (See Grimshaw 1990 for suggestions to this effect.)

In addition, the conceptual conditions in (18) may apply even in the absence of syntactic structure. Relevant examples have been discussed by Schachter (1976) and Williams (1985). For instance, in *those promises PRO to leave*, PRO is bound by the promiser, even though the determiner occupies the position where one would have to locate a controlling NP. In the present theory, the implicit argument is *explicit* in conceptual structure and serves as the binder for PRO. Conversely, Williams observes that in *John submitted Harry to Sue's scrutiny*, *Harry* serves as binder for the Patient of *scrutiny*—Harry is necessarily understood as the person Sue is scrutinizing. Yet there is no evidence for the presence of a PRO within the nominal (*Sue's scrutiny of PRO*), and in fact such a PRO would violate GB binding theory. Within the present account, the binding takes place purely in conceptual structure, where all arguments must be present in order to express the meaning.

The treatment of *dress* proposed here reflects on an issue mentioned in section 1.4: the homogeneity of lexical and extralexical principles of grammar. Reflexivization in English is obviously an extralexical principle, a subcase of rule (18). But the structure that results from applying (18) to (17)—the binding of the variable ξ to the subject—is identical to the structure of *Bill dressed*, in which the binding comes as part of the lexical entry of the verb. A case intermediate between these two is presented by Romance reflexive clitics, which, following Grimshaw 1982, are not free morphemes like English reflexives. Rather, the rule of reflexivization in Romance languages is a morphological rule that alters the form of lexical entries: it adds a reflexive clitic to the verb in the phonology and deletes an NP from the subcategorization frame in the syntax. In conceptual structure (in our terms), the rule deletes the index corresponding to the NP deleted in the syntax and substitutes into that argument an α bound to the subject—in short, it effects just the alternation that appears in the two forms of English *dress* seen in (15). Thus in this case a productive lexical rule has as output the same form of structure as the English extralexical rule. In a sense, it is this common effect that motivates calling both of them rules of reflexivization.[7]

Recasting the binding theory in terms of argument binding need not necessarily affect any of the syntactic content of the theory. All presently known syntactic conditions on binding may well still be valid. At the same time, though, (1) it permits semantic content to enter into the conditions on reflexives, and (2) it permits a homogeneous treatment of binding in cases where either binder or bindee or both is an implicit argument, a serious problem for a purely syntactic binding theory. Thus semantic effects on control and reflexivization will be not some curious intrusion of semantics into syntax but rather a natural concomitant of the way rules work in the correspondence rule component.

3.4 Appendix: Thematic Conditions on Control

Under the present treatment, reflexives are of course not the only items subject to principle (18): PRO must also be treated in terms of argument binding. Like reflexives, PRO has the conceptual structure [ξ], that is, "Bind me." Thus one would expect semantic conditions to appear in the theory of control. This section reviews evidence that this is the case.

As it happens, Gruber's theory of thematic relations first attracted my attention because it provides an approach to problems of control in examples like (21)–(22).

(21) a. John$_i$ gave Sue$_j$ orders PRO$_j$ to leave.
     b. John$_i$ got from Sue$_j$ orders PRO$_i$ to leave.

(22) a. John$_i$ gave Sue$_j$ a promise PRO$_i$ to leave.
     b. John$_i$ got from Sue$_j$ a promise PRO$_j$ to leave.

The problem is that these are all structurally identical in the relevant respects, so there is no apparent syntactic condition that can determine the proper antecedent for PRO.

However, the sentences differ in the positions of Source and Goal in a way appropriate to predict the results. Intuitively, it is part of the meaning of *order* that the recipient (or Goal) of an order is under obligation to perform the action described by the complement clause; it is part of the meaning of *promise* that the issuer (or Source) of a promise undertakes an obligation to perform the action described by the complement. This difference, crossed with the difference in θ-roles between *give* and *get*, correctly predicts the control properties of (21)–(22): the subject of the complement of *order* should be controlled by the Goal of the speech-act—the indirect object of *give* or the subject of *get*; the subject of the complement of *promise* should be controlled by the Source of the speech-act—the subject of *give* or the oblique object of *get from*.

This approach was sketched in Jackendoff 1972 and elaborated in Jackendoff 1974. If it is correct, thematic roles play an important role alongside syntactic structure in regulating control, especially in nominals. Similar conclusions have since been reached by Cattell (1984), Williams (1985), Chierchia (1988), and Farkas (1988).

In a review of Jackendoff 1972, Hust and Brame (1976) take issue with this conclusion, offering the single counterexample (23) to the claim that thematic roles help determine control.

(23) Bill was promised to be allowed to leave.

Here the recipient of the promise controls the complement subject, contrary to the analysis above. On these grounds, Hust and Brame (and many subsequent writers) dismiss the whole notion of thematic involvement in control.

However, the issue is not so simple. Notice that control by the recipient of a promise is restricted to a class of complements that is very tiny—and also syntactically and semantically extremely coherent:

(24) a.   Bill was promised to be permitted to leave.
    b.   *Bill was promised to permit Harry to leave.
    c.   *Bill was promised to get permission to leave.
    d.   *Bill was promised to leave the room.
    e.   *Bill was promised to be hit on the head.
      etc.

That is, the recipient of a promise seems to be able to control the complement subject only when (1) the complement is passive, (2) the complement subject is the recipient of permission from the Source of the promise, and (3) the Source of the promise is an implicit argument. In the parallel nominal, the same conditions apply:

(25) a.   Harry$_i$'s promise to Bill$_j$?PRO$_i$/*PRO$_j$ to be allowed to leave
    b.   the promise to Bill$_j$ PRO$_j$ to be allowed to leave

Thus the account of (23) seems inevitably to involve semantic information of some sort, though more subtly than in my original treatment of (21)–(22).[8]

Oehrle (1975, forthcoming) has also suggested counterexamples to the strongest account of (21)–(22), namely that thematic roles in a nominal are *always* determined by those in the matrix clause. In (26), for instance, *the director* can be either kicker or source of permission to kick; *the dancer* can be either kicker, "kickee," or interested observer. Only one of these combinations could be predicted by the strongest account.

(26) The director gave the dancer a kick.

Again, this requires a deeper account of (21)–(22), but it does not eliminate the contribution of thematic roles. In particular, in the reading of *kick* in which both the director and the dancer are characters involved in the action of kicking, the director must be understood as the kicker and the dancer as "kickee"; the reverse is impossible. By contrast, in the parallel reading of *kick* in (27), the roles of director and dancer are reversed, just as in (21)–(22).

(27) The director got a kick from the dancer.

Thus the problem presented by Oehrle is really one of refining the conditions under which the thematic roles assigned by the matrix verb affect those of the complement, not one of finding an altogether different theory. I conclude that indeed control cannot be accounted for in entirely syntactic terms—that semantic factors are inevitably involved. In a theory that encodes binding as a purely syntactic relation, such a conclusion is strange and to be avoided, as it threatens the autonomy of syntax. However, in the present theory, binding is a relation stated over conceptual structure and established by means of some conjunction of syntactic and semantic properties. It is therefore altogether natural that one should find semantic effects on control.

Chapter 4

Unifying Lexical Entries

How do you encode an argument structure.

As observed in section 1.5, an important problem for the theory of the lexicon—and especially for the learnability of the lexicon—is how to unify related uses of a lexical item into a single entry. This chapter will propose two abbreviatory conventions that permit certain alternations to be expressed within single lexical entries. (Further alternations will be taken up in part III.)

We should note that there are already two mechanisms in place for unifying the syntactic frames in which a lexical item occurs. First, potential *modifiers* of a lexical item are not encoded anywhere in its lexical entry. So, for example, the alternations in (1) have no reflex at all in the lexical entry of the verb *buy*.

(1) a. Harry bought a yoyo in Chicago.
    b. Harry bought a yoyo on Tuesday.
    c. Harry bought a yoyo impulsively.
       etc.

Hence the possibility of using *buy* with place, time, and manner expressions *Only alterations in* is not part of its lexical entry at all. Rather, only alternations in *argument* *argument st.* *structure* have to be encoded. *have to be encoded*

The one alternation in argument structure that we have already accounted for is optional expression of an argument, as in the examples given in (2).

(2) a. Harry bought a yoyo ⟨from Marcia⟩.
    b. Sue drank ⟨the martini⟩.

We have encoded such alternations in more or less traditional terms. The verb's subcategorization feature contains an optional position; if filled, it is coindexed to a conceptual argument; if unfilled, the conceptual argument becomes implicit.

4.1 Optional Outer Functions

(1) and (2), of course, hardly exhaust the full range of syntactic alternations. For another prominent case, consider the alternation of senses in the prepositions *under* and *over* in (3)–(4).

(3) a. The mouse is under the table.
   b. The mouse ran around under the table.
   c. The mouse ran under the table and stayed there.
   d. The mouse ran under the table into a hole in the wall.

(4) a. The plane is now over the city.
   b. The plane flew around over the city.
   c. The plane came over the city and started skywriting there.
   d. The plane flew over the city towards the mountains.

The (a) examples illustrate the preposition being used as a Place-function that satisfies the Place argument of *be*, as shown in (5a). In the (b) examples, the PP also denotes a Place; this time the Place is a restrictive modifier, giving the overall location of the Event, as shown in (5b).

(5) a. $[_{\text{Event}}$ BE $([_{\text{Thing}}$ MOUSE], $[_{\text{Place}}$ UNDER $([_{\text{Thing}}$ TABLE])])]

   b. $\left[\begin{array}{l} \text{GO } ([_{\text{Thing}} \text{ MOUSE}], [_{\text{Path}} \text{ AROUND}]) \\ _{\text{Event}} \ [_{\text{Place}} \text{ UNDER } ([_{\text{Thing}} \text{ TABLE}])] \end{array} \right]$

However, in the (c) sentences, the PP denotes instead the Path of motion, which terminates at the Place denoted by the Place sense of the PP. In this reading, *the table* and *the city* are Goals of motion. Thus if the Place sense of *under* is (6a), this Path sense is (6b).

(6) a. $[_{\text{Place}}$ UNDER $([_{\text{Thing}} \quad]_j)]$
   b. $[_{\text{Path}}$ TO $([_{\text{Place}}$ UNDER $([_{\text{Thing}} \quad]_j)])]$

In the (d) sentences, the PP also expresses a Path of motion, but *the table* and *the city* are not Goals. Rather, the PP denotes a route that the Theme traverses on the way to its Goal (the hole and the mountains respectively). Thus this sense is formalized as (6c).

(6) c. $[_{\text{Path}}$ VIA $([_{\text{Place}}$ UNDER $([_{\text{Thing}} \quad]_j)])]$

These alternations with *under* and *over*, though common among English prepositions, are not due to general rules of construal, because many Place prepositions do not undergo them. *At* has only a Place sense; it is supplanted by *to* in the Goal sense and perhaps *by* in the Route sense (though *by* is more like VIA NEAR). *In* has a Place sense and a Goal sense (where it is synonymous with *into*), but not a Route sense; the sense VIA IN is expressed by *through*. *With* has only a Place sense, compared to *next to*, which has a Place and a Goal sense but no Route sense. And so on.

It is therefore necessary to encode the Goal and Route senses of *under* and *over* in the lexicon: one must learn that these senses are specifically available for these words.[1] These senses of *under* and *over* are related in the following way: the Place sense provides a "conceptual core" that remains constant in all three senses; the conceptual core can optionally be elaborated by embedding it as an argument of either of the Path-functions TO and VIA.

We would therefore like to express these optional elaborations as part of the preposition's lexical entry. Unfortunately, the standard notation for optionality is awkward to apply here, since what is optional is a nonconstituent—a constituent minus an argument. (7) illustrates.

(7) $\langle [_{\text{Path}} \text{ TO } (\rangle [_{\text{Place}} \text{ UNDER } ([_{\text{Thing}} \quad]_j)] \langle)] \rangle$

What we really want is something like "inside-out" bracketing: we would like to bracket the "core" constituent and make everything *outside* the brackets optional. One way to do this would be to use inverted brackets, $\rangle, \langle$, renotating (7) as (8).

(8) $[_{\text{Path}} \text{ TO } (\rangle [_{\text{Place}} \text{ UNDER } ([_{\text{Thing}} \quad]_j] \langle)]$

This is better but still hard to interpret, given our habits in reading brackets. I will therefore notate optional outer arguments with something a bit easier to read: a dashed underline, as in (9).

(9) $[_{\underline{\text{Path}}} \underline{\text{TO}} \underline{([_{\text{Place}} \text{ UNDER } ([_{\text{Thing}} \quad]_j)])}$

The dashed line still has to include the right-hand parenthesis and bracket at the end, but at least it avoids the obnoxious crossing of bracketed material in (7) and the sense of disorientation I find in reading (8).

Since *under* actually has *three* senses, (9) has to be further generalized to (10).

(10) $\left\{ \begin{matrix} [_{\text{Path}} \text{ TO} \\ [_{\text{Path}} \text{ VIA} \end{matrix} \right\} ([_{\text{Place}} \text{ UNDER } ([_{\text{Thing}} \quad]_j)])]$

Here the braces are not so pretty either, but they will have to do, for reasons to become apparent in a moment.

The notation in (10), then, abbreviates the three senses in (6a, b, c). As the LCS of *under*, it says that the morpheme *under* can correspond to any of these expressions in the conceptual structure of a sentence.

A second alternation in prepositional senses is illustrated in (11).

(11) a. Bill ran up the hill/down the road/through the tunnel.
     b. Bill's house is up the hill/down the road/through the tunnel (from here).

The PP in (11a) denotes a Path of motion; that in (11b) is an argument of *be*, so it must be a Place. In the case of *under*, the Path reading is an elaboration of a core Place reading, but this time the relation appears to be the other way around: Bill's house is located in terms of a Path that extends up the hill, down the road, or through the tunnel. This core Path can in fact be further fleshed out by the modifier *from here*, which specifies the Path's initial point. Thus the reading of the PP *through the tunnel* in (11b) might be specified as (12).

(12) [$_{Place}$ AT-END-OF ([$_{Path}$ VIA ([$_{Place}$ IN ([$_{Thing}$ TUNNEL])])])]

The core of *through* is therefore the Path-function VIA IN, with an optional outer Place-function AT-END-OF. (13) uses the dashed underline notation to express the alternate conceptual structures of *through*.

(13) [$_{Place}$ AT-END-OF ([$_{Path}$ VIA ([$_{Place}$ IN ([$_{Thing}$]$_j$)])])]

To make life more interesting, *over* also exhibits this Place sense based on its Path sense, for instance in *Bill's house is over the hill from here*. (Interestingly, *under* does not, even in a pragmatically promising situation such as **The subway is under the harbor from here*, in the sense that one must pass under the harbor to get to the subway.) This elaboration of *over* has to be built on the VIA sense: it means "at the end of a Path that passes over (VIA OVER) the hill." Incorporating this elaboration yields a fuller LCS for *over*, which iterates the dashed underline notation and expresses four senses.[2]

(14) $\left\{ \begin{array}{l} [_{Path} \text{ TO} \\ [_{Place} \text{ AT-END-OF} ([_{Path} \text{ VIA} \end{array} \right\}$ ([$_{Place}$ OVER ([$_{Thing}$]$_j$)])])]

We next turn to two applications of the dashed underline notation to verbs. There are many verbs of English, for instance those in (15), that alternate between a State reading and an Event reading.

(15) a. The weathervane pointed north.
  b. The enemy surrounded the city.
  c. Bill stood on the table.
  d. Snow covered the hills.

Other such verbs are *hide, shelter, block, support, face,* and *sit*. The State reading of these verbs emerges if a duration phrase like *for hours* is appended to the sentences in (15). The Event reading emerges if a rate adverb like *quickly* is inserted preverbally. The fact that both modifiers cannot be inserted at once (**The weathervane quickly pointed north for hours*) shows that the two readings are distinct.

The relation between the two readings is intuitively clear: the Event *(inchoative)* reading describes a change taking place whose final state is the State reading—the familiar inchoative relation. Anticipating the more detailed argumentation in section 5.3, we will formalize the inchoative as an elaboration of Event into the function INCH, whose sole argument is a State. INCH maps its argument into an Event that terminates in that State:

(16) $[\text{EVENT}] \rightarrow [_{\text{Event}} \text{ INCH ([STATE])}]$

Given the function INCH, we can express the two senses of (15a) as (17a) and (17b).

(17) a. $[_{\text{State}} \text{ ORIENT } ([_{\text{Thing}} \text{ WEATHERVANE}], [_{\text{Path}} \text{ NORTH}])]$
  b. $[_{\text{Event}} \text{ INCH } ([_{\text{State}} \text{ ORIENT } ([_{\text{Thing}} \text{ WEATHERVANE}],$
  $[_{\text{Path}} \text{ NORTH}])])]$

Again, this is a lexically specified alternation. Not every stative verb has a homophonous inchoative. The inchoative of *have*, for instance, is not *have* but (probably) *get*; that of *know* seems to be *find out*. Thus the alternation, when it exists, must be encoded in lexical entries. Using the dashed underline notation, we can give the LCS of *point* the form (18).

(18) $[_{\text{Event}} \underline{\text{INCH}} ([_{\text{State}} \underline{\text{ORIENT}} ([_{\text{Thing}} \quad]_i, [_{\text{Path}} \quad]_j)])]$

(- - - -) indicates that don't need to be filled out

A second and possibly more controversial application of the dashed underline notation to verbs is the causative alternation. Consider a typical case such as *slide* in (19a, b).

(19) a. The box slid down the stairs.
  b. Bill slid the box down the stairs.

In order for Argument Fusion to apply properly, the conceptual structures for the two senses must be (20a, b) respectively.

(20) a. $[_{\text{Event}} \text{ GO } ([_{\text{Thing}} \quad]_i, [_{\text{Path}} \quad]_k)]$
  b. $[_{\text{Event}} \text{ CAUSE } ([_{\text{Thing}} \quad]_i, [_{\text{Event}} \text{ GO } ([_{\text{Thing}} \quad]_j, [_{\text{Path}} \quad]_k)])]$

These *almost* can be combined using the dashed underline notation. This time the elaboration of the core reading is not just a function but a function plus one of its arguments, the Agent. The difficulty lies in the designation of the external argument: in the noncausative version the external argument is the Theme, but in the causative it is the Agent. Omitting the offending indices for the moment, the two senses can be combined as (21).

(21) $[_{\text{Path}} \underline{\text{CAUSE}} ([_{\text{Thing}} \quad], [_{\text{Event}} \text{ GO } ([_{\text{Thing}} \quad], [_{\text{Path}} \quad]_k)])]$

One possible solution to this difficulty is provided by the Unaccusative Hypothesis (Perlmutter 1978; Burzio 1986). The idea is that the Agent is coindexed *i* with subject position and that—in both causative and noncausative versions—the Theme is coindexed *j* with the object position. With this configuration of indices, Argument Fusion maps the causative reading of (21) into the correct surface form, but it maps the noncausative reading into *e slid the box down the stairs*, where *e* is an empty subject. The object is then promoted to subject position in the course of derivation from underlying to surface structure, producing the surface form (19a). Chapter 11 will propose another way out, which replaces the rigid coindexing of syntactic and conceptual argument positions with a more flexible linking convention, so that Argument Fusion can map directly to the surface syntactic order.

4.2 Multiple Argument Structures

Consider next the verb *climb*, whose use of a preference rule system was discussed in section 1.7.2. *Climb* appears in three syntactic contexts: with a null complement, with a direct object, and with a PP.

(22) a. Joe climbed (for hours).
  b. Joe climbed the mountain.
  c. Joe climbed $\begin{cases} \text{down the rope.} \\ \text{along the ridge.} \\ \text{through the tunnel.} \\ \text{etc.} \end{cases}$

As observed in section 2.2, the conceptual structure for the transitive case (abstracting away from various complications) is (23).

(23) $[_{\text{Event}} \text{GO} ([_{\text{Thing}} \quad]_i, [_{\text{Path}} \text{TO} ([_{\text{Place}} \text{TOP-OF} [_{\text{Thing}} \quad]_j])])]$

However, the PP-complement does not entail that the subject reaches the top of anything—it specifies only that the subject is traversing some Path described by the PP (in a clambering manner). The null complement leaves the Path totally unspecified. In particular, it too does not imply that the subject got to the top of anything (compare to intransitive *enter*, which implies that the subject went into something).

To express this alternation, we adopt an abbreviatory convention introduced in Jackendoff 1985. In this notation, the index for the postverbal argument appears in two different positions in the verb's LCS, but the two positions are marked as mutually exclusive by enclosing them in curly brackets. The lexical entry for *climb* then looks like (24).[3]

(24) $\begin{bmatrix} \text{climb} \\ \text{V} \\ \underline{\qquad} \langle \text{XP}_j \rangle \\ [_{\text{Event}} \text{GO} ([_{\text{Thing}} \quad]_i, [_{\text{Path}} \{ \text{TO} ([_{\text{Place}} \text{TOP-OF} ([_{\text{Thing}} \quad]_j)]) \}_{\{j\}})] \end{bmatrix}$

The Path-constituent in (24) abbreviates the two possibilities in (25).

(25) a. [$_{Path}$ TO ([$_{Place}$ TOP-OF ([$_{Thing}$]$_j$)])]
      b. [$_{Path}$]$_j$

To see how (24) works, consider how Argument Fusion applies to the sentences in (22). Start with the transitive case (22b). *The mountain* is of the conceptual category Thing. Since Argument Fusion must combine it with an indexed constituent of category Thing, only the realization of the Path given in (25a) is possible. Thus (22b) says that Joe went to the top of the mountain. On the other hand, a PP-complement such as the one in (22c) is of the conceptual category Path and therefore must be fused with realization (25b) of the Path. Hence there is no implication of reaching the top of anything. Finally, in the case of a null complement, neither choice of *j* can be satisfied, so the Path is indeterminate.

The subcategorization feature in (24) stipulates merely an optional post-verbal phrase of arbitrary major phrasal category. This simplification is possible because of the selectional restrictions of the verb: only an NP or a PP can correspond to a conceptual constituent of the proper category. Things must always be expressed in English by NPs; Paths in the unmarked case are expressed by PPs.

However, there is a further, marked possibility: a small class of nouns such as *way* and *route* map into Paths instead of Things. Notice what happens when these nouns head the direct object of *climb*:

(26) We can get down there by climbing this $\begin{Bmatrix} \text{route.} \\ \text{way.} \end{Bmatrix}$

(26) shows that, in these cases, unlike with other direct objects, climbing need not imply getting to the top of anything. The reason is that the NP *this route/way* expresses a Path; hence it must fuse with realization (25b) of the Path-constituent, which does not contain TO TOP-OF. In other words, *this route/way* behaves semantically like a PP, even though its syntax is clearly that of an NP. The interpretation of *climb this route* is therefore predicted by lexical entry (24), without further ado. There is, for example, no need to advert to an idiosyncratic rule of preposition deletion or an empty preposition in order to account for the interpretation.

Another verb that works much like *climb* is *jump*. To *jump a fence* or *jump a gorge* means roughly "jump *over* NP"; that is, the Path-function VIA OVER is incorporated. But with a PP-complement, any Path is possible: *jump toward Bill*, *jump around the corner*, *jump through the hoop*. Moreover, *jump right this way* (where *right* excludes the irrelevant manner reading "in this fashion") does *not* incorporate *over*. Thus the treatment of *climb* generalizes to this verb as well.

A subtly different combination of multiple arguments appears in the verb *pass*.[4] Syntactically, it looks the same as *climb*:

(27) a. The train passed.
   b. The train passed the station.
   c. The train passed $\left\{ \begin{array}{l} \text{through the tunnel.} \\ \text{under the bridge.} \\ \text{etc.} \end{array} \right\}$

The conceptual structure for the transitive case, like that of *climb*, incorporates Path- and Place-functions; it means roughly "go via near":

(28) $[_{\text{Event}} \text{GO} ([_{\text{Thing}} \quad]_i, [_{\text{Path}} \text{VIA} ([_{\text{Place}} \text{NEAR} ([_{\text{Thing}} \quad]_j)])])]$

However, the PP-complement differs from that of *climb* in that it is subject to a selectional restriction: as (29) shows, Source, Goal, and Direction expressions are ungrammatical.

(29) *The train passed $\left\{ \begin{array}{l} \text{(away) from the station.} \\ \text{to the station.} \\ \text{toward the station.} \\ \text{northward.} \end{array} \right\}$

With a few possibly idiomatic exceptions such as *pass from sight*, the PP-complements of *pass* are restricted to Routes—essentially Paths whose Path-function is VIA.

This combination of argument structures can be expressed by placing curly brackets slightly differently than in (24):

(30) $\left[\begin{array}{l} \text{pass} \\ \text{V} \\ \underline{\hspace{1cm}} \langle \text{XP}_j \rangle \\ [_{\text{Event}} \text{GO} ([_{\text{Thing}} \quad]_i, [_{\text{Path}} \text{VIA} ([_{\text{Place}} \{\text{NEAR} ([_{\text{Thing}} \quad]_j)\}])]_{\{j\}})] \end{array} \right]$

The Path-constituent here abbreviates the two possibilities shown in (31).

(31) a. $[_{\text{Path}} \text{VIA} ([_{\text{Place}} \text{NEAR} ([_{\text{Thing}} \quad]_j)])]$
   b. $[_{\text{Path}} \text{VIA} ([_{\text{Place}} \quad])]_j$

The difference from *climb* appears in (31b). Whereas in (25b) the variable *j* is stipulated only as a Path, in (31b) it is stipulated as a Path whose Path-function is VIA. This further stipulation makes it impossible to fuse this constituent with the interpretation of PPs such as those in (29), which have different Path-functions.

This verb illustrates an important advantage of the approach to selectional restrictions proposed in section 2.3. The very same marker, VIA, plays two apparently different roles in the verb *pass*. In realization (31a), it appears as an incorporated Path-function, altogether parallel to the incorporated functions TO IN in *enter*. But in realization (31b), it plays the role of a selectional restriction on the PP-complement. In the present approach, this falls out naturally. When VIA is *outside* the indexed constituent, as in (31a), it is information supplied solely by the verb—which is what is meant by an incorporated function. When VIA is *inside* the indexed constituent, as in (31b), it interacts with the information supplied by the PP-complement—which is what is meant by a selectional restriction. No further distinctions need to be invoked.

Moreover, the difference between *pass* and *climb* in expressed simply by the placement of the inner curly brackets. Because those in *climb* include the Path-function TO, TO drops out if the outer *j* is chosen. By contrast, the Path-function VIA in *pass* is not within the inner curly brackets, so it remains as a selectional restriction if the outer *j* is chosen.

A case similar to *pass* is *cross*. Cross NP$_j$ means roughly "go over NP$_j$ to other side of NP$_j$"; the rather complex Path-function "across" has been incorporated. Cross PP$_j$ puts a corresponding selectional restriction on PP$_j$ that permits *cross over the river* and *cross to the other side* but not **cross toward the house, *cross around the car,* or **cross up the stairs*. (Other possibilities such as *cross between the signs* describe the overall location of the event of crossing and are hence not relevant.) Evidently this verb's possibilities are formalized much like those of *pass*. In fact, the Path-function incorporated in transitive *cross* is similar enough to that in transitive *jump* that the two verbs constitute a near-minimal pair in the behavior of their PP-complements: *jump* imposes no selectional restriction, but *cross* does. This difference is nicely expressed in the present formalism.

Yet another case is the verb *put*, everyone's standard example of a verb that subcategorizes an obligatory PP. What has not been so widely remarked is this verb's curious selectional restriction on the PP argument.[5] It appears that this argument must express either a Place or else a Path whose function is TO. Examples of the former case are (32a),[6] of the latter (32b).

(32) a. George put the book $\begin{cases} \text{at the corner of the bed.} \\ \text{with the telephone.} \end{cases}$

   b. Martha put the book $\begin{cases} \text{into the drawer.} \\ \text{onto the counter.} \end{cases}$

On the other hand, expressions of Source (33a), Direction (33b), and Route (33c) are impossible—and, oddly enough, so is the preposition *to* itself (33d).

(33) a. *Groucho put the book from the shelf.
   b. ?*Harpo put the book toward the bed.
   c. ?*Chico put the book through the tunnel.
   d. *Gummo put the book to the floor.[7]

The notations developed here permit a relatively straightforward account of this selectional restriction. (34) is the entry for *put*; (35) spells out the options for the Path abbreviated by the curly brackets.

$$(34) \quad \left[\begin{array}{l} \text{put} \\ \text{V} \\ \underline{} \text{ NP}_j \text{ PP}_k \\ [_{\text{Event}} \text{ CAUSE } ([_{\text{Thing}} \quad]_i, [_{\text{Event}} \text{ GO } ([_{\text{Thing}} \quad]_j, \\ [_{\text{Path}} \text{ TO } ([_{\text{Place}} \quad]_{\{k\}})]_{\{k\}})])] \end{array} \right]$$

(35) a. $[_{\text{Path}} \text{ TO } ([_{\text{Place}} \quad]_k)]$

   b. $[_{\text{Path}} \text{ TO } ([_{\text{Place}} \quad])]_k$

In realization (35a), the verb means "cause to go to a place." The PP argument is coindexed with the Place-constituent and therefore must itself express a Place. This is the case illustrated in (32a). In realization (35b), on the other hand, the PP argument is fused with the whole Path-constituent. In order for the result of fusion to be well formed, the PP must express a Path (1) whose Path-function is TO and (2) whose argument is a Place. The first of these requirements is sufficient to rule out (33a, b, c), whose Path-functions are FROM, TOWARD, and VIA respectively. (33d) is ruled out by the second requirement, since the structure of its PP is (36).

(36) $[_{\text{Path}} \text{ TO } ([_{\text{Thing}} \text{ FLOOR}])]$

On the other hand, the PPs in (32b) have the requisite structure to satisfy (35b):[8]

(37) a. $[_{\text{Path}} \text{ TO } ([_{\text{Place}} \text{ IN } ([_{\text{Thing}} \text{ DRAWER}])])]$

   b. $[_{\text{Path}} \text{ TO } ([_{\text{Place}} \text{ ON } ([_{\text{Thing}} \text{ COUNTER}])])]$

The upshot of this analysis is that the disjunctive selectional restriction on the PP of *put* follows from a disjunctive argument structure. Unlike the previous cases, this disjunction does not show itself in the syntax, since both Places and Paths are expressed by PPs. Nevertheless, it is a genuine, if subtle, case of multiple argument structures, and its properties follow from the present account of selectional restrictions and the curly bracket notation. In particular, we see again that a marker, in this case TO, functions in one realization as an incorporated function and in the other as a selectional restriction, just because of where the alternative choices of index happen to fall in the verb's semantic structure.

For a final case of an alternation involving the curly bracket notation, let us return to the verb *dress*, discussed in section 3.3. (38a) is the entry given there for transitive *dress*; (38b) is the entry for intransitive *dress*.

(38) (= (3.15))

a.
$$\begin{bmatrix} \text{dress} \\ \text{V} \\ \underline{\qquad} \text{NP}_j \langle \text{PP}_k \rangle \\ [\text{CAUSE ([ ]}_i, [\text{GO ([ ]}_j, [\text{TO [IN [CLOTHING]]}_k])])] \end{bmatrix}$$

b.
$$\begin{bmatrix} \text{dress} \\ \text{V} \\ \underline{\qquad} \langle \text{PP}_k \rangle \\ [\text{CAUSE ([ ]}^\alpha_i, [\text{GO ([}\alpha], [\text{TO [IN [CLOTHING]]}_k])])] \end{bmatrix}$$

Unlike transitive and intransitive *eat*, these forms cannot be collapsed into a single entry by just making the NP argument optional: the intransitive form does not just make the Theme implicit but rather binds the Theme to the Agent.

The curly bracket notation permits us to unify these two entries as (39).

(39)
$$\begin{bmatrix} \text{dress} \\ \text{V} \\ \underline{\qquad} \langle \text{NP}_j \rangle \langle \text{PP}_k \rangle \\ [\text{CAUSE ([ ]}^\alpha_i, [\text{GO ([\{}\alpha\}]_{\{j\}}, [\text{TO [IN [CLOTHING]]}_k])])] \end{bmatrix}$$

The crucial constituent here is the Theme. Following the conventions of the curly bracket notation, this constituent has two mutually exclusive possibilities: either it is coindexed to the direct object, or else it is bound to the Agent. In turn, if it is bound to the Agent, an NP object cannot be linked to it. Hence the bound reading appears just when the verb is used intransitively. This is exactly the desired alternation of interpretations.

4.3 Remarks

The examples in this chapter are, I believe, representative of the kinds of idiosyncratic alternations of argument structure that appear in the lexicon. Lexical theory must have enough expressive power to capture and differentiate the range of possibilities. For example, it is not enough to say that *climb, jump, pass,* and *cross* all undergo a lexical process that changes an oblique argument into a direct object: as we have seen, there are differences both in the character of their oblique arguments and in the functions they incorporate in the transitive case. Likewise, a theory that treats lexical argument structure as a list of primitive θ-roles cannot account for the relation between the realizations of *pass*. In transitive *pass*, VIA serves as a determinant of the NP argument's θ-role—perhaps the NP would receive the primitive θ-role "Landmark." However, when *pass* takes a PP-complement, VIA serves as a selectional restriction on the argument—an aspect of the verb's representation totally outside the system of θ-roles. In the present approach, where θ-marking amounts to coindexation with positions in conceptual structure, the generalization between these two cases falls out naturally. Finally, the distinction between the argument structures of *put* makes no difference at all in the syntax, only in the selectional restrictions on the PP. We have seen, though, that it is otherwise quite like the alternation in the verbs *pass* and *cross* and should therefore be represented similarly. The present theory assimilates the two cases; it is hard to see how they would be related in a separate level of argument structure.

To close this chapter, I want to mention briefly the more productive lexical processes that have often been treated in terms of alternations in argument structure. In the present theory, such alternations can be expressed in terms of manipulations on the indices in the verb's LCS.

For example, consider the lexical rule that forms passive participles from verbs. The essential modification that this rule performs on the LCS of the verb is to delete i, the index that marks the external argument. By virtue of this deletion, the "logical subject" becomes an implicit argument, precisely parallel to all other lexically specified implicit arguments: all that we know about this individual is what is specified in the verb's selectional restriction.[9] In GB Theory, this is all that needs to be said: the absence of i means that the subject is not a θ-position, and the independent alterations of the participle's case-marking properties will trigger movement of the object into subject position. In a theory such as LFG (Bresnan 1982b), where the passive is purely lexical, one of the other indices in the verb's conceptual structure must be changed to i so that the argument in question will appear in subject position. The point is that one does not need a separate level on which to perform these manipulations on indices. They can be carried out directly on conceptual structure. Thus both idiosyncratic and productive alternations in argument structure can be formulated in the present framework without loss of generality.

A last remark to close part I: one important thread of these chapters has been to compare a fine-grained theory of argument structure, where thematic roles appear as positions in a detailed conceptual representation, with a coarse-grained theory, where argument structure appears as a list annotated with thematic roles, or as a set of diacritics marked on syntactic structure. In order for a sentence to be understood, of course, the fine-grained representation—the conceptual structure—must exist in any event, so the issue is whether a coarse-grained argument structure is necessary as well. We have seen that the coarse-grained structure is unnecessary for the statement of the syntax-semantics correspondence, and impossible to specify in an insightful way for only slightly complex lexical entries. Further, it obscures relations among multiple argument structures of lexical entries, relations that emerge naturally in the fine-grained representation.

One reason that people have adopted coarse-grained approaches to argument structure, I suspect, is that, in the absence of a full-blown theory of conceptual structure, one still needs *some* expression of θ-roles. But adopting a coarse-grained theory as a temporary shortcut is quite a different matter from adopting it as a codification of a level of mental representation. I have shown here that the latter approach misses many important generalizations, even if the former is for the moment often unavoidable. At the same time, the theory of Conceptual Semantics begins to provide some hope that a fine-grained theory of some generality and rigor can be formulated.

PART II

Mostly on the Problem of Meaning

Chapter 5
Some Further Conceptual Functions

5.1 Introduction to Part II

The conceptual functions listed in (2.1)—GO, STAY, BE, ORIENT, EXT, and CAUSE—account for a substantial fraction of the verbs of spatial motion and location of English and can be extended to a wide range of other semantic fields (section 1.6.2; S&C, chapter 10). However, many other conceptual domains, even within the spatial field, do not appear to reduce easily to any combination of these functions and must therefore be posited as additional elaborations of the conceptual system. This part of the book will examine some such classes, work out their conceptual structures, and show that they have distinct syntactic properties as well.

Beyond the particular issues of semantic description that are raised by these conceptual domains, two general questions constantly arise. The first is to what extent new conceptual functions ought to be added as simple primitives in their own right, and to what extent they should be added by elaborating old primitives in terms of a feature system. In the areas examined in this chapter, the solution adopted is the addition of primitives. However, in chapter 6, it turns out to be more interesting to posit feature elaboration of existing spatial primitives. Chapter 7 arrives at a combination of the two solutions. At the moment I can offer no overall recipe; I think the answer in any particular case must be decided by sensitive practice, in the hope that a more comprehensive picture will emerge at some point in the future.

The second general question raised in these analyses is to what extent conceptual functions receive a consistent syntactic expression—in particular whether one can maintain the position that a thematic role always corresponds to the same syntactic role. We will see, especially in chapter 6, that the correspondence has roughly the characteristics of morphological correspondences—that is, that there is something like an unmarked realization for certain arguments of certain semantic functions, but that there are lexical exceptions to the pattern.

5.2 Verbs of Manner of Motion and Configuration

The sentences in (1) describe motion of an object but do not imply traversal of a Path.

(1) a. Willy wiggled.
     b. Debbie danced.
     c. The top spun.
     d. The flag waved.

Compare (1) to (2), where there is an implicit Path.

(2) a. Emma entered.
     b. Aaron approached.
     c. Leon left.

The fact that there are no Paths in (1), even as an implicit argument, suggests that these verbs are not cases of GO, which specifically takes a Thing and a Path argument. How then should these verbs be analyzed?

Each of the verbs in (1) expresses a different idiosyncratic manner of motion, of a sort not easily decomposable into features. It is hard to imagine features, for example, that might distinguish wiggling from other possible motions, say wriggling. Peterson (1985) argues that there is a general ontological category of "natural actions," parallel to the class of natural kinds. Like natural kinds, natural actions are difficult to describe in words but easy to point out (or in the case of natural actions, demonstrate). The difficulty of decomposing natural actions into plausible features, moreover, parallels the difficulty of decomposing the shapes of natural kinds— for instance, what sort of features could possibly encode the shape of a swan's neck? Section 1.7.1 suggested that both the (stereotypical) shapes of objects and the (stereotypical) spatial configurations of natural actions are not encoded at all in the essentially algebraic (featurelike) format of conceptual structure. Rather, they are represented in a quasi-geometrical format, a suitable extension of Marr's (1982) 3D model level of representation for the visual system. If this is the case, visual distinctions of "manner of motion" (or at least a great many of them) are not the business of conceptual structure at all; conceptual structure has to encode primarily an appropriate argument structure, linked in the lexicon to a more detailed spatial structure encoding.

What is the appropriate argument structure? The sentences in (1) describe only the internal motion of the subject, with no implications with respect to their location, change of location, or configuration with respect to any other object. This suggests that, unlike the previous Event- and State-functions, the function in question takes a single argument. Following a suggestion of Carter (1984), we will analyze the sentences in (1) as instances of a function of the form (3).

(3) [_Event_ MOVE ([_Thing_   ])]

To be sure, at least some of the verbs in this class can appear with a Path-expression:

(4) a. Willy wiggled out of the hole.
    b. Debbie danced into the room.

Section 10.3 will argue that sentences like (4) express a conceptual structure that includes both a MOVE-function and a GO-function; the subject is an argument of both functions, but the Path-expression is an argument of the GO-function alone. Thus the manner-of-motion aspect of these sentences can be isolated in the single-argument MOVE-function.

As evidence that this is the correct analysis, Talmy (1985) notes that Spanish disallows expressions of (completed) Path with the translations of these verbs:

(5) *La botella floto   a la   cueva.
    the bottle floated to the cave

The translations must rather include both a verb of external motion (GO) and a participle expressing manner of motion (MOVE):

(6) La botella entro   a la   cueva flotando.
    the bottle moved-in to the cave   floating

Yoneyama (1986) observes that Japanese similarly prohibits expressions of Goal with manner-of-motion verbs (though certain other Path-expressions are possible, for somewhat obscure reasons):

(7) a. ?John-wa   eki-e   hashitta.
       John-TOP station-to ran
       (John ran to the station.)
    b. ?John-wa   kishi-e   oyoida.
       John-TOP shore-to swam
       (John swam to shore.)

However, if these verbs are compounded with the verb *iku* (GO), Goal-expressions are permitted:

(8) a. John-wa   eki-e   hashitte-itta.
       John-TOP station-to running-went
    b. John-wa   kishi-e   oyoide-itta.
       John-TOP shore-to swimming-went

Since conceptual structure is by hypothesis universal, we want the differences among these languages to appear solely in their means for expressing conceptual structures, that is, in the correspondence rules between conceptual structure and syntax—including the lexicon. Talmy suggests that the difference is that English, unlike Spanish, permits a GO-function optionally to be incorporated into a manner-of-motion verb. Section 10.3 will propose a specific rule that accomplishes this incorporation.

Carter (1984), who points out parallel facts from French, argues that, for the purposes of language learning, English must present the marked case. If French, Spanish, and Japanese are the unmarked case, the possibility of incorporation in English can be learned from positive evidence, namely the existence of sentences like (4). On the other hand, if English were the unmarked case, the impossibility of incorporation in French, Spanish, and Japanese would have to be learned from negative evidence that a monolingual English speaker finds highly unexpected, namely the ungrammaticality of (5) or (7). This suggests that the present analysis, which separates the GO component of (4) from the MOVE component, is motivated on syntactic as well as semantic grounds, and that their conflation into a single verb in (4) is licensed by a language-particular rule of English.

In addition to verbs like those in (1) that clearly express manner of motion of an object, one might also consider cases such as (9) as possible instances of MOVE.

(9) a. Lila laughed.
    b. Sparky sneezed.

Alternatively, these might be analyzed as a variety of GO-verb, roughly as "emit a laugh/sneeze," where laughs and sneezes are kinds of sounds. Such an analysis is especially attractive in the case of *laugh*, which can frame a direct quote, a sentence emitted by the subject:

(10) "We're out of trouble now," she laughed/*sneezed.

On the other hand, there is reason to believe that emission of sound is not part of the core meaning of these verbs. For instance, one can laugh or sneeze silently; hence the emission of a sound is not a necessary condition. Furthermore, although a loudspeaker or a computer can be said to emit sounds or even talk, it is odd to speak of one laughing or sneezing: the bodily action seems essential. Hence *laugh* and *sneeze* appear to genuinely fall into the class of MOVE-verbs (or some closely related single-argument class), with the emission of a characteristic sound as a default accompaniment. This contrasts with a pure verb of sound-emission such as *rumble*, which does not go with any characteristic action and can be attributed to any sound-emitting object.

Parallel to the Event-verbs describing manner of motion, there is a class of intransitive stative verbs that describe internal spatial configuration of their Themes. (These were analyzed in *S&C* as BE-verbs.)

(11) Sally stood/sat for hours on end.

These verbs can of course occur with locative expressions (*Sally stood/sat on the wall*). Such constructions will be analyzed as a combination of the configuration-function with a BE-function, just as the sentences in (4) are a combination of manner of Motion with a GO-function. These verbs can also occur inchoatively (*Sally stood up/down*). The next section will take up the structure of the inchoative cases.

We will call the one-place function that expresses configuration CONF, as in (12).

(12) $[_{State}$ CONF $([_{Thing}$ $])]$

As in the case of manner-of-motion verbs, the distinctions among various CONF-verbs will not necessarily be expressed in conceptual structure; rather, their details may well appear only in a more geometric spatial representation.

5.3 Inchoative

As observed in section 4.1, many verbs of English, for instance those in (13), alternate between a State reading and an "inchoative" Event readily; the latter is understood as an Event whose termination is the State reading:

(13) ($=$ (4.15))
    a. The weathervane pointed north.
    b. The enemy surrounded the city.
    c. Bill stood on the table.
    d. Snow covered the hills.

In *S&C*, inchoatives are treated implicitly as instances of the function GO, as in (14b).

(14) a. The light is red.
      $[BE_{Ident}$ ([LIGHT], $[AT_{Ident}$ $([_{Property}$ RED])])]
      ($=$ *S&C*, 195, (10.14a))
    b. The pages yellowed.
      $[GO_{Ident}$ ([PAGES], $[TO_{Ident}$ $([_{Property}$ YELLOW])])]
      ($=$ *S&C*, 195, (10.15a))

In other words, the Event reading contains a GO TO-function where a corresponding State reading such as (14a) contains BE AT. However, this analysis will not work in general. For instance, the State reading of (13a) is (15), which does not contain a BE-function at all.

(15) [$_\text{State}$ ORIENT ([WEATHERVANE], [$_\text{Path}$ NORTH])]

If a GO-function were substituted into (15), the resulting conceptual structure would be "the weathervane moved/traveled northward," which is entirely wrong. For another example, (16a) can describe either the past extent of the railroad, the favored reading in (16b), or a stage in the construction of the railroad, the favored reading in (16c).

(16) a. The railroad reached Kansas City.
     b. The railroad used to reach Kansas City, till they tore it up.
     c. The railroad finally/soon reached Kansas City.

The extent reading in (16b) is a State, and the "stage of construction" reading in (16c) is an Event that is evidently the inchoative of the State: "the railroad soon came to reach Kansas City." The State reading has the conceptual structure (17).

(17) [$_\text{State}$ EXT([RAILROAD], [$_\text{Path}$ TO ([K.C.])])]

However, the Event reading (16c) cannot be created by substituting GO for EXT; the resulting reading would be "the railroad traveled/moved to Kansas City," clearly an incorrect result. (*Reach* does have this transitional sense in sentences like *Joe finally reached Kansas City*, where Joe is undergoing motion.)

A similar problem occurs in (13b). The State sense of *surround* means EXT AROUND; that is, the Theme is asserted to extend all the way around its reference object. The Event sense of *surround* does not mean "travel around," as it would if EXT were changed to GO. (That meaning is expressed by something like *circumnavigate*.) Rather, it means "assume a position that extends all the way around the reference object."

Evidently a more general solution to the problem of inchoatives is necessary. Taking the bull by the horns, we introduce a function that maps a State into an Event:

(18) [$_\text{Event}$ INCH ([$_\text{State}$])]

Using this function, the inchoative counterparts of (14a), (15), and (17) are given in (19a,b,c).

(19) a. [$_\text{Event}$ INCH ([$_\text{State}$ BE$_\text{Ident}$ ([LIGHT], [AT ([RED])])])]
     b. [$_\text{Event}$ INCH ([$_\text{State}$ ORIENT ([...], [...])])]
     c. [$_\text{Event}$ INCH ([$_\text{State}$ EXT ([...], [...])])]

For the present, we will regard the function INCH as a primitive; in Jackendoff (in preparation) it will be composed into a bundle of more general features.

As seen in section 4.1, INCH makes it possible to account for the ambiguity of the sentences in (13); we regard the lexical entries of *point, surround, stand,* and *cover* as having two alternative conceptual structures, one encoding the State reading

$[_{State} X]$

and the other encoding the Event reading

$[_{Event} INCH ([_{State} X])]$.

This dual representation is abbreviated by the dashed underline notation, in parallel to the numerous prepositions (*over, under, between, here,* etc.) that express either

$[_{Place} X]$

or

$[_{Path} TO ([_{Place} X])]$.

It might be observed that there now is an apparent redundancy in the system, in that (20a) and (20b) appear to encode the same Event.

(20) a. $[_{Event} GO ([X], [_{Path} TO ([_{Place} Y])])]$
      b. $[_{Event} INCH ([_{State} BE ([X], [_{Place} Y])])]$

Is the redundancy necessary? If it can be eliminated, there is the possibility of reducing the stock of conceptual primitives, always a desideratum in the absence of evidence to the contrary.

But in fact there *is* evidence to the contrary. We have already seen that the INCH-function cannot be reduced to a GO-function—for when it applies to an ORIENT-State or an EXT-State instead of a BE-State, the resulting reading is quite distinct from anything that can be expressed by a GO-function.

The opposite possibility, that GO can be reduced to INCH (BE), has appeared in its essence many times in the literature (e.g. Schank 1973; Dowty 1979; Hinrichs 1985): it amounts to the view that going to a place is nothing more than coming to be at that place. *S&C,* section 9.2, gives three arguments against such a reduction. The first is that GO can occur not only with explicit Goals but also with a wide variety of Path-functions:

(21) The train traveled {
to Chicago.
down the track.
along the river.
toward the mountain.
through the tunnel.
away from the station.
etc.
}

Only in the first of these cases can the movement be described as coming to be at someplace. That is, the full distribution of GO reveals a generality within which going *to* is only a special case.

The second argument against reducing GO to INCH BE is that many GO-verbs (for example *reach* and *go* itself) can appear also as expressions of extent:

(22) a. The road reaches Kansas City.
      b. The track goes by the mountain.
      c. The fence goes along the river.

These expressions cannot be reduced to an Event of coming to be at a place at a particular time; rather, they are States and thereby devoid of change over time. Moreover, as seen in (16c), they can themselves serve as arguments of INCH. In order to capture the generalization between the extent and motion readings of these verbs, then, the motion readings cannot be treated as inchoatives of a State—there is no available parallel treatment for the extent reading.[1]

The third argument for the nonreducibility of GO to INCH BE is that motion must be a primitive in spatial cognition anyway—we can perceive an object as in continuous motion without knowing anything about the endpoints of its motion. It moreover appears (Marr 1982) that the visual system contains specialized motion detectors that are rather independent of the channels that individuate and localize objects. If motion is a primitive even in elementary aspects of visual cognition, why should conceptual structure be so stingy as to provide no way to encode it?

My conclusion is that GO and INCH are two independent functions of conceptual structure and that they happen to overlap in their application in the one instance shown in (20). In many particular cases, it is relatively easy to determine which function is being encoded. Here are three criteria.

1. If the verb in question appears with a range of Path-prepositions (e.g. those in (21)), it is likely a GO-verb.
2. If the verb in question appears in an Extent sense (e.g. (22)), it is likely a GO-verb. (Recall that EXT is a featural variant of GO.)
3. If the verb in question has two senses that are related by the inchoative relation (e.g. (13)), it is likely an INCH-verb.

This still leaves a range of cases where analysis is indeterminate. A number of these will appear in chapter 6. For an immediate example, consider whether the analysis of the verb *yellow* as GO TO in (14b) ought to be changed to INCH BE. Criteria 1 and 2 obviously do not apply. In fact, neither does criterion 3, which speaks of a *verb* having two related senses. Verbal *yellow* could contain the reading of adjectival *yellow* in the Place argument of either (20a) or (20b).

I find this particular case unresolved for the moment, but in the similar case of *cool* there is some evidence. Consider the difference between (23a) and (23b).

(23) a. Bill stood on the table for hours.
     b. The metal cooled for hours.

In (13c), *stand* has an inchoative reading; but, as seen in (23a), it lacks this reading when modified by a durative expression like *for hours*. Rather, only the State of standing on the table can take place over a period of time. By contrast, (23b) describes a continuous process of becoming cooler and cooler; in other words, the verb fundamentally expresses a change over time and not the achievement of a state. This argues that the verb *cool* expresses a GO-function, meaning roughly "continuously change temperature toward the direction of coolness."

The point of this example is not to give a definitive analysis for every possible case in which a choice arises between a motion reading and an inchoative reading. Rather, I have tried to show in the course of this section that many particular cases are decidable on grounds of lexical and semantic distribution, so that the apparent redundancy shown in (20) is not reason to judge the theory vague or untestable. It is a matter for future research to resolve ambiguous cases as they arise—and moreover to discover what evidence the language learner might use to resolve them.

5.4 Kinds of Conceptual Clause Modification

This section will lay out a partial taxonomy of functions that convert a State or Event into a restrictive modifier of another State or Event. Such functions are syntactically most transparent when they appear as subordinating conjunctions that turn sentences into restrictive modifiers. These cases can be used as a foundation for analyzing situations where the syntax is more opaque to direct conceptual analysis.

There is of course a wide variety of modifying subordinate clauses. One important type is *means* expressions, for which the most standard marker is the preposition *by*:

(24) a. John got into the room *by coming through the window.*
     b. John won the award *by performing a clever trick.*

Related PP constructions with *by means of* and *through* have roughly the same conceptual connection; the object of the preposition is construed as describing some sort of Action that is the means to the accomplishment of the main Event:

(25) a. John got the award *through his cleverness.*
     b. John got the award *by means of a clever trick.*

Using BY to encode the subordinating function, we can represent the conceptual structure of (24a) as (26).

(26) $\begin{bmatrix} \text{GO ([JOHN], [TO [IN [ROOM]]])} \\ \text{[BY [GO ([JOHN], [VIA [IN [WINDOW]]])]]} \end{bmatrix}$

The main clause of (24a) maps into the "main conceptual clause" of (26); the subordinate clause of (24a) maps into the argument of BY. In turn, BY plus its argument is a restrictive modifier of the main conceptual clause.

A second type of modifying clause is a *cause* expression, where we find the characteristic markers *because (of)*, *from*, and *of*:

(27) a. John got the award because he did something clever.
      b. John got the award because of his good looks.
      c. John turned yellow from eating carrots.
      d. John died $\begin{cases} \text{from the ravages of excludiosis.} \\ \text{of excludiosis.} \end{cases}$

Note that means expressions are answers to *How did such-and-such happen?* whereas cause expressions are answers to *Why did such-and-such happen?* and are therefore a variety of *reason*.

Using FROM to encode the subordinating function for cause expressions, we get a conceptual structure (28) for (27c), for example.

(28) $\begin{bmatrix} \text{GO}_{\text{Ident}} \text{ ([JOHN], [TO [YELLOW]])} \\ \text{[FROM [EAT ([JOHN], [CARROTS])]]} \end{bmatrix}$

Another sort of answer to *Why?* is an expression of *purpose*, *goal*, or *rationale*, normally encoded as an infinitival, *in order to*-phrase, or *for*-phrase. (See Faraci 1974 for a detailed taxonomy.)

(29) a. John earned the award (in order) to please his mother.
      b. We brought Bill to the doctor to be examined.   (*in order to be examined)
      c. The railings were built for our protection.

Purposes differ from causes in their entailments. Specifically, the sentences in (27) entail that John did something clever, has good looks, ate too many carrots, and was ravaged by excludiosis. By contrast, the sentences in (29) do not entail that John pleased his mother, that the doctor actually examined Bill, or that the railings actually protected us. Rather, the most that can be said is that the purpose is conceptualized by the speaker as the intended result of the Action of the main clause. In turn, the intention may be the speaker's; alternatively, it may be attributed to the (explicit or implicit) Agent of the sentence, as is the case in the sentences in (29).

Let us use FOR to encode the subordinating function for purpose clauses. Then sentence (30a) receives conceptual structure (30b).

(30) a. Bill obtained the book (in order) to give it to Harry.

b. $$\begin{bmatrix} \text{CAUSE ([BILL], } [\text{GO}_{\text{Poss}} \text{ ([BOOK], [TO [BILL]])])} \\ [\text{FOR } [\text{GO}_{\text{Poss}} \text{ ([BOOK], } \begin{bmatrix} \text{FROM [BILL]} \\ \text{TO [HARRY]} \end{bmatrix})]] \end{bmatrix}$$

A fourth kind of subordination appears in a wide variety of syntactic guises. Perhaps a good way to begin thinking about it is to compare expressions of accompaniment such as (31a,b) with simple conjunction as in (31c).

(31) a. Bill came with Harry.
    b. Harry came with Bill.
    c. Bill and Harry came.

Although (31a) and (31b) both entail (31c), (31c) says nothing about the relationship between Bill's coming and Harry's coming—they could have come independently. By contrast, (31a,b) express some mutual dependence between Bill's coming and Harry's, though they are inexplicit about the nature of this dependence. In particular, it is not necessary that either event is the cause of the other, as it is in, say, *Bill came because Harry did*.

In addition, (31a,b) differ in whose coming is "foregrounded." In these sentences, where the two events involved are commensurate, it is hard to see much function for the foregrounding. On the other hand, there is a distinct difference in (32).

(32) a. Bill came with an urgent message.
    b. An urgent message came with Bill.

I won't try to characterize this difference, but will only note it as circumstantial evidence to motivate another kind of conceptual subordination, which I will denote by the traditional term *accompaniment*.[2] Accompaniment is a kind of subordination (1) that is asymmetrical and (2) that implies a relation between the main and subordinate conceptual clauses (a) closer than mere conjunction but (b) something less than full causation.

A simple case where an accompaniment phrase clearly expresses a State or "conceptual clause" is (33).

(33) Bill entered the room $\begin{cases} \text{a. with a smile on his face.} \\ \text{b. without a smile on his face.} \end{cases}$

The *with-* and *without-*phrases here correspond to States in conceptual structure: "Bill had a smile on his face"; "Bill didn't have a smile on his face."[3] The connection to the main clause is highly nonspecific: is it "Bill entered the room *and* he had a smile on his face," or "When Bill entered the room, he had a smile on his face," or something else? There is no ready paraphrase with a full clause.

Next notice the parallel of (34) to (33).

(34) Bill entered the room $\begin{cases} \text{a.} & \text{smiling at Harry.} \\ \text{b.} & \text{without smiling at Harry.} \end{cases}$

(34a) and (34b) bear much the same relationship to each other as (33a) and (33b): the second is the negative of the first (with perhaps an additional presupposition about what might have been expected). This suggests that the absence of *with* in (34a) is nothing but a syntactic idiosyncrasy, possibly even something so trivial as a *with*-deletion before gerundives. Whatever the syntactic account, the paradigmatic relation between (33) and (34) suggests that they have similar conceptual forms, in particular that they both have a modifier of accompaniment.

Let us use WITH to encode the subordinating function of accompaniment. Then (35a) has the conceptual structure (35b).

(35) a. Bill entered the room without smiling.
   b. $\begin{bmatrix} \text{GO ([BILL], [TO [IN [ROOM]]])} \\ \text{[WITH [NOT SMILE ([BILL])]]} \end{bmatrix}$

A fifth subordinating function appears in (36), expressed by *for*.

(36) a. Susan promoted Phil *for* having discovered a new reflexive construction in Quechua.
   b. The police imprisoned Harold *for* stealing the computer code.
   c. Kitty Hofman, for instance, had been given a black eye by Carter Davis when she kicked him in the groin *for* dunking her head in a punch bowl *for* calling him a son of a bitch *for* telling her she looked like something the cat dragged in. (John O'Hara, *Appointment in Samarra*, Random House 1934, chapter 4)

The relation between the main clause and the *for* + gerundive in these examples is one of "exchange." Roughly speaking, the Agent in the main clause is performing an action that he or she deems of value appropriate to match the value of the action of the Agent in the subordinate clause. For example, in (36a) Susan considers a promotion to be of a value appropriate to match Phil's discovery. The matched values may be either positive or negative, as seen by comparing the positive (36a) to the negative (36b). If the two characters do not deem their respective actions to be of commensurate value, the result may be cycles of retribution, as seen in (36c).

Note that this relation of exchange is not a causal relation: Phil's discovery doesn't *cause* Susan to promote him. Nor is it necessarily a temporal relation between the two Events. In all the cases in (36), the main clause Event takes place after the subordinate clause Event, but in (37) the reverse is the case.

(37) I'll give you $10 today for mowing the lawn next week.

Rather, the exchange relationship seems to involve a voluntary act of social cognition, based on an ability to assess and compare the values of disparate acts. It thereby lies at the conceptual foundation of many aspects of legal and economic systems.

Using EXCH to notate the subordinating function of exchange, (38a) has the conceptual structure (38b).

(38) a. Bill gave Harold $5 for mowing the lawn.

   b. $\begin{bmatrix} \text{CAUSE ([BILL], [GO ([\$5], [TO [HAROLD]])])} \\ \text{[EXCH [MOW ([HAROLD], [LAWN])]]} \end{bmatrix}$

The similarities of the first four subordinators discussed here to spatial functions, I assume, is not coincidental. In particular, BY appears to be a form of VIA; FROM a variety of the usual FROM; FOR a variety of TO or TOWARD; and WITH a variety of the spatial WITH as in *Harry is with Bill*. This is what motivates my cavalier appropriation of spatial functions for this new purpose, though obviously further refinement is necessary.

For a further bit of evidence, consider the similarity of the subordinating functions to the NP modifiers in (39).

(39) a. a trip by train   (means)
   b. a trip from London   (source)
   c. a trip to Timbuktu   (goal)
   d. a trip with Harry   (accompaniment)

Notice especially the fact that if the trip is in progress, it must involve taking a train, having left London, and being with Harry. On the other hand, the trip need not actually reach the goal of Timbuktu. That is, the inferences associated with these modifiers parallel the inferences associated with subordinate clauses; in particular, the nonimplicative character of purpose clauses parallels the nonimplicative character of the goal phrase in (39c). In short, there is more than morphological similarity that suggests that the subordinators BY, FROM, FOR, and WITH are related to spatial counterparts. (On the other hand, I have not found a spatial counterpart for EXCH.)

A further issue concerns the conceptual category of the modifying constituents. Is [BY [GO...]] an Event, some variety of Circumstantial Place or Path, or what? Again, this is an important question for the overall characterization of conceptual structure. Since it will not play a role in what is to follow, though, I will leave it open.

Chapter 6

Some Featural Elaborations of Spatial Functions

6.1 Distributive Location

As a preliminary to the topic of this section, consider the restrictions on the determiner of the subject in (1).

(1) a. $\left\{\begin{array}{l} \text{Water} \\ \text{??Some water} \\ \text{The water} \end{array}\right\}$ was rushing out of the faucet.

b. $\left\{\begin{array}{l} \text{People} \\ \text{??Some people} \\ \text{*A person} \\ \text{The people} \end{array}\right\}$ was/were streaming into the room.

These sentences seem to convey the sense of an unbounded stream of water or people.[1] From a larger perspective one might view their boundaries, but not from the perspective expressed here. That is, *water* and *people* denote *media* in the sense discussed in section 1.6.3. As pointed out there, a medium can consist either of a substance like *water*, which has no internal organization, or of an aggregate like *people*, which is organized in terms of minimal units, in this case an individual person. The zero determiner on an expression of medium leaves it unbounded; the determiner *some* imposes a boundary, so that the NP denotes a closed or bounded form.

Notice that the definite article is acceptable in (1). This might be taken as evidence against the claim that the subject denotes an unbounded medium—but only under the assumption that *the* is a bounding expression. However, an alternative interpretation of the article is that it performs only a deictic function; in these cases it designates a previously known *medium* instead of a previously known *object*. In other words, under this interpretation, the definite/indefinite distinction is orthogonal to the closed form/medium distinction and does not affect the analysis of (1).

The sense of unboundedness in (1a, b) is heightened by the use of progressive aspect, which in a sense takes a snapshot of an event in progress whose temporal boundaries are not in view. If progressive is replaced by simple past, the event may be viewed as temporally bounded. As a result, the amount of water and the number of people is also bounded, and so *some* is acceptable. Compare (1) and (2).

(2) a. $\left\{\begin{array}{l}\text{Water}\\\text{Some water}\\\text{The water}\end{array}\right\}$ rushed out of the faucet.

b. $\left\{\begin{array}{l}\text{People}\\\text{Some/fifty people}\\\text{The people}\end{array}\right\}$ streamed into the room.

Turning to the main topic of this section, observe that similar determiner constraints appear in location sentences that employ a small class of English prepositions such as *all over*, *all along*, and *throughout*:

(3) a. $\left\{\begin{array}{l}\text{Water}\\\text{*Some water}\\\text{*A puddle of water}\\\text{The water}\end{array}\right\}$ was all over the floor.

   There was $\left\{\begin{array}{l}\text{water}\\\text{*some water}\\\text{*a puddle of water}\end{array}\right\}$ all over the floor.

b. $\left\{\begin{array}{l}\text{Telephone poles were}\\\text{*A telephone pole was}\\\text{*Some telephone poles were}\\\text{The telephone poles were}\end{array}\right\}$ all along the road.

   There was/were $\left\{\begin{array}{l}\text{telephone poles}\\\text{*a telephone pole}\\\text{*some telephone poles}\end{array}\right\}$ all along the road.

c. $\left\{\begin{array}{l}\text{?Raisins were}\\\text{*A raisin was}\\\text{*Some raisins were}\\\text{The raisins were}\end{array}\right\}$ throughout the pudding.

   There was/were $\left\{\begin{array}{l}\text{raisins}\\\text{*a raisin}\\\text{*some raisins}\end{array}\right\}$ throughout the pudding.

Compare these with (4), where ordinary prepositions of location appear.

(4) a. $\left\{\begin{array}{l}\text{*Water}\\\text{A puddle of water}\\\text{Some water}\\\text{The water}\end{array}\right\}$ was on the floor.

$$\text{There was} \left\{ \begin{array}{l} \text{water} \\ \text{a puddle of water} \\ \text{some water} \end{array} \right\} \text{on the floor.}$$

b.
$$\left\{ \begin{array}{l} \text{*Telephone poles} \\ \text{A telephone pole} \\ \text{Some telephone poles} \\ \text{The telephone poles} \end{array} \right\} \text{was/were along/beside the road.}$$

$$\text{There was/were} \left\{ \begin{array}{l} \text{telephone poles} \\ \text{a telephone pole} \\ \text{some telephone poles} \end{array} \right\} \text{along/beside the} \qquad \text{road.}$$

c.
$$\left\{ \begin{array}{l} \text{*Raisins} \\ \text{A raisin} \\ \text{Some raisins} \\ \text{The raisins} \end{array} \right\} \text{was/were in the pudding.}$$

$$\text{There was/were} \left\{ \begin{array}{l} \text{raisins} \\ \text{a raisin} \\ \text{some raisins} \end{array} \right\} \text{in the pudding.}$$

(I have no explanation for why *Raisins were throughout the pudding* is questionable, nor for why the *there*-construction permits bare NPs.)

Two observations can be made about the contrast between (3) and (4). First, in (3), the pattern of acceptable determiners and the possibility of only plural or mass nouns is much like that in (1). Second, the meanings of (3) and (4) are different. The sentences in (4) simply assert the location of the subject with respect to the object of the preposition. Those in (3), however, assert that the subject in some sense extends over the whole space subtended by the object of the preposition. For instance, (4a) just locates some body of water somewhere within the area of the floor, but (3a) says that the floor has water everywhere on it. (4b) could be satisfied by a single pile of poles stacked beside the road, but (3b) requires the poles to be distributed (fairly evenly) over the road's length. (4c) locates raisins in the pudding, but (3c) asserts that the pudding is thick with them.

To make the semantic differences clearer, append *somewhere* to the sentences in (3) and (4). It is acceptable in (4) (e.g. *A telephone pole was along the road somewhere*) but totally out in (3) (*Telephone poles were all along the road somewhere*). This fits our informal semantic description: if the poles are distributed over the road's length, they cannot be localized somewhere within it.

What do these differences have to do with the constraints on the subject? In ordinary expressions of location such as (4), the Theme is conceptualized as a closed form with its own intrinsic boundaries. Thus to assert its location does not affect its form. By contrast, the Themes in (3) are conceptualized as *media*—either substances, as in (3a), or aggregates, as in (3b, c). These sentences not only locate the medium but also specify its form, in terms of the form of the object of the preposition. For example, the water in (3a) takes its form from that of the surface of the floor. The aggregate of poles in (3b) takes its form from the road and hence is spread out linearly. The aggregate of raisins in (3c) takes its form from that of the pudding. Hence, as in (1), only expressions of unbounded media (definite or indefinite) are possible.

In the case of a substance taking a form, as in (3a), the meaning is perfectly clear: the substance is found in every place in the proper relation to the reference object, in this case *on* or *over the floor*. In the case of an aggregate, a little more explanation is necessary. By parallelism with substances, one might expect aggregates to be densely packed. This is fine if one is thinking of a basket of apples, but not, for example, if one is thinking of a line of telephone poles. In fact, all that seems necessary for a collection of individuals to count as a medium is that they be fairly uniformly distributed. The *density* of the distribution is a purely pragmatic matter—for instance, people all along a road are likely to be more densely packed than tunnels all along a road. From the point of view of conceptualizing them as aggregate media, though, they are both equally acceptable. Nor does the density of the medium need to be uniform: *There were tunnels all along the road, but especially in the mountains.* Here the density is taken to be greater in the mountains, but there is no region or neighborhood of the road that is entirely free of them.

This means that in (3b), for instance, one can think of the medium of telephone poles as occupying the entire length of the road, even though the poles may be 100 meters apart. They just happen to form a sparse medium. Likewise, in (3c), there is some pragmatically determined density of raisins that licenses the assertion. Whatever the total number of raisins, (3c) says that they are not localized in one part of the pudding but rather are more or less uniformly distributed.

I will refer to the kind of location expressed in (4) as *ordinary* location and to that in (3) as *distributive* location. Given their basic similarity—they are after all both expressions of location, with nearly identical syntactic structure—it would be of interest to differentiate them by means of a binary feature in conceptual structure. This feature could then be used to correlate the expression of medium in the subject with the use of the special prepositions appearing in (3).

Let us call the feature [±*distributive*], with the negative value [−dist] (ordinary location) being the unmarked case. We can then contrast *on the floor* and *all over the floor* as in (5).

(5) a. on the floor
       [$_{\text{Place}}$ ON$_{-\text{dist}}$ [$_{\text{Thing}}$ FLOOR]]

b. all over the floor

[$_\text{Place}$ ON$_\text{+dist}$ [$_\text{Thing}$ FLOOR]]

This formalization captures the fact that *on* and *all over* describe the same spatial relation to the reference object (here, the floor), namely contact with its surface. They differ only in that *on* expresses an ordinary location and *all over* a distributive location. Similarly, *along* and *all along* will be ordinary and distributive counterparts, as will *in* and *throughout*.

It appears that *all over* and *all along* are semi-idiomatic combinations recorded in the lexicon as such. In particular, *all over*, which implies contact with the reference object, is closer in meaning to *on* than it is to ordinary *over*, which does not imply contact. Similarly, *throughout* supplants *all in*. Some other combinations are *all around*, which is distributive *around*, *all across* (distributive *across*), and *all through*, which seems essentially the same as *throughout*.

To explore the uses of distributive location a little further, compare the sentences in (6).

(6) a. Paint ran all over the wall.
    b. Felix ran all over the field.

(6a) can be seen as a motional counterpart to *Paint was all over the wall.* The paint, viewed as a medium in motion, comes to occupy the region subtended by the wall. This sentence thus expresses a distributive *Path* traveled by the medium, so the feature [+dist] is carried up from the Place-to the Path-constituent:

(7) Paint ran all over the wall.

[$_\text{Event}$ GO ([$_\text{Thing}$ PAINT], [$_\text{Path}$ TO$_\text{+dist}$ [$_\text{Place}$ ON$_\text{+dist}$ [WALL]]])]

On the other hand, (6b) does not mean that Felix ended up subtending the entire area of the field (heaven forfend!). Rather, he is seen as an object of closed form that follows a single, nondistributive Path. The Path, however, eventually winds through most of the region subtended by the field (again, as in the poles all along the road, more or less densely or sparsely). Thus this time the Path constituent is [−dist], tracing out a route through a region viewed as [+dist]:

(8) Felix ran all over the field.

[$_\text{Event}$ GO ([$_\text{Thing}$ FELIX], [$_\text{Path}$ VIA$_\text{−dist}$ [$_\text{Place}$ ON$_\text{+dist}$ [FIELD]]])]

(Note that changing the Place to [−dist] in (8) gives the conceptual structure for *Felix ran over/across/through the field*.)

With a notion of distributive location and motion we are in a position to describe the well-known differences in meaning between (9a) and (9b) and between (10a) and (10b).

(9) a. $\left\{\begin{array}{l}\text{Bees}\\\text{A million bees}\\\text{The bees}\end{array}\right\}$ swarmed in the garden.

b. The garden swarmed with $\left\{\begin{array}{l}\text{bees.}\\\text{*a million bees.}\\\text{?the bees.}\end{array}\right\}$

(10) a. Felix loaded $\left\{\begin{array}{l}\text{books}\\\text{some books}\\\text{the books}\end{array}\right\}$ onto the truck.

b. Felix loaded the truck with $\left\{\begin{array}{l}\text{books.}\\\text{?*some books.}\\\text{the books.}\end{array}\right\}$

As noted by Fillmore (1968), Chomsky (1972), Anderson (1971), and others, the (b) sentences have a sense of "completiveness": the garden is full of bees, the truck is full of books. This sense is lacking in the (a) sentences.

Now note the determiner restriction in (9)–(10): one can comfortably add a bounding expression like *some* only in the (a) sentences. This suggests that the difference is one of ordinary versus distributive location. If the (b) sentences express distributive location, two facts follow: first, that bounding expressions cannot occur in the Theme; second, that the Theme completely occupies the space subtended by the reference object— precisely the observed difference in meaning. In short, the two word orders possible with these verbs differ in which kind of location they predicate. Moreover, the fact that *fill* occurs only in the (b) frame (the distributive frame) is then related to what *fill* means, namely that every location within the filled object comes to be occupied. (We will return to these verbs in chapter 8.)

6.2 Verbs of Touching

Let us next consider verbs that express not only an object's location but also its actual physical contact with another object and—even stronger— its attachment to another object. The notions of contact and attachment, although intuitively closely related, do not seem to be reducible one to the other. Nor does either of them reduce immediately to pure spatial location. Rather, there is a chain of implication: X *is attached to* Y implies X *is in contact with* Y, which in turn implies X *is located at* Y. The reverse implications of course do not hold. This section will deal with the verbs of touching and the next with the verbs of attachment.

The simplest verbs of touching are probably *touch* and *contact*. In simple present tense (11a) they express a state of contact; in past tense

(11b) they are ambiguous between a State reading and an inchoative Event.

(11) a. The tree touches the house.
          The wire contacts the switch.

d finished state?

   b. The tree touched the house $\begin{cases} \text{for years. (State)} \\ \text{suddenly. (Event)} \end{cases}$

       The wire contacted the switch $\begin{cases} \text{for a second. (State)} \\ \text{suddenly.   (Event)} \end{cases}$

Other verbs of contact, such as *hit, prick, strike, bump, knock,* and *kick,* have only an Event reading. Thus simple present is ruled out with these verbs, except as stage directions or "hot news" (in the sense of McCawley (1981)); moreover, in the past tense the durative expression *for 2 minutes* forces a repetitive reading on the sentence:

(12) a. *The tree hits the house.
          *The pin pricks his skin.

   b. The tree hit the house $\begin{cases} \text{?for 2 minutes. (repetition)} \\ \text{suddenly.} \end{cases}$

       The pin pricked his skin $\begin{cases} \text{?for 2 minutes. (repetition)} \\ \text{suddenly.} \end{cases}$

   There are two possible ways in which these verbs could be added into the system. The first way would be to introduce a new spatial State-function [$_{\text{State}}$ TOUCH (X, Y)]. The verbs in (11) would express this function directly, with an optional inchoative function; the verbs in (12) would be obligatorily inchoative. The second way would be to introduce a new feature opposition across the board in the field of spatial location, say Location versus Contact (or [$\pm$ *contact*]). I will argue that the latter alternative is correct, then show what analysis follows for (11)–(12).

   The main reason for not treating contact as a primitive expressed by the verbal system is that it shows up also in the prepositional system. There are at least two locational prepositions of English, *on* and *against,* that imply contact with the reference object. These contrast with *in, next to, alongside, above,* and so on, which say nothing about contact:

(13) a. The fly is on the wall.
          The ladder is against the wall. $\Big\}$ (contact)

   b. The fly is in the box.
          The ladder is next to the wall. $\Big\}$ (no necessary contact)

Thus a semantic feature [$\pm$contact] might well be involved in differentiating these prepositions.

   Moreover, among the Path-prepositions, *into* has a relevant ambiguity:

(14) a. The cockroach ran into the wall.
      b. Bill ran into the wall.

The most salient reading of (14a) is of the cockroach passing through a hole into the interior of the wall; that of (14b) is of Bill coming into violent contact with the surface of the wall. Again, the feature [±contact] appears necessary to discriminate the two. Let us formalize the distinction as (15).

(15) a. *Noncontact* into
          [$_{Path}$ TO ([$_{Place}$ IN$_{-contact}$ ([   ])])]
      b. *Contact* into
          [$_{Path}$ TO ([$_{Place}$ AT$_{+contact}$ ([   ])])]

(The nonspecific location function AT is used in (15b) because no further distinctions seem to be necessary.)

Given this feature of Places, verbs of contact could be formalized as conceptual functions that incorporate [±contact] Place-functions. *Touch*, for instance, would have the structure (16), plus, optionally, an inchoative.

(16) NP$_i$ touch NP$_j$.
      [$_{State}$ BE ([   ]$_i$, [$_{Place}$ AT$_{+contact}$ ([   ]$_j$)])]

However, this solution is not fine-grained enough. Most if not all the verbs of contact permit a further location expression describing the point of contact, as in (17a, b). By contrast, ordinary verbs of location and motion used with prepositions of contact do not allow this extra phrase, as seen in (17c).

(17) a. Harry is touching Bill *on the nose.* Ste+(
          The wire is contacting the switch *in the wrong place.*
      b. The tree hit the house *just under the bedroom window.*
          The arrow hit the target *right in the middle.*
          The pin pricked him *on/in the finger.*
      c. *The ladder is against the wall *under the window.*   (where *under the window* is the point of the ladder's contact)
          *Bill ran into Harry *on/in the knee.*

In order to distinguish which verbs permit this "secondary locative," some feature must be introduced into their lexical entries. Since the relevant feature appears to be whether the verb explicitly specifies contact, it would seem appropriate to generalize the feature [±contact] from the prepositional system to the verbal system.

Under this proposal, (16) is elaborated slightly into (18).

(18) NP$_i$ touch NP$_j$.
      [$_{State}$ BE$_{+contact}$ ([   ]$_i$, [$_{Place}$ AT$_{+contact}$ ([   ]$_j$)])]

In other words, the original idea for a new primitive function TOUCH ⟋⟍ reduces essentially to the introduction of $BE_{+contact}$, an elaboration of the previously existing system. We can consider [− contact], which designates pure location, to be the unmarked value of the feature, and it will in fact not be marked from here on out. The marked value, [+ contact], will be abbreviated by the subscript c.

Next consider the verb *hit*, one of the contact verbs that always designates an Event. Given the introduction of [± contact] as a feature on the main spatial functions, there are two possible ways to analyze *hit*: either as a verb of motion (19a) or as an inchoative (19b).

(19) NP_i hit NP_j.
   a. $[_{Event}\ GO_c\ ([\quad]_i,\ [_{Path}\ TO\ [_{Place}\ AT_c\ [\quad]_j]])]$
   b. $[_{Event}\ INCH\ [_{State}\ BE_c\ ([\quad]_i,\ [_{Place}\ AT_c\ [\quad]_j])]]$

(The analyses in (19a, b) attempt to capture only the "core meaning" of *hit*, as in *The ball hit the wall*. Other senses will be elaborated from this one in section 7.6.)

Which of these analyses of *hit* is correct? Consider what *hit* means: motion of the Theme culminating in contact with the reference object. Under the inchoative analysis (19b), this meaning follows automatically. By contrast, under the motion analysis (19a), it is necessary to stipulate that GO_c has this meaning. There is nothing in principle against such a stipulation, but GO_c might just as well specify, for example, motion while in continuous contact with the reference object. Now it just so happens that another class of contact verbs, for instance *stroke* and *scratch*, has exactly this latter reading. These verbs occur in much the same syntactic pattern as other verbs of contact, including the secondary locative:

(20) a. Beth stroked the cat on the neck.
   b. The thorns scratched Harry on/in the leg.

The verbs *rub* and *brush* appear in parallel contexts but also allow a PP-complement alone, specifying a Path of contact:

(21) a. The cat brushed by/along/against Harry's leg.
   b. The shirt rubbed on/against my elbows.

Thus this class of verbs permits the variety of Paths one would expect with a genuine GO-function, highlighting by contrast the narrowness of impact verbs like *hit*. We conclude that the proper analysis for *hit* is as an inchoative and that the slot in the conceptual paradigm provided by the new function GO_c is filled by the rather different verbs in (20) and (21).

We conclude that the contact verbs fall into the three categories in (22).

(22) a. *Pure contact:* NP_i touch/contact NP_j.
   $[_{State}\ BE_c\ ([\quad]_i,\ [_{Place}\ AT_c\ [\quad]_j])]$

    b. *Impact:* NP$_i$ hit/strike NP$_j$.
      [$_{Event}$ INCH [$_{State}$ BE$_c$ ([   ]$_i$, [$_{Place}$ AT$_c$ [   ]$_j$])]]
    c. *Moving contact:* NP$_i$ stroke/scratch NP$_j$.
      [$_{Event}$ GO$_c$ ([   ]$_i$, [$_{Path}$ VIA$_c$ [$_{Place}$ AT$_c$ [   ]$_j$])])]

It is interesting to contrast a verb of impact such as *hit* with the verb *bounce*. As observed above, *hit* specifies motion culminating in contact. By contrast, *bounce* specifies travel that is interrupted by an impact and that continues in a new direction. *Bounce* has quite a different syntactic pattern from *hit*: one cannot say **The ball bounced the floor* parallel to *The ball hit/struck the floor*. Moreover, *bounce* can occur with a full range of PP-complements (*The ball bounced along the road/through the hole/toward Harry*) as well as with no complement at all (*The ball bounced again*). This suggests that *bounce* does not have the same conceptual structure as the verbs of impact. Rather, it behaves more like an ordinary manner-of-motion verb, for which the defining characteristic of the manner of motion is contact and rebound at an intermediate point in the Path of motion.

Similarly, we can contrast the verbs of moving contact with the verb *slide*, which also expresses motion of the Theme while in contact with a surface. *Slide*, like *bounce*, appears not in the typical syntactic frame for contact verbs (**The skater slid the ice*) but rather in the usual frame for manner-of-motion verbs (*The skater slid on the ice/into the barn/through the tunnel; The skater slid again*). The difference between *slide* and *stroke*, although intuitively clear, is difficult to pin down. Very roughly, although both specify motion and contact, the contact is in some sense more "central" to the meaning of *stroke*, whereas the motion is more "central" to the meaning of *slide*. *Roll* is similar to *slide*: the surface upon which the Theme rolls need not be mentioned at all, and the grammatical pattern is that of an ordinary manner-of-motion verb. Thus *bounce* and *slide* fall under the class of MOVE-verbs discussed in section 5.2; their occurrence with Paths of motion will be treated in section 10.3.

Returning to the overall class of verbs that specify contact "centrally," the analyses in (22) leave two problems. The first is that at the moment the verbs of impact (22b) have exactly the same structure as inchoatives of verbs of pure contact (22a). But in fact there is a distinction between them that has a grammatical reflex in English: only the impact verbs allow a secondary locative with the preposition *in*:

(23) a. Bill touched Harry on/*in the nose.
      b. Bill hit Harry in the nose.

There are a number of possibilities for differentiating these two classes. Here are four. (1) There is a simple feature [± *impact*] that is positive in the impact verbs and negative in the inchoative contact verbs. Such a solution, however, seems crude, and a solution with more structural integrity would clearly be preferable. (2) Impact verbs may include an additional conceptual function that specifies that the Theme is in motion—that is, *hit* NP_j means roughly "come into contact with NP_j by moving to NP_j." (3) The distinction between the two classes may be localized in the role of Patient. Anticipating developments in chapter 7, this role is orthogonal to the thematic roles discussed so far. (24) shows that the two verb types contrast in the standard test for the Patient role and that only the direct object of impact verbs is a Patient.

(24) a.   What happened to the tree was the car hit it.
　　 b.   ??What happened to the tree was the car touched it.

Thus the impact verbs would mark their object as a Patient and the contact verbs would not. (4) Patienthood in impact verbs may not simply be a stipulation but may follow from their expressing exertion of a force on the reference object. This feature of exerting force is also found in verbs such as *push* and *pull*, whose objects are also Patients. Such a conceptual feature would therefore be of more general applicability than the [+impact] feature suggested above. I do not want to decide here which of these proposals is the correct way to distinguish impact verbs from inchoative contact verbs. Whichever proves most desirable, there will be a distinction between the lexical entries of *touch* and *hit* that can condition the choice of preposition in (23).

The second problem with the analyses in (22) is this: although the feature [+contact] distinguishes the verbs that allow a secondary locative from those that do not (as in (17)), this feature does not tell us *how* the secondary locative is attached when [+contact] is present. I will stipulate, without any strong evidence, that the secondary locative is a modifier of the BE- or GO-function. Sample structures appear in (25).

(25) a.   Harry is touching Bill on the nose.

$$\begin{bmatrix} \text{BE}_c \text{ ([HARRY], [}_{\text{Place}} \text{ AT}_c \text{ [BILL]]})\\ _{\text{State}} \text{ [}_{\text{Place}} \text{ ON ([NOSE])]} \end{bmatrix}$$

　　 b.   The tree hit the house under the window.

$$\begin{bmatrix} \text{INCH} \begin{bmatrix} \text{BE}_c \text{ ([TREE], [}_{\text{Place}} \text{ AT}_c \text{ [HOUSE]]})\\ _{\text{State}} \text{ [}_{\text{Place}} \text{ UNDER ([WINDOW])]} \end{bmatrix}\\ _{\text{Event}} \end{bmatrix}$$

　　 c.   Beth stroked the cat on the neck.

$$\begin{bmatrix} \text{GO}_c \text{ ([BETH], [VIA}_c \text{ [AT}_c \text{ [CAT]]]})\\ _{\text{Event}} \text{ [}_{\text{Place}} \text{ ON ([NECK])]} \end{bmatrix}$$

In order to construct these structures, there must be a general formation rule of conceptual structure that licenses the new modifier. The rule is roughly of the form (26).

(26) $[F_c ([_{Thing} X], [P ([_{Thing} Y])])]$
$$\Rightarrow \begin{bmatrix} F_c ([_{Thing} X], [P ([_{Thing} Y])]) \\ [_{Place} G ([PART OF Y])] \end{bmatrix}$$

This rule stipulates the following facts: (1) The secondary locative is available only with verbs that explicitly express contact, so that the sentences in (17c), whose verbs are [−contact], are ungrammatical. (2) The secondary locative is a Place, not a Path, so we do not get such things as *Bill hit Fred into the nose. (3) The point of contact must be a part of the object being contacted, to rule out such things as *Bill hit Fred in his sister. The rule leaves open, however, whether the contact function is BE or GO and whether its second argument is a Place or a Path.

(26), the general form of the licensing rule within the theory of Conceptual Semantics, is a definite improvement over old-time solutions that did such things as transformationally derive Bill hit Fred in the nose from Bill hit Fred's nose. From the evidence in the above discussion it should be easy to construct an argument why such a solution is impossible, so I will not spell it out.

One might feel however that (26) is still overly stipulative and that a truly explanatory theory of conceptual structure would derive much of it on more general principles. Indeed, it is possible that some of its conditions might be eliminated. For instance, the expression PART OF Y might follow automatically from the way this modifier maps into spatial representation, and it would therefore not have to be stipulated in (26) itself. However, for the sake of explicitness I have included all this information, leaving potential simplifications for future research.

6.3 Verbs of Attachment

The state of attachment is expressed most directly by a verb such as adhere or stick.[2] (27) is either a State or the inchoative of a State.

(27) The gum adhered/stuck to the table.

The neutral preposition of attachment is to. However, a secondary locative is also possible on occasion (28a), and there are other variants (28b, c, d).

(28) a. The gum stuck to Bill above the eyebrow.
   b. The gum stuck on the table.
   c. The gum stuck next to the table.   (i.e. stuck to something else that was next to the table)
   d. The gum stuck under the table.   (ambiguous: either to underside of table or to something underneath table)

A much wider range of these verbs are causative inchoatives:

(29) Harry stuck/attached/fastened/connected/glued/nailed/pinned the
      gum to Bill above the eyebrow.

Many of the verbs in the class, for instance *glue, nail,* and *pin,* incorporate
the instrument with which the Theme is attached to the reference object.
A further class of relevant verbs are those of *de*tachment. Here the
characteristic preposition is *from,* and a secondary locative is impossible:

(30) Harry detached/unglued/disconnected/unfastened the bit of paper
      from Bill (*above the eyebrow).

The beginning of section 6.2 mentioned the implicative relationship
among expressions of attachment, contact, and location: attachment to X
implies contact with X, which in turn implies location at X. The relation
between contact and location was captured by encoding contact as a
special marked form of location. We can extend this process by considering
attachment a special marked form of contact. The hierarchy of features then
looks like (31).

(31)

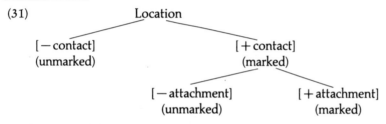

The verbs of detachment provide evidence for this schema. Notice that
remove can be substituted into (30), preserving the sense of detachment.
However, *remove* allows a further range of possibilities that sound pragmatically ludicrous with verbs of detachment:

(32) Harry $\begin{Bmatrix} \text{removed} \\ \text{!detached} \end{Bmatrix} \begin{Bmatrix} \text{the bird from the cage.} \\ \text{the milk from the cup.} \\ \text{the leaves from the sidewalk.} \end{Bmatrix}$

Thus detachment appears to be a special case of removal or taking away.
Under schema (31), this relationship can be captured by marking *detach* with
[+contact, +attachment] in the relevant structural position(s) but leaving
remove unspecified. (The argument would be stronger if alongside verbs of
cessation of location and of detachment there were verbs of cessation of
contact, say **untouch.* I have been unable to find any but do not know
whether this is a principled gap or an accidental one. Given the present
proposals, I am forced to regard it as accidental.)
Let us therefore analyze the state of attachment as parallel to the state
of contact, only adding the extra feature [+attachment]. (Again, I will

notate the marked values of the features as c and a. If c and a are absent, the intended value is the unmarked one ($[-$contact$]$ and $[-$attachment$]$).)

(33) NP_i sticks/adheres to NP_j.

   $[_{State} BE_{c,a} ([\quad]_i, [_{Place} AT_{c,a} [\quad]_j])]$

The secondary locative is automatically available with these verbs, then, because they have a $[+$contact$]$ State-function, satisfying the conditions of rule (26).

   We are then faced with a choice of analyses for *attach*, parallel to that for *hit* in the previous section: it may be either the causative of an inchoative (34a) or the causative of a verb of motion (34b).

(34) NP_i attach NP_j to NP_k.

   √a. $[_{Event} CAUSE ([\quad]_i, [_{Event} INCH [_{State} BE_{c,a} ([\quad]_j, [AT_{c,a} [\quad]_k])]])]$
   b. $[_{Event} CAUSE ([\quad]_i, [_{Event} GO_{c,a} ([\quad]_j, [TO [AT_{c,a} [\quad]_k]])])]$

For much the same reasons as with *hit*, the inchoative solution (34a) appears better. There are no alternative Paths available for verbs of attachment, nor can anything be said about intermediate steps in the process of attachment. Such narrowness of possibilities is more consistent with the inchoative analysis.

   Moreover, recall the interpretation attributed to GO_c in the previous section: this is the structure for verbs such as *stroke* and *scratch* that specify motion of the Theme while in contact with the reference object. A parallel for attachment verbs would be a verb that specified the Theme moving along the surface of the reference object but attached to it all the while. Although such a notion is pragmatically possible (for instance to describe the motion of a typewriter carriage or perhaps a piston), I am unable to think of a verb of English that specifically expresses it. Rather, we tend to make do with the more general verb *slide*. In short, the situation characterized as (34b) does not have the properties associated with the verb *attach*, again pointing to the inchoative analysis (34a) as the correct one.

   Turning to the verbs of detachment, we expect an analysis in which one element of the attachment structure is reversed or negated. There are three possibilities for the element in question: (1) INCH could be reversed to an element TERM(inate); that is, the verbs could express the termination of a state of attachment. (2) BE could be negated; that is, the verbs could express the beginning of a state of nonattachment. (3) AT could be reversed or negated; that is, the verbs could express the beginning of a state of location other than attachment.

   Of these three possibilities, the third provides the best opportunity for a localized account of the preposition choice. In a number of other cases, *from* appears as a Place-function that expresses the negation of a position:

(35) a. You have to stay out from under the table.
   b. Bill kept Harry from the cookies.

This use of *from* appears to be a special case of its occurrence in Place-expressions like *down the road from here*, which section 4.1 analyzed as "terminus of a Path originating here and extending down the road." The only difference in (35) is that the direction of the Path ("down the road") is omitted. We therefore tentatively analyze this *from* as (36), using the AT-END-OF operator of section 4.1.

(36) [$_{Place}$ AT-END-OF ([$_{Path}$ FROM ([$_{Thing/Place}$])])]

In the verbs of detachment, the point of origin with *from* must indicate attachment. We can express this by making the argument of *from* the Place [AT$_{c,a}$ ([THING])]. Putting these pieces together, we get the following analysis of detachment verbs:

(37) NP$_i$ detach NP$_j$ from NP$_k$.
   [$_{Event}$ CAUSE ([   ]$_i$, [$_{Event}$ INCH [$_{State}$ BE ([   ]$_j$, [$_{Place}$ AT-END-OF
                    [$_{Path}$ FROM [$_{Place}$ AT$_{c,a}$ [$_{Thing}$]$_k$]])])])]

Note that BE is not [+ contact, + attachment] in (37), because the final state is not one of attachment. Rather, attachment is specified only as part of the origin of the Path. The presupposition that NP$_j$ was previously attached to NP$_k$ comes out of the logic of the inchoative: for this state to come to pass, the reverse had to be the case before the event took place.

The fact that BE in (37) is not [+ contact, + attachment] provides an incidental dividend: the structure (37) thereby does not meet the structural description of rule (26), which licenses secondary locatives. Hence this analysis predicts correctly that secondary locatives are ungrammatical with verbs of detachment, as seen in (30).

A remaining issue: Where is the instrument of attachment—the glue or nails—integrated into the conceptual structure of these verbs? There are two reasons to believe it is not an ordinary instrument: (1) The inferences are different. A hammer helps someone make the picture come to be attached to the wall, but the nails keep the picture attached to the wall without outside intervention. (2) Ordinary instruments do not incorporate into verbs of detachment. One can *hammer* a picture to a wall, but one cannot **unhammer* it, though one may *unglue* it. I leave the resolution for future research.

Bringing together the past two sections, we have seen the virtues of treating contact and attachment not as new primitive functions but as featural elaborations of location. Some aspects of the verbs of contact and location remain unexplained, for instance the fact that the contact verbs are transitive but the attachment verbs use the preposition *to*, and that there are verbs of detachment but none of ceasing to touch. It should be noted, though, that these differences between the two classes are not totally regular. For instance, the contact verb *touch* has a causative that borrows the syntax of attachment verbs (*John touched the powder to his lips*); and the attachment verb *join* has a noncausative transitive form, parallel to contact verbs (*John joined the crowd*). Such exceptional cases bring out the closeness between the two classes despite their syntactic differences.

It should also be mentioned that these classes include a substantial number of the spatial verbs that permit intransitives with reciprocal interpretations:

(38) a. *Contact*
Harry and Sue touched/kissed/hit/collided/rubbed/bumped.   (but **struck/contacted*)
b. *Attachment*
The hoses stuck/connected/joined.   (but **attached/glued*)

Another important class of reciprocal verbs, including *mix* and *combine*, appears to be a generalization of the contact verbs, specifying contact throughout a volume instead of on a surface.

6.4 Verbs of Material Composition

Another class of verbs not treated in *S&C* describes the composition and decomposition of material objects.[3] The verbs of composition are typically causative. Some allow expression of either Source or Goal (39a); others allow only a Source-expression (39b).

(39) a. Sam made/formed/built/assembled $\begin{Bmatrix} \text{a house from/out of bricks.} \\ \text{the bricks into a house.} \end{Bmatrix}$

   Sam put $\begin{Bmatrix} \text{the house together from bricks.} \\ \text{the bricks together into a house.} \end{Bmatrix}$

b. Same constructed/erected/manufactured/produced/created
   $\begin{Bmatrix} \text{a house from/out of bricks.} \\ \text{*the bricks into a house.} \end{Bmatrix}$

Form and *make* also appear noncausatively, in both stative and inchoative variants:

(40) a. The three lines $\begin{Bmatrix} \text{form} \\ \text{make} \end{Bmatrix}$ a triangle.   (stative)

b. The three lines suddenly $\begin{Bmatrix} \text{formed} \\ \text{made} \end{Bmatrix}$ a triangle.   (inchoative)

Many verbs of *decomposition* appear in both inchoative and causative variants (41a, b); only the causative is possible with others (41c, d). All of these permit a Goal-expression; none permits a Source (41e).

(41) a.   The bowl broke/split/cracked/splintered/crumbled/divided/
                                    shattered into a thousand pieces.
       b.   Maggie broke/split/cracked/splintered/crumbled/divided/
                                    shattered the bowl into a thousand pieces.
       c.   *The bowl ground/pulverized/chopped/disassembled into
                                                      little pieces.
            *The bowl took apart into little pieces.   (*except as middle)
       d.   Maggie ground/pulverized/chopped/disassembled the bowl into
                                                      little pieces.
            Maggie took the bowl apart into little pieces.
       e.   *Ernie broke/split/ground/disassembled a thousand pieces out of
                                                      the bowl.

Still other verbs of decomposition totally incorporate the Goal-expression
and at best reluctantly permit it to be expressed as a PP:

(42) Harry destroyed/demolished/wrecked the car (*into bits).

   As in the previous sections, from an analysis of the stative case we can
derive the other cases by standard techniques. So the primary question is
the conceptual structure of (40a). The difference between this semantic field
and all other fields of spatial verbs is that in this field the two NPs are
semantically related as parts and whole instead of being separate objects. It
is therefore necessary to introduce a new conceptual element to encode this
relationship. As in the case of contact verbs, we could simply invent a new
primitive, say

$[_{State} \text{FORM} ([\ \ ]_i, [\ \ ]_j)]$,

that serves this purpose in the system. However, it again proves more
interesting to ask whether more structure can be teased out.
   The semantic field of S&C to which the verbs of composition show the
closest resemblance is the Identificational field, which is used to categorize
objects and ascribe properties to them. As with the verbs of material
composition, the two NPs related by the verb do not designate distinct
objects:

(43) a.   The coach $\begin{Bmatrix} \text{changed} \\ \text{turned} \end{Bmatrix}$ into a pumpkin.

      b.   Tom became a renegade.

Rather, in this field the Theme is referential, and the "reference object"
denoted by the predicate nominal is a category or type (see S&C, section
10.2). Moreover, the syntactic patterns characteristic of this field are in part
the same as those for composition verbs, especially the use of into as the
standard preposition of Goal.

A particularly close alliance appears in the case of the verbs *make* and *create*, which have the following pattern in the Identificational field, parallel to (39a) in the compositional field:

(44) a. An MIT education made $\left\{\begin{matrix} \text{me (into) a linguist.} \\ \text{a linguist out of me.} \end{matrix}\right\}$

b. An MIT education creates linguists out of mathematicians.

Pairs like (45) seem especially close in meaning.

(45) a. Sam made/created the house out of wood/bricks.   (composition)
b. Sam made/created the house out of an old barn.   (identification)

It is also worth notice that the two fields have similar determiner restrictions (noted in part for the Identificational field by Gruber (1965) and discussed briefly in *S&C*, page 207):

(46) a. Sam made/built/assembled $\left\{\begin{matrix} \text{the bricks into a house.} \\ \text{*bricks into the house.} \end{matrix}\right\}$

b. Sam made/built/assembled/created $\left\{\begin{matrix} \text{a house out of the bricks.} \\ \text{the house out of bricks.} \end{matrix}\right\}$

(47) a. Sam made/converted/changed/transformed
$\left\{\begin{matrix} \text{the barn into a house.} \\ \text{*a barn into the house.} \end{matrix}\right\}$

b. Sam made/created $\left\{\begin{matrix} \text{a house out of the barn.} \\ \text{the barn out of a house.} \end{matrix}\right\}$

It is not clear how this determiner restriction is to be accounted for, but it suggests that the two fields share some aspects of their logical organization.

It develops, then, that the field of material composition is best worked into the system not by inventing a new conceptual function out of whole cloth but by subsuming it with Identification under a supercategory that might go under the name *Character*. By contrast with the various subcategories of Location discussed in the previous sections, or with Possession, predicates of Character tell about the object itself: what category it belongs to and what properties it has (Identification), and what it is made of (Composition):

(48)

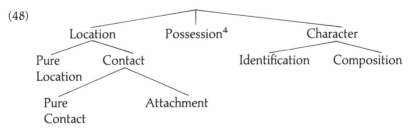

Having established the overall place of this semantic field in the system, we return to the analysis of the verbs within the field. We have claimed that this field is not built up of its own idiosyncratic primitives but is a part of the standard system of thematic functions. This means that the statives must be analyzed as a variety of the function BE, with a Theme and a "reference object."

I will notate the semantic field feature as *Comp*, bearing in mind that it has the further analysis shown in (48). There are two possible analyses for BE_{Comp}, given in (49). They differ in which NP is taken to be Theme and which "reference object."

(49) The three lines form/make a triangle.
    a. [$_{State}$ BE_{Comp} ([3 LINES], [$_{Place}$ AT [TRIANGLE]])]
    b. [$_{State}$ BE_{Comp} ([TRIANGLE], [$_{Place}$ AT [3 LINES]])]

Which of these is correct? Here are three arguments that (49a) is the proper analysis.

First, in the inchoative version of *form*, shown in (50), the direct object may be replaced by a PP-complement and is hence a clear expression of Goal; moreover, the subject of the inchoative is understood as undergoing change and is hence Theme.

(50) The three lines suddenly formed (into) a triangle.

Since the inchoative and stative forms of a verb usually have the same syntactic argument structure, we can conclude that a parallel analysis should be adopted for (49). Structure (49a) assigns them the correct roles, whereas (49b) reverses them.

Second, the object of stative *make* and *form* is constrained by the determiner restrictions observed in (46) that are characteristic of the Goal-expression in inchoatives:

(51) a.   The three lines make/form a triangle.
    b.   ?*Three lines make/form the triangle.

The principles that enforce this restriction (whatever they are) would be most generally stated if the conceptual structures of statives and inchoatives were of parallel form, namely with the subject as Theme and the object as reference object. Thus (49a) is again the preferable analysis.

Third, there happens to be a verb for which (49b) appears to be the proper structure:

(52) The triangle consists of three lines.

Here *three lines* appears in a PP, a sign of reference object status, and *the triangle* appears as subject, a frequent sign of Theme status. Moreover, with this verb the determiner restrictions apply in reverse:

(53) *A triangle consists of the three lines.

In short, *consist* seems best analyzed as (49b).

We see then that, although sentences describing composition always involve a relationship between a whole and its parts, there is not a constant mapping from these elements to thematic relations. There are two ways to encode composition: parts as Theme, whole as reference object (49a), and the reverse (49b). Lexical items differ in which encoding they express. Hence a further feature must be added in conceptual structure to distinguish (49a) from (49b), and lexical entries must specify a value for this feature in order to determine the thematic relations they assign. Let us set up this feature as a diacritic on the field feature Comp, as follows:

(54) a. $[_\text{State} \text{BE}_{\text{Comp}^+} ([X], [AT [Y]])] \Rightarrow$ Y are parts of X
(Theme is whole, reference object is parts)

b. $[_\text{State} \text{BE}_{\text{Comp}^-} ([X], [AT [Y]])] \Rightarrow$ X are parts of Y
(Theme is parts, reference object is whole)

That is, $\text{BE}_{\text{Comp}^+}$ and $\text{BE}_{\text{Comp}^-}$ have opposite mapping of whole and parts to thematic relations. Using this refinement of the feature Comp, we see that *form* and *make* in (49) express $\text{BE}_{\text{Comp}^-}$, and *consist* in (52) expresses $\text{BE}_{\text{Comp}^+}$.

In nonstative sentences of composition and decomposition, the same distinction can be observed. Sentences of composition with a Source-expression (such as (55a)) have the whole completed unit as Theme and are therefore Comp$^+$; those with a Goal-expression (such as (55b)) have the parts as Theme and are therefore Comp$^-$. Notice that nearly all verbs of composition are either Comp$^+$ alone (as in (39b)) or permit either version of Comp (as in (39a)).

(55) a. Sam built/assembled/constructed/created the house out of bricks.
(Comp$^+$: Theme = whole)

b. Sam built/assembled the bricks into a house.   (Comp$^-$: Theme = parts)

Verbs of decomposition are all Comp$^+$, as seen in the contrast (41b,e).

(41) b. Maggie broke/split/... the bowl into a thousand pieces.
(Comp$^+$: Theme = whole)

e. *Ernie broke/split/... a thousand pieces out of the bowl.
(Comp$^-$ Theme = parts)

Next comes the usual question: are the inchoatives genuine inchoatives, that is, INCH BE-verbs, or are they GO-verbs? Unfortunately, the evidence here is equivocal. Our standard argument, based on the lexical relation between stative and inchoative *form* and *make*, suggests that they are genuine inchoatives. Under this analysis, the three classes of change-of-composition verbs shown in (55a), (55b), and (41b) receive the following structures:

(56) a. Sam built the house out of bricks.
  [CAUSE ([SAM], [INCH [BE$_{Comp^+}$ ([HOUSE], [AT [BRICKS]])]])]
  b. Sam assembled the bricks into a house.
  [CAUSE ([SAM], [INCH [BE$_{Comp^-}$ ([BRICKS], [AT [HOUSE]])]])]
  c. Sam broke the bowl into pieces.
  [CAUSE ([SAM], [INCH [BE$_{Comp^+}$ ([BOWL], [AT [PIECES]])]])]

These are inadequate in a number of ways. The most glaring is that (56a) and (56c) are exactly the same structure; that is, there is no difference between *building* X *out of* Y and *breaking* X *into* Y. Moreover, under this analysis, (56a) and (56c) should mean roughly "Sam caused the house to come to consist of bricks" and "Sam caused the bowl to come to consist of pieces," which are both off the mark. In addition, there is no apparent role for the difference between the prepositions *out of/from* in (56a) and *into* in (56c).

Trying the GO alternative, we get the following structures for the three types of change of composition:

(57) a. Sam built the house out of bricks.
  [CAUSE ([SAM], GO$_{Comp^+}$ ([HOUSE], [FROM [BRICKS]])])]
  b. Sam assembled the bricks into a house.
  [CAUSE ([SAM], [GO$_{Comp^-}$ ([BRICKS], [TO [HOUSE]])])]
  c. Sam broke the bowl into pieces.
  [CAUSE ([SAM], [GO$_{Comp^+}$ ([BOWL], [TO [PIECES]])])]

This analysis provides the proper range of distinctions. The verbs of composition and decomposition are differentiated, and the prepositions *into* and *out of* correspond to the Path-functions TO and FROM in the correct way.

In fact, even the choice of the preposition *into* is partly motivated in analysis (57). In normal locational use, it decomposes as TO IN. But notice that there is also a use of *in* that expresses a state of decomposition:

(58) a. The house is in pieces/ruins.
  b. The book is in three parts.

Thus in (57c), we can see the change as taking an object *to* "in pieces." In other words, *into* decomposes as TO IN again, but this time in a different sense of *in*.

We are then left with the problem of why the verbs *form* and *make* can be both stative and inchoative. Does this undermine the original argument in section 5.3 for the INCH-function? Or does it mean only that more sensitive evidence is called for? If the latter, though, how does the language learner know which analysis to choose? I leave these troubling issues open for now. The tension in the theory between INCH BE and GO is an important one, and I would rather live with it for a while to see how it develops than rush to an over-hasty Occamic solution.

6.5 Conclusion(s)

What has been learned from these exercises in conceptual description?

The classes of verbs and prepositions treated in this chapter constitute, I believe, a substantial subset of the purely spatial concepts that were omitted from the *S&C* system of thematic relations. They have all proven to be featural extensions of the previous system. The next chapter will discuss a further set of extensions, in the CAUSE system. But it seems to me that the major classes do not go on forever: at least within the spatial system, the number of distinct conceptual categories of predicates is, if not small, at least manageable. Thus there appears to be some hope for a fairly comprehensive coverage.

We have found that the best way to formalize the conceptual structure of many of these classes is not just to add more primitive functions to the system. Rather, the treatment of verbs and prepositions of distributive location, contact, attachment, and composition involves developing the primitive semantic fields of *S&C* into coherent feature systems. In other words, the system as a whole has not just gotten bigger: it has come to acquire more structure, as might be expected of something as rich as human cognition.

Each of the semantic classes investigated here is realized with a characteristic syntactic structure; that is, there appears to be a canonical mapping from each particular variant in conceptual structure to a standard syntactic argument structure. For instance, the verbs of contact typically are transitive, the verbs of attachment typically appear with the preposition *to*, and the verbs of composition typically appear with the prepositions *out of/from* for Source and *into* for Goal. In each class, there are exceptional cases in which a different mapping appears, but on the whole the canonical patterns are remarkably well observed. In a way, these regularities and subregularities of the semantics-to-syntax mapping resemble those of the syntax-to-phonology mapping for inflectional categories of English such as past tense and plural.

Within each class of verbs, some verbs realize a broader range of syntactic and semantic possibilities than others: some are only stative or only causative inchoative, but some can be stative, inchoative, or causative inchoative. For instance, *touch* is a great deal broader than *strike*; *stick* is broader than *glue*; *make* is broader than *disassemble*. Some of these variations may be principled. For instance, the verb *glue* essentially involves an instrument, the glue; since instrument is a modifier of causation, we would not expect this verb to appear noncausatively. On the other hand, there seems no essential reason why *pulverize*, "turn to dust," is only causative, while *vaporize*, "turn to vapor," can be noncausative as well. So the syntactic and semantic restrictions on lexical items cannot be expected to be totally explained; there is a point where the quest for explanatory adequacy must leave off.

To determine the boundaries of explanation rather than mere description, it is necessary to consider the behavior of each individual verb within the context of the overall class to which it belongs. The class as a whole and its place in the larger system must be examined in detail in order to lay out the place of a verb within the system. Only then can one judge whether a particular fact about the verb is principled or idiosyncratic, regular or exceptional. Cross-linguistic study is important here, of course: if the same apparently idiosyncratic fact appears in language after language, something is being missed. Conversely, if an apparently principled fact is violated in other languages, the principle must be questioned.

These are elementary points of linguistic methodology. My point in repeating them here is only to emphasize that they are just as germane to semantics as to syntax and phonology. I have tried here to lay out some steps toward sorting out the principled from the idiosyncratic in a few semantic fields beyond those of *S&C*; it remains for further investigation to determine whether the correct generalizations have been drawn.

Chapter 7
The Action Tier and the Analysis of Causation

7.1 The Roles Actor and Patient; the Action Tier

The last two chapters motivated enrichments in conceptual structure that do not change its overall texture. This chapter will open up the expressive power of the theory somewhat more radically, along the lines of tier theory in recent phonology.

Let's start with the verb *hit*. What are the thematic roles in (1)?

(1) a. Sue hit Fred.
　　b. The car hit the tree.
　　c. Pete hit the ball into the field.

In (1a), *Sue* is evidently the Agent. But what is *Fred*? I have seen it said that *Fred* is the Theme, because it is the thing affected. But that is not the definition of Theme—"thing in motion or being located." Such an analysis derives, I think, from the notion of Theme as a default case-marker, like Fillmore's (1968) Objective case. As pointed out in section 2.2, such a notion makes no sense within the theory of thematic relations as originally conceived and as pursued here.

The proper thematic analysis comes from looking at (1b), where *the car* is clearly in motion and *the tree* is its endpoint, hence the Goal. By analogy, *Fred* is Goal in (1a) and the Theme is *Sue* (or, more precisely, Sue's hand). However, this analysis fails to generalize properly with (1c), where *the ball* is clearly in motion and therefore ought to be Theme. So how do we express the relationship among these three uses of *hit*?

A notion missing from the theory of thematic relations in *S&C* and earlier sources (back to Gruber 1965) is that of "affected entity"—the traditional role of Patient. A rough-and-ready test for this role is the ability of an NP to appear in the frame (2).

(2) $\left\{ \begin{array}{l} \text{What happened} \\ \text{What Y did} \end{array} \right\}$ to NP was . . .

Using this test, we can see that the direct objects in all the examples in (1) are Patients:

(3) a. What happened to Fred was Sue hit him.
    b. What happened to the tree was the car hit it.
    c. What happened to the ball was Pete hit it into the field.

However, their being Patients does not eliminate their other roles: it is still necessary to specify what moves where under whose agency. Hence Patient is a potential role independent of and supplementary to the other roles.

Note that the role Patient is not predictable from the other thematic roles. Although the Goal *the tree* is a Patient in (1b), not all Goals are Patients, as seen in (4a). Nor are all Patients Goals, since in (1c) the Patient is *the ball* (Theme), not *the field* (Goal), as seen in (4b,c).

(4) a. *What Bill did to the room was enter it.
    b. What Pete did to the ball was hit it into the field.
    c. *What Pete did to the field was hit the ball into it.

The distribution of Patients vis-à-vis other thematic roles finds a parallel in the distribution of Actors ("doers of the action"). If we pick out Actors by the test frame (5), we find Actors in Source (6a), Theme (6b), and Goal (6c).

(5) What NP did was...

(6) a. The sodium emitted electrons.   (What the sodium did was emit electrons.)
    b. Bill ran down the hill.   (What Bill did was roll down the hill.)
    c. The sponge absorbed the water.   (What the sponge did was absorb the water.)

This situation, then, has a flavor not unlike that of recent phonological theory, in which representations are organized into independent tiers. Adapting suggestions of Culicover and Wilkins (1986) and Talmy (1985), let us suppose that conceptual roles fall into two tiers: a *thematic tier* dealing with motion and location, and an *action tier* dealing with Actor-Patient relations. Staying for a moment with a description in terms of informal annotation, we might find analyses like those in (7).

(7) a. Sue   hit   Fred.
        Theme   Goal   (thematic tier)
        Actor   Patient   (action tier)
    b. Pete   threw the ball.
        Source   Theme   (thematic tier)
        Actor   Patient   (action tier)
    c. Bill   entered the room.
        Theme   Goal   (thematic tier)
        Actor   (action tier)

d. Bill received a letter.
   Goal   Theme   (thematic tier)
                                (action tier)

We see in these examples different combinations of thematic and actional roles. In particular, *enter* has an Actor but no Patient, as seen in (4a), and, as seen in (8), *receive* has neither Actor nor Patient.

(8) a. *What Bill did was receive a letter.
    b.? *What happened to Bill was he received a letter.
         (OK only with surrounding context in which the letter in turn has some unfortunate effect)[1]
    c. *What happened to the letter was Bill received it.

This is all well and good for a first approximation, but as was stressed in chapter 2, mere annotation of syntactic structure is inadequate. What we really need is a *functional* representation that has Actor and Patient as argument positions, parallel to the treatment of Theme, Source, and Goal.

To that end, we introduce a new formal elaboration of Events in the action tier. Regarding the schemas (2.1c,e) (GO, STAY, and CAUSE), (5.3) (MOVE), and (5.18) (INCH) as expansions of the thematic tier, we can supplement them with (9).

$$(9) \quad [\text{EVENT}] \rightarrow \begin{bmatrix} \cdots \\ \text{AFF} (\langle[\text{THING}]\rangle, \langle[\text{THING}]\rangle) \end{bmatrix}$$

AFF ("affect") is an additional mainstream function alongside the thematic functions. The first argument of this function is the Actor; the second is the Patient. For example, *The car hit the tree* now receives the conceptual structure (10).

$$(10) \quad \begin{bmatrix} \text{INCH} [\text{BE}_c ([\text{CAR}], [\text{AT}_c [\text{TREE}]])] \\ _{\text{Event}} \text{AFF} ([\text{CAR}], [\text{TREE}]) \end{bmatrix}$$

Up until this point, all conceptual functions have had a fixed number of arguments. If the Path argument of GO, for instance, is not filled syntactically, we still understand the Theme as traversing a Path, for example in *Bill entered*. However, as (9) indicates, AFF has the curious property of having two optional arguments. If the Patient is missing, the sentence still may have an Actor, as seen in (7c), and there is no sense of an "implicit Patient." Hence the existence of a Patient of action is not obligatory.

The optionality of the Actor role in (10) is seen from the action tier of certain intransitive verbs such as *roll*, whose subject passes the test for either Actor or Patient:

(11) a. What Bill did was roll down the hill.
     b. What happened to Bill was he rolled down the hill.

In (11a), as in (7c), there is no sense of an implicit Patient. Conversely, in (11b) there is no sense of an implicit Actor whose action caused Bill's rolling—it just may have been one of those things. In such a case perhaps it would be better to say Bill is the *Undergoer* rather than the *Patient*, but the sense "affected by the Event" remains. Hence (11b) appears to be a case where only the second argument of AFF is present. The lexical entry for *roll*, then, must permit the Theme to be identified on the action tier as either Actor or Patient. *Roll* contrasts with, for instance, *enter* or *march*, whose Themes can only be Actor:

(12) a. What Bill did was $\begin{cases} \text{enter the room.} \\ \text{march down the hall.} \end{cases}$

   b. *What happened to Bill was he $\begin{cases} \text{entered the room.} \\ \text{marched down the hall.} \end{cases}$[2]

We need a convention for notating AFF when only one of its arguments is present; a notation like (13a) would be ambiguous. Accordingly, (13b) will be used when there is only an Actor and (13c) when there is only a Patient/Undergoer. These are distinguished from the case where there is an implicit Actor or Patient, for which we will also have need. These will be notated as in (13d) and (13e) respectively.

(13) a. [AFF ([X])]   (X = Actor or Patient?)
   b. [AFF ([X]),   ]   (X = Actor only)
   c. [AFF (, [Y])]   (Y = Patient only)
   d. [AFF ([   ], [Y])]   (implicit Actor)
   e. [AFF ([X], [   ])]   (implicit Patient)

The action tier enables us to dissect the traditional notion of Agent into a number of independent parts (as has been suggested by Dowty (1988), for example).[3] One sense of Agent, "extrinsic instigator of action," is captured by the role "first argument of CAUSE," an element in the thematic tier. However, a second sense is "volitional actor." This appears, for instance, in the well-known ambiguity of *Bill rolled down the hill*, where Bill may or may not be performing the action willfully. Generally, it seems that any Actor, if animate, is subject to this ambiguity, unless the verb specifically selects for a volitional Agent, as do, for instance, *buy* and *look*.

Jackendoff 1972 was rightly criticized (Comrie 1975; Kac 1975; Rosenberg 1975) for encoding volitional Agents in terms of CAUSE, so that the ambiguity was represented as in (14).

(14) Bill rolled down the hill.
   a. *Volitional*
      [CAUSE ([BILL], [GO ([BILL], [DOWN [HILL]])])]
   b. *Nonvolitional*
      [GO ([BILL], [DOWN [HILL]])]

Such an account requires an optional CAUSE-function in the lexical entry of every action verb. Worse, it obscures the difference between willful agency and extrinsic instigation. *The wind rolled the ball down the hill* has a extrinsic instigator that is not volitional; the volitional reading of (14) has a willful agent but no extrinsic instigator. In addition, the first argument of CAUSE is itself subject to the volitional ambiguity, since *Bill rolled the ball down the hill* has a (preferred) volitional reading. In short, the roles "extrinsic instigator" and "volitional actor" are independent and cannot be encoded identically.

A more adequate approach in the present framework is to permit the function AFF a feature elaboration [± *volitional*], or [± vol]. It is just when an animate NP has the Actor role that volitionality becomes an issue. So, for example, *deliberately* (volitional) and *accidentally* (nonvolitional) can be inserted in (7a,b,c) and (11a) but not (7d) or (11b). *Bill rolled down the hill* can thus be associated with three possible action tiers, as shown in (15).

(15) Bill rolled down the hill.

$$\left[\begin{array}{l} \text{GO ((BILL], [DOWN [HILL]])} \\ \left\{\begin{array}{l} \text{a. } \text{AFF}_{+vol}\text{ ([BILL], }\quad) \\ \text{b. } \text{AFF}_{-vol}\text{ ([BILL], }\quad) \\ \text{c. } \text{AFF (}\quad, \text{[BILL])} \end{array}\right\} \end{array}\right]$$

(willful doer)
(nonwillful doer)
(undergoer)

The markedness conditions on [± vol] are slightly tricky. As mentioned a moment ago, there are plenty of verbs that require [+ vol] Actors; some, like *die*, require [− vol] Actors. When a verb is unmarked for volitionality (like *roll*), an animate subject is *preferably* interpreted as volitional, although this preference is easily overridden by other information. Finally, if the Actor is inanimate, [− vol] must be selected for consistency.

To sum up the dissection of the notion Agent, we see that it breaks into three semi-autonomous parts: doer of action (first argument of AFF), volitional Actor (first argument of AFF$_{+vol}$), and extrinsic instigator (first argument of CAUSE).

Section 2.3 mentioned the possibility of a general linking rule that correlates agentivity with subject position. Which of the three subnotions of Agent is relevant to this rule? In English, if there is an Actor on the action tier, it is invariably subject; on the thematic tier, the subject is instigator if there is one, and otherwise usually Theme. Thus the constancy of association goes specifically with the Actor role.

If there is a Patient in a transitive sentence, it tends to be associated with direct object position in English. Some of the relevant facts are presented by Anderson (1977) (who unfortunately uses the term *Theme* rather than *Patient* for "affected entity," perpetrating a certain amount of confusion that has persisted in the literature). Comparing the two syntactic frames of verbs like *load* and *smear*, we find differences in which argument can be taken as Patient:

(16) a. i.   What Bill did to the books was load them on the truck.
             What Bill did to the paint was smear it on the wall.
       ii. ?What Bill did to the truck was load the books onto it.
            ?What Bill did to the wall was smear paint on it.
     b. i.   *What Bill did to the books was load the truck with them.
            ?*What Bill did to the paint was smear the wall with it.
       ii.   What Bill did to the truck was load it with books.
             What Bill did to the wall was smear it with paint.

The thematic relations in each case are the same: the books go onto the truck, the paint goes onto the wall. The change is in which entity is viewed as most directly "affected" by Bill's action, and the direct object has a stronger claim on the role in either case. Thus the action tier is strongly implicated in choice of objects as well as subjects. We return to this issue periodically in this chapter and more definitively in chapter 11.

7.2 Varieties of Causation

Talmy (1985) shows that the standard notion of causation can be fruitfully decomposed into a number of features, each of which is subject to parametric variation. Changing the values of the parameters yields a whole family of concepts related to causation such as hindering, overcoming, letting, helping, and resisting. The next few sections are devoted to incorporating Talmy's insights into the present framework.[4]

Talmy's fundamental idea is that causation is one instance of a broad system of concepts he calls *force-dynamics*. Force-dynamic concepts involve the interaction of two characters. One of these characters, the *agonist*, has a tendency toward performing or not performing some action; this tendency is opposed by the other character, the *antagonist*. Standard causation is the case in which the antagonist gets his/her/its way, and so the agonist ends up acting differently than his/her/its natural tendency. So, for example, in *Harry forced Sam to go away*, Sam, the agonist, has an inherent tendency (or desire) not to go away; Harry, the antagonist, opposes this tendency, and the outcome is that Sam indeed leaves.

This overall conception can be formalized nicely in the present theory. Consider the conceptual structure of *Harry forced Sam to go away*, including the action tier. (Section 7.7 works out the control relations in terms of argument binding; for now, I will just duplicate HARRY and SAM in all the θ-roles in which they are understood.)[5]

(17) Harry forced Sam to go away.

$$\begin{bmatrix} \text{CAUSE ([HARRY], } \begin{bmatrix} \text{GO ([SAM], [AWAY])} \\ \text{AFF ([SAM],} \quad) \end{bmatrix}) \\ \text{AFF ([HARRY], [SAM])} \end{bmatrix}$$

Talmy's agonist-antagonist dyad shows up on the action tier. The agonist is Patient—the person on whom force is being applied. The antagonist is Actor—the person applying the force. Instead of Talmy's notion of "agonist's tendency," we have the notion "what the antagonist is trying to bring about," namely the Effect ⟨for⟩ Sam to go away.[6] The inference rule for CAUSE, (1.27), allows us to infer that the Effect takes place, so the outcome is Sam's leaving, just as Talmy describes it.

A slightly different combination appears in *Harry prevented Sam from going away*. Here everything is the same except that Harry's effort is directed toward Sam's *not* leaving. (18) shows this case.

(18) Harry prevented Sam from going away.

$$\begin{bmatrix} \text{CAUSE ([HARRY], [NOT } \begin{bmatrix} \text{GO ([SAM], [AWAY])} \\ \text{AFF ([SAM],} \quad) \end{bmatrix}]) \\ \text{AFF ([HARRY], [SAM])} \end{bmatrix}$$

Talmy's approach becomes more interesting when we consider verbs that express the same force-dynamic oppositions as *force* and *prevent* except that there is a different outcome:

(19) a. Harry pressured/urged/goaded Sam to go away,

$$\left\{ \begin{array}{l} \text{and he did go away.} \\ \text{but he didn't go away.} \end{array} \right\}$$

b. Harry impeded/hindered Sam's going away,

$$\left\{ \begin{array}{l} \text{and in the end Sam didn't go away.} \\ \text{but Sam did go away.} \end{array} \right\}$$

In these examples, Harry and Sam again form an antagonist-agonist dyad. In (19a), as with *force*, Harry is trying to bring about Sam's going away; in (19b), as with *prevent*, Harry is trying to bring about Sam's not going away. The difference is that in these sentences the Effect is only potential: as can be seen from the continuations, we cannot infer whether the Effect took place or not. Another way of seeing this is to note that *successfully* and *unsuccessfully* can be inserted after the subject in (19), whereas only *successfully* can be inserted before *force* and *prevent*, and it is somewhat redundant there:

(20) a. Harry $\left\{ \begin{array}{l} \text{successfully} \\ \text{unsuccessfully} \end{array} \right\}$ $\left\{ \begin{array}{l} \text{urged Sam to leave.} \\ \text{impeded Sam's leaving.} \end{array} \right\}$

b. Harry $\left\{ \begin{array}{l} \text{?successfully} \\ \text{*unsuccessfully} \end{array} \right\}$ $\left\{ \begin{array}{l} \text{forced Sam to leave.} \\ \text{prevented Sam from leaving.} \end{array} \right\}$

To encode the similarity of the force-dynamic configurations but the difference in outcomes, let us introduce a more general function CS that contains a "success parameter." We will use the notation CS^+ to encode application of force with a successful outcome; this case supplants the previous notation CAUSE. We will use CS^u for application of force with an undetermined outcome. Thus *force* (17) and *prevent* (18) will be CS^+, and *pressure* and *impede* will be CS^u. In turn, *pressure* and *impede* differ in that the latter incorporates a negation in the potential Effect, just like *prevent*:

(21) a. Harry pressured Sam to go away.

$$\left[\begin{array}{l} CS^u\,([\text{HARRY}], \left[\begin{array}{l}\text{GO ([SAM], [AWAY])}\\ \text{AFF ([SAM],\quad)}\end{array}\right]) \\ \text{AFF ([HARRY], [SAM])} \end{array}\right]$$

b. Harry impeded Sam's going away.

$$\left[\begin{array}{l} CS^u\,([\text{HARRY}], [\text{NOT} \left[\begin{array}{l}\text{GO ([SAM], [AWAY])}\\ \text{AFF ([SAM],\quad)}\end{array}\right]]) \\ \text{AFF ([HARRY], [SAM])} \end{array}\right]$$

A different configuration appears in the verbs *manage, succeed, try,* and *fail*:

(22) a. Harry managed to go away/succeeded in going away.
    b. Harry tried to go away.
    c. Harry failed to go away.

In each of these, Harry is exerting effort toward leaving. *Manage* and *succeed* have a positive outcome, *try* has an undetermined outcome, and *fail* has a negative outcome. Only *try* permits the adverbs *successfully* and *unsuccessfully*, which determine the outcome as they did with *impede* and *urge*. Since the three verbs all involve exertion of effort and differ in outcome, it would be nice to assimilate them to CS. What makes them different from the previous verbs is that they lack an explicit agonist-antagonist dyad; if anything, Harry is opposed only by implicit obstacles.

The representation in (23) seems appropriate for *try*.

(23) Harry tried to go away.

$$\left[\begin{array}{l} CS^u\,([\text{HARRY}], \left[\begin{array}{l}\text{GO ([HARRY], [AWAY])}\\ \text{AFF ([HARRY],\quad)}\end{array}\right]) \\ \text{AFF ([HARRY],\quad)} \end{array}\right]$$

This says that Harry, the Actor, is exerting effort toward leaving, but the outcome is indeterminate. (Alternatively, we might want to include an implicit Patient, roughly [OBSTACLES], in the outer action tier, though this seems rather ad hoc: an *obstacle* is defined functionally, as something that must be overcome—essentially, as a Patient in this position.) *Manage* and *succeed* then differ from *try* only in having CS^+ instead of CS^u. *Fail* requires a third value of the success parameter, which we can encode as CS^-.

(Notice, by the way, that CS⁻ is not the same as CS⁺ ... NOT. The latter would mean that Harry's efforts are directed toward not going away and that those efforts are successful; *avoid* might be a lexicalization of this concept.)

All the verbs mentioned so far in this section are pure causatives; the Effect or potential Effect appears as an infinitival or gerundive complement. Of course, there are many causative verbs that express both a CS-function and an Effect. For the most part, these verbs (*roll, break, open, kill,* etc.) express the function CS⁺ (= CAUSE); that is, they have positive outcomes. Some of the differences between such lexical causatives and the phrasal causatives of this section are discussed in section 7.8.

But I have also come across a few lexical causatives with other values of the success parameter. Consider (24).

(24) Amy pushed/pulled (on) the door as hard as she could,

$$\left\{\begin{array}{l}\text{and it finally opened.}\\\text{but it wouldn't budge.}\end{array}\right\}$$

Here there is a standard force-dynamic interaction between *the door* (agonist) and *Amy* (antagonist), with undetermined outcome. As the continuations show, we cannot infer whether the door moved or not. The difference between *push* and *pull* is in whether the antagonist's force is directed away from or toward the antagonist. So X *push (on)* Y is essentially "X CSᵘ Y to go away from X," and X *pull (on)* Y is "X CSᵘ Y to go toward X." (The transitive forms with Path, such as *Amy pushed/pulled Bill out the window,* do of course have a positive outcome. Chapter 10 will treat them as resultative constructions with core *push/pull* as means modifiers.) It is also conceivable that *miss* (as in *The arrow missed the target*) can be analyzed as "fail (CS⁻) to hit," providing a third value for the success parameter in lexical causatives.

To sum up so far, we have encoded Talmy's force-dynamic configuration through a combination of the thematic and action tiers, using the functions CS and AFF. One of the parameters in causation, the success parameter, is notated as a superscript +, *u*, or − on the function CS. Standard causation, previously notated as CAUSE, is now CS⁺.

7.3 Varieties of Dyadic Interaction; the Role Beneficiary

7.3.1 Verbs of Helping and Letting

A second parameter in Talmy's force-dynamic theory concerns the character of the interaction between the two protagonists. In all the cases presented so far, the two have been in opposition. However, a different configuration appears in verbs like *help, assist,* and *aid*: the two characters are striving for the same potential Effect. With these verbs, the direct object no longer passes the standard test for Patient. The appropriate preposition is *for* instead of *to*; the object might be characterized as a Beneficiary:

(25) What Harry did for/?*to Sam was help him go away.

Yet another configuration appears in verbs like *let, allow,* and *permit.* Here the situation is conceptualized as a *potential* opposition between antagonist and agonist that is not realized. This nonrealization of opposition can be volitional, as in *Amy let Bill go to the movies*: this is understood as a decision by Amy not to obstruct Bill's action. Alternatively, it can be nonvolitional, as in *The window let the light come in*: here it is the window's mere existence that eliminates the potential obstruction to the light. With these verbs of letting, the direct object again does not pass the standard test for Patient; it's odd to say *What Harry did to Sam was let him come in.* With both protagonists animate, a *for* of Beneficiary seems all right:

(26) What $\begin{Bmatrix} \text{Harry} \\ \text{*the window} \end{Bmatrix}$ did $\begin{Bmatrix} \text{for} \\ \text{*to} \end{Bmatrix} \begin{Bmatrix} \text{Sam} \\ \text{*the light} \end{Bmatrix}$ was let $\begin{Bmatrix} \text{him} \\ \text{it} \end{Bmatrix}$ come in.

Since we have localized Talmy's dyadic opposition as the two arguments of AFF in the action tier, it makes sense to express these new dyadic relations as variations in the action tier. I will renotate the relation of opposition, so far just AFF, as AFF$^-$: the second argument is negatively affected (Patient). The relation of helping will be notated AFF$^+$: the second argument is positively affected (Beneficiary). The relation of letting will be notated as AFF^0, or nonopposition.

In principle, AFF$^+$ and AFF^0 ought to occur with all the varieties of CS, just as AFF$^-$ was shown to in the last section. The verbs of helping appear to me to vary between CS^u and CS$^+$, depending on the form of the complement:

(27) *Verbs of helping*: AFF$^+$ (HARRY, SAM)
  a. *Infinitival complement*
     Harry helped Sam wash the dishes,
     $\begin{Bmatrix} \text{and they finished quickly.} \\ \text{but they didn't finish.} \end{Bmatrix}$ (CS^u)
  b. *Gerundive complement*
     Harry assisted/aided Sam in washing the dishes,
     $\begin{Bmatrix} \text{and they finished quickly.} \\ \text{??but they still didn't finish.} \end{Bmatrix}$ (CS$^+$)
  c. *Implicit complement*
     Harry helped/aided/assisted Sam,
     $\begin{Bmatrix} \text{and they finished quickly.} \\ \text{but they didn't manage to finish.} \end{Bmatrix}$ (CS^u)

The other combination, AFF$^+$ and CS$^-$, is pragmatically bizarre: it would imply that through the Agent's help, the Beneficiary fails to perform a desired task. Not surprisingly, I cannot find any verb that means that.

The verbs of letting display a similar pattern: if someone is allowed to do something, there is a strong presumption but not a logical inference that he or she did it. Hence these verbs are predominantly CS^u (28a). On the other hand, inanimate letting is more likely to be construed as CS$^+$ (28b).

(28) *Verbs of letting*: AFF^0 (HARRY, SAM)
  a. Harry let Sam leave/allowed Sam to leave,
$$\begin{cases} \text{and so Sam left.} \\ \text{but for some strange reason, Sam didn't leave.} \end{cases} \quad (CS^u)$$
  b. The cracks in the wall let the light come in,
$$\begin{cases} \text{and so the room was not entirely dark.} \\ \text{*but the light still didn't come in.} \end{cases} \quad (CS^+)$$

The combination of AFF^0 and CS$^-$, something failing to happen as a result of being permitted, is again pragmatically bizarre (though perhaps imaginable with a parent as Actor and a perversely rebellious teenager as Beneficiary).

In general, because AFF$^+$ and AFF^0 are less stereotypical force-dynamic interactions than AFF$^-$, it is probably to be expected that they have less highly differentiated lexical realizations. There are certainly fewer verbs of helping and letting than of causing. However, alongside the pure verbs of helping and letting cited above, there are a few that incorporate these forms of interaction along with another function. *Guide*, for instance, means roughly "help to go along a Path"; *support*, "help to stay up"; *promote*, "help to advance." Among the verbs of letting, *release* means roughly "let go out/away"; *drop*, "let fall"; *admit*, "let enter."

7.3.2 Verbs of Possession

Perhaps the most prominent appearance in English of the Beneficiary role, though, is in verbs of transfer of possession. The Goal of possession, especially in indirect object position (29a), is construed as Beneficiary.

(29) What Harry did for Sam was $\begin{cases} \text{a.} & \text{give him a book.} \\ \text{b.} & \text{?give a book to him.} \end{cases}$

Thus double-object *give* has the conceptual structure (30).

(30) Harry gave Sam a book.
$$\begin{bmatrix} CS^+ \ ([HARRY], [GO_{Poss} \ ([BOOK], \begin{bmatrix} FROM \ [HARRY] \\ TO \ [SAM] \end{bmatrix})]) \\ AFF^+ \ ([HARRY], [SAM]) \end{bmatrix}$$

On the thematic tier of (30), Harry causes (CS$^+$) a book to change possession from him to Sam; on the action tier, Harry benefits Sam, that is, acts positively on him. By contrast, *give NP to NP* prefers an action tier with the Theme as some sort of quasi Patient:

(31) a.   What Harry did with/*to/*for the books was give every one of them to Sam.

b.   ?What Harry did with the books was give Sam every one of them. (this form used to avoid *give Sam it*, which is out on independent prosodic grounds)

Hence the "dative shift" verbs have an alternation in the action tier not unlike that of the locative alternation with *load*, seen in (16).

Since *give* is the causative of *receive*, the latter must have the conceptual structure (32).

(32) Sam received a book.
$$\begin{bmatrix} GO_{Poss}\ ([BOOK],\ [TO\ [SAM]]) \\ AFF^+\ (\quad,\ [SAM]) \end{bmatrix}$$

The action tier in (32) says that Sam benefits from this Event, without implicating any specific Actor who benefits him. It thus parallels the specification of Undergoer in (15c), *Bill rolled down the hill*, where Bill is adversely affected by the Event but there is no particular Actor that has brought the Event about.

The parallelism actually cuts a little deeper. *Sam got a book* shares a reading with (32), in which Sam is passive Beneficiary of the Event. But it also has another reading in which Sam initiates the action, as in *Sam went and got a book* or *What Sam did was get a book*. Hence *get*, like *roll*, has an ambiguous action tier, in which the subject is either the first or the second argument of AFF. Since AFF is AFF$^+$ this time, the latter reading casts the subject as Beneficiary rather than Undergoer.

We now may begin to see why there should be a dative alternation with verbs of possession in particular. The subject and the NP immediately following the verb are the canonical positions for action tier roles. The use of an indirect object, then, is a means of canonically marking the Beneficiary role. (We return to this matter in chapter 11.)

We can also begin to understand the use of *give* as a light verb, as in *give X a kiss*, *give X a kick*. What is being preserved of the regular verb *give* is its action tier, in which X is the second argument. In fact, the switch from Beneficiary in *give X a kiss* to Patient in *give X a kick* now comes simply by neutralizing the sign of AFF in the light verb and filling it in from the nominal. The fact that these constructions are much worse in the *to-NP* form—?*give a kiss to X, ?*give a kick to X*—now follows from the observation made in (29) that the *to-NP* form has a different action tier. Since the action tier is the crucial part of the light verb *give*, it must remain intact.

7.3.3 Verbs of Reaction

Consider the following trio of verbs:

(33) a. Sam gave in to Harry('s pressure on him).
     b. Sam withstood Harry('s pressure on him).
     c. Sam resisted Harry('s pressure on him).

As Talmy observes, the force-dynamic configuration here is that Harry is trying to get Sam to do something; that is, Sam is agonist and Harry antagonist. However, the sentences are set from Sam's point of view: they describe the nature of Sam's *reaction* to Harry. They differ in whether Harry gets his way. With *give in*, Harry at length succeeds; with *withstand*, Harry fails; with *resist*, the outcome is undetermined but can be settled by use of *successfully* or *unsuccessfully*. In other words, these differences correlate with the three possible values of the success parameter in CS: *give in* is CS^+; *withstand* is CS^-; *resist* is CS^u.

But what is the action tier? The usual two possibilities present themselves: we can introduce a new primitive function or we can differentiate one of the old ones with features. This time, for simplicity, I will introduce a new function

REACT ([X], [Y]),

"X reacts to Y." Using this function, (33c) receives this representation:

(34) Sam resisted Harry.
$$\begin{bmatrix} CS^u \ ([HARRY], [_{Event} \quad]) \\ REACT^- \ ([SAM], [HARRY]) \end{bmatrix}$$

The thematic tier of (34) is clear: Harry is exerting effort toward the realization of some implicit Event, with undetermined outcome. The action tier represents the force-dynamic interaction between Harry and Sam with respect to this implicit Event. In the action tier, the function REACT is sort of a mirror image of AFF. This time the agonist, and the one on whom the negative effect falls, is the first argument (a case of $REACT^+$ will appear presently). The antagonist, the Instigator of the CS-function, is the second argument. In other words, the functional roles have been reversed. What has been preserved thereby is the mapping to syntax: the first argument is mapped to subject position and the second to object position.

An alternative approach would be to use the function AFF for these verbs and reverse the mapping from the action tier to syntactic structure. However, there is a sense that verbs of reaction add something to the meaning beyond a change of viewpoint. They imply a more active role for the agonist than does the essentially passive Patient role. For instance, the contrastive *but* in (35) indicates that resistance is more than being a recipient of pressure, even though *pressure* and *resist* are both CS^u verbs.

(35) Harry pressured Sam to leave, but Sam resisted.

In addition, the *do* test shows that a Reactor is a kind of Actor:

(36) What Sam did was resist/withstand/give in to Harry.

And certainly the rhetoric of political and social resistance has stressed its active character.

This suggests that we should consider AFF and REACT alternative realizations of a more abstract function, just as CAUSE is one realization of the more abstract function CS. I suspect this is ultimately the right approach, but I won't explore the issue any further here.

7.4 Temporal Relations between the Cause and the Effect

Another parameter of causation involves the temporal relation between the Cause (or Instigator's action) and the Effect. Consider the contrast between (37a) and (37b).

(37) a. Bill dragged the car down the road.
      b. Bill threw the ball into the field.

In (37a) Bill's dragging is temporally coextensive with the motion of the car; by contrast, in (37b) Bill's throwing only initiates the ball's motion. Interestingly, these two possibilities were noted already by Michotte (1954), according to whom these are the principal variants in the perception of physical causation. Michotte called the kind of causation seen with *drag* "entraining" and that seen with *throw* "launching."

This difference can be simply encoded as a feature on the causative function. Adopting Michotte's terminology, we will notate the feature as a subscript *entrain* versus *launch* on CS, as shown in (38). (39) shows two parallel forms of letting.

(38) a. Bill dragged the car down the road.   (entraining)
$$\begin{bmatrix} CS_{entrain}^{+} \ ([BILL], [GO \ ([CAR], [DOWN \ [ROAD]])]) \\ AFF^{-} \ ([BILL], [CAR]) \end{bmatrix}$$
      b. Bill threw the ball into the field.   (launching)
$$\begin{bmatrix} CS_{launch}^{+} \ ([BILL], [GO \ ([BALL], \begin{bmatrix} FROM \ [BILL] \\ TO \ [IN \ [FIELD]] \end{bmatrix})]) \\ AFF^{-} \ ([BILL], [BALL]) \end{bmatrix}$$

(39) a. The valve let the water out.   (entraining)

$$\begin{bmatrix} CS_{entrain}{}^+ \ ([VALVE], [GO \ ([WATER], [OUT])]) \\ AFF^0 \ ([VALVE], [WATER]) \end{bmatrix}$$

b. Bill released the bird from the cage.   (launching)

$$\begin{bmatrix} CS_{launch}{}^+ \ ([BILL], [GO \ ([BIRD], [FROM \ [CAGE]])]) \\ AFF^0 \ ([BILL], [BIRD]) \end{bmatrix}$$

It appears that this feature distinction occurs only with CS^+, that is, successful causation. In indeterminate and failed causation, the Effect is not asserted to have taken place, so there can't be a temporal relation between the Cause and the Effect.[7]

7.5 Extensions of Force-Dynamics to Logical Verbs and Psych-Verbs

All of the force-dynamic interactions presented so far have been Events. Next, we should observe that there are also *stative* force-dynamic interactions. (40) gives a few examples.

(40) a. This fence constrains the cattle.
b. This hole lets the water out.
c. This highway leads (you) to Tucson.
d. The windowshade blocks the light.

The use of simple present tense here is a clue that the sentences are either stative or generic (though it is not entirely clear which). One's intuition is that the subjects of these sentences don't actively do anything—they are just there, and their presence inhibits or facilitates movement of things that happen to come in contact with them. Such effects seem sufficient to characterize them as some sort of Actor, since they pass the *do* test, given in the appropriate tense: *What this fence does is constrain the cattle.*

Very tentatively, we can formalize this sort of interaction as stative CS and AFF, as in (41).

(41)   This hole lets the water out.

$$\begin{bmatrix} CS^u \ ([HOLE], [GO \ ([WATER], [OUT])]) \\ {}_{State} \ AFF^0 \ ([HOLE], [WATER]) \end{bmatrix}$$

(41) contrasts minimally with the ongoing Event *This hole is letting the water out*, which in the present analysis differs only in the substitution of Event for State.

This sets the stage for an analysis of verbs of logical relation in terms of force-dynamics, as suggested by Talmy and hinted at in Jackendoff 1976. They are of course all stative. (42) presents a sample.

(42) a. X entails/implies/leads to Y.   (cause)
b. X rules out/precludes Y.   (cause . . . not)

    c. X permits/is consistent with Y.   (let)
    d. X reinforces/supports Y.   (help)

It is interesting that this set includes the "help" verbs *reinforce* and *support*, which strictly speaking are not considered verbs of logical relation but which in fact play a prominent role in argumentation. They emerge clearly in the present analysis as members of the same family of vocabulary as *entail* and *imply*.

It has also been observed (e.g. Lakoff 1972; Talmy 1985) that the modals *must* and *may* pair up conceptually with the verbs *require* and *permit*, which are verbs of causing and letting respectively. Suppose, then, that we think of *must* as a version of stative AFF$^-$ and *may* as a version of stative AFF^0. In this analysis, the subject of the sentence plays the role of agonist, and the sentence minus the modal is the potential Effect. The trick in the analysis is identifying the antagonist. It is always an implicit argument: something like logic, morality, the present situation (these three being varieties of the epistemic use of the modal), or some contextually understood authority (the root use of the modal). Such a conceptual analysis, of course, calls for a highly noncanonical mapping between conceptual structure and syntax, and hence for extra-special care in its execution— more than can be provided in the present context. I therefore leave it as suggestive speculation.

A final intriguing possibility is the application of the action tier to the differentiation of Experiencer verbs. A well-known bifurcation of these verbs, going back in the generative literature to Chomsky 1965, Postal 1971, and Lakoff 1970, concerns whether the Experiencer is (1) in object or oblique position, as with *please*, *matter*, and *strike*, or (2) in subject position, as with *like*, *admire*, and *regard*. Another parameter concerns whether the affect is positive, as in *please* and *like*, negative, as in *displease* and *hate*, or neutral, as in *strike* and *regard*. Finally, a third parameter concerns whether the verb is stative or eventive; many verbs with Experiencer objects are ambiguous and the difference is signaled by tense and aspect:

(43) a. Thunder frightens Bill.   (stative)
      b. Harry (deliberately) frightened Bill.   (eventive)

Suppose we think of the Experiencer as the person affected by the State or Event, that is, as a kind of Patient. This provides the key to an analysis in terms of the action tier. Under this approach, the verbs with Experiencer in object or oblique position include the function AFF, which canonically maps the Patient into object position. Those with Experiencer in the subject can be thought of as giving the subject's *reaction* to the stimulus; that is, their action tier contains REACT—which canonically maps the Patient into subject position. The second parameter, polarity of affect, is then represented by the sign of AFF or REACT; we will have to add a value *u* for the neutral cases (it is not the same as the value *0*, which designates letting). Finally, the third parameter is the State versus Event variation observed in (43). (44)–(45) give some sample analyses of the action tier in these terms; a full analysis including the thematic tier will have to wait for some other occasion.

(44) a. X pleases Y. $[_{State} \text{ AFF}^+ ([X], [Y])]$
       b. X displeases Y. $[_{State} \text{ AFF}^- ([X], [Y])]$
       c. X (suddenly) frightened Y. $[_{Event} \text{ AFF}^-_{\pm vol} ([X], [Y])]$
       d. X strikes Y as crazy. $[_{State} \text{ AFF}^u ([X], [Y])]$
       e. X matters to Y. $[_{State} \text{ AFF}^u ([X], [Y])]$

(45) a. Y likes X. $[_{State} \text{ REACT}^+ ([Y], [X])]$
       b. Y fears/hates X. $[_{State} \text{ REACT}^- ([Y], [X])]$
       c. Y regards X as crazy. $[_{State} \text{ REACT}^u ([Y], [X])]$

The interest of this analysis, I think, lies in the parallel that it draws between the *please-like* alternation and the *pressure-resist* alternation. The reversal of grammatical relations follows from a conceptual difference that independently is known to have a strong effect on grammatical roles.

These extensions of the action tier, of course, push the notion of causation well beyond the physical domain. In fact, the examples used in sections 7.2 and 7.3 were chosen freely from the fields of physical force (*push, roll*) and social interaction (*pressure, urge*). Many of the verbs mentioned are ambiguous between the two fields (*force, resist, let*). The verbs of logical relations, the modals, and the Experiencer verbs introduce new fields of causation, sometimes using the very same lexical items (e.g. *lead to, permit, support, reinforce, strike*). Thus the force-dynamic domain yields a further application of the semantic field parameter in conceptual structure, beyond the extensions of thematic roles discussed in section 1.6. The observed generalizations, particularly in the logical domain, have little to do with the nature of the world out there, but a great deal to do with the nature of conceptualization, that is, the Universal Grammar of concepts.

I can't resist a last remark on the verbs of logical relation. If the present analysis is correct, verbs of logical relation express an abstract form of force-dynamic interaction, not too distantly related to verbs that express pushing things around in space. It is interesting that Piaget (1970) arrives at a similar hypothesis. He claims that concepts of logical relation, which appear relatively late in child development, are abstractions of concepts involved in motor activity, which appear very early. While one doesn't have to accept Piaget's theory of how development takes place, this particular point resonates with the present analysis. And I think Piaget's conclusion deserves to be taken seriously: that logical concepts, often taken to be the core of rational thought—the thing a theory of concepts must explain first—are really derivative. The real core of thought, according

to Piaget, involves the principles by which we understand the physical world—cognitive principles that in evolutionary terms are much older than logic. To be slightly contentious, this conclusion demotes the logical vocabulary to a small and rather eccentric concern in semantic theory, while elevating the conceptualization of the physical world to a much more prominent status. _d perception?_

7.6 The Role Instrument; Unifying the Uses of *Hit*

The action tier provides an interesting way of encoding the traditional role Instrument. Consider standard examples of Instruments such as the *with*-phrases in (46). In both these sentences, the subject is Actor and the object is Patient.

(46) a. Phil opened the door with a key.
     b. Sam broke the window with a hammer.

In general, the characteristics of an Instrument are: (1) it plays a role in the means by which the Actor accomplishes the action (notice that Instrumental *with NP* can often be paraphrased with *by means of NP*); (2) the Actor acts on the Instrument; (3) the Instrument acts on the Patient. More subtly, it is the fact that the Actor acts on the Instrument that results in the Instrument acting on the Patient. However, it is left open to pragmatics to determine exactly how the Actor uses the Instrument and exactly what the Instrument does to the Patient.

We can encode this information rather nicely by assigning the Instrument NP a role within a means expression that modifies the core sentence. This means expression is completely vague in terms of thematic roles; it basically contains only action tier information. (47a,b) are the conceptual structures for (46a,b) respectively.

(47) a. $\begin{bmatrix} CS^+ \ ([PHIL], [INCH \ [BE \ ([DOOR], [OPEN])]]) \\ AFF^- \ ([PHIL], [DOOR]) \\ [BY \begin{bmatrix} CS^+ \ ([PHIL], [AFF^- \ ([KEY], [DOOR])]) \\ AFF^- \ ([PHIL], [KEY]) \end{bmatrix}] \end{bmatrix}$

     b. $\begin{bmatrix} CS^+ \ ([SAM], [GO_{Comp^+} \ ([WINDOW], [TO \ [\quad]])]) \\ AFF^- \ ([SAM], [WINDOW]) \\ [BY \begin{bmatrix} CS^+ \ ([SAM], [AFF^- \ ([HAMMER], [WINDOW])]) \\ AFF^- \ ([SAM], [HAMMER]) \end{bmatrix}] \end{bmatrix}$

In these structures, BY is the function that turns Events into means modifiers (section 5.4). The Event in turn is a causative relation. For instance, the means expression in (47a) says that Phil, acting on the key, caused the key to act on the door, without saying any more about what the particular actions were. That is, the Instrument is stipulated as an intermediary in the Actor's action.

Notice that under this analysis, the role Instrument, like other thematic roles, is defined structurally: it is a conceptual constitutent that appears in a means expression of the sort seen in (47). Section 9.2 will discuss how the syntactic phrase *with NP* comes to be mapped into this structure.[8]

Let us now at last return to the verb *hit*. The beginning of this chapter introduced three uses of *hit* and showed that they have in common the fact that the object is Patient:

(1) a. Sue hit Fred.
    b. The car hit the tree.
    c. Pete hit the ball into the field.

However, we did not deal with the fact that *the tree* seems to be Goal in (1b) and *the ball* Theme in (1c). The time has come to make good on that omission. The simplest case, (1b), comes out as (48).

(48) The car hit the tree.
$$\begin{bmatrix} \text{INCH [BE}_c \text{ ([CAR], [AT}_c \text{ [TREE]])])} \\ \text{AFF}^- \text{ ([CAR], [TREE])} \end{bmatrix}$$

That is, by virtue of the car's coming to be in contact with the tree, it comes to act on the tree.

Next consider *Sue hit Fred with a stick*. *With a stick* here appears to be an ordinary Instrumental; that is, we should have a partial structure of the form (49).

(49) [BY $\begin{bmatrix} \text{CS}^+ \text{ ([SUE], [AFF}^- \text{ ([STICK], [FRED])])} \\ \text{AFF}^- \text{ ([SUE], [STICK])} \end{bmatrix}$]

However, we cannot just add this as a modifier of a structure like (48), since what comes into contact with Fred is not Sue but the stick. Thus the conceptual structure has to be (50).

(50) Sue hit Fred with a stick.
$$\begin{bmatrix} \text{CS}^+ \text{ ([SUE], [INCH [BE}_c \text{ ([STICK], [AT}_c \text{ [FRED]])])])} \\ \text{AFF}^- \text{ ([SUE], [FRED])} \\ \text{[BY} \begin{bmatrix} \text{CS}^+ \text{ ([SUE], [AFF}^- \text{ ([STICK], [FRED])])} \\ \text{AFF}^- \text{ ([SUE], [STICK])} \end{bmatrix} \text{]} \end{bmatrix}$$

Notice the relation between the senses of *hit* in (48) and (50). The "core" conceptualization, that of an object coming in contact with another object, forms the thematic tier of (48); it appears as a subpart of the thematic tier in (50). The stick in (50) plays the standard role of an Instrument, but in addition it functions as Theme of the main action. This extra function is lexically specific to *hit*.

Next let us omit the explicit instrument from (50), giving us (1a), *Sue hit Fred*. The object in motion is now Sue's hand; this is an incorporated Theme and Instrument, which serves as default if nothing else is named. The structure is otherwise identical to (50). Again, this extension of meaning is lexically specific to *hit*. *Kick*, for example, selects the foot as default Instrument and cannot substitute an Instrument that is very different: *Bill kicked Harry with his left foot/*a stick*.

Finally, here is the most complex case, (1c):

(51) Pete hit the ball into the field ⟨with a stick⟩.

$$
\left[
\begin{array}{l}
\text{CS}_{\text{launch}}{}^{+}\ ([\text{PETE}],\ [\text{GO}\ ([\text{BALL}],\ [\text{TO}\ [\text{IN}\ [\text{FIELD}]]])]) \\
\text{AFF}^{-}\ ([\text{PETE}],\ [\text{BALL}]) \\
\left[\text{BY}
\begin{array}{l}
\text{CS}^{+}\ ([\text{PETE}],\ [\text{INCH}\ [\text{BE}_{c}\ ([\langle\text{STICK}\rangle],\ [\text{AT}_{c}\ [\text{BALL}]])]]) \\
\text{AFF}^{-}\ ([\text{PETE}],\ [\text{BALL}]) \\
\left[\text{BY}
\begin{array}{l}
\text{CS}^{+}\ ([\text{PETE}],\ [\text{AFF}^{-}\ ([\langle\text{STICK}\rangle],\ [\text{BALL}])]) \\
\text{AFF}^{-}\ ([\text{PETE}],\ [\langle\text{STICK}\rangle])
\end{array}
\right]_{1}
\end{array}
\right]
\end{array}
\right]
$$

This elaborates the form of *hit* in (50) by adding the motion of the ball after it is hit. The main conceptual clause is standard "launching" causation. Its means modifier is parallel to (50)—a causation containing an instrumental means modifier. If the Instrument is expressed, it plays the same role in the structure as it did in (50); if it is left out, some Instrument is still implicit (though this time it is not the hand in the default case).

This sense of the verb *hit*, then, is a further elaboration of the core meaning (48): in addition to a character operating the missile, it adds a subsequent trajectory for the object struck. In other words, the three senses of *hit* are the core (48), an outer elaboration (50), and a second layer of outer elaboration (51). The two elaborations together can be combined in the lexical entry of *hit*, using a double application of the dashed underline notation of section 4.1, suitably generalized.[9]

Note that these elaborations must be in part lexically specified. For example, the verb *strike* can be substituted for *hit* in (48) and (50) without changing the sense appreciably, but it cannot be substituted into (51):

(52) a.   The car struck the tree.
     b.   Sue struck Fred with a stick.
     c.   *Pete struck the ball into the field (with a stick).

Thus *hit* and *strike* must be differentiated in the lexicon according to whether the superordinate elaboration in (51) is possible.

These elaborations of *hit* explain the superficially strange behavior of its thematic relations observed in (1). *The ball* in (51) is a Goal, just like the direct objects in (48) and (50), preserving the generality of the lexical structure. But in addition a superordinate Event has been erected in which it is the Theme. Thus we are dealing not with a change from Goal to Theme but with the creation of a further layer of θ-roles.

Returning to a motive of chapters 2 and 3, notice that structures like (51) make it completely impossible to regiment θ-roles into any kind of list form. There are two Themes and two Goals; *Pete* is Instigator and Actor of three Events; *the ball* is Theme of one Event, Goal of another, and Patient in three positions; *a stick* appears in three positions, as Theme, Actor, and Patient. However, the present theory of θ-roles extends without stress to hierarchical conceptual structures; each argument in (51) has a distinct θ-role, defined purely by its position in the structure as a whole.

7.7 Argument Binding in Force-Dynamic Verbs

With the introduction of the action tier, it becomes altogether routine for NPs to satisfy multiple θ-roles, one and often more on each tier. This section applies the notation of argument binding, introduced in chapter 3, to representative force-dynamic verbs, showing how they may be formulated so as to satisfy the Linking Condition (or Neo-θ-Criterion, (3.12)). In addition, I will work out some cases of multiple frames for these verbs, making use of the abbreviatory principles introduced in chapter 4.

As an important preliminary, observe that the binding relations between CS and the action tier are highly constrained, evidently as part of the meaning of CS and AFF. The standard causative interaction looks like (53).

(53) $\begin{bmatrix} \text{CS} ([\alpha], [\text{AFF} ([\beta], \quad)]) \\ \text{AFF} ([\quad]^{\alpha}, [\quad]^{\beta}) \end{bmatrix}$

That is, the Actor is also Instigator, and the Patient or Beneficiary is Actor of the (potential) Effect. (54) illustrates.

(54) Sam$_i$ forced Harry$_j$ to go away.

$\begin{bmatrix} \text{CS}^{+} ([\alpha], \begin{bmatrix} \text{GO} ([\beta], [\text{AWAY}]) \\ \text{AFF} ([\beta], \quad) \end{bmatrix}) \\ \text{AFF}^{-} ([\text{SAM}]^{\alpha}_i, [\text{HARRY}]^{\beta}_j) \end{bmatrix}$

Configuration (53) is a subpart of (54). Notice that the linking to syntax is accomplished through the action tier of the main clause, and that all other argument positions are bound by these two. As mentioned in section 7.1, the reason for choosing the action tier roles as the ones to link is that they provide a more regular mapping to syntactic positions than the thematic tier—an issue we return to in chapter 11.

The configuration in (53) appears equally in verbs of causation such as *force*, in verbs of helping and letting, and in verbs of hindering. Hence it is independent of the value of the success parameter on CS (+ or u) and of the polarity of AFF (−, +, or 0).

A second major configuration for force-dynamic verbs appears in *try*, *fail*, and *succeed*:

(55) $\begin{bmatrix} \text{CS } ([\alpha], [\text{AFF } ([\alpha], \quad)]) \\ \text{AFF } ([\quad]^\alpha, \quad) \end{bmatrix}$

Here the Actor is again Instigator, but this time there is no Patient, and the Actor is also Actor of the (potential) Effect. (56) illustrates.

(56) Sam$_i$ tried go away.

$\begin{bmatrix} \text{CS}^u \ ([\alpha], \begin{bmatrix} \text{GO } ([\alpha], [\text{AWAY}]) \\ \text{AFF } ([\alpha], \quad) \end{bmatrix}) \\ \text{AFF } ([\text{SAM}]^\alpha_i, \quad) \end{bmatrix}$

A third configuration appears in verbs of resistance:

(57) $\begin{bmatrix} \text{CS } ([\beta], [\text{AFF } ([\alpha], \quad)]) \\ \text{REACT } ([\quad]^\alpha, [\quad]^\beta) \end{bmatrix}$

In this case, the Instigator is bound to the *second* argument of REACT, and the Actor of the potential Effect is bound to the first argument of REACT. That is, the Instigator β is exerting effort toward α's doing something, and α is reacting against β. (58) provides an illustration.

(58) Sam$_i$ resisted going away.

$\begin{bmatrix} \text{CS}^u \ ([\beta], \begin{bmatrix} \text{GO } ([\alpha], [\text{AWAY}]) \\ \text{AFF } ([\alpha], \quad) \end{bmatrix}) \\ \text{REACT } ([\text{SAM}]^\alpha_i, [\quad]^\beta) \end{bmatrix}$

Here the Instigator is entirely implicit, but its multiple roles are still indicated by the argument binding.

Given these configurations, we can work out lexical entries for some of the force-dynamic verbs. Let's begin with *force* in the frame *force NP to VP*, as in (59). I will assume that it can specify the syntactic form of its complement, in particular that it has a *to*-complementizer; the details of this specification are irrelevant for now.

(59) $\begin{bmatrix} \text{force} \\ \text{V} \\ \underline{\quad\quad} \text{NP}_j \text{ to } S_k \\ \begin{bmatrix} \text{CS}^+ \ ([\alpha], [_{\text{Event}} \text{AFF } ([\beta], \quad)]_k) \\ {}_{\text{Event}} \text{AFF}^- ([\quad]^\alpha_i, [\quad]^\beta_j) \end{bmatrix} \end{bmatrix}$

The conceptual structure here is a straightforward specialization of (53). The trick is in the way it is mapped to syntax. The Effect constituent is coindexed with the complement clause. But it is also subject to the selectional restriction that (1) it is an Event and (2) its Actor is bound to the Patient of the superordinate Event. The result is that *force* (1) prohibits stative complements and (2) requires coreference between its object and its complement subject. The only way to achieve this second requirement, of course, is to have a PRO subject. That is, the present theory's approaches to selectional restrictions and to binding together permit a natural specification of the well-known condition of obligatory control with *force*.

Some necessary refinements: (1) *Force* also permits in its complement the verb *resist*, whose action tier is REACT rather than AFF. Since clearly REACT and AFF are related, *force* should actually specify the features they have in common rather than AFF. (2) *Force* can occur with passive complements, as in *Sam forced Harry to be examined by the doctor*, and with normally stative verbs, as in *Sam forced Harry to seem stupid*. But in these cases, Harry *is* understood as an Actor in the complement clause; that is,

AFF ([HARRY],   )

is *added* to the interpretation of the complement. This is exactly the behavior observed with selectional restrictions in chapter 2, so these apparent counterexamples suggest that the present treatment is indeed on the right track.

Force also occurs in another syntactic frame, with an NP-PP complement. Consider an example like *Bill forced the ball through the hole*. In this sentence, *force* behaves like a lexical causative instead of a periphrastic causative: the Effect is physical motion of the Patient along the Path designated by the PP. Here is an entry that combines these two uses by means of the curly bracket notation of section 4.2:

(60)
$$
\begin{bmatrix}
\text{force} \\
\text{V} \\
\underline{\quad} \text{ NP}_j \ \{\text{PP}_k\} \ \{to\ S_k\} \\
\begin{bmatrix}
\text{CS}^+ \ ([\alpha], \begin{bmatrix} \{\text{GO} \ ([\beta], [_{\text{Path}} \quad]_k)\} \\ \text{AFF} \ ([\beta], \quad) \end{bmatrix}_{\{k\}}) \\
_{\text{Event}}\text{AFF}^- \ ([\ \ ]^\alpha_i, [\ \ ]^\beta_j)
\end{bmatrix}
\end{bmatrix}
$$

The curly bracket notation in (60) abbreviates two lexical conceptual structures, one already seen in (59) and the other shown in (61).

(61)
$$
\begin{bmatrix}
\text{CS}^+ \ ([\alpha], \begin{bmatrix} \text{GO} \ ([\beta], [_{\text{Path}} \quad]_k) \\ \text{AFF} \ ([\beta], \quad) \end{bmatrix}) \\
_{\text{Event}} \text{AFF}^- \ ([\ \ ]^\alpha_i, [\ \ ]^\beta_j)
\end{bmatrix}
$$

The alternative with the outer k fills in the Effect just as in (59). The other, shown in (61), fills in the Effect as an Event of motion whose Theme is β and whose Path is the PP-complement of *force*. In this version *force* resembles other lexical causatives like *roll NP PP*. Thus this lexical entry combines two conceptual structures in much the same way we saw with verbs like *pass* and *cross* in section 4.2: certain material, in this case AFF ([β],   ), functions as incorporated conceptual structure in one frame and as a selectional restriction in the other.

This treatment of *force* extends to a number of other force-dynamic verbs, including *coerce* and causative *get* in the causatives, *help* and *assist* in the helping verbs, and *let* and *allow* in the letting verbs. All allow either a *to*-VP complement or a PP that serves as Path of an incorporated spatial motion function:

(62) Sam coerced/got/helped/assisted/let/allowed Harry
$$\begin{cases} \text{(to) talk about the war.} \\ \text{out of the room.} \end{cases}$$

Notice that this combination of frames provides an important argument against the position (to be discussed in the Appendix to this chapter) that periphrastic and lexical causatives are essentially different. *Force* and the verbs in (62) function as lexical causatives in the NP-PP frame and as periphrastic causatives in the NP-S frame. Only if the two kinds of causatives are basically the same can we account for the fact that so many lexical items appear in both classes.[10]

Next let us turn to *try*. In the frame *try to VP*, its LCS can be encoded as (63).

(63)
$$\begin{bmatrix} \text{try} \\ \text{V} \\ \underline{\quad} \; to \; S_j \\ \begin{bmatrix} \quad CS^u \; ([\alpha], \; [_{Event} \; AFF \; ([\alpha], \quad)]_j)' \\ _{Event} \; AFF_{+vol} \; ([\quad]^\alpha_i, \quad) \end{bmatrix} \end{bmatrix}$$

This entry encodes the fact that trying is taken to be a voluntary action toward the accomplishment of some Effect. In addition, just as with *force*, the Effect is stipulated to be an action whose Actor is bound—this time to the Actor of the main clause instead of the Patient. This selectional restriction, then, accounts for the obligatory subject control with this verb.

Another frame of *try* is *try for NP*, where NP is something that potentially benefits the Actor. Here is an attempt on this frame:

(64)
$$\begin{bmatrix} \text{try} \\ \text{V} \\ \underline{\quad} \; for \; NP_j \\ \begin{bmatrix} \quad CS^u \; ([\alpha], \; [_{Event} \; AFF^+ \; ([\quad]_j, \; [\alpha])])' \\ _{Event} \; AFF_{+vol} \; ([\quad]^\alpha_i, \quad) \end{bmatrix} \end{bmatrix}$$

This has a nonstandard configuration, in which the Effect is some unspecified Event of NP_j benefiting the Instigator. (63) and (64) cannot be combined by any of the abbreviatory notations of chapter 4. This may indicate either that I don't yet have the entries right or that I don't yet have the abbreviatory notations right. In any event, the similarity of the two entries is obvious. (Note that neither *attempt* nor *fail* nor *succeed* has a frame like *try for NP*, so perhaps the generalization is not so very natural after all. *Win*, *gain*, and *achieve* might be candidates for a CS^+ counterpart of *try for*.)

A different pattern appears in the verbs of resistance, where we have the possibilities in (65).

(65) Sam resisted $\left\{\begin{array}{l}\text{a. Harry.}\\ \text{b. talking about the war.}\\ \text{c. Harry's trying to push him around.}\\ \text{d. Harry's leaving the party.}\end{array}\right\}$

In (65a), the direct object is the antagonist, the second argument of REACT. In (65b), the gerundive is the potential Effect, and its subject is obligatorily controlled by the subject of *resist*. (65c) and (65d) are syntactically parallel but semantically different. In (65c), *Harry's trying to push him around* is an Event that Sam is reacting against; it is best analyzed as an Event playing the role of antagonist. (It is a counterpart of the gerundive serving as antagonist in *Harry's trying to push him around finally forced Sam to leave.*) (65d), on the other hand, evokes a scenario in which Sam is capable of getting Harry to leave the party, someone is trying to get Sam to make Harry leave, but Sam doesn't want to. Hence *Harry's leaving the party* is part of the potential Effect.

Here is a lexical entry that incorporates all these possibilities:

(66) $\begin{bmatrix}\text{resist}\\ \text{V}\\ \underline{\hspace{1cm}}\text{ NP}_j\\ \begin{bmatrix}\text{CS}^u\;([\beta],\begin{bmatrix}\{\text{CS}^+\;([\alpha],\;[_{\text{Event}}\quad]_j)\}\\ \text{AFF}\;([\alpha],\quad)\end{bmatrix}_{\{j\}})\\ \text{REACT}^-\;([\quad]^\alpha_i,\;[\quad]^\beta_{\{j\}})\end{bmatrix}\end{bmatrix}$

This is an elaboration of the REACT pattern (57). There are three alternatives in the curly brackets this time, broken out separately in (67).

(67) a. $\begin{bmatrix}\text{CS}^u\;([\beta],\;[\text{AFF}\;([\alpha],\quad)])\\ \text{REACT}^-\;([\quad]^\alpha_i,\;[\quad]^\beta_j)\end{bmatrix}$

b. $\begin{bmatrix}\text{CS}^u\;([\beta],\;[\text{AFF}\;([\alpha],\quad)]_j)\\ \text{REACT}^-\;([\quad]^\alpha_i,\;[\quad]^\beta)\end{bmatrix}$

c. $\begin{bmatrix}\text{CS}^u\;([\beta],\begin{bmatrix}\text{CS}^+\;([\alpha],\;[_{\text{Event}}\quad]_j)\\ \text{AFF}\;([\alpha],\quad)\end{bmatrix})\\ \text{REACT}^-\;([\quad]^\alpha_i,\;[\quad]^\beta)\end{bmatrix}$

(67a) is the case in which the object of *resist* is the antagonist—either (65a), with a Thing as antagonist, or (65c), with an Event as antagonist. (67b) is the case in which the object of *resist* is the potential Effect, that is, (65b). Because this frame has the selectional restriction

AFF ([α],   ),

the complement has obligatory subject control. (67c) introduces a subordinate CS-function, whose Effect is indexed to the direct object of *resist*. This is (65d), in which Sam is resisting bringing about Harry's leaving.

Notice how the binding conditions here are independent from the coindexing to syntax. In (65b) and (65d), the antagonist is an implicit argument, but its multiple roles are still linked by binding. Similarly, in (65a) and (65c), the Effect is an implicit argument, but the fact that its Actor is bound to the agonist is still expressed by the binding network.

These formalizations of lexical entries are illustrative of the patterns found in force-dynamic verbs. As in the verbs of contact and attachment in the last chapter, we seem to find a characteristic syntactic pattern for each subclass of these verbs, with some marked variation remaining within the subclasses. For example, *try*, *fail*, and *manage* share the *to*-VP complement, but *succeed* uses an *in* + gerundive complement. The verbs of resisting share large portions of the pattern shown in (65), but *withstand*, for instance, has only the (a) and (c) frames, not the (b) and (d) frames. The verbs of hindering have yet another set of patterns, not worked out here. The point of the exercises in this section, though, is to show that this regimented variety of syntactic patterns maps into an even more highly constrained set of variations in conceptual structure. Most of the variety lies in the placement of the indices for the verb's complements and in which conceptual arguments are left implicit.

7.8 Appendix: Lexical versus Periphrastic Causatives

A distinction has frequently been noted in the literature (Fodor 1970; Shibatani 1976; McCawley 1978; Comrie 1985; Gergely and Bever 1986; Pinker 1989) between the "direct" causation of lexical causatives such as *break* Y and *kill* Y and the potential of "indirect" causation in periphrastic causatives such as *cause* Y *to break* and *cause* Y *to die*. The difference appears in contrasts like (68).

(68) a. Bill $\begin{Bmatrix} \text{??broke the window} \\ \text{caused the window to break} \end{Bmatrix}$ by startling the guy who was fixing it.

     b. Bill $\begin{Bmatrix} \text{??killed Harry} \\ \text{caused Harry to die} \end{Bmatrix}$ on Tuesday by giving him poison on Monday.   (after Fodor 1970)

     c. The warm sun $\begin{Bmatrix} \text{??grew the tomatoes.} \\ \text{made the tomatoes grow.} \end{Bmatrix}$

A number of independent explanations converge on this result. First, there is a "stereotypy effect." As McCawley (1978) points out, if there is a potential overlap between a lexical item and a phrasal counterpart, the lexical item tends to be used for the more central instances of the concept and the phrase for less central instances. For example, *pink* is related to *red* in the same way that *light green* is related to *green*, and it usurps much of the territory that would otherwise be covered by *light red*. The latter phrase is therefore restricted to relatively unusual cases. McCawley suggests that the same is true of *kill* versus *cause to die*: direct action is more stereotypical, hence better characterized by the unitary word *kill*, while *cause to die* is reserved for less direct cases.

A second factor comes from the presence of the extra clause in the periphrastic causatives. This extra clause permits two sets of modifiers where the single-clause lexical causatives permit only one. For example, in *Bill killed Harry on Monday*, the temporal phrase can only be a modifier of the event as a whole, whereas in *Bill caused Harry to die on Monday* it may modify either the whole event or the event denoted by the subordinate clause, creating the possibility of expressing temporally distant causation, as in (68b).

A third factor is that the lexical causative may include idiosyncratic information as a modifier of the CS-function or as selectional restrictions on its arguments; such lexically specific information is not available with a general periphrastic causative. This appears to be the case in (68c), which requires an animate Instigator. Compare causative *grow* to *stunt* ("prevent/hinder from growing"), which has no such selectional restriction: *The hot sun/Bill stunted the tomatoes*. Similarly, many lexical causatives have idiosyncratic (stereotypical) manners. For instance, causative *jump* is applied primarily to horses being ridden by the Instigator. Intransitive *smoke*, "give off smoke," has a highly specialized causative, which can have only cigars, cigarettes, pipes, and the like as Patient, and which specifies that the Patient is caused to give off smoke by putting in the mouth and puffing. Fodor (1981) points out that *paint* is more specific than "cause to become covered with paint," in that one is not *painting* the brush that one dips in the paint in order to paint the wall, even though the brush does become covered with paint. (He does not offer a better analysis, given that his goal is to show it *can't* be analyzed; see section 1.8) The point, then, is that such idiosyncratic information frequently differentiates a lexical causative from the corresponding periphrastic causative, making it narrower in any number of lexically specific ways.

Among all these factors, then, there seems to be ample room for explaining the greater "directness" of causation in lexical causatives.

PART III
Mostly on the Problem of Correspondence

Chapter 8
Adjuncts That Express an Incorporated Argument

8.1 Introduction to Part III

We have been exploring two problems simultaneously: the Problem of Meaning and the Problem of Correspondence. The Problem of Meaning is to develop a theory of conceptual structure that is sufficiently expressive for the semantic distinctions among sentences and for the inferences that sentences support. The Problem of Correspondence is to state a theory of the relation between conceptual structures and syntax—including a theory of lexical entries, for, as stressed in chapter 1, lexical entries are correspondence rules too. This part of the book will concentrate on the latter problem.

One's overall methodological assumption ought to be, presumably, that the correspondence rules—including the lexicon—are maximally simple, within the constraint that they must map from a universal conceptual structure to a language-particular syntax. The impulse to simplify the correspondence rules lies behind many proposals in many theories of grammar, such as the Katz-Postal Hypothesis (1964) in the Standard Theory, which claims, in present terms, that Deep (D-) Structure is the only syntactic structure visible to the correspondence rules; the theory of Logical Form, in which quantifier embedding in syntax is mirrored precisely in conceptual structure; the θ-Criterion of GB Theory and the Biuniqueness Principle of LFG, according to which syntactic arguments are matched one-to-one with conceptual arguments; the strict compositionality of Montague Grammar; and the Grammatical Constraint of S&C, essentially an injunction to prefer simple correspondence rules to complex ones.

In terms of the simplification of lexical entries, an ideal situation would be one in which conceptual relations were reflected directly and uniformly in syntactic relations. This would permit us to formulate lexical entries just in terms of their syntactic category and their conceptual structure, since both the subcategorization feature and the syntactic position corresponding to each conceptual argument would be predictable on general principles. This idealization finds expression in Case Grammar (Fillmore 1968), in GB Theory as the Uniformity of Theta Assignment Hypothesis (Baker

1988), and in Relational Grammar as the Universal Alignment Hypothesis (Rosen 1984; Perlmutter and Postal 1984).

Unfortunately, the true story is not so simple. There are many apparent mismatches between conceptual arguments—even *expressed* conceptual arguments—and syntactic positions. How is one to cope with the numerous deviations from ideal correspondence? To take a well-worn example that has already arisen here, consider the mismatch between syntactic and conceptual relations in an optionally causative verb such as *open*, whose Theme appears as subject of the intransitive form and as object of the transitive form. There are basically three strategies for describing this case, and within them further substrategies.

Syntactic Strategy. One can preserve the simplicity of the lexical entry by claiming that the Theme always has the same underlying syntactic position. The mismatch must then be localized in the relation between underlying and surface syntax, through the application of syntactic movement. This approach appears in Case Grammar (where the Theme of *open* is always underlying Objective case), in Generative Semantics (McCawley 1968a; Lakoff 1970—Theme is always underlying subject), and in Relational Grammar and GB Theory versions of the Unaccusative Hypothesis (Perlmutter 1978; Burzio 1986—Theme is always underlying object).

Lexical Strategy. One can claim that there are two lexical forms of *open*, one for each syntactic frame. The cost of duplicating entries can then be reduced by either of two substrategies. (1) *Lexical Abbreviation*: The two lexical forms can be combined by means of abbreviatory notations. We did this in many instances in chapters 2 and 4, using optional arguments (angle bracket notation), optional outer functions (dashed underline notation), and alternative argument structures (curly bracket notation). (Section 4.2 showed, however, that the two frames of *open* could not be combined by any of these techniques, without further appeal to the Unaccusative solution.) (2) *Lexical Rule*: One can introduce a lexical rule that creates or relates a pair of syntactic frames. In the case of *open*, such a rule will express the possibility of a zero-affix causative in English, such that the Theme appears in subject position in the noncausative form of the verb and in object position in the causative form. The Lexical Rule Strategy has appeared prominently in LFG (Bresnan 1982a), in Marantz 1984, and in my own work on lexical redundancy rules (Jackendoff 1975), among others. Whichever substrategy we adopt, the result of relating the two syntactic frames lexically is to render unnecessary the use of a syntactic movement to produce the surface forms.

Correspondence Rules Strategy. One can localize the complexity in correspondence rules external to the lexical item. Under this approach, the lexical entry does not completely specify in which syntactic frames it appears and how these frames are matched to conceptual structure. Rather, various extralexical rules help establish this mapping. The subset of these rules germane to the case of *open* might say something to the effect that (1) if there is an Agent, it appears in subject position; (2) if there is a Theme, it appears as object if subject position is occupied, otherwise as subject. (This is the "Theme Rule" of Anderson 1977.) More generally, such *linking rules* might appeal to some sort of "thematic hierarchy" to determine the (unmarked) syntactic realization of conceptual roles. Since Anderson 1977, this approach has been explored in Carter 1984, Foley and Van Valin 1984, Grimshaw 1987, and Bresnan and Kanerva 1989, among others. Under this strategy, there is again no need to invoke a syntactic movement to derive the surface forms. Rather, in combination with either version of the Lexical Strategy, we can simply specify that a causative argument may be added to *open*, without saying how this argument changes the syntactic form. We develop a version of this approach in chapter 11.

More generally, for any particular pair of lexical frames we may discover, it is an empirical problem to decide which of these strategies—or which combination of them—is best in terms of descriptive adequacy and optimal constraint on the theory of grammar. It might for example turn out best to express the passive alternation by means of syntactic movement but the causative alternation by means of a correspondence rule—or, less probably, vice versa. To find out the proper disposition of any of these alternations, one must explore the options in detail. Lamentably, the practice in the literature for the most part has been to match a highly formalized syntactic structure with a highly informal conceptual structure, specified only in taxonomic terms such as Agent, Patient, and Theme. Such practice tacitly discourages consideration of solutions other than those using the Syntactic Strategy, since any solution that makes essential use of properties of conceptual structure will by necessity be imprecise and informal.

We have already seen how a highly articulated theory of conceptual structure can yield interesting accounts of lexical alternations. Many of these alternations, especially those involving the curly bracket notation, had syntactic solutions back in the early days of transformational grammar, when one could conceive of things like lexically specified movements and preposition deletions. However, through the attempt to codify such lexically specific rules (especially in Lakoff 1970), it eventually became clear that this was the wrong way to deal with such alternations, in that it led to an unconstrained theory of transformations (Chomsky 1972; Jackendoff 1972). When the dust had settled, the Extended Standard Theory for many good reasons prohibited lexically governed movements and deletions.

The favored account then became lexical rules, especially in LFG (Bresnan 1982a). But theories of lexical rules do not really have much to say about the lexically very specific alternations we encountered in chapters 4 and 7, dealing more with semiproductive alternations like the causative. The reason for this, I think, is that there is not enough information in just the syntax and the list of θ-roles to specify properly the relations between frames that we observed with *climb, pass, put, force*, and so on. A more articulated conceptual structure is necessary in order to pick out what the frames have in common and how they differ.

We have already mentioned some alternations in which the Correspondence Rule Strategy is clearly the preferred solution, namely those that involve restrictive modifiers. As pointed out in section 1.5, we would not want the alternations in (1) to be accounted for by the Lexical Strategy.

(1) a. i. Bill ate an apple.
         ii. Bill ate an apple on Tuesday.
     b. i. Sue read *Syntactic Structures*.
         ii. Sue read *Syntactic Structures* in the library.
     c. i. Lucy left the room.
         ii. Lucy left the room quickly.

At the risk of belaboring the obvious, let us see what the Lexical Strategy would have to say here. Under the Lexical Abbreviation substrategy, the lexical entries for *eat, read*, and *leave* would include optional subcategorizations for time, place, and manner phrases. Under the Lexical Rule substrategy, a lexical rule would create lexical entries with the (ii) frames from the entries with the (i) frames. Now it was argued in the earliest treatment of lexical subcategorization (Chomsky 1965, 101–102) that this is the incorrect approach to these constructions, and that time, place, and manner phrases should not be part of verbal subcategorization. But, then, *what licenses the interpretation of these phrases?* It has always, I think, been tacitly understood that these phrases are integrated into the sentence's interpretation by different correspondence rules than are strictly subcategorized arguments. Chapter 2 codified this difference in the Restrictive Modifier Rule, a principle that operates in different contexts than Argument Fusion. So this is a case where the Correspondence Rule Strategy is favored over the Lexical Strategy.

Most of the alternations we have dealt with so far, though, have been cases of the Lexical Abbreviation substrategy, in which alternative argument structures are encoded in a verb's or preposition's entry. What these cases have in common is that the syntactic arguments express conceptual arguments that are part of the head's LCS; this correspondence is guaranteed by Argument Fusion.

This chapter and the next two discuss alternations in which *not* all syntactic arguments are licensed by the head. In order to license these arguments, new correspondence rules, alternatives to Argument Fusion, will be necessary. The benefit of introducing these "adjunct rules" will be a simplification of lexical entries: the extra arguments will not have to appear as optional alternatives in subcategorization frames. In other words, we will be playing off an account in terms of the Correspondence Rule Strategy against one in terms of the Lexical Strategy. Occasionally, when there is a syntactic alternative of interest, we will deal with that too.

Maybe I am a little old-fashioned, but I am interested in ending up with a syntactic theory in which movement of arguments is minimized—where what you see is what you get. This contrasts with recent work that adopts the Syntactic Strategy, for instance Baker 1988, Belletti and Rizzi 1988, and Larson 1988, in which a good deal of rearrangement takes place between D-Structure and S-Structure. I am trying a different tack, the Correspondence Rule Strategy, to see how complex the linking rules have to be in order to map as closely as possible into the surface form. It is only when we have explicit versions of both views, pushing both to their limits, that we can debate their relative merits and incorporate the insights of both into the proper synthesis.

Two remarks before we proceed. First, I am using the term *adjunct* for the present to include any phrase in VP not licensed by the verb. This is as yet informal. Just as terms like *selectional restriction* and *θ-role* received more technical explication in chapter 2, so will *adjunct*. In particular, section 8.7 will sharpen the term in a way that goes somewhat against the grain of standard usage but has theoretical advantages in explaining the form of the lexicon.

Second, I have been assuming all along and will continue to assume through these three chapters a traditional *Aspects*-style treatment of subcategorization features. It is not there just as a convenient anachronism. Much current theory, especially GB Theory, assumes that subcategorization is redundant and need not be specified in lexical entries, because, it is claimed, the θ-Criterion plus Case theory guarantees the right number of syntactic arguments in the right places (Stowell 1981). This claim, however, is an important part of what is at issue here: How much of the syntactic structure of a sentence *can* be predicted by its head, and how much is to be attributed to other factors? The best way to gauge this, at least for my purposes here, is to retain subcategorization features in the theory, then see (1) how much we can pare them down and (2) how much of what is left is semantically predictable. We will then be in a position in chapter 11 to better evaluate the status of subcategorization features.

8.2 *Fill* and *Cover*

Fill and *cover* occur in the following paradigms:

(2) a.   Water filled the tank.   (stative or inchoative)
    b.   *Bill filled water (into) the tank.

    c.   Bill filled the tank (with water).   (causative inchoative)
    d.   The tank filled (with water).   (inchoative only)

(3) a.   Snow covered the ground.   (stative or inchoative)
    b.   *Bill covered a tarpaulin (on) the ground.
    c.   Bill covered the ground (with a tarpaulin).   (causative inchoative).
    d.   *The ground covered (with snow).

Other verbs with the same paradigm as *cover* are *surround* and *saturate*; *adorn* and *decorate* are similar except that the inchoative in form (a) is (for me) marginal.

    Looking first at the (a) cases, we see that in the inchoative reading the entity that changes location—the Theme—is expressed in subject position. The direct object then plays the role of reference object. Since there is an inchoative alternation, we want the basic form of the verbs to be stative, with an optional outer function INCH for the inchoative. Thus the basic conceptual structure for these verbs is (4), using the dashed underline notation of section 4.1.

(4) $[_{\text{Event}} \underline{\text{INCH}} [_{\text{State}} \text{BE} ([_{\text{Thing}} \quad], [_{\text{Place}} \quad])]]$

    One thing that distinguishes *fill* and *cover* from other verbs of inchoative location is that they incorporate a "distributive location" in the sense of section 6.1. Let us notate distributive location with the subscript d, and ordinary location without it. Then *fill* says that the Theme is/comes to be everywhere *in* (IN_d) the volume subtended by the reference object, which is taken as a container; *cover* says that the Theme is/comes to be *all over* (ON_d) the reference object; *surround* says that the Theme is/comes to be *all around* (AROUND_d) the reference object; and *saturate* says that a liquid Theme is/comes to be *throughout* (IN_d) the reference object. This means that the conceptual structures for the verbs in (2a) and (3a) are as given in (5), where i indexes the subject and j the object, as usual. (For the sake of notational simplicity, I revert for now to structures without the action tier and to CAUSE instead of CS$^+$; I ignore the selectional restriction that the Theme of *fill* is a container.)

(5) a. fill
      $[_{\text{Event}} \underline{\text{INCH}} [_{\text{State}} \text{BE} ([\quad]_i, [_{\text{Place}} \quad \text{IN}_d [\quad]_j])]]$
    b. cover
      $[_{\text{Event}} \underline{\text{INCH}} [_{\text{State}} \text{BE} ([\quad]_i, [_{\text{Place}} \quad \text{ON}_d [\quad]_j])]]$

    The causatives of these verbs, however, do not exhibit the usual alternation in which the Theme moves into object position, yielding forms like (2b) and (3b). Rather, the reference object remains in object position, and the Theme either disappears entirely or is expressed as a *with*-phrase, as seen in (2c) and (3c). In the case of *fill*, this causative can be seen as a regular derivation from an alternative version of the inchoative shown in (2d); but such a variant does not exist for *cover* (3d).

In formulating the lexical entries for the forms in (2c), (3c), and (2d), then, the issue arises of how to treat the *with*-phrase. This *with* does not alternate with other prepositions and has no clear spatial meaning (such as accompaniment); hence, under our assumptions so far, it appears to be lexically specified by the verb. That is, the lexical entry for causative *cover* has to include the preposition as part of its syntactic structure, as in (6).

(6)
$$\begin{bmatrix} \text{cover} \\ \text{V} \\ \underline{\qquad} \text{ NP}_j \langle [_{PP} \text{ with NP}_k] \rangle \\ [\text{CAUSE} ([\quad]_i, [\text{INCH} [\text{BE} ([\quad]_k, [\text{ON}_d [\quad]_j])])])] \end{bmatrix}$$

Similar tactics of Lexical Abbreviation will be necessary for the *with*-phrases in both variants of *fill*.

Although it is hardly unknown for a verb to specify a preposition in one of its complements, for example *depend on, attach to, believe in,* it would still be nice to eliminate this specified *with* from the entry of *cover*. As we will see, the use of a *with*-phrase as an expression of Theme is widespread in English, so it would miss a generalization not to encode it in more general fashion, thereby simplifying the lexical entries of all verbs involved.

Toward stating a rule that captures this generalization, let us simplify the entry of *cover* to (7), in which the Theme is an implicit argument.

(7)
$$\begin{bmatrix} \text{cover} \\ \text{V} \\ \underline{\qquad} \text{ NP}_j \\ [\text{CAUSE} ([\quad]_i, [\text{INCH} [\text{BE} ([\quad], [\text{ON}_d [\quad]_j])])])] \end{bmatrix}$$

The rule we want can be stated informally as (8). (A similar rule is proposed by Rappaport and Levin (1988) and by Rappaport, Levin, and Laughren (1988).) (9) is a more formal statement.

(8) With-*Theme Adjunct Rule* (version 1)

In a sentence containing *with* NP in the VP, if the Theme position is not indexed in the verb's lexical entry, then the object of *with* can be interpreted as Theme.

(9) With-*Theme Adjunct Rule* (version 2)

If V corresponds to [... BE ([X], ...) ...], with [X] unindexed, and NP corresponds to [Y],

then [$_S$ ... [$_{VP}$ V ... [$_{PP}$ with NP] ...] ...] may correspond to

[... BE ($\begin{bmatrix} X \\ Y \end{bmatrix}$, ...) ...], where $\begin{bmatrix} X \\ Y \end{bmatrix}$ is the fusion of [X] and [Y].

To see how (9) works, consider again (3c), *Bill covered the ground (with a tarpaulin)*. Using lexical entry (7), Argument Fusion will create the partial conceptual structure (10).

(10) [CAUSE ([BILL], [INCH [BE ([ ], [ON$_d$ [GROUND]])]])]

If the *with*-phrase is not present, the conceptual structure remains (10), "Bill caused something to come to be all over the ground." If the *with*-phrase is present, however, (9) comes into play. The verb *cover* meets the structural description of the rule: it contains a BE-function with unindexed Theme. The sentence is of the requisite syntactic form. Hence the reading of the object of *with* can be fused into the Theme position to yield structure (11), the desired reading for the sentence.

(11) [CAUSE ([BILL], [INCH [BE ([TARPAULIN], [ON$_d$ [GROUND]])]])]

For a slightly different case, consider the inchoactive *fill* in (2d), *The tank filled with water*. This variant of the verb has the entry (12).

(12) $\begin{bmatrix} \text{fill} \\ \text{V} \\ \rule{2cm}{0.4pt} \\ \text{[INCH [BE ([ ], [IN}_d\text{ [ ]}_i\text{])]]} \end{bmatrix}$

Under the present account, the *with*-phrase does not have to be mentioned in the subcategorization; syntactically the verb is a pure intransitive. Argument Fusion inserts the reading of the subject into the reference object argument. In addition, though, (2d) meets the structural description of the adjunct rule, so structure (13) can be derived for the sentence.

(13) [INCH [BE ([WATER], [IN$_d$ [TANK]])]]

This is identical to the structure derived for the inchoative reading of *Water filled the tank*, where both *water* and *the tank* are arguments. Thus we have alternate routes to the same conceptual structure, depending on whether the NPs in the sentences are arguments or adjuncts.

(9) stipulates only that the *with*-phrase *may* be interpreted as the Theme, not that it *must* be interpreted as the Theme. The reason is that there are at least two other interpretations of *with*-phrases: as instruments (*Bill filled the tank with a hose*) and as accompaniments (*The tank filled with a gurgling sound*). We do not want these *with*-phrases to be interpreted as the Theme of *fill*. Rather, each of them is integrated into the interpretation by means of a different correspondence rule. The overall constraint on interpretation, of course, is that each syntactic constituent of the sentence must be consis-

tently integrated *somehow* into the conceptual structure of the sentence. (Instrumentals will be treated in section 9.2.)

The *With*-Theme Adjunct Rule stated in (9), then, provides a new mechanism in the correspondence rule component to match NP readings with the verb's argument positions, distinct from the mechanisms of subcategorization plus Argument Fusion. The rule may be thought of as a rule of "constructionally determined" meaning composition, contrasting with Argument Fusion, which might be thought of as "lexically determined" meaning composition. Rule (9) is also distinct from the constructionally determined Restrictive Modifier Rule (2.18), in that it affects the conceptual structure of the main conceptual clause determined by the verb's LCS. That is, *with NP* in this construction is not a restrictive modifier.

An alternative way of thinking of rule (9)—but still as a correspondence rule—is as a context-sensitive rule for one meaning of the preposition *with*. For still another alternative, we may think of *with* as an oblique case-marker that marks Themes, and (9) as the rule that licenses this interpretation. All these interpretations of the rule seem apt; we return to these alternative characterizations in chapter 11. Meanwhile, I leave readers free to choose whichever characterization helps them understand the situation.

Still another alternative is the Lexical Rule Strategy of the previous section. On this view, the *With*-Theme Adjunct Rule could be formulated instead as a lexical rule that adds coindexed positions to lexical entries. In such form, we could think of the rule as converting entry (7) into entry (6) before the verb is inserted into the sentence. Interpretation (11) would then be derived directly from the syntactic structure by Argument Fusion. At the moment there is little to decide between these strategies—they make essentially the same structural distinctions. I leave it to the interested reader to restate the rule in lexical format.

Here I have chosen the form in (9) over the lexical formulation because I would like to explore the consequences of interpreting argument positions without the use of subcategorization. The question at issue is the balance of power between two kinds of rules in the grammar: lexical rules and extralexical correspondence rules. The grammar needs at least one extralexical rule—Argument Fusion—to link syntactic and conceptual arguments. If the *With*-Theme Adjunct Rule is a lexical rule defined over verb entries, Argument Fusion remains the only correspondence rule that performs this function. However, the *With*-Theme Adjunct Rule as formulated in (9) provides an additional principle of linking that is not encoded in lexical entries of verbs. The proper balance of power between the two kinds of rules can be determined only by attempting to formulate various processes in both ways and observing the consequences. Toward such a determination, I am deliberately choosing the less-used path.

8.3 *Butter, Powder, Water, Ice,* and *Frost*

Next consider the sizable class of denominal verbs in English in which the root noun stands for an incorporated Theme. The verbs *butter, powder,* and *water* are typical examples of one subclass of these. In *S&C* and section 2.3 they were analyzed as meaning "cause N to go onto." Given the last section's analysis of *cover* (not given in *S&C*), we see that an even more appropriate paraphrase is "cover with N" or, more primitively, "cause N to come to be all over."

The principle that creates such denominal verbs in English is obviously lexical rather than syntactic (e.g. it is not a syntactic rule of the form "adjoin object to verb," as in Baker's (1988) account of Noun Incorporation in Mohawk and other languages). As evidence, note (1) that the rule is not totally productive—although one can understand new coinages—and (2) it is phonologically and semantically partially irregular, as seen from verbs like *ice, frost,* and one sense of *line* ("cover with *icing/frosting*," not "cover with *ice/frost*", "cover *the inside* of a coat with a *lining*," not "cover a coat with a *line*").

We will therefore consider the verb *butter* to be a lexical item of its own, conceptually a specialized version of *cover*. Its lexical entry is (14).

$$(14) \quad \begin{bmatrix} \text{butter} \\ [_V \text{ N}] \\ \underline{\quad\quad} \text{NP}_j \\ [\text{CAUSE ([\quad]}_i, [\text{INCH [BE ([BUTTER], [ON}_d [\quad]_j])]])] \end{bmatrix}$$

In this entry, the subject is mapped into the Agent position and the object is mapped into the Goal; the Theme is unindexed and therefore completely incorporated into the reading of the verb.

Notice, though, that something akin to the Theme may appear in a *with*-phrase, as in (15).

(15) We buttered the bread with cheap margarine/with soft, creamy unsalted butter.

In (15), cheap margarine is what we put on the bread; that is, the *with*-phrase seems to play the role incorporated into the verb in entry (14). (It is evidently *not* an instrument: cheap margarine is not what we put butter on the bread with.) The problem then is, What is this *with*-phrase and how does it come to be integrated into the interpretation in the way it does? The answer is that (15) meets the structural description of the *With*-Theme Adjunct Rule (9), so that the *with*-phrase is fused with the incorporated theme BUTTER. That is, the *with*-phrase comes to function as Theme even though it is not licensed as such by the LCS of the verb.

Butter, powder, water, ice, frost, and *line* pattern like causative *cover.* On the other hand, the verbs *ice up* and *steam up* pattern like inchoative *fill:*

(16) a. The windshield iced up (with tiny crystals).
　　 b. The bathroom steamed up (with clouds of steam).

The lexical entry (17) enables us to apply the adjunct rule to (16a) in exactly the way it applies to (2d). (I have fudged the syntactic treatment of the particle *up* in (17); see section 11.4 for a more satisfactory version.)

(17) $\left[\begin{array}{l} \text{ice up} \\ \text{[}_V \text{ N] Prt} \\ \underline{\hspace{3cm}} \\ \text{[INCH [BE (([ICE], [ON}_d \text{ [}]_i\text{]))]]} \end{array}\right]$

One effect of adding a *with*-phrase to a sentence containing a denominal verb such as *butter* is to change BUTTER from an implicit argument to a selectional restriction on the Theme. To make this point clearer, observe that (18a) is anomalous and that the object of *with* in (18b) is understood as being a buttery substance. (Margarine, I assume, counts as a buttery substance.)

(18) a. # We buttered the bread with pineapple juice.
　　 b. 　We buttered the bread with that stuff you bought yesterday.

This is exactly what would be expected from the fusion of BUTTER with the object of *with.*

On the other hand, (19a, b) are odd.

(19) a. ?We buttered the bread with butter.
　　 b. ?We buttered the bread with something.

Unless the object of *with* in (19a, b) is used contrastively (*We didn't butter it with MARGARINE, stupid—we buttered it with BUTTER*), the sentences sound oddly redundant. In general, the *with*-adjunct is felicitous only if it adds nonredundant information. Where is this effect to be localized?

There seem to be two possibilities: (1) nonredundancy is part of the operation of fusion; (2) nonredundancy is specified as part of the adjunct rule itself. If (1) is the case, nonredundancy ought to be a condition not only on the *With*-Theme Adjunct Rule but also on optional arguments that are filled by Argument Fusion. Since (20a, b) are all right, we have to reject (1). (On the other hand, my judgments are spotty; (20c) seems rather odd.)

(20) a. He drank some liquid.
　　 b. He drank something.
　　 c. ?He paid Bill some money for the book.

Tentatively, then, I will make the nonredundancy condition part of the adjunct rule; it will turn out to be a general characteristic of all the adjunct rules we develop.

The nonredundancy condition is easily added to the rule, yielding the form (21).

(21) With-*Theme Adjunct Rule* (version 3)
       If V corresponds to [... BE ([X], ...) ...], with [X] unindexed, and NP corresponds to [Y],

       then [$_s$ ... [$_{vp}$ V ... [$_{pp}$ with NP] ...] ...] may correspond to

       [... BE ($\begin{bmatrix} X \\ Y \end{bmatrix}$, ...) ...], where $\begin{bmatrix} X \\ Y \end{bmatrix}$ is the fusion of [X] and [Y] and

       is distinct from [X].

The sentences in (19) fail this last condition; otherwise everything proceeds as before.

This analysis provides further evidence for the conclusion in section 2.3 that selectional restrictions are nothing but semantic information that a verb supplies about its arguments. There we dealt with examples where an implicit argument alternates with an explicit argument (for instance *drink* and *pay*); we saw that the selectional restrictions on the explicit argument are identical to the content of the implicit argument. In the present case, an implicit argument is supplanted by an adjunct, and the selectional restriction on the adjunct is identical to the content of the implicit argument.

8.4 *Empty, Uncover,* and *Skin*

However, (21) needs further refinement. Many of the verbs discussed so far have "opposites" that do not permit the Theme to be encoded in a *with*-phrase:

(22) a. The tank emptied (*with water). }
       b. Bill emptied the tank (*with water).} (cf. *fill*)
       c. Bill uncovered the field (*with a tarpaulin).   (cf. *cover*)
       d. Bill skinned the banana (*with its smooth yellow skin).   (cf. *butter*)

Empty, but not *uncover* or *skin*, permits the Theme to be expressed instead by means of an *of*-adjunct:

(23) a.   The tank emptied of water.
       b.   Bill emptied the tank of water.
       c.   *Bill uncovered the field of a/the tarpaulin.
       d.   *Bill skinned the banana of its smooth yellow skin.

How are these facts to be accounted for? The hypothesis to be pursued here is as follows:

(24) a. The *With*-Theme Adjunct Rule is formally constrained to apply only to "positive" verbs.

   b. The verbs in (22) are all "negative" in some sense and so do not satisfy the conditions of the *With*-Theme Adjunct Rule.

   c. The "negativity" of *uncover* and *skin* is encoded in a formally different fashion from that of *empty*.

   d. The *of*-phrase in (23a, b) is interpreted by a different adjunct rule, whose structural description applies only to the form of "negativity" present in *empty*.

Toward developing such an analysis, let us consider first the *un*-verbs. Section 6.3 discussed the relation between verbs of attachment (such as *attach*) and verbs of detachment (such as *detach*). Among these were morphologically related pairs such as *fasten/unfasten, glue/unglue*, and *pin/unpin*. In order best to account for the complement structures of the verbs of detachment, we proposed the conceptual structures in (25) for these verbs.

(25) a. attach, fasten, glue:
      [CAUSE ([X], [INCH [BE$_{c,a}$ ([Y], [AT$_{c,a}$ [Z]])])])]

   b. detach, unfasten, unglue
      [CAUSE ([X], [INCH [BE ([Y],
      [AT-END-OF [FROM [AT$_{c,a}$ [Z]]]])])])]

In particular, one implication of this analysis is that the *un*- prefix in *unfasten* and *unglue* can be treated conceptually as inserting the Place-function

AT-END-OF [FROM [   ]]

into the verb's structure. We can maintain this generalization for the case of *uncover* by making a parallel insertion in the lexical entry for causative *cover*. This yields the lexical entry (26) for *uncover*; its syntactic pattern is different from that of the verbs of detachment largely because its argument indexation is different.

(26) ⎡ uncover
     ⎢ [$_V$ Af V]
     ⎢ ——— NP$_j$
     ⎢ [CAUSE ([   ]$_i$, [INCH [BE ([   ],
     ⎣   [AT-END-OF [FROM [ON$_d$ [   ]$_j$]]])])])] ⎤

Next consider the denominal verbs of removal such as *skin, scale, milk, weed*, and one reading of *dust*. They appear to have essentially the same structure as *uncover*, even though they lack the negative prefix. (In fact, some denominal verbs of removal *do* have a negative prefix, for instance *declaw, defang, de-ice, defrost, defrock, unmask, disrobe*, and *disembowel*.) Under the assumption that these structures parallel *uncover, skin* has the entry (27).

(27)
$$\begin{bmatrix} \text{skin} \\ [_V \text{ N}] \\ \underline{\quad\quad} \text{ NP}_j \\ [\text{CAUSE ([\ ]}_i, [\text{INCH [BE ([SKIN]},} \\ \qquad\qquad\qquad [\text{AT-END-OF [FROM [ON}_{c,a} [\quad]_j]]])])] \end{bmatrix}$$

Another class of denominal verbs is illustrated in (28).

(28) a. The chimney smoked (*with/*of a strong sulfurous smoke).
   b. The soup steamed (*with/*of clouds of steam).

These verbs are of the conceptual form "smoke/steam came from (in) x," certainly not "smoke/steam came not to be in x"; that is, these are verbs of motion rather than inchoatives. The entry of this reading of *smoke* is therefore (29).

(29)
$$\begin{bmatrix} \text{smoke} \\ [_V \text{ N}] \\ \underline{\quad\quad} \\ [\text{GO ([SMOKE], [FROM [IN [\ ]}_i]])] \end{bmatrix}$$

In order to satisfy clause (c) of hypothesis (24), *empty* must have a structure distinct from any of these. We will therefore posit a structure of the form (30) for the causative form of *empty* illustrated in (23b). (In the pure inchoative of *empty*, the outer CAUSE-function is absent, and *i* replaces the *j* in (30).)

(30)
$$\begin{bmatrix} \text{empty} \\ \text{V} \\ \underline{\quad\quad} \text{ NP}_j \\ [\text{CAUSE ([\ ]}_i, [\text{INCH [NOT BE ([\ ], [IN}_d [\quad]_j])]])] \end{bmatrix}$$

At the moment I have no direct evidence to offer that (30) is the correct structure for *empty*. However, assuming the differences between (26), (27), (29), and (30), we can state an *Of*-Theme Adjunct Rule that applies only to *empty*, not to the others:

(31) *Of-Theme Adjunct Rule*
   If V corresponds to [... NOT BE ([X], ...) ...], with [X] unindexed, and NP corresponds to [Y],
   then [$_S$ ... [$_{VP}$ V ... [$_{PP}$ of NP] ...] ...] may correspond to
   [... NOT BE ($\begin{bmatrix} X \\ Y \end{bmatrix}$, ...) ...], where $\begin{bmatrix} X \\ Y \end{bmatrix}$ is distinct from [X].

In order to finish the analysis proposed in (24), it remains to restrict the *With*-Theme Adjunct Rule so it cannot apply to any of the "opposite" verbs. Essentially, the rule must be stated in such a way that neither the

NOT in *empty*, not the complex Place-function in *uncover*, nor the GO in *smoke* can squeeze into the structural description of the rule. (32) is a possible statement.

(32) With-*Theme Adjunct Rule* (version 4)

If V corresponds to [... [BE ([X], [F ([$_\text{Thing}$])])] ...],
with [X] unindexed, and NP corresponds to [Y],
then [$_\text{S}$ ... [$_\text{VP}$ V ... [$_\text{PP}$ with NP] ...] ...] may correspond to
[... [BE ($\begin{bmatrix} X \\ Y \end{bmatrix}$, [F ([$_\text{Thing}$])])] ...], where $\begin{bmatrix} X \\ Y \end{bmatrix}$ is distinct from [X].

This differs from (21), the previous version of the rule, in two respects. First, a left bracket has been placed next to BE, so that a NOT cannot precede it in the State-function. Second, a specifically simple Place-function is mentioned in the rule, so a complex location like that in *uncover* cannot be used. The range of possibilities, then, encompasses all the verbs we have encountered so far that permit a *with*-Theme adjunct and excludes those that disallow it.

The adjunct rules in (31) and (32), then, enable us to make a structural distinction among the various verbs with incorporated themes. Only some of these verbs admit Theme-adjuncts, and those that do not are that way because they fail to meet the structural descriptions of both rules. In turn, the two rules formally specify the conditions when an *of*-adjunct rather than a *with*-adjunct appears. One certainly might want more in the way of an explanation for why these verb classes differ, and further justification of the proposed conceptual structures that differentiate them, but at least there is now a formal description over which issues of explanation can be debated.[1]

As a further note on the *With*- and *Of*-Theme Adjunct Rules, it should be observed that the *with*- and *of*-adjuncts of Theme occur with adjectives that are morphologically related to the verbs we have discussed:

(33) a. The table is/seems/stayed [$_\text{AP}$ covered with flowers].
   b. The room is/seems/stayed [$_\text{AP}$ all steamed up with clouds of freon vapor].
   c. The sink is/seems/stayed [$_\text{AP}$ empty of water].

Evidently the adjunct rules (31) and (32) should be generalized to apply to these cases too. (For those speakers who do not accept (33c), only the *With*-Theme Adjunct Rule needs to be generalized.) On the syntactic side of the rules, all that is necessary is a generalization of V and its projections to A and its projections, using syntactic features and X-bar theory. On the conceptual structure side, we can assume that the adjectives have essentially the same conceptual structure as the related verbs, plus or minus an operator or two. Thus, pending a full treatment of the conceptual structure of deverbal adjectives, it seems safe to assume that a suitable generalization of these rules to APs does not pose a formidable technical problem.

8.5 Bottle, Pocket, and Package

Another class of denominal verbs mentioned in section 2.3 includes *bottle*, *pocket*, and *package*. This class incorporates the noun as Goal rather than as Theme of the verb's conceptual structure. For instance, (34a) means "put wine into bottles"; the other examples in (34) are parallel.[2]

(34) a. Fred bottled the wine.
     b. Herb deftly pocketed the money.
     c. We finally packaged the potato chips.

The structure of the verb *bottle* is thus (35a) (if it is a GO-verb) or (35b) (if it is an INCH BE-verb).

(35)
$$\left[\begin{array}{l} \text{bottle} \\ [_V \text{ N}] \\ \underline{\hspace{2em}} \text{ NP}_j \\ \left\{\begin{array}{l} \text{a. } [\text{CAUSE } ([\quad]_i, [\text{GO } ([\quad]_j, [\text{TO } [\text{IN } [\text{BOTTLE}\langle S\rangle]]])])] \\ \text{b. } [\text{CAUSE } ([\quad]_i, [\text{INCH } [\text{BE } ([\quad]_j, [\text{IN } [\text{BOTTLE}\langle S\rangle]]])])] \end{array}\right\} \end{array}\right]$$

However, the verbs in (34) also allow PP-complements that fill in more details about the Theme's final location:

(36) a. Fred bottled the wine in tall green bottles/*in bottles.
     b. Herb deftly pocketed the money in his left pocket/*in his pocket.
     c. We finally packaged the potato chips in air-cushioned packets/*in packages.

Like the *with*-adjuncts, these can be omitted from the verb's subcategorization frame, at the price of adding another adjunct rule:

(37) *PP-Adjunct Rule*
     If V corresponds to [... GO/BE (..., [X]) ...], with [X] unindexed, and PP corresponds to [Y],
     then [$_S$ ...[$_{VP}$ V ... PP ...] ...] may correspond to
     [... GO/BE (..., $\begin{bmatrix} X \\ Y \end{bmatrix}$) ...], where $\begin{bmatrix} X \\ Y \end{bmatrix}$ is distinct from [X].

Whichever conceptual structure is assigned to the verb *bottle* in (35), rule (37) will apply in (36a) to fuse the interpretation of the PP *in tall green bottles* into the unindexed Place-constituent of the verb. On the other hand, the PP *in bottles* is not distinct from the implicit argument, so the rule does not apply felicitously.

Rule (37) has been stated extremely generally—so generally, in fact, that it can apply to *any* optional PP Place- or Path-complement. This means that verbs of motion or location that take optional PPs need not mention this fact in their subcategorization. So, for example, *throw* can be listed as a simple transitive with an implicit Path: its entry can be simplified from (38a) to (38b).

(38) a.
$$\begin{bmatrix} \text{throw} \\ \text{V} \\ \underline{\qquad} \text{NP}_j \, \langle \text{PP}_k \rangle \\ \text{[CAUSE ([\quad]}_i, \text{[GO ([\quad]}_j, \text{[}_{\text{Path}} \quad \text{]}_k)])] \end{bmatrix}$$

b.
$$\begin{bmatrix} \text{throw} \\ \text{V} \\ \underline{\qquad} \text{NP}_j \\ \text{[CAUSE ([\quad]}_i, \text{[GO ([\quad]}_j, \text{[}_{\text{Path}} \quad \text{]})])] \end{bmatrix}$$

In other words, lexical entries need to mention in their subcategorization frames only those Place- and Path-complements that are *obligatory* or that assign idiosyncratic prepositions.

Rule (37) also permits a Path specified by a verb to be augmented with further PP-adjuncts. For instance, the verb *enter*, as noted at many points previously, incorporates the Path-function TO IN. Yet it is possible to add a Route-phrase as adjunct, as in (39).

(39) Bill entered the room *through the window/along the west side.*

Such PPs can simply be added into the Path specification by means of rule (37), yielding conceptual structures with compound Paths like (40).

(40) [GO ([BILL], $\begin{bmatrix} \text{TO [IN [ROOM]]} \\ \text{VIA [IN [WINDOW]]} \end{bmatrix}$)]

Thus the PP-Adjunct Rule permits interpretation of a wide variety of Place- and Path-PPs that previously could not be integrated into the readings of sentences, and moreover permits the simplification of a large number of lexical entries of verbs that take PP-complements.

8.6 *Load, Spray, Pack, Stuff, Clear,* and *Drain*

Sections 6.1 and 7.1 mentioned the well-known class of "locative alternation" verbs (Fillmore 1968; Anderson 1971, 1977; Rappaport and Levin 1985; Levin and Rappaport 1986). These are relevant in the present context because one member of the alternation includes a *with*-Theme adjunct:

(41) a. Bill loaded hay onto the truck.
     b. Bill sprayed paint onto the wall.

    c. Bill packed books into the boxes.

    d. Bill stuffed groceries into the bag.

(42) a. Bill loaded the truck (with hay).

    b. Bill sprayed the wall (with paint).

    c. Bill packed the boxes (with books).

    d. Bill stuffed the bag (with groceries).

As often observed, the thematic relations of these two forms ought to be essentially the same—Bill is performing the same action in both cases. However, as also often observed, the forms in (42) are for the most part "completive" or "perfective" in a way that the forms in (41) are not. For instance, if Bill has *loaded the truck with hay*, the truck is full of hay; this is not necessarily the case if Bill has *loaded hay onto the truck*. This difference in meaning, it may be recalled, was the evidence in Anderson 1971 and Chomsky 1972 against using a syntactic movement strategy to account for the alternation.

    I have encountered two proposals for predicting this completive sense. One, found in Tenny 1987 for instance, tries to connect completiveness with *the truck* being in object position, by analogy with the complete consumption of the apple in *Bill ate the apple* versus the noncompletion in *Bill ate at the apple*. The other proposal, found in Rappaport and Levin 1985 and Pinker 1989, connects completiveness with the fact that *the truck* is Patient when it is in object position: in order to be "affected," it must end up fully loaded.

    I do not find either of these accounts totally convincing. First, a number of my informants have observed that *spray* in the form (42b) is not necessarily completive: the wall ends up with paint on it, but not necessarily with paint all over it (though the suggestion is perhaps stronger in (42b) than in (41b)). Thus the NP-*with*-NP frame does not invariably imply completiveness. Second, the association of Patient with direct object is not invariable, since (43) is not too bad.

(43) ?What Bill did to the $\begin{Bmatrix} \text{truck} \\ \text{wall} \end{Bmatrix}$ was $\begin{Bmatrix} \text{load books onto it.} \\ \text{spray paint onto it.} \end{Bmatrix}$

(43) is not necessarily completive; hence the connection of affectedness to completiveness cannot be sustained either.

    A third reason surfaced in section 6.1, where it was observed that the object of *with* in the completive form displays the determiner constraints characteristic of a Theme being located in a distributive location:

(44) (= (6.10))

    a. Felix loaded $\begin{Bmatrix} \text{books} \\ \text{some books} \\ \text{the books} \end{Bmatrix}$ onto the truck.

b. Felix loaded the truck with $\left\{\begin{array}{l}\text{books.}\\ \text{?*some books.}\\ \text{the books.}\end{array}\right\}$

This suggests that the proper account of the completive reading is that it involves a distributive location: the books completely occupy the relevant space in the interior of the truck. Thus *load, pack,* and *stuff* in this frame are elaborations of *fill:* "cause to come to be in$_d$." *Spray* is identical except that it lacks the distributive feature and instead incorporates an ordinary location function; hence it is not necessarily completive.[3]

This leads to the following entries for *load* and *spray* in the NP-*with*-NP frame.

(45) a. $\left[\begin{array}{l}\text{load}\\ \text{V}\\ \underline{\quad}\ NP_j\\ \text{[CAUSE ([\ ]}_i, \text{[INCH [BE ([\ ], [IN}_d\text{/ON}_d\text{ [\ ]}_j\text{])])])}\end{array}\right]$

   b. $\left[\begin{array}{l}\text{spray}\\ \text{V}\\ \underline{\quad}\ NP_j\\ \text{[CAUSE ([\ ]}_i, \text{[INCH [BE ([\ ], [ON [\ ]}_j\text{])])])}\end{array}\right]$

In these entries, the Theme is not coindexed to the syntax, and the reference object is coindexed to the direct object. As a result, the *with*-phrases in (42) meet the structural description of the *With*-Theme Adjunct Rule and come to be interpreted as Theme. Hence the hay ends up in the truck, the paint ends up on the wall, and so forth. (This approach is also suggested by Rappaport and Levin (1988).)

It remains to address the relationship between the NP-*with*-NP frame (42) and the NP-PP frame (41). There are two conceptual structure differences between them. First, of course, is the distributive-nondistributive difference in many of the verbs (though not in *spray,* for example). The second is that in NP-PP frames, these verbs appear to be verbs of motion rather than inchoatives, since they occur with a wide variety of Path-prepositions: we have consistently taken the use of the Path-prepositions *into* and *onto* as strong evidence that the verb in question is a GO-verb rather than an INCH BE-verb.

The relation between the frames, then, does not appear to be a simple case of multiple frames like *climb* or *pass* (section 4.2). Rather, some relation of elaboration is called for, much as in the case of *hit* (section 7.6). Levin and Rappaport (1989) suggest that the NP-PP frame represents the core reading and the NP-*with*-NP frame is an elaboration: *Bill loaded the truck with hay* is roughly "Bill filled the truck with hay by loading hay onto the truck." Another possibility starts with *load the truck* as core, and the NP-PP frame as elaboration. On this model, *Bill loaded hay onto the truck* is roughly "Bill put hay onto the truck in order to load the truck with hay." Pinker (1989) suggests that locative alternation verbs may vary in which member of the alternation is the conceptual core. I leave the issue open, pointing out only that the present formalization helps sharpen the questions.

The locative alternation occurs also with some verbs of removal, such as *clear* and *drain*. The Theme-adjunct with these verbs is an *of*-phrase, paralleling *empty*:

(46) a. Bill cleared (the/some) dishes from the table.
      b. Bill drained (the/some) water out of the sink.

(47) a. Bill cleared the table (of (the/*some) dishes).
      b. Bill drained the sink (of (the/*some) water).

The same differences between the two variants obtain: the sentences in (47) are "completive" and have the determiner constraints of distributive location, but this is not the case in (46). Either *the dishes* or *the table* may be Patient in (46a), but only *the table* may be Patient in (47a) (*What Bill did to (the) dishes was clear the table of them*). We can therefore give the verb forms in (47) an analysis like that of *empty*, meeting the structural description of the *Of*-Theme Adjunct Rule:

(48) $$\begin{bmatrix} \text{clear} \\ \text{V} \\ \underline{\quad}\text{ NP}_j \\ [\text{CAUSE} ([\quad]_i, [\text{INCH} [\text{NOT BE} ([\quad], [\text{ON}_d [\quad]_j])])]) \end{bmatrix}$$

Note also that *drain*, like *empty*, has a noncausative inchoative variant (*The sink drained (of water)*); *clear* lacks this variant. This form of *drain* simply lacks the outer CAUSE-function, but the *Of*-Theme Adjunct Rule applies identically.[4]

8.7 Obligatory Adjuncts: *Rid, Provide, Present, Deprive, Swarm,* and *Teem*

One of the reasons it has been plausible to maintain that *with-* and *of*-adjuncts are not subcategorized is that they are optional. However, there exist some verbs that evidently require these adjuncts to be present. For example, *rid* is very much like the causative variant of *empty* (30), except that its *of*-adjunct is obligatory:

(49) a. Bill rid the room of insects.
      b. *Bill rid the room.

Since, almost by definition, obligatory phrases in the VP must be subcategorized, it appears that *rid* must revert to a more complicated lexical form

(50) in which the *of*-phrase is subcategorized—the sort of entry we rejected for *cover* back in section 8.2. ((50) omits the interesting selectional restriction on the Theme argument that it be considered somehow objectionable to the Agent or to the speaker.)

$$(50) \begin{bmatrix} \text{rid} \\ \text{V} \\ \underline{\hspace{2em}} \text{NP}_j \, [_{PP} \text{ of NP}_k] \\ [\text{CAUSE} ([\quad]_i, [\text{INCH} [\text{NOT BE} ([\quad]_k, [\text{ON}_d/\text{IN}_d \, [\quad]_j])])])] \end{bmatrix}$$

Thus this particular *of*-phrase is not interpreted by the *Of*-Theme Adjunct Rule, even though it has exactly the same interpretation as the *of*-adjunct of *empty*—an apparent loss of generality.

One way to recapture the generalization is to make use of a formal possibility of the notation that has not yet been exploited. We have so far assumed that every subcategorized phrase in the syntactic structure of a lexical item must bear an index that relates it to an argument in conceptual structure. Suppose, however, that we drop this requirement. Then, just as arguments in the conceptual structure of a lexical item can remain unindexed to the syntax, so subcategorized phrases in the syntactic structure of a lexical item can remain unindexed to the semantics—as long as some other way can be found to integrate them into the interpretation.

Following up this idea, suppose we drop the indices k in (50) to get the form in (51).

$$(51) \begin{bmatrix} \text{rid} \\ \text{V} \\ \underline{\hspace{2em}} \text{NP}_j \, [_{PP} \text{ of NP}] \\ [\text{CAUSE} ([\quad]_i, [\text{INCH} [\text{NOT BE} ([\quad], [\text{ON}_d/\text{IN}_d \, [\quad]_j])])])] \end{bmatrix}$$

This entry says that *rid* requires an object and an *of*-phrase; it specifies how the object is mapped into conceptual structure, but it does not say how to interpret the *of*-phrase. However, the conceptual and syntactic structures both meet the conditions for application of the *Of*-Theme Adjunct Rule, so the *of*-phrase can be properly interpreted as Theme.

This tactic may or may not be a notational trick, but it is a way to accomplish the desired result of interpreting the *of*-phrases with *rid* and *empty* by means of exactly the same principle. Looked at a different way, this solution is a way of saying that *rid* is lexically simpler than a hypothetical lexical item *shmid* with the same interpretation as *rid* but a different specified preposition. That is, the pattern in (51) ought to be easier to learn than would be a pattern like (52) with the same meaning.[5]

(52) a. Bill shmid the room at insects.
     b. *Bill shmid the room.

It should be observed that, if correct, this solution in terms of an "obligatory adjunct" severely blurs the distinction between "syntactic arguments" and "adjuncts." If a "syntactic argument" is supposed to be a phrase whose θ-role is specified by the verb, and an adjunct is supposed to be an optional phrase not specified by the verb, the *of*-phrase with *rid* falls in the cracks: it is syntactically required by the verb but receives its θ-role by a nonlexical principle. I personally have no problem with accepting such a result. The argument-adjunct distinction, while it has been useful as a rough-and-ready criterion, has on the whole simply been assumed. If it should turn out that a more precise treatment of the distinction reveals intermediate cases, so what? That is, I believe that objecting to this treatment of *rid* on the grounds that it undermines what was assumed to be a clear distinction amounts to little but an assertion of dogma.

It is also worth considering how *rid* might be treated in a theory that dispenses with lexical subcategorization features, on the grounds that they are (allegedly) predictable from lexical conceptual structure. (As mentioned in section 8.1, this is the prevalent theory of subcategorization in the GB Theory tradition since Stowell 1981, using the θ-Criterion to predict the syntactic pattern.) In such a theory, the entry of *rid* still has to specify that (1) there is a noncanonical mapping of conceptual arguments to the syntax, in that the reference object is mapped into direct object position and the Theme is mapped into an oblique position; (2) the oblique argument is obligatory rather than optional; (3) the preposition of the oblique argument is *of*; and (4) this *of* rather than some other preposition is predictable from the conceptual analysis of *rid*. These are exactly the distinctions between *rid* and other lexical items captured in the present analysis. I am not familiar with an attempt to describe a similar situation in terms of the θ-Criterion and Case-marking; however, as far as I can see, the very same distinctions must be made. The question, then, is what formal mechanisms for making them are most explanatory. The present approach, which retains subcategorization features, works out very neatly; moreover, it strengthens the thesis of autonomy of syntax, in that a lexical entry's syntactic structure is to a certain extent cut loose from its conceptual structure. It remains to be seen how a theory without subcategorization will fare by comparison. (See section 11.4 for further discussion.)

There are other verbs for which a similar problem arises. For example, a number of verbs display a paradigm much like that of *cover, surround,* and *saturate,* with the exception that the causative requires the presence of the *with*-phrase.

(53) a.   Snow capped the mountain.
       Trees lined the street.   (stative; inchoative marginal)
       Jewels encrusted the throne.

b. *The storm capped snow (on) the mountain.
   *The town planner lined trees (along) the street.
   *The dwarves encrusted jewels (on) the throne.
c. The storm capped the mountain with snow.
   The town planner lined the streets with trees.
   The dwarves encrusted the throne with jewels.
d. *The storm capped the mountain.
   *The town planner lined the streets.
   *The dwarves encrusted the throne.

(Note the difference between this verb *line* and the one in *The tailor lined the coat*, mentioned in section 8.3; they are evidently different lexical items.)

Evidently some minimal difference must be specified between the lexical entries of these verbs and those of the verbs discussed in sections 8.2 and 8.3. The solution for *rid* applies nicely: *cap, line,* and *encrust* subcategorize an unindexed *with*-phrase, which is interpreted by the *With*-Theme Adjunct Rule; by contrast, the entries of *cover* and *surround* omit mention of the *with*-phrase altogether.

Another such case appears in the possessional field. *Provide, present,* and *furnish,* instead of undergoing the usual dative alternation expected in this field, have the alternation shown in (54).

(54) a. Bill provided/presented/furnished some books (to the students).
     b. Bill provided/presented/furnished the students with some books.
     c. *Bill provided/presented/furnished the students. (* on Goal reading of *students*)

These contrast with *supply*, which has the same alternation, but for which the counterpart of (54c) is acceptable. (This rules out any attempt to explain (54c) based on eliminating ambiguities in parsing: why shouldn't the same argument pertain to *supply*?)

(55) a. Bill supplied some books (to the students).
     b. Bill supplied the students with some books.
     c. Bill supplied the students. (OK on Goal reading)

Similar contrasts appear in the verbs of possessional deprivation. *Rob* and *cheat* have an optional *of*-phrase that is interpreted as Theme, but *deprive* requires the *of*-phrase:

(56) a. Bill robbed/cheated/deprived Harry of his money.
     b. Bill robbed/cheated/*deprived Harry.

Again the treatment of the contrast between *empty* and *rid* is applicable: *provide, present, furnish,* and *deprive* will have an "obligatory adjunct," but *supply, rob,* and *cheat* will not.[6]

Yet another case involves verbs often discussed in conjunction with the locative alternation:

(57) a. Bees swarmed in the garden.
     b. Spiders crawled on the floor.

(58) a. The garden swarmed with bees.
     b. The floor crawled with spiders.

Again, the variants in (58) are more "holistic" or "completive" than those in (57): the bees are everywhere in the garden, the spiders are all over the floor. This aspect of the meaning certainly cannot be attributed to the difference in grammatical relations, since *fill* and *cover* have the same "completive" property but grammatical relations opposite to those in (58):

(59) a. Bees filled the garden.
     b. Spiders covered the floor.

Within the present theory, the completive aspect of the forms in (58) is stated directly in the verbs' lexical entries: these variants incorporate a distributive Place-function, just like *fill* and *cover*. As in one of the variants of *fill* (*The tank filled with water*), the reference object happens to appear in subject position.

The reason these verbs are relevant here is that the *with*-phrases in (58) are obligatory: **The garden swarmed, *The floor crawled*. Again, the solution appears to be to specify an obligatory but unindexed *with*-phrase in the verb's syntactic structure:

$$
(60) \left[\begin{array}{l} \text{swarm} \\ \text{V} \\ \underline{\hspace{1cm}} \ [_{\text{PP}} \ \text{with NP}] \\ [\text{BE} \ ([\quad], [\text{IN}_{\text{d}} \ [\quad]_i])] \end{array} \right]
$$

The *With*-Theme Adjunct Rule will then apply in (58a) to interpret the *with*-phrase as Theme.

It remains to relate the forms in (58) to those in (57). As in the case of the locative alternation, I wish to claim that the two forms have different conceptual structures and that the existence of both forms is a matter of lexical knowledge. As evidence, note that the verb *run* occurs freely in the form parallel to (57) but is semantically restricted in the form parallel to (58). Contrast (61a, b) with (61c, d); I will not investigate what the relevant restriction is.

(61) a. Puppies ran in the garden.
     b. *The garden ran with puppies.
     c. Blood ran in the river.
     d. The river ran with blood.

On the other side, the verb *teem* occurs only in a form parallel to (58), not to (57), although it seems to mean much the same as *swarm*:

(62) a. *Bees teemed in the garden.
     b. The garden teemed with bees.

And the verb *buzz* occurs with certain subjects in both forms and with other subjects in only the *with*-variant:

(63) a. Bees buzzed in the garden.
     b. The garden buzzed with bees.
     c. *Excitement buzzed in the garden.
     d. The garden buzzed with excitement.[7]
     e. *The garden buzzed.

This suggests that the difference between the forms in (57) and (58) is lexically specific and that it is a matter not just of different syntactic structures but of different associated conceptual structures as well. As in the case of the locative alternation, I beg off for now on a description of the relationship between the two conceptual structures.

8.8 The Passive By-Phrase

In various theories of argument structure, one of the major changes of the passive is to delete the verb's external argument. As observed in sections 2.3 and 4.3, the present framework's counterpart of argument structure is the system of indices in the verb's lexical entry that link its syntactic and conceptual arguments. Hence, corresponding to other theories' deletion of the external argument, the formation of a passive participle in the present framework will delete the index i that links a conceptual argument to subject position.

The upshot is that the passive participle has an unindexed (implicit) argument where the active verb has an indexed position. So, for instance, transitive *sink* has the LCS (64a), and the past participle *sunk* has (64b).[8]

(64) a. [CAUSE ([$]_i$, [GO ([$]_j$,
            [DOWN FROM SURFACE OF WATER])])]
     b. [CAUSE ([ ], [GO ([$]_j$,
            [DOWN FROM SURFACE OF WATER])])]

Hence *The ship was sunk* has an implicit Agent in conceptual structure that is available for binding the subject of the complement in the well-known example *The ship was sunk to collect the insurance*.

This chapter's treatment of *with-*, *of-*, and PP-adjuncts leads directly to a treatment of the passive *by*-phrase. In brief, we have only to state an adjunct rule that fuses the reading of the object of *by* into the unindexed argument left by the deletion of *i*. That is, just like our other three adjunct rules, it fills in the reading of an implicit argument. The passive *by*-phrase cannot occur in an active sentence, then, because there is no unindexed argument it can fill in—just as the *With*-Theme Adjunct Rule cannot apply if the verb has an explicit Theme.

The only trick in stating the rule is finding the correct conditions for the conceptual structure part of the rule. In previous cases the adjunct filled in a specific thematic role—Theme in the *With*- and *Of*-Theme Adjunct Rules, and Path in the PP-Adjunct Rule. This time the adjunct does not play any specific thematic role—it gets whatever role the external argument has. However, we appear not to have to provide the adjunct rule with a "memory" of what was deleted, as there is still a structural characterization of the external argument position.

Anticipating the discussion of chapter 11, notice that the external argument of nearly every verb we have examined is the first argument of the *action* tier, if there is one. Space precludes going through all the potential problems here, especially since the action tier is not yet very well articulated. But for a first approximation, let us adopt this characterization. (65) states the rule in terms of the action tier.

(65) *Passive By-Adjunct Rule*

If V-*en* corresponds to $\left[\begin{array}{l} \ldots \\ \text{AFF ([X] } \ldots) \end{array}\right]$, with [X] unindexed,

and NP corresponds to [Y],

then [$_S$ ... [$_{VP}$ V-*en* ... [$_{PP}$ by NP] ...] ...] may correspond to

$\left[\begin{array}{l} \ldots \\ \text{AFF } (\left[\begin{array}{l} X \\ Y \end{array}\right] \ldots) \end{array}\right]$, where $\left[\begin{array}{l} X \\ Y \end{array}\right]$ is the fusion of X and Y.

Some comments:

1. I have stated the rule specifically in terms of the passive participle form of the verb. This perhaps could be simplified, but it is not a big issue.

2. The rule does not mention the passive auxiliary *be*. Thus it should be adaptable to other contexts where passive VPs occur, for instance *The ship got sunk by a torpedo*, *The admiral had the ship sunk by the Air Force*, and *The ship sunk by the Air Force miraculously appeared in Harry's bathtub*. The syntactic part of the rule has to be adjusted to accommodate whatever the syntax of these constructions should turn out to be (for instance, is the passive VP immediately dominated by S or not?).

3. As in the treatment of *try* and *force* in section 7.7, AFF here should be generalized to include REACT. This will permit the passives of verbs such as *resist* and *withstand*. Since AFF and REACT also appear in statives, the rule applies to the passives of stative verbs such as *imply* and *like* as well.

4. The rule should also be able to fill in the *by*-phrase in the passive of *receive*, whose external argument is Beneficiary—the *second* argument of AFF, according to section 7.3. However, in this case there is no *first* argument of AFF. So we could adjust the rule as in (66).

(66) If V-*en* corresponds to $\begin{bmatrix} \dots \\ \text{AFF} (\langle, \rangle [X] \dots) \end{bmatrix}, \dots$

Here the angle brackets around the comma indicate that the argument [X] may be either the first argument of AFF or else, if there is no first argument, the second. A somewhat baroque notation, but it does the trick.

5. It is not yet clear whether every passivizable verb has an action tier. That has to remain for future research. In particular, I would not yet be inclined to use the passive as a criterion for the action tier. That would be begging the question. If the action tier characterization cannot be sustained, some other structural description must be sought for the rule.

6. The passive *by*-phrase in nominals, for instance *the destruction of the city by the enemy*, is not licensed by this rule. Rather, as shown by Rappaport (1983) and Grimshaw (1988) (among others) and illustrated in (67), the *by*-phrase in nominals is more strictly agentive.

(67) a. Bill is liked by Harriet.
          *the like/liking of Bill by Harriet
      b. This solution was resisted by Bill.
          *the resistance to this solution by Bill
      c. The answer was known by Bill.
          *the knowledge/knowing of the answer by Bill

An appropriate structural description for the nominal *by*-phrase will likely refer to the presence of CS coindexed with the first argument of AFF⁻ in an Event, that is, a much more restricted situation than the sentential passive *by*-phrase. However, I will not explore the details here.

This completes our discussion of adjuncts that fill in thematic relations in the main conceptual clause of the verb. We now go on to more exotic cases.

Chapter 9

Adjuncts That Express an Argument of a Modifying Conceptual Clause

9.1 Three Kinds of *For*-Adjuncts

Consider the *for* of *beneficiary*, found in sentences like (1).

(1) a. Bill sang a song for Mary.
    b. Bill sold a book to Harry for Mary.

In (1), the object of *for* receives the benefit of the action the subject performs. This contrasts with the *for* of *benefit*, seen in (2).

(2) a. Bill sang a song for fun.
    b. Bill bought/rented an airplane from Harry for fun.
    c. Bill sold a book to Harry for fun.

Here the object of *for* is the benefit that the subject intends to receive by performing the action.

Both of these *for*'s have been called "benefactive," but it is clear that they must be distinguished. In fact, the ambiguity of (3) turns on precisely this distinction.

(3) Bill would do anything for a pretty face.

On the benefit reading of *for*, Bill wants the benefit of having or getting a pretty face; on the beneficiary reading, Bill wants to do anything that will benefit someone with a pretty face.

A third kind of *for* was mentioned in section 3.1 in connection with verbs of exchange such as *buy, pay, rent, sell,* and *trade*. With these verbs, the object of *for* denotes the Theme of the countertransfer:

(4) a. Bill bought/rented a lawnmower from Harry for $25.
    b. Bill sold/rented a lawnmower to Harry for $25.
    c. Bill paid $25 to Harry for a lawnmower.
    d. Bill traded a lawnmower to Steve for a weedeater.

In each case, the direct object is changing possession from one character to the other, and the object of *for* is changing possession in the other direction. I will call this the *for* of *exchange*; it is restricted to sentences expressing change of possession.

The *for* of exchange must not be confused with the *for* of benefit. Compare (2b, c) to (4a, b). In (2b), Bill is the one who is going to have fun; in the most salient reading of (4a), Harry is the one who gets the $25. In (2c), either Harry or Bill can be construed as anticipating having fun; in the most salient reading of (4b), Bill unambiguously gets the $25. More generally, the *for* of benefit goes to either the Actor or the Beneficiary of the main clause; the *for* of exchange always goes to the Source of the main clause.

The distinction between benefit and exchange *for* is responsible for an ambiguity in (4a, b): there is a less salient reading in which Bill is to be given $25 by some unspecified agent, as reward for carrying out the action of buying from or selling to Harry. Since in each case $25 is the benefit that Bill will receive from his action, this reading is the *for* of benefit.

The distinction between *beneficiary* and exchange *for* is responsible for the ambiguity in (5).

(5) Bill obtained some food for his dog.

On the exchange reading, Bill has traded his dog for food; on the beneficiary reading, Bill obtained the food with the intention of giving it to his dog.

There are of course various other *for*'s, which we needn't distinguish at the moment. Some involve intended goals or purposes (6a–e); one is temporal (6f); I am not sure how to characterize (6g).

(6) a. Bill headed for home.
    b. Bill tried for a new job.
    c. Bill looked for Harry.
    d. Bill aimed for the target.
    e. What is this machine for?
    f. The movie lasted for six hours.
    g. What do you do for a stiff neck?

As usual, the present approach dictates that these *for*'s cannot be distinguished in conceptual structure with mere taxonomic labels. We need to give structural characterizations of their readings. Toward such a characterization, the next section will sketch the *for*'s of beneficiary and benefit, leaving for the two sections after that a more detailed consideration of the *for* of exchange.

9.2 The Conceptual Structure of the *For*'s of Beneficiary and Benefit; the Instrumental

Let us first consider (1a), *Bill sang a song for Mary*. We can characterize Mary's beneficiary role as the second argument of the action tier function AFF^+, that is, a partial conceptual structure of the adjunct is (7).

(7) $[AFF^+ (\quad , [MARY])]$

To incorporate this into the reading of the sentence as a whole, we must ask (1) how (7) is attached to the main conceptual clause expressed by *Bill sang a song*, and (2) whether there is an Actor as well as Beneficiary in (7).

Dealing with these in order, it appears that the appropriate structural connection is to treat (7) as a modifier linked by the subordinating FOR-function of purpose or intent (section 5.4). For one thing, this motivates the use of the preposition *for*—in this case, it expresses FOR plus other material. In addition, notice the entailments of the *for* of beneficiary: one can say, for instance, *Bill sang a song for Mary, but it turned out that she didn't hear it*. Evidently Bill intends the song for Mary's ears, but that does not entail that the intention was realized. This is just the inference pattern expected with the modifying function FOR.

Turning to the second question, if there is an Actor, it is surely the Actor of the main conceptual clause, in this case *Bill*. On the other hand, we may be able to get away without specifying an Actor in (7). At the moment I am not clear what criteria internal to conceptual structure would decide.

There is, however, a formal difference of some consequence in the correspondence rules. If no Actor is specified in (7), the lexical entry for the *for* of beneficiary can be given as (8): it is just a preposition that incorporates an Event-function, in the same way that various Path-prepositions incorporate Place-functions.

(8) $\begin{bmatrix} \text{for} \\ \text{P} \\ \underline{\quad} \; NP_j \\ [FOR \; [_{Event} \; AFF^+ (\quad , [\quad]_j)]] \end{bmatrix}$

This entry will combine with the main conceptual clause as a restrictive modifier, giving (9) as the conceptual structure for (1a). (SING and SONG are clearly approximations.)

(9) $\begin{bmatrix} \text{SING ([BILL], [SONG])} \\ \text{AFF ([BILL], \quad)} \\ [FOR [AFF^+ (\quad , [MARY])]] \end{bmatrix}$

If, however, we wish to make *Bill* the Actor in the modifying Event, a binding relation must be established. We can do this by using a correspondence rule on the model of the adjunct rules of the last chapter:

(10) For-*Beneficiary Adjunct Rule*

If V corresponds to $\begin{bmatrix} \cdots \\ \text{AFF} ([X], \ldots) \end{bmatrix}$

and NP corresponds to [Y],

then [$_S$ ... [$_{VP}$ V ... [$_{PP}$ for NP] ...] ...] may correspond to

$\begin{bmatrix} \cdots \\ \text{AFF} ([X]^\alpha, \ldots) \\ [\text{FOR} [\text{AFF}^+ ([\alpha], [Y])]] \end{bmatrix}$.

This rule will produce a conceptual structure for (1a) just like (9), except that BILL binds an argument in the Actor position of the lower AFF.

The change from (8) to (10) seems like a drastic increase in complexity just to include an Actor whose necessity in any event is somewhat unclear. (Section 11.9 will reduce the disparity somewhat but not altogether.) Still, pending further evidence, I leave the issue open.

In the case of the *for* of benefit there is no choice. Consider (2a), *Bill sang a song for fun*. Here *Bill* picks up an extra role not present in *Bill sang a song*, namely the (intended) receiver of fun. As usual, the extra role has to be encoded in conceptual structure by binding *Bill* to an argument in the appropriate structural position. In order to establish this binding, which appeals to the internal structure of the verb, we will have to use an adjunct rule rather than a simple lexical correspondence rule.

In order to state the rule, we must determine the conceptual structure associated with the *for* of benefit. The proper subordinating function again appears to be FOR, motivated by (1) the choice of preposition and (2) the entailment pattern, which suggests intended rather than necessarily realized benefit. One can say, for instance, *Bill sang a song for fun, but in fact he didn't enjoy it a bit*—that is, he didn't turn out to have fun after all.

Next we must determine what conceptual structure is subordinated under FOR. Roughly, the intended Event seems to be that the Actor come to *have* the object of *for*, benefiting thereby. This yields the following conceptual structure for (2a):

(11) $\begin{bmatrix} \text{SING} ([\alpha], [\text{SONG}]) \\ \text{AFF} ([\text{BILL}]^\alpha, \quad) \\ [\text{FOR} \begin{bmatrix} \text{INCH} [\text{BE}_{\text{Poss}} ([\text{FUN}], [\text{AT} [\alpha]])] \\ \text{AFF}^+ (\quad , [\alpha]) \end{bmatrix}] \end{bmatrix}$

An adjunct rule that produces this structure is given in (12).

(12) For-*Benefit Adjunct Rule*

If V corresponds to $\begin{bmatrix} \cdots \\ \text{AFF} ([X], \ldots) \end{bmatrix}$

and NP corresponds to [Y],

then $[_S \ldots [_{VP} V \ldots [_{pp} \text{ for NP}] \ldots] \ldots]$ may correspond to

$$\begin{bmatrix} \ldots \\ \text{AFF } ([X]^\alpha, \ldots) \\ [\text{FOR} \begin{bmatrix} \text{INCH } [\text{BE}_{\text{Poss}} ([Y], [\text{AT } [\alpha]])] \\ \text{AFF}^+ (\quad , [\alpha]) \end{bmatrix}] \end{bmatrix} \cdot$$

This precisely encodes the informal characterization above: whatever action the Actor performs, it is with the intended purpose of coming to have the object of *for* and thereby being positively affected.

As noted above, there are instances in which the *for* of benefit can assign the benefit to the Beneficiary (or possibly the Goal) of the main conceptual clause instead of to the Actor. A case in point is (2c), in which Harry may be the intended recipient of fun. This could be incorporated into (12) by using curly bracketed binders—either the Actor or the Beneficiary—or it could be a separate, as yet uncharacterized rule. I leave the issue open.

While examining this class of adjuncts, we might as well also sketch the adversative *on*, as in *My car broke down on me*. This is sort of an opposite of the beneficiary *for*: the object of *on* is negatively rather than positively affected by the main Event. There is one other difference between adversative *on* and beneficiary *for*. As we have seen, beneficiary *for* expresses an intended beneficiary who does not necessarily receive the benefit. By contrast, adversative *on* entails the negative effect: it is strange to say ?*?My car broke down on me, but it didn't have any effect on me* (except perhaps in a sense of ironic or studied nonchalance, where one is denyi g significance to the effect).

In formalizing the adversative *on*, we can adapt the structure of beneficiary *for*, making two changes corresponding to the observed differences. First, instead of AFF$^+$, whose second argument is a Beneficiary, adversative *on* will have AFF$^-$, whose second argument is a Patient or Undergoer. Second, the subordinating function cannot be FOR, whose entailments are wrong. A possible substitute is WITH, which indicates accompaniment; alternatively, we might want something stronger, say RESULTING-IN. For now, I leave the question open. The main point is that the adversative can be encoded with a simple structure entirely parallel to the beneficiary. (13) gives the structure for *My car broke down on me* (where the main conceptual clause is an approximation).

(13) $\begin{bmatrix} \text{BREAK-DOWN } ([\text{MY CAR}]) \\ [\text{WITH } [\text{AFF}^- (\quad , [\text{ME}])]] \end{bmatrix}$

As in beneficiary *for*, the question arises whether there ought to be an Actor in the subordinate Event, say the car in (13). The existence of adversatives with impersonal subjects, for instance *It rained on me*, suggests that there is not, since such sentences have no Actor in the main Event that could bind the lower Actor. (Compare to ?*It was sunny for me, where the *For*-Beneficiary Adjunct Rule *does* require binding by the main clause Actor.) The rule for adversative *on*, which derives (13), then parallels either (8) or (10), depending on how the issue of binding is resolved. There should be no need to state it at this point.[1]

So far, then, we have explored the semantic properties of three kinds of *for*-adjuncts and formalized two of them. Though various details remain to be explored, it appears that these two as well as the adversative *on* are closely related: they all introduce a modifying Event of which the object of the adjunct's preposition is an argument; the two *for*-adjuncts also bind the Actor of the main conceptual clause to another argument of the modifier.

This formal machinery also permits us to state a rule for interpreting instrumental phrases. Following the analysis of section 7.6, *Phil opened the door with a key* receives the conceptual structure (14).

(14) (= (7.47a))
$$\begin{bmatrix} CS^+ \ ([PHIL], [INCH \ [BE \ ([DOOR], [OPEN])])]) \\ AFF^- \ ([PHIL], [DOOR]) \\ [BY \begin{bmatrix} CS^+ \ ([PHIL], [AFF^- \ ([KEY], [DOOR])]) \\ AFF^- \ ([PHIL], [KEY]) \end{bmatrix}] \end{bmatrix}$$

This says that Phil, acting on the door, caused it to become open; Phil did this by acting on the key, causing the key to act on the door.

Binding all the occurrences of like arguments together, this becomes (15).

(15) $$\begin{bmatrix} CS^+ \ ([\alpha], [INCH \ [BE \ ([\beta], [OPEN])])]) \\ AFF^- \ ([PHIL]^\alpha, [DOOR]^\beta) \\ [BY \begin{bmatrix} CS^+ \ ([\alpha], [AFF^- \ ([\gamma], [\beta])]) \\ AFF^- \ ([\alpha], [KEY]^\gamma) \end{bmatrix}] \end{bmatrix}$$

This configuration is now similar to that of the *for*-adjuncts: the object of the preposition is an argument in a modifying means clause, and all other arguments in the means clause are bound to arguments in the main conceptual clause. Accordingly, we can state an adjunct rule for the instrumental that formally parallels those for the *for*-adjuncts:

(16) *Instrumental Adjunct Rule*

If V corresponds to $\begin{bmatrix} \ldots \\ AFF^- \ ([X], [Y]) \end{bmatrix}$

and NP corresponds to [Z],

then [$_S$ ...[$_{VP}$ V ... [$_{PP}$ with NP] ...] ...] may correspond to

$$\begin{bmatrix} \ldots \\ AFF^- \ ([X]^\alpha, [Y]^\beta) \\ [BY \begin{bmatrix} CS^+ \ ([\alpha], [AFF^- \ ([\gamma], [\beta])]) \\ AFF^- \ ([\alpha], [Z]^\gamma) \end{bmatrix}] \end{bmatrix}.$$

This differs from the previous cases primarily in that *two* arguments of the main conceptual clause—both the Actor and the Patient—have been bound down into the modifying clause.

9.3 *Buy*, *Pay*, and *Sell*

We next look at the *for* of exchange, which has similar but more complex characteristics. Let us first attempt to fill out the conceptual structure of *buy*, building on the sketch in section 3.1. We need to make explicit both transfers of possession; hence a representation for *buy* must include at least the information in both (17a) and (17b).

(17) X buy Y from Z for W.

a. $[GO_{Poss} ([Y], \begin{bmatrix} FROM [Z] \\ TO [X] \end{bmatrix})]$ (transfer)

b. $[GO_{Poss} (\begin{bmatrix} W \\ MONEY \end{bmatrix}, \begin{bmatrix} FROM [X] \\ TO [Z] \end{bmatrix})]$ (countertransfer)

How are these Events to be combined into a single lexical entry? One clue comes from the difference between *buy* and *pay*. Notice that *X paid W to Z for Y* involves exactly the same changes of possession as *X bought Y from Z for W*. The difference involves a "foregrounding" of one element of the transaction or the other: *buy* foregrounds the transfer of goods, *pay* the transfer of money. In turn, the foregrounded transfer determines the grammatical relations imposed by the verb: the Theme of the foregrounded transfer appears as direct object, the preposition *from* or *to* is appropriate to the direction of the foregrounded transfer, and the Theme of the background-grounded transfer is relegated to the *for*-phrase.

Accordingly, let us encode the foreground-background distinction of *buy* and *pay* in a way that mirrors its syntactic realization. We will make the foregrounded Event the main conceptual clause in conceptual structure, and the backgrounded Event a subordinate Event embedded in a modifier. The appropriate subordinating function this time is EXCH; the relation between the two Events is one of judged equivalence of value. Moreover, as is characteristic of EXCH, the two transfers need not be simultaneous: one can pay in advance for something one receives later, or alternatively "buy now, pay later." Under either of these conditions, there is a time interval between the transfers during which the Source of the uncompleted transfer is *under obligation* to the Goal to complete the transaction. The verb *owe* pertains to the conditions during this time interval.

Using this approach, we can express the difference between *buy* and *pay* as in (18).

(18) a. X buy Y from Z for W.

$$
\left[
\begin{array}{l}
GO_{Poss}\ ([Y],\ \begin{bmatrix} FROM\ [Z] \\ TO\ [X] \end{bmatrix}) \\[2ex]
[EXCH\ [GO_{Poss}\ (\begin{bmatrix} W \\ MONEY \end{bmatrix},\ \begin{bmatrix} FROM\ [X] \\ TO\ [Z] \end{bmatrix})]]
\end{array}
\right]
$$

b. X pay W to Z for Y.

$$
\left[
\begin{array}{l}
GO_{Poss}\ (\begin{bmatrix} W \\ MONEY \end{bmatrix},\ \begin{bmatrix} FROM\ [X] \\ TO\ [Z] \end{bmatrix}) \\[2ex]
[EXCH\ [GO_{Poss}\ ([Y],\ \begin{bmatrix} FROM\ [Z] \\ TO\ [X] \end{bmatrix})]]
\end{array}
\right]
$$

These contain exactly the same Event-functions with the same arguments, reflecting their basic similarity. They differ only in which of the conceptual clauses is primary and which subordinate.

As mentioned in section 3.1, these verbs are quintessential violations of the θ-Criterion as generally understood: both X and Z have (at least) double roles in the structures in (18). However, argument binding permits us to limit indexing of the syntactic phrases to a single occurrence of each character. Using argument binding, we get the following lexical entries for *buy* and *pay*.[2]

(19) a.
$$
\left[
\begin{array}{l}
buy \\
V \\
\underline{\hspace{2em}}\ NP_j\langle from\ NP_k \rangle\ \langle for\ NP_m \rangle \\[1ex]
\left[
\begin{array}{l}
GO_{Poss}\ ([\ \ ]_j,\ \begin{bmatrix} FROM\ [\ \ ]^{\alpha}_{\ k} \\ TO\ [\ \ ]^{\beta}_{\ i} \end{bmatrix}) \\[2ex]
[EXCH\ [GO_{Poss}\ ([MONEY]_m,\ \begin{bmatrix} FROM\ [\beta] \\ TO\ [\alpha] \end{bmatrix})]]
\end{array}
\right]
\end{array}
\right]
$$

b.
$$
\left[
\begin{array}{l}
pay \\
V \\
\underline{\hspace{2em}}\ NP_j\langle to\ NP_k \rangle\ \langle for\ NP_m \rangle \\[1ex]
\left[
\begin{array}{l}
GO_{Poss}\ ([MONEY]_j,\ \begin{bmatrix} FROM\ [\ \ ]^{\alpha}_{\ i} \\ TO\ [\ \ ]^{\beta}_{\ k} \end{bmatrix}) \\[2ex]
[EXCH\ [GO_{Poss}\ ([\ \ ]_m,\ \begin{bmatrix} FROM\ [\beta] \\ TO\ [\alpha] \end{bmatrix})]]
\end{array}
\right]
\end{array}
\right]
$$

These lexical structures correctly express the difference between foreground and background Events in *buy* and *pay*, and furthermore express the proper relation of syntactic structure to the primary Event. The extra roles played by the giver and receiver are expressed by the binding of arguments, independent of the linking to syntactic structure. Thus, for example, even if the *from*-phrase is omitted after *buy*, the binding of the implicit arguments is still in force, designating the Source of the primary transfer and the Goal of the secondary transfer as being the same character, as desired.

Although *buy* and *pay* have been differentiated, *buy* as it stands has not been differentiated from *sell*, which also has the transfer of goods as primary and transfer of money as subordinate. As has frequently been remarked, the difference between *buy* and *sell* lies in which character is foregrounded: the receiver or the provider of goods respectively. This foregrounding is of course reflected syntactically in the choice of subject: the subject of *buy* is Goal and the subject of *sell* is Source. The usual way to express this difference, which I will adopt without argument, is to consider the subject an extrinsic Instigator, that is, to have a CAUSE-function outermost in the representation. Under this analysis the conceptual structures of *buy*, *sell*, and *pay* would look like this:

(20) a. buy

$$[\text{CAUSE } ([\ \ ]^{\alpha}_{i}, \begin{bmatrix} \text{GO}_{\text{Poss}} ([\ \ ]_{j'} \begin{bmatrix} \text{FROM} [\ \ ]^{\beta}_{k} \\ \text{TO} [\alpha] \end{bmatrix}) \\ [\text{EXCH } [\text{GO}_{\text{Poss}} ([\text{MONEY}]_{m'} \begin{bmatrix} \text{FROM} [\alpha] \\ \text{TO} [\beta] \end{bmatrix})]] \end{bmatrix})]$$

b. sell

$$[\text{CAUSE } ([\ \ ]^{\alpha}_{i}, \begin{bmatrix} \text{GO}_{\text{Poss}} ([\ \ ]_{j'} \begin{bmatrix} \text{FROM} [\alpha] \\ \text{TO} [\ \ ]^{\beta}_{k} \end{bmatrix}) \\ [\text{EXCH } [\text{GO}_{\text{Poss}} ([\text{MONEY}]_{m'} \begin{bmatrix} \text{FROM} [\beta] \\ \text{TO} [\alpha] \end{bmatrix})]] \end{bmatrix})]$$

c. pay

$$[\text{CAUSE } ([\ \ ]^{\alpha}_{i}, \begin{bmatrix} \text{GO}_{\text{Poss}} ([\text{MONEY}]_{j'} \begin{bmatrix} \text{FROM} [\alpha] \\ \text{TO} [\ \ ]^{\beta}_{k} \end{bmatrix}) \\ [\text{EXCH } [\text{GO}_{\text{Poss}} ([\ \ ]_{m'} \begin{bmatrix} \text{FROM} [\beta] \\ \text{TO} [\alpha] \end{bmatrix})]] \end{bmatrix})]$$

9.4 The *For*-Exchange Adjunct Rule

The lexical entries in (19) are unusual in that they have four indexed arguments; so far we have been able to keep the indices down to two or occasionally three. It would also be desirable to eliminate some of the complexity in the verbs' subcategorization frames.

The *from*-phrase with *buy* and the *to*-phrase with *sell* and *pay* are totally regular expressions of Path, so they can be interpreted by means of the PP-Adjunct Rule of section 8.5. This permits us to remove the first PP from each of the subcategorization frames in (19) and the index k from each of the conceptual structures.

What about the *for*-phrase? As we saw in the last section, this is a phrase with a specialized meaning, evidently restricted to verbs of change of possession. Section 3.1 observed that the use of this *for*-phrase is however not restricted to verbs of exchange such as *buy* and *pay*. Rather, it can also occur with simple verbs of change of possession such as *obtain, receive,* and *get*. When it appears with these verbs, though, it converts the sentence into an expression of exchange—that is, this *for*-phrase alone can induce the construction of a conceptual clause of countertransfer:

(21) Bill obtained/got/received $5 from Harry for the book.

I have chosen main verbs in (21) in which the subject is Goal of the primary transfer. This was done in order to show that the *for*-phrase is not the *for* of benefit, which is always understood as going to the subject (or in some cases Goal). Rather, in the most salient reading of (21), Harry (the Source of the primary transfer) ends up with the book, just as with the *for* of exchange verbs. (There are of course other readings, for instance one in which Harry is contributing money toward Bill's buying a book; this probably is a *for* of benefit.)

It would be strange for simple verbs of change of possession to include in their lexical entries an optional subordinate conceptual clause of exchange, to be invoked just in case a *for*-phrase is present. Rather, it would be preferable to treat the *for*-phrase as an adjunct that adds its own contribution of a subordinate conceptual clause to the meaning of the sentence. Here is a rule with the desired effect:

(22) For-*Exchange Adjunct Rule*
      If V corresponds to [... [GO$_{Poss}$ (...) ...] ...]
      and NP corresponds to [Y],
      then [$_S$ ...[$_{VP}$ V ... [$_{PP}$ for NP] ...] ...] may correspond to the
      fusion of the reading of V with

$$\left[... \begin{bmatrix} GO_{Poss}\ (...,\ \begin{bmatrix} FROM [\quad]^\alpha \\ TO [\quad]^\beta \end{bmatrix}) \\ [EXCH\ [GO_{Poss}\ ([Y],\ \begin{bmatrix} FROM\ [\beta] \\ TO\ [\alpha] \end{bmatrix})]] \end{bmatrix} ... \right].$$

How will this rule work? Consider first a simple verb of change of possession such as *obtain*. This has the lexical entry (23).

(23) $$\begin{bmatrix} \text{obtain} \\ \text{V} \\ \underline{\quad\quad}\ NP_j \\ [CAUSE\ ([\quad]^\alpha_i,\ [GO_{Poss}\ ([\quad]_j,\ [TO\ [\alpha]])])] \end{bmatrix}$$

In the sentence *Bill obtained $5 for the book,* the verb subcategorizes only the direct object. However, the verb also satisfies the structural description of rule (22), so the rule inserts all the extra detail of an exchange into the reading of the sentence to get (24). (Binding indices have been changed to β and γ to preserve distinctness in the notation.)

(24) Bill obtained \$5 for the book.

$$[\text{CAUSE ([BILL]}^\alpha, \begin{bmatrix} \text{GO}_{\text{Poss}} \text{ ([\$5], } \begin{bmatrix} \text{FROM [\quad]}^\beta \\ \text{TO [}\alpha]^\gamma \end{bmatrix}) \\ [\text{EXCH [GO}_{\text{Poss}} \text{ ([BOOK], } \begin{bmatrix} \text{FROM [}\gamma] \\ \text{TO [}\beta] \end{bmatrix})]] \end{bmatrix})]$$

Now return to verbs that explicitly specify exchange, such as *buy*. Since the *for*-phrase is now treated as an adjunct, it can be omitted from the verb's subcategorization frame, simplifying the lexical entry of *buy* to (25).

(25)
$$\begin{bmatrix} \text{buy} \\ \text{V} \\ \underline{\quad} \text{NP}_j \\ [\text{CAUSE ([\quad]}^\alpha_i, \begin{bmatrix} \text{GO}_{\text{Poss}} \text{ ([\quad]}_{j'} \begin{bmatrix} \text{FROM [\quad]}^\beta \\ \text{TO [}\alpha] \end{bmatrix}) \\ [\text{EXCH [GO}_{\text{Poss}} \text{ ([MONEY], } \begin{bmatrix} \text{FROM [}\alpha] \\ \text{TO [}\beta] \end{bmatrix})]] \end{bmatrix})] \end{bmatrix}$$

In *Bill bought the book for \$5*, the countertransfer due to the *For*-Exchange Adjunct Rule will be fused with that due to the lexical entry of the verb. The only new information added by the *for*-phrase, then, will be a value \$5 fused with MONEY.

Note how this fusion accounts for the ungrammaticality of **Bill bought \$5 for the book*. When this sentence is interpreted, the adjunct rule fuses BOOK with the selectional restriction MONEY imposed by *buy* on the Theme of the countertransfer. Hence the sentence is anomalous. By contrast, no such selectional restriction is imposed by the simple verbs like *obtain*, so books are perfectly acceptable as the Theme of the countertransfer in (21).

Notice also how argument binding facilitates the statement of rule (22). As the rule is stated, the binding of Source and Goal of the primary transfer to Goal and Source respectively of the countertransfer is completely independent of the syntactic expressions for these characters. Thus, for example, in (24) the Source of the \$5 is totally implicit—but whoever it is, argument binding ensures that the same character gets the book.

Similarly, *pay* and *sell* put the Source of the primary transfer in subject position, whereas *buy* and *obtain* put the Goal of the primary transfer there. But this difference in syntactic indexing has no bearing on the binding of α and β, which is totally within conceptual structure. That is, the countertransfer will always be in the direction opposite to the primary transfer, no matter what character appears in subject position.

In fact, this works even with simple verbs of change of possession. Here, for example, is the lexical entry of *give* (ignoring the "dative-shifted" version):

(26)
$$
\begin{bmatrix}
\text{give} \\
\text{V} \\
\underline{\qquad} \text{ NP}_j \, [_{PP} \text{ to NP}_k] \\
[\text{CAUSE} ([\quad]^{\alpha}{}_i, [\text{GO}_{Poss} ([\quad]_j, \begin{bmatrix} \text{FROM } [\alpha] \\ \text{TO } [\quad]_k \end{bmatrix})])]
\end{bmatrix}
$$

When *give* is followed by a *for*-phrase, the usual exchange interpretation appears. Here is the result of applying (22) in a typical case:

(27) I'll give this book to you for only \$5.
$$
\begin{bmatrix}
\text{[CAUSE } ([I]^{\alpha}, & \begin{bmatrix} \text{GO}_{Poss} ([\text{BOOK}], \begin{bmatrix} \text{FROM } [\alpha]^{\beta} \\ \text{TO } [\text{YOU}]^{\gamma} \end{bmatrix}) \\ [\text{EXCH } [\text{GO}_{Poss} ([\$5], \begin{bmatrix} \text{FROM } [\gamma] \\ \text{TO } [\beta] \end{bmatrix})]] \end{bmatrix})]
\end{bmatrix}
$$

The interpretation here is derived in exactly the same way as the other cases, even though Source and Goal positions are opposite to the way they are with *receive* and *obtain*. (Alternatively, this could be construed as a *for* of benefit; I have for the most part restricted myself to examples with Source as subject just to eliminate this ambiguity.)

The *For*-Exchange Adjunct Rule, then, is a rule of interpretation that fills in a highly specialized bundle of conceptual structure particular to expressions of change of possession. It interprets the *for*-phrase as expressing the Theme of a countertransfer, whether or not the verb itself expresses a countertransfer. At the same time, it enables us to simplify the syntactic structure of all verbs of exchange, omitting the *for*-phrase and its associated index from the subcategorization feature. The conceptual structure, of course, remains the same—that's what makes them verbs of exchange.

9.5 "*For*-Dative" and "*To*-Dative" Adjuncts

Having dealt in section 9.2 with the *for* of beneficiary, it now makes sense to consider another construction that has always been recognized as closely related: the so-called *for*-dative. Sentences such as those in (28) are near enough in meaning to those in (29) that they used to be considered transformationally related (and in recent work such as Baker 1988 and Larson 1988 this possibility has been revived). Hence the term *for*-dative for the construction.

(28) a. Susan made Francine a picture.
     b. Enrico sang Helen a song.

    c. Carol bought Walt a car.
    d. Beulah, peel me a grape!   (from a Mae West movie)

(29) a. Susan made a picture for Francine.
    b. Enrico sang a song for Helen.
    c. Carol bought a car for Walt.
    d. Beulah, peel a grape for me!

As shown by Green (1974), Oehrle (1975), and others, the two constructions are not semantically equivalent, casting doubt on any putative relationship between them that involves only syntactic movement. Moreover, there is no overt dative case in English. So the construction is doubly misnamed. Accordingly, for terminological clarity, I will call the construction in (28) the *beneficiary NP construction*; *Francine* in (28a) will be called the *beneficiary NP*, and *a picture* will still be called the *object NP*.

Here are the two basic reasons why the *for*-beneficiary and the beneficiary NP constructions are not semantically equivalent. First, the beneficiary NP construction carries the implication that the object NP is intended for the benefit of the beneficiary NP. The *for*-beneficiary carries no such restriction: rather, the action as a whole is intended for the benefit of the beneficiary NP. Relevant contrasts appear in (30)–(31).

(30) a. *Bill removed Harold the garbage.
    b. *Nancy fought the king the dragon.
    b. *Beth jumped Harriet the puddle.

(31) a. Bill removed the garbage for Harold.
    b. Nancy fought the dragon for the king.
    c. Beth jumped the puddle for Harriet.

As a result, the *for*-beneficiary permits a wider range of possibilities, even in cases where the beneficiary NP is grammatical. For instance, (29c) may mean either that Walt ends up having the car or that Carol is acting as Walt's agent, but (28c) permits only the former reading.

This constraint is sometimes said to be that the beneficiary NP must come to *have* the object NP. This interpretation is rather forced in some cases, though: it is rather strange to say that Helen *has* the song in (28b), for example. The somewhat broader category of benefit seems more apt. Also, it need not be the case that the beneficiary actually receives the benefit, as seen in (32).

(32) a. Enrico sang Helen a song, but she wasn't listening.
    b. Beulah peeled Mae a grape but then accidentally dropped it in the toilet.

All that seems necessary is the subject's *intention* that the beneficiary receive the benefit.

The second constraint on the beneficiary NP construction is that the action of the subject has to be one of creation (e.g. *make*), performance (*sing*), making available (*buy*), or preparation (*peel*). The *for*-beneficiary is much freer. (33)–(34) (due to Jane Grimshaw) illustrate the contrast.

(33) a. Sue fixed a drink for Dick/fixed Dick a drink.
      b. Sue fixed the radiator for Dick/*fixed Dick the radiator.

(34) a. Sue poured some coffee out for Dick/poured Dick out some coffee.
      b. Sue poured some cement for Dick/*poured Dick some cement.

Intuitively, fixing a drink is creating a new entity, the drink; fixing a radiator is performing an operation on some preexisting object. Similarly, pouring some coffee creates a cup of coffee; pouring cement does not create a new entity. (Note that if the new entity is named, the sentence is all right, for instance *The builders poured us a new sidewalk.*) The formal means at hand do not immediately suggest a way to state this constraint so as to include all the relevant cases. I will therefore have to content myself with an informal statement of this part of the meaning of the construction.

The beneficiary NP, apart from its syntactic position, has all the hall-marks of the adjuncts we have been studying in this chapter. First, it is always optional. Second, there is no conceivable reason why an intended beneficiary should be part of the lexical conceptual structure of verbs like *make, sing, buy, peel, fix,* or *pour*. Third, it adds a piece of meaning quite similar to that of a known adjunct, the beneficiary *for*. Fourth, like the exchange *for*, it only occurs with a certain restricted class of verb meanings. This suggests that, even though it is a bare NP in immediately postverbal position—traditionally assumed to be *the* stereotypical configuration for arguments—we should take a deep breath and try to account for it by means of an adjunct rule:

(35) *Beneficiary NP Adjunct Rule*
      If V corresponds to [CREATE/PREPARE ([X], [Y])],
      and NP corresponds to [Z],
      then [$_S$ ... [$_{VP}$ V NP ...] ...] may correspond to
$$\begin{bmatrix} \text{CREATE/PREPARE ([X], [Y]}^\alpha) \\ \text{[FOR [AFF}^+ \text{ ([}\alpha\text{], [Z])]]} \end{bmatrix}.$$

The characterization of the verb in (35), as mentioned above, is informal. The characterization of the modifier, though, is fully formal; the difference between it and the modifier in the *for*-beneficiary concerns the binding of the first argument of AFF. In the *for*-beneficiary, the first argument of the purpose clause is bound to the actor of the main clause; in this construction it is bound to the object being created or prepared. This accounts for the differences observed in (30)–(31).

The syntactic part of this rule puts the beneficiary NP in the right place; one consequence is a displacement of the object NP away from its usual location next to the verb. Section 11.9 will show a way to accomplish this apparent "demotion."

The other "dative" NPs in English, of course, are the so-called *to*-datives, for example the inner NP in *give Bill a book*. These also have a long history of being analyzed as transformationally related to PPs, this time with *to*. Yet, as shown in the sources cited above, there are significant semantic disparities between the two constructions, which make a purely syntactic relationship between them hard to defend.[3]

I would like to show that the so-called *to*-datives cluster into two distinct classes with different properties. In one class, the "true *to*-datives," the inner NP is indeed an argument of the verb. In the other class, the inner NP is rather an adjunct that I will call the *recipient NP* adjunct. Most of the disparities that have been noted pertain only to the latter class. Thus by making this division I hope to provide a more adequate account of the construction in general.

The most notable problem for a syntactic account of the *to*-dative alternation concerns a difference in meaning: in the ditransitive construction, the inner NP must be the intended possessor of the second NP, but this restriction does not obtain in the NP-*to*-NP construction. Thus, for example, (36a) is all right with either *Bill* or *New York*, but (36b) is good only with *Bill*, because *New York* is not a possible possessor. (There is however a reading in which *New York* is construed as something like "the people in the New York office," in which case the sentence is all right again.)

(36) a. Joan sent the package to Bill/to New York.
     b. Joan sent Bill/*New York the package.

Again, most discussion of this restriction claims that *actual* possession must be achieved. As in the beneficiary NP, *intended* possession is sufficient, as can be seen from examples like (37).

(37) Joan sent Bill the package, but he never got it.

Inspection of the cases in which this semantic difference appears, for example the verbs in (38a), reveals that the verbs are all fundamentally spatial, not possessional: they all appear to be verbs of putting something in motion. They can all occur with a wide variety of spatial PPs, as seen in (38b), or with just the Theme NP, as in (38c). On the other hand, the Goal NP can never occur alone in the complement, as seen in (38d).

(38) a.   Sam sent/threw/kicked/hurled/hit Bill the ball.
    b.   Sam sent/threw/kicked/hurled/hit the ball to Sandy/out the window/into the park/away.
    c.   Sam sent/threw/kicked/hurled/hit the ball.
    d.   *Sam sent/threw/kicked/hurled/hit Bill.   (in relevant sense)

From these facts, we see that the basic LCS for *throw* (39) (= (8.38b)) generalizes to the whole class. In this LCS, the subject and object are arguments, but the PP is an adjunct, fused into the Path-constituent by the PP-Adjunct Rule (8.37).

(39) [CAUSE ([   ]$_i$, [GO ([   ]$_j$, [$_{Path}$])])]

Pinker (1989) notes a further restriction on this class of verbs. Contrast (38) with (40).

(40) a.   *Sam pushed/pulled/dragged Bill the ball.
    b.   Sam pushed/pulled/dragged the ball (to Bill).

The difference, according to Pinker, is that the verbs in (38) describe causation of the *inception* of motion, whereas those in (40) describe continuous causation of motion. In present terms, this is the difference between "launching" causation and "entraining" causation (section 7.4). We have expressed this difference formally in the features of CS, subscripting the relevant cases as CS$_{launch}$. (Two exceptions to Pinker's generalization, though, are *bring* and *take*, which are spatial verbs of entrained motion.)

Considering only this class of verbs, then, the indirect object has the behavior of an adjunct: it is optional; it is not part of the core meaning of the verb; it depends on an idiosyncratic semantic stipulation on the verb; and its meaning, intended possession, is clearly in the family of adjuncts considered in this chapter.

By contrast, another class of *to*-dative verbs displays different behavior. They are all possessional verbs to start with, and in the NP-PP form the only possible preposition is *to* (with idiomatic exceptions such as *give away* and *give out*), as seen in (41b). Some of them, though not all, permit the Goal NP to appear alone in the complement, as seen in (41c).

(41) a.   Adam gave Debbie a book.
        Adam served Debbie her dinner.
        Adam told Debbie a long story.
        Adam paid Debbie $5.

$$
\text{b.}\quad
\left\{
\begin{array}{l}
\text{Adam gave a book} \\
\text{Adam served dinner} \\
\text{Adam told a long story} \\
\text{Adam paid \$5}
\end{array}
\right\}
\left\{
\begin{array}{l}
\text{to Debbie.} \\
\text{*out the window.} \\
\text{*down the road.} \\
\text{*into the fire.}
\end{array}
\right\}
$$

    c.   Adam served/told/paid/*gave Debbie.

The only discernible difference in meaning was in fact noted in section 7.3.2: in the ditransitive form, the Goal is easier to construe as Beneficiary:

(42) (= (7.29))

What Harry did for Sam was $\begin{Bmatrix} \text{a.} & \text{give him a book.} \\ \text{b.} & \text{?give a book to him.} \end{Bmatrix}$

In section 7.3.2, we used this difference in the action tier to explain why ditransitive *give* can be used more comfortably as a light verb than *give* with NP-*to*-NP:

(43) a.   Sam gave Harry a kiss/a kick.
     b.   ?*Sam gave a kiss/a kick to Harry.

This disparity between the two frames in turn has nothing to do with the class of verbs illustrated in (38).[4]

In this second class of *to*-dative verbs, then, the indirect object acts a great deal more like a normal argument: it has something to do with the core meaning of the verb, transfer of possession, and, aside from a difference in the action tier, plays a role indiscernible from the object of *to*. I will therefore call these verbs *true to-datives*. We return to their analysis in sections 11.5 and 11.7.

This clears the way for a fairly simple statement of the adjunct rule responsible for the sentences in (38a):

(44) *Recipient NP Adjunct Rule*
     If V corresponds to $[CS_{launch} \ ([X], [GO \ ([Y], [_{Path} \qquad])])]$
     and NP corresponds to $[Z]$,

     then $[_S \ \ldots \ [_{VP} \ V \ NP \ \ldots] \ \ldots]$ may correspond to
     $\begin{bmatrix} CS_{launch} \ ([X], [GO \ ([Y]^\alpha, [_{Path} \ TO \ [Z]^\beta])]) \\ [FOR \ [GO_{Poss} \ ([\alpha], [TO \ [\beta]])]] \end{bmatrix}$.

The only novelty in this rule is that it specifies a spatial Path. This Path is what makes the ditransitive sentences apparently synonymous with the NP-*to*-NP sentences. But in addition, the spatial Goal is bound to the role of intended possessor, adding the observed difference in meaning between the two cases.

We now have two adjunct rules that fill the same "dative" NP position. This parallels the situation observed with *for*-adjuncts, where we found three different conceptual realizations. Just to make sure the two rules are distinct, note that (45) is ambiguous.

(45) The secretary wrote the boss a letter.

On one reading, the boss is intended to receive the letter; this is the recipient NP adjunct. On the other reading, the secretary is writing a letter for the boss's benefit or on the boss's behalf; this is the beneficiary NP adjunct.

It is not too hard to imagine a rule syntactically similar to (35) or (44) that is however sensitive to some affix on the verb. This presents the possibility of an account of "applicative" constructions in various languages, such as have been discussed by Baker (1988), Bresnan and Kanerva (1989), Bresnan and Moshi (1988). Baker advocates an approach based on movement rules, a contemporary version of the old dative shifts; Bresnan, Kanerva, and Moshi work out an account in terms of lexical rules that add arguments. The present approach, while formally closer to that of Bresnan, Kanerva, and Moshi, keeps the extra NPs out of lexical argument structure, as we did earlier with *with*-adjuncts. It remains to be seen whether the special effects of applicatives observed in these papers can emerge naturally from the present account.

And now for something completely different.

9.6 Depictive Predication

There is a class of adjuncts that has been widely discussed under the term *predication* or *secondary predication* (where *primary prediction* is taken to be the relation between a subject and its VP) (Rothstein 1983; Williams 1980; Culicover and Wilkins 1984; Carrier and Randall, forthcoming; Napoli 1989). The clearest cases of these adjuncts are APs that (1) appear in VPs, (2) are not subcategorized by the verb, and (3) are predicated of one of the NPs in the clause. Here are three standard examples:

(46) a. Bill chewed the meat nude.
     b. Bill chewed the meat raw.
     c. Bill chewed his knuckles raw.

On the most salient readings of these, *nude* is predicated of *Bill* in (46a), *raw* is predicated of *meat* in (46b), and *raw* is predicated of *knuckles* in (46c). (46b) and (46c) further differ on their most salient readings, in that in (46b) the meat is asserted to be raw when Bill chews it or when he begins to chew it, whereas in (46c) Bill's knuckles are asserted to have become raw as a result of Bill's chewing. Following Rothstein, we will call cases like (46b) *depictive predication* and cases like (46c) *resultative predication*. We will put off resultative predication to sections 10.4–10.5, for the moment concentrating on depictives.

(46a) is also depictive (Bill is nude as he chews the meat), but the AP is predicated of the subject rather than the object. As is by now well known, it is possible to get both kinds of depictives in a single sentence, with the subject depictive following the object one:

(47) a.   Bill ate the meat raw nude.
     b.   *Bill ate the meat nude raw.

Various people have suggested therefore that subject and object depictives are attached at different points in the tree, perhaps as in (48); Culicover and Wilkins (1984) present a number of syntactic arguments for this structure.

(48) [$_S$ Bill [$_{V''}$[$_{V'}$ ate the meat raw] nude]]

For many of the authors listed above, the implication behind the use of the term *predication* for this construction is that there is a single *syntactic* relation that unifies these cases with subject-to-VP predication. Thus it makes sense to speak of the *subject* of the predication as that NP to which the AP applies. However, the approach taken here will be to leave the syntax alone, seeking the commonality at the level of conceptual structure. Accordingly, I will reserve the term *subject* for the standard syntactic relation, and instead speak of the *host* of a secondary predication. Thus in (48) *the meat* is the host of *raw* and *Bill* is the host of *nude*.

Some analyses (Williams; Culicover and Wilkins) express the predication relation by coindexing the predicate with its host:

(49) Bill$_i$ ate the meat$_j$ raw$_j$ nude$_i$

The general approach in GB Theory (Chomsky 1981) makes use of a "small clause" whose subject is PRO, which in turn is coindexed with the host by the usual binding principles:

(50) Bill$_i$ ate the meat$_j$ [PRO$_j$ raw] [PRO$_i$ nude]

The analysis in (50) has (what is taken to be) the virtue of preserving the θ-Criterion, in that each NP has exactly one θ-role. By contrast, in the analysis in (49), *Bill* is both Agent of *eat* and Theme of *nude*, and *meat* is both Patient of *eat* and Theme of *raw*, violating the θ-Criterion. However, chapter 3 has shown that preserving the θ-Criterion is hardly a pressing desideratum in the present approach, so this motivation for (50) over (49) is not especially strong for us here. In addition, Rothstein (1983) and Williams (1983) present some arguments against the feasibility of (50) under GB Theory-internal assumptions about the government of PRO.

On the other hand, coindexing of the sort in (49) is not very informative. The two coindexed phrases are linked, but the interpretation of this linkage is not the usual coreference. *Bill* is not coreferential with *nude*, for example —*Bill* refers to a Thing and *nude* if anything to a Property. Rather, the interpretation of the coindexing is obviously that the AP is predicated of the NP—a different conceptual relation than coreference or argument binding.

In addition, both approaches fail to specify the semantic connection between the secondary predication and the reading of the main clause. This relationship is described informally but plays no role in the analysis of the coindexing. (Carrier and Randall's (forthcoming) analysis of resultatives is an exception, as we will see later.) So our first problem here will be to spell out the conceptual structure of depictives.

The structure of the predication itself is not difficult: it is simply a BE-function whose arguments are the host and the predicate AP. So, for instance, the predications in (48) have the forms in (51).

(51) a. [BE$_{Ident}$ ([BILL], [AT [NUDE]])]
     b. [BE$_{Ident}$ ([MEAT], [AT [RAW]])]

How is this conceptual clause attached? Its relation to the main conceptual clause seems to be the sort of nonspecific mutual dependence that we encoded in section 5.4 as a modifier of accompaniment: if Bill eats meat raw, it is not necessarily that he eats it *because* it is raw or *when(ever)* it is raw, and certainly not *by means* of its being raw; and yet it is more than that he eats meat and it happens to be raw. These intuitions are the symptoms of accompaniment, formalized by means of the subordinating function WITH. We will therefore encode *Bill ate the meat raw* as (52).

(52) Bill ate the meat raw.
$$\begin{bmatrix} \text{EAT ([BILL], [MEAT])} \\ \text{[WITH [BE}_{Ident}\text{ ([MEAT], [AT [RAW]])]]} \end{bmatrix}$$

This structure contrasts with other cases that have sometimes also been called secondary predication. In particular, verbs like *consider* and *find* subcategorize the secondary predicate and treat it as part of the argument structure. *Bill considered/found Amy smart* does not mean "Bill considered/found Amy because of/depending on her being smart" but rather "Bill thought/found that Amy is smart." In other words, the meaning of the sentence does contain the BE-function, with *Amy* as host and *smart* as predicate, but this BE-function is an argument rather than a modifier:

(53) Bill considers/finds Amy smart.
     [THINK/FIND ([BILL], [BE$_{Ident}$ ([AMY], [AT [SMART]])])]

As evidence for this difference, notice that the AP can be questioned in (53) but not in depictive predicates: *How smart does Bill consider Amy?* but not *How raw did Bill eat the meat?* Similarly, consider perception verbs in constructions such as *Bill saw Harry running in the park.* On one reading, *running* is predicated of *Harry* as part of the main verb's meaning, and one can ask *Where did Bill see Harry running?* However, our interest here is not in these cases. We are specifically concerned with the cases in which the predicate AP is *not* subcategorized but is rather treated semantically as the reference object of a modifying conceptual clause. (The literature recognizes this distinction clearly but usually does not provide a semantic account of the difference parallel to (52) versus (53).)

Rothstein (1983, section 5.1) points out two restrictions on depictive predicates. (Similar conditions appear in Bresnan 1982d.) The first is that the predicate must express a potentially transitory property of the host. Thus (54a) is strange because tastiness is in some sense a more permanent property of the meat than rawness; (54b) is strange because height is assumed to be permanent. On the other hand, in the context of *Alice in Wonderland*, where Alice is always changing height, (54c) is fairly acceptable with *Alice* as host of the predicate.

(54) a. *Bill ate the meat tasty.
     b. *Bill ate the meat tall.
     c. Alice met the White Rabbit tall.

This restriction is a consequence (albeit informal) of the present analysis. The WITH connection between the predication and the main Event is one of nonspecific mutual dependence. If the predicate were one that could not potentially change, there would be no way that the performance of the main Event could depend on whether or not the predication obtained. Here only potentially changeable predicates can enter into structure (52).

The second restriction Rothstein brings up concerns the impossibility of *John* serving as host in the sentences in (55), despite the pragmatic plausibility of such a reading.

(55) a. Mary gave John the book drunk.
     b. The nurse gave John the medicine sick.

She claims that the restriction is that the host cannot be a Goal but must rather be an Agent or Patient; hence the indirect object cannot be host of a depictive predication. However, the sentences in (56) are acceptable, even though *John* is Goal in (56a) and *the bread* is Goal as well as Patient in (56b) (recall that X *butter* Y means "X cause butter to come to be all over Y").

(56) a. John received the letter drunk.
     b. Bill buttered the bread warm.

Thus Rothstein's proposed constraint is incorrect; I leave the proper formulation open.

There seem as well to be other semantic constraints on direct objects serving as hosts. For instance, the sentences in (57) seem odd even if pragmatically plausible. (Thanks to Richard Oehrle for some of these.)

(57) a. ?*Bill only sings songs unpopular.
     b. ?Bill filled the cup dirty.

    c. ?*Bill entered the room noisy.

    d. ?*Bill is seeking his lost car unharmed.

In addition, I have come across a few cases in which the object of a preposition can serve as host of a depictive predication, so the construction is not constrained simply to subjects and objects:

(58) a. You can count on John even drunk.

    b. What do you make of John drunk?

I will not pursue these further restrictions here.

Let us now state the correspondence rule that accounts for the interpretation of depictive predication. We will first formulate it in a version that states the syntactic relation of host to predicate explicitly:

(59) *Depictive Predicate Adjunct Rule* (version 1)

If NP corresponds to [X] and AP corresponds to [Y], then either of the configurations (a) or (b)

    a. $[_S \text{ NP } \dots [_{V''} \text{ V}' \dots \text{ AP}] \dots]$

    b. $[_S \dots [_{V'} \dots \text{ NP AP }] \dots]$

may correspond to

$$\left[\begin{array}{l} \text{F} (\dots \text{ [X]}^\alpha \dots) \\ _{\text{Event}} [\text{WITH } [\text{BE}_{\text{Ident}} ([\alpha], [\text{AT } [Y]])]] \end{array} \right].$$

In (59), the NP host is an argument of the main conceptual clause, and it is bound to the Theme of the secondary predicate; the AP is the reference object in the secondary predicate. The argument binding in (59) achieves in conceptual structure the effect intended by (50), the GB Theory treatment of the binding relation, but without invoking any PRO or small clause in the syntax.

Notice that sentence (48) meets the structural description of (59) in two different ways, one corresponding to each of the syntactic configurations in the rule. Thus each secondary predicate leads to the construction of its own WITH-clause in conceptual structure: there is no prohibition against two of them appearing in tandem.

Suppose instead that the potential relationship of host to predicate is determined by some syntactic principle such as c-command (Williams) or bijacency (Culicover and Wilkins), and that this relationship is marked by a syntactic rule, as presumed in analysis (49). Then the adjunct rule does not itself have to specify the syntactic structural description in such detail; it has only to invoke the host-to-predicate relationship established by the extrinsic syntactic rule. Let us notate the relationship with cosuperscripted numerals in syntactic structure (so as not to confuse it with the subscripts of syntax-to-semantics coindexing). (59) can then be simplified to (60).

(60) *Depictive Predicate Adjunct Rule* (version 2)
If NP corresponds to [X] and AP corresponds to [Y],
then [$_S$ ... NP^1 ... AP^1 ...] may correspond to

$$\left[\begin{array}{l} \text{F} (... \text{[X]}^\alpha ...) \\ _{\text{Event}} \text{[WITH [BE}_{\text{Ident}} \text{([}\alpha\text{], [AT [Y]])]]} \end{array}\right].$$

I leave unstated in (60) the proper form of the restrictions on the host as well as any further semantic restrictions on the construction.

I am inclined to think that (60) rather than (59) is the correct form of the rule. The reason is that there appear to be other correspondence rules that depend on the very same syntactic relation, here notated as cosuperscripting. The most prominent is the relation between an expletive *it* and an S'-complement. Consider the cases in (61).

(61) a. It bothers everyone that/when/if you sing out of tune.
b. Sue likes it very much that/when/if you tickle her.
c. Sue would prefer it strongly if you would leave.
d. You can depend on it without a doubt that Bill will be drunk.
e. What do you make of it that Bill is drunk?

The subordinate clauses in (61) all satisfy the argument role whose place is marked by *it*: subject in (61a), object in (61b, c), object of a verbally specified preposition in (61d, e). This relationship used to be expressed by extraposition of the S' from the position in question, following Rosenbaum (1967). However, as pointed out by Emonds (1976), the use of *if*- and *when*-clauses in at least some of these cases casts doubt on the extraposition analysis, since these clauses never appear in subject position. Moreover, there are plenty of languages in which even *that*-clauses never appear in subject position. (See Postal and Pullum 1988 for more facts like (61b–e).)

In Jackendoff 1977, section 4.8, it is argued therefore that the ability of the clause to function as an argument is established by an interpretive relation between the clause and the expletive. The basic form of the rule in present terms is something like "Fuse the conceptual structure of the S' with that of the expletive." Since the expletive has *no* conceptual structure, the result is that the S' functions as an argument in place of the expletive.

This rule, however, needs a syntactic structural description: in what relative syntactic configurations is this fusion of S' and *it* possible? Interestingly, the contexts seem very close to those for depictive predication. Compare (61) to (62).

(62) a. Bill bothers everyone even sober.
b. Sue likes Bill even drunk.
c. Sue prefers Bill even drunk.

d. You can depend on Bill even drunk.
e. What do you make of Bill drunk?

That is, the interpretation of "extraposed" S'-complements and of depictive predicates, though quite different in their effects in conceptual structure, depend on essentially the same syntactic configuration. (Section 11.10 formulates the rule that interprets (61); Williams (1980) also notes the parallelism between depictive predication and "extraposed" complements.)

This observation suggests two conclusions. First, the identification of the requisite syntactic configuration is independent of which interpretive rule is going to make use of it. Thus it makes sense to factor the syntactic configuration out of the depictive predication rule, as has been done in (60), rather than duplicating it in two or more rules. Second, if the configuration for "extraposed" S'-complements is to be generalized with that for depictive predicates, this is further evidence against an actual extraposition transformation (as if more were needed). There is no way that a movement of S' and an interpretive rule, coindexing, or whatever for depictive predication could be construed as forming a natural class of rules, whereas two correspondence rules sharing a common syntactic configuration is altogether common. It remains to be seen whether this analysis can be extended to other "extraposition" phenomena such as extraposed relative clauses and especially degree clauses (see Jackendoff 1977, chapter 8).

A last comment on depictive predication. It is often observed that depictive predication can also be produced with a PP or predicate NP rather than an AP:

(63) a. Bill entered the room in a good mood and left it out of sorts.
b. Bill entered the room a pauper and left it a rich man.

The generalization of (59) or (60) to such cases is on the whole obvious. Curiously, though, predicate NPs allow only the subject as host, not the object. For instance, (64a) and (64b) can have either *Bill* or *Harry* as host, but in (64c) only *Bill* can be host.

(64) a. Bill encountered Harry happy.
b. Bill encountered Harry out of sorts.
c. Bill encountered Harry a pauper.

Similarly, gerundive accompaniment constructions, mentioned briefly in section 5.4, are related to secondary predication (see the next section). But they differ among themselves in whether they allow subject and object hosts or only subjects:

(65) a. Bill encountered Harry leaving the room.   (subject or object)
b. Bill encountered Harry without leaving the room.   (subject only)[5]

Overall, the facts seem to be that for the most part subject hosts are always possible, whereas object hosts are highly restricted by a number of syntactic and semantic criteria. This suggests that secondary predication with object host is not really the same phenomenon as with subject host, and that it may well be a mistake to combine the two kinds of secondary predication into a single rule as we have done. Rather, one should perhaps have two separate rules to account for them, the rule for subject host being essentially as stated above, but that for object host containing a much more detailed structural description. Again, I leave further investigation of the issue for future research.

What we have accomplished here, though, is an explicit statement of the conceptual structure associated with secondary predication and a preliminary statement of the correspondence rule that relates it to the syntax. Like all the other adjuncts discussed in this chapter, the secondary predicate AP proves to be one argument of a modifying conceptual clause, one or more of whose other arguments are bound to an argument of the main conceptual clause. These kinds of adjuncts, then, form a natural class that contrasts with the adjuncts discussed in chapter 8, all of which involved filling in an implicit argument in the primary structure of the verb.

9.7 Appendix: Control in Gerundive Secondary Predicates

As a side issue, but also as a preliminary step toward a more complete account of control, let us consider briefly how control is established in gerundive secondary predicates like (65a). The problem is this: unlike *happy* and *out of sorts* in (64), the gerundive *leaving the room* has an external argument that is left unfilled. This argument must somehow get bound to the host of the predicate.

There are two different syntactic approaches to this problem. In the approach required in GB Theory for satisfaction of the θ-Criterion (and presumed by various other accounts), *leaving the room* is a clause whose subject is PRO. In the other approach (LFG; Generalized Phrase Structure Grammar; Farmer 1984; Culicover and Wilkins 1984), the VP *leaving the room* is not dominated by S and therefore has no syntactic subject. I will work out a solution for each in turn.

First, suppose that, following the GB Theory approach, the syntactic structure of (65a) is (66). Assume that the gerundive is in V'', so that *Bill* will be host.

(66) [$_S$ Bill [$_{V''}$ [$_{V'}$ encountered Harry] [$_S$ PRO leaving the room]]]

The issue is how PRO is marked coreferential with *Bill*.[6]

In the present approach, we can take the conceptual structure of PRO to be a bound argument ξ, parallel to the structure of reflexive pronouns proposed in section 3.3. Then the conceptual structure of the subordinate clause in (66) is given in (67).

(67) PRO leaving the room
      [$_{Event}$ GO ([ξ], [FROM [IN [ROOM]]])]

The Depictive Predicate Adjunct Rule as stated in (59) or (60) cannot apply to this as it stands, for two reasons: (1) the predicate is a clause rather than an AP; (2) the conceptual structure of the predicate is an Event rather than a Property, so it cannot serve as a location argument of BE$_{Ident}$ in the conceptual structure of the construction as a whole. The first of these problems is easily remedied by generalizing the syntactic part of the rule's structural description to include gerundives as well as APs and PPs. As for the second, there is another semantic field, Circumstantial, in which the second argument of BE *is* an Event rather than a Property. (See *S&C*, section 10.2.) In the Circumstantial field, the meaning of X being located at Y is that X is a participant in the Event or State Y. Thus the appropriate generalization of the adjunct rule is to permit it to introduce a BE$_{Circ}$ rather than a BE$_{Ident}$ just in case the predicate expresses an Event.

Without pursuing the formal niceties of these modifications to the rule, we can see that they would together yield a structure (68) for (65a).

(68) Bill encountered Harry leaving the room.
$$\left[\begin{array}{l} \text{ENCOUNTER ([BILL]}^{\alpha}\text{, [HARRY])} \\ \text{[WITH [BE}_{Circ} \text{ ([}\alpha\text{], [AT [GO ([}\xi\text{],} \\ \qquad\qquad\qquad\qquad\qquad \text{[FROM [IN [ROOM]]])])]])]} \\ \text{Event} \end{array} \right]$$

Here *Bill* is bound to the Theme of BE$_{Circ}$, but it has not yet been connected to the Theme of GO.

However, this second connection follows essentially from the conceptual structure of BE$_{Circ}$. What was just said about the meaning of the Circumstantial field is captured (at least in part) by the following well-formedness condition:

(69) [BE$_{Circ}$ ([X]$^{\alpha}$, [$_{Place}$ AT [$_{Event/State}$ F (... [α] ...)]])]

(69) says that the Theme of BE$_{Circ}$ must bind an argument within the Place, corresponding to the idea that circumstantial location with a State or Event amounts to being a character in that State or Event.

Now consider what happens when this well-formedness condition is imposed on (68), that is, when the full structure of BE$_{Circ}$ is filled in. Just the desired binding relation is added to the structure, yielding (70), in which control is explicit.

(70)
$$\left[\begin{array}{l} \text{ENCOUNTER ([BILL]}^{\alpha}\text{, [HARRY])} \\ \text{[WITH [BE}_{Circ} \text{ ([}\alpha\text{]}^{\beta}\text{, [AT [GO ([}\beta\text{],} \\ \qquad\qquad\qquad\qquad\qquad \text{[FROM [IN [ROOM]]])])]])]} \\ \text{Event} \end{array} \right]$$

Notice that the two binding relations encoded by α and β are independent. This has a useful consequence. Suppose that the gerundive predicate is in V' instead of V'', and that it therefore takes *Harry* as host. Then the adjunct rule assigns the binder α to HARRY instead of BILL. In turn the bound α serves as binder for β, which determines control of the predicate. As a result, control of the gerundive shifts along with the choice of host, because of the chaining of the two binding relations.

Next let us turn to the alternate syntactic analysis, in which the gerundive is *not* a clause with PRO subject. In this case, the syntactic structure of (65a) on the reading with *Bill* as host is (71).

(71) [$_S$ Bill [$_{V''}$ [$_{V'}$ encountered Harry] [$_{VP}$ leaving the room]]]

As it turns out, the only new problem faced by this analysis is how to apply Argument Fusion to the gerundive. The second clause of Argument Fusion (rule (2.13)) says: "If H is a verb, fuse the conceptual structure of the subject into the constituent indexed i in H's LCS." Since there is no subject, this part of Argument Fusion cannot apply. However, suppose we generalize this clause of the rule as in (72).

(72) *Argument Fusion* (external argument clause)
  b. If H is a verb, fuse the conceptual structure of the subject, *if there is one*, into the constituent indexed i in H's LCS. Otherwise, fuse a bindee [ξ] into this position.

The upshot of this rule will be to produce the conceptual structure (67) for the VP *leaving the room*, and everything else will proceed as before. In other words, we have again created in conceptual structure the missing argument that the more standard theory of control expresses in the syntax as PRO— but we have done so without actually invoking any syntactic empty category.

I leave open which syntactic theory of gerundives is correct and how to adapt the latter theory to broader issues of control. In particular, (72) beckons toward a general account of obligatory control in which the complement of *try*, for example, lacks a syntactic subject (along the syntactic lines of LFG and Generalized Phrase Structure Grammar, and following a strongly semantic conception of obligatory control as advocated in, for instance, Jackendoff 1972 and Farkas 1988). Notice that the analyses of obligatory control in section 7.7 can be adapted readily to a bare VP complement treatment under this proposal. I will resist tackling this extremely important and extremely complex issue here (though section 11.8 carries it a little further). I have shown, in any event, that an explicit formal treatment of control in depictive gerundive predicates can be developed with PRO or without it. Thus nothing in the present analysis hangs on the eventual general theory of control.

Chapter 10

Adjuncts That Express Arguments of a
Superordinate Conceptual Clause

The adjuncts discussed in the previous two chapters supplement the existing argument structure of the verb with further arguments. As a result, these adjuncts add to but do not alter the syntactic structure determined by the verb. The constructions to be examined in this chapter are more radical: it turns out that the adjunct rather than the verb determines the syntax of the VP, in violation of the standard correspondences established by Argument Fusion.

10.1 *Babe Ruth Homered His Way into the Hearts of America*

Consider the examples in (1), which illustrate what I will call the *way-construction*.

(1) a. Bill belched his way out of the restaurant.
    b. Harry moaned his way down the road.
    c. Sam joked his way into the meeting.

This construction severely violates the argument structure of the verb. As seen in (2), the verbs in (1) normally cannot appear with NP and PP-complements.

(2) a. *Bill belched (a belch) out of the restaurant.
    b. *Harry moaned (a long serious moan) down the road.
    c. *Sam joked (many jokes) into the meeting.

What licenses this bizarre behavior?

Let us begin by establishing the surface syntax of the *way*-construction. It is useful to contrast it with a superficially similar construction using a measure phrase, shown in (3).

(3) Bill belched all the way/the whole way out of the restaurant.

In the *way*-construction, the material after the verb does not prepose (4a); by contrast, *all the way out of the restaurant* does prepose and therefore must form a constituent (4b).

(4) a. *His way out of the restaurant, Bill belched.
   b. All the way/The whole way out of the restaurant, Bill belched.

An adverb may be inserted after *way* in the *way*-construction, indicating a constituent break (5a); it is impossible in the measure phrase construction (5b).

(5) a. Bill belched his way noisily out of the restaurant
   b. *Bill belched all the way noisily out of the restaurant.

On the other, an adverb may *not* be inserted after the verb in the *way*-construction (6a) but *may* appear after the verb in the measure phrase construction (6b).

(6) a. *Bill belched noisily his way out of the restaurant.
   b. Bill belched noisily all the way out of the restaurant.

This suggests that the constituent structure of the *way*-construction is as given in (7a), where *his way* occupies the position of an ordinary direct object and *out of the restaurant* is a separate PP under VP. By contrast, the measure phrase construction has the structure (7b).

(7) a. Bill [$_{VP}$ belched [$_{NP}$ his way] [$_{PP}$ out of the restaurant]]
   b. Bill [$_{VP}$ belched [$_{?P}$ all the way out of the restaurant]]

Next consider the verbs that appear in the *way*-construction. A vast range of intransitive action verbs are acceptable:

(8) a. We ate our way across the U.S.
   b. Sue whistled her way through the tunnel.
   c. The barrel rolled its way up the alley.

On the other hand, the transitive variants of the verbs in (8) are unacceptable in the *way*-construction, as seen in (9).

(9) a. *We ate hot dogs our way across the U.S.
   b. *Sue whistled a tune her way through the tunnel.
   c. *Bill rolled the barrel its way up the alley.

This syntactic requirement of intransitivity is very strictly observed in the *way*-construction. Consider minimal pairs like (10) and (11): *homer* is synonymous with *hit a home run*, and *fan* in the relevant sense is synonymous with *strike out*. (11) (due to Dick Oehrle) further shows that the verb not only must be intransitive but in fact must have an absolute zero complement.

(10) a. Babe Ruth homered his way into the hearts of America.
   b. *Babe Ruth hit home runs his way into the hearts of America.

(11) a.   Mickey Mantle fanned his way into the Hall of Fame.
   b. *Mickey Mantle struck out his way/struck his way out into the Hall of Fame.

On the other hand, the examples in (12) are unacceptable.

(12) a. *The window opened/broke its way into the room.
   b. *Bill hid/crouched his way into the room.
   c. *Bill slept/fell/blushed his way to New York.

There appear to be two semantic constraints on the choice of verb that together account for the difference between these and the previous cases. The first constraint is that the verb must be capable of being construed as a *process*. By "capable of being construed as a process," I mean that the verb either is inherently a process verb (e.g. *eat, whistle, roll*) or else describes a repeated bounded event (e.g. *belch, joke, homer*). *Open* and *break* in (12a) are nonrepeatable events; *hide* and *crouch* in (12b) are stative or unrepeatable inchoative. Thus these verbs do not satisfy the process constraint.

This constraint still does not account for the unacceptability of (12c), though, since sleeping, falling, and blushing are presumably processes and so should be acceptable. My speculation is that the verb must express a process with some kind of internal structure. Repetition of a bounded action is one such sort of internal structure; rolling and eating, which are inherently processes, also involve internal motion on the part of the actor. On the other hand, sleeping and falling are inherently homogeneous processes and so do not satisfy the constraint. *Blush* is ambiguous: on the most prominent reading it means "maintain a blushing countenance" and is therefore homogeneous. Marginally, though, *Bill blushed for hours* can convey repeated blushing; and on this reading, *Bill blushed his way out of the room* seems to me possible. Note also that the regrettably sexist example *Sue slept her way to the top* implies not just homogeneous snoozing but repeated acts.

I will not try to formalize this constraint here.[1] (A class of cases in which it may not obtain is mentioned in note 2.) The main point is that the choice of verb in the *way*-construction is constrained by both syntactic considerations, as seen in (8)–(11), and semantic considerations, as seen in (12). The semantic factors, which in themselves seem fairly natural, are not reducible in any obvious way to syntactic properties.

Intuitively, what is going on in the *way*-construction can be revealed more clearly by examining its close paraphrases. For example, (13a–f) paraphrase (1a–c) and (8a–c).

(13) a. Bill went out of the restaurant belching.   (= (1a))
   b. Harry went down the road moaning.   (= (1b))

   c. Sam went into the meeting joking. *or*
      Sam got into the meeting by joking. $(= (1c))$
   d. We went across the U.S. eating. *or*
      We got across the U.S. by eating. $(= (8a))$
   e. Sue went through the tunnel whistling. *or*
      Sue got (herself) through the tunnel by whistling. $(= (8b))$
   f. The barrel went up the alley rolling. $(= (8c))$

In these paraphrases, the correspondence between syntactic and conceptual argument structure is much more regular. The main verb of the *way*-construction appears in a subordinate clause, accompanied by its proper complement structure, that is, nothing. The PP of the *way*-construction appears as a Path of the main verb *go* or *get*. The paraphrases thus correspond in a more canonical way to a conceptual structure that contains a subordinate conceptual clause of accompaniment. The conceptual structure of (13a), for instance, is (14).

(14) $\begin{bmatrix} \text{GO ([BILL], [TO [EXTERIOR-OF [RESTAURANT]]])} \\ \text{[WITH [BELCH ([BILL])]]} \end{bmatrix}$

   The paraphrases in (13) suggest that the *way*-construction ought to be regarded as a calque, in which the unexpressed conceptual structure GO is imposed on the conceptual structure of the verb. So, just as the constructions discussed in chapter 9 add a subordinate conceptual clause whose main function is not expressed syntactically, the *way*-construction adds an unexpressed *superordinate* conceptual function, in effect demoting the meaning of the lexical verb to a subordinate accompaniment or means modifier. Here is a first approximation to a correspondence rule with the desired effect:

(15) Way-*Adjunct Rule* (version 1)

   If V corresponds to $\begin{bmatrix} \text{AFF ([X]}_i, \quad) \\ -\text{BOUNDED} \\ \text{Y} \end{bmatrix}_{\text{Event}}$,   (i)

   Then $[_{\text{VP}} \text{V} [_{\text{NP}} \text{NP}_j\text{'s way}] \text{PP}_k]$ may correspond to   (ii)

$$\begin{bmatrix} \text{GO ([}\alpha\text{]}_j, [_{\text{Path}} \quad]_k) \\ \text{AFF ([} \quad]^\alpha_i, \quad) \\ \text{[WITH/BY} \begin{bmatrix} \text{AFF (}\begin{bmatrix} \alpha \\ X \end{bmatrix}, \quad) \\ -\text{BOUNDED} \\ \text{Y} \end{bmatrix}] \end{bmatrix}_{\text{Event}}.$$ (iii)

   Let us see how this rule applies to derive (14) as the conceptual structure of (1a), *Bill belched his way out of the restaurant*. First, *belch* is an action verb, as indicated by the test frame *What Bill did was belch.* Thus it meets the selectional restriction

$$[AFF ([X], \quad)]$$

in line (i) of the rule. Second, *belch* can be construed as a process—the repetition of individual belches. The process requirement is notated here as $-$BOUNDED; a process is an unbounded Event, while accomplishments and achievements are bounded Events (see section 1.6.3 and Jackendoff, in preparation). Finally, Y is simply a variable notating the rest of the verb's meaning. Thus *belch* satisfies the structural description of line (i) of (15).

Line (ii) of rule (15) stipulates a particular syntactic form for the VP, which allows it to apply to (1), (8), (10a), and (11a) but not to (2), (9), (10b), and (11b). Thus the syntactic restrictions on the *way*-construction are explicit in the rule, as in previous adjunct rules.

Since both the syntactic and conceptual parts of the structural description are satisfied by (1a), the VP of (1a) may be placed in correspondence with the conceptual structure of line (iii) of the rule. The coindexing of syntactic and conceptual structures in lines (ii) and (iii) indicates that the reading of the PP *out of the restaurant* satisfies the Path-variable and that the reading of the subject *Bill* satisfies the external argument. (Alternatively, the coindexing could be omitted from the Path-constituent, and the PP-Adjunct Rule (8.37) could match it up with the PP. This is in fact probably the correct treatment, but I will keep everything overly explicit for now.) So far, then, the following can be derived:

$$(16) \quad \begin{bmatrix} \text{GO } ([\alpha]_j, [_{\text{Path}} \text{ TO [EXTERIOR-OF [RESTAURANT]]}]_k) \\ \text{AFF } ([\text{BILL}]^{\alpha}{}_i, \quad) \\ \\ \text{[WITH/BY } \begin{bmatrix} \text{AFF } (\begin{bmatrix} \alpha \\ X \end{bmatrix}, \quad) \\ -\text{BOUNDED} \\ \text{BELCH} \end{bmatrix}] \\ _{\text{Event}} \end{bmatrix}$$

There remains the treatment of *his* in (1a). In (16), the binding indicated by the α's stipulates that the Actor and Theme of the superordinate Event and the Actor of the subordinate Event are the same individual; that is, Bill is both belching and going out of the restaurant. However, notice also that the Theme of GO is coindexed *j* with the possessive NP in line (ii). The only way to simultaneously satisfy both this coindexing and the binding to the Actor is to use a bound pronoun *his* in the syntax. Thus the need for both binding and coindexing rules out examples like **Bill belched Harry's way into the room.* (This solution is also applicable in idioms with bound pronouns such as *lose one's cool* and *crane one's neck*, as well as in those with obligatory reflexives such as *perjure oneself* and *behave oneself*. It parallels the treatment of obligatory control in section 7.7, where simultaneous coindexing and binding forced an NP subject to be PRO.)

Rule (15) as stated permits either WITH or BY to be chosen freely as the appropriate subordinating function. The choice actually appears to be principled. Only some of the sentences in (1) and (8) permit the *by* paraphrase, as seen in (13). The rest of the *by* paraphrases are odd. Consider for instance ?*Bill got out of the restaurant by belching*. This sentence, if acceptable, suggests that Bill deliberately belched, as a trick to escape from the restaurant. And under such odd circumstances, (1a) can be similarly interpreted. My guess is that the means (or *get . . . by*) interpretation is appropriate just in case the lexical verb is taken as volitional, and otherwise the accompaniment (*go . . . ing*) interpretation is chosen. Belching, moaning, and (for a barrel) rolling are nonvolitional, so only the accompaniment reading is available. By contrast, joking, eating, and whistling are volitional, so either reading is possible. I do not at the moment have any formalization to offer for this systematic variation. However, it suggests that WITH and BY are conceptually closely related and that the choice between them in the *way*-construction is conditioned by the presence or absence of the feature [vol] in

AFF ([X],   ).[2]

One oddity of the *way*-construction is its profound incompatibility with the passive:

(17) *His way was belched out of the restaurant by Bill.

Within the present theory (sections 4.3, 8.8), constructing a passive requires (1) deleting the index i that marks the external argument, so that subject position is not filled and not θ-marked; and (2) moving into subject position either another argument or (in the case of "Exceptional Case Marking" or "Object Raising" verbs) an NP within a sentential argument. *Belch* and the other verbs in (1) and (8) have no internal arguments that can be moved into subject position; nor do they have sentential arguments from which a movable NP can be extracted. In particular, *his way* is not an argument of *belch* but rather only a phrase that happens to be in object position. It parallels the nonobject *the bucket* in the idiom *kick the bucket*, which likewise cannot undergo passive. In addition, the construction is subject to the constraint on passivizing bound pronouns that prohibits *His teeth were gnashed (by Bill).*[3] Hence (17) violates two independent constraints on the passive.

Next notice that in rule (15) the noun *way* apparently drops out of the interpretation of the sentence: it seems to be treated simply as a meaningless syntactic marker for the *way*-construction. This cannot be the whole story, though, since one can insert adjectival modifiers on *way*:

(18) a. Bill belched his miserable way out of the restaurant.
   b. Sam joked his insidious way into the meeting.
   c. The barrel rolled its ponderous way up the alley.

In the paraphrases, these adjectives turn up as manner adverbs, as in (19), or as absolutives, as in (20).

(19) a. Bill went miserably out of the restaurant, belching.
   b. Sam insidiously got into the meeting by joking.
   c. The barrel went ponderously up the alley, rolling.

(20) a. Bill, miserable, went out of the restaurant belching.
   b. Sam, insidious (as ever), got into the meeting by joking.
   c. The barrel, ponderous (as an elephant), went up the alley rolling.[4]

I will not pursue the modifications necessary to incorporate these adjectives into rule (15) (especially since I have no conceptual structure analysis of the absolutive paraphrases). The important thing to notice, though, is that there is an actual inversion of head-subordinate relations. The adjective that modifies *way* is in a syntactically fairly subordinate position, yet it corresponds conceptually to a modifier of the superordinate conceptual Event. This then confirms our sense that the *way*-construction violates the otherwise rock-solid correspondence of subordination relations in syntactic and conceptual structure.

A final wrinkle in the *way*-construction is that a few verbs occur idiomatically in it. The ones I have encountered are *wend* and *worm*, which occur only in idiomatic *way*-constructions, plus *thread*, *make*, and *work*, which have special meanings in the *way*-construction. What makes these cases special is that they do not have paraphrases like (13):

(21) a. Bill wended/wormed/threaded/made/worked his way down the narrow alley.
   b. *Bill went down the narrow alley wending/worming/threading/ making/working.
   c. *Bill got down the narrow alley by wending/worming/threading/ making/working.

Rather, each verb adds a manner to the basic meaning of the *way*-construction: *wend one's way* means roughly "go in a leisurely and/or irregular manner," *worm one's way* means "go in a wormlike fashion," *thread one's way* means "go along a twisted path among obstacles," *make one's way* means "go in a deliberate and/or careful fashion," and *work one's way* means "go in a deliberate and/or effortful fashion."[5]

10.2 Alternative Approaches to the *Way*-Construction

The *way*-construction is a fairly outrageous example of mismatch between syntactic and conceptual structure, in three respects. (1) The relative embedding of syntactic and conceptual constituents is altogether different. In particular, the main verb of the sentence appears as a subordinate conceptual Event. (2) The lexical verb does not have a Path argument, yet a Path-PP is licensed. Moreover, *NP's way* in direct object position is not licensed by the verb, nor does it express an argument. (3) The functions GO and AFF in the main conceptual clause are not expressed by any lexical item in the sentence (except perhaps *way*).

In the last section, the properties of the *way*-construction were attributed to the construction-specific correspondence rule (15) that incorporates characteristics (1)–(3). Let us now step back a little and ask about other possible accounts of the mismatch.

Suppose one wished to adopt the Syntactic Strategy of section 8.1 to account for this construction: keep the match of conceptual structure to underlying syntax simple, preserve the θ-Criterion, and localize the mismatch in a mapping from underlying to surface structure. In such an approach, the *way*-construction would be the result of some sort of verb-raising transformation, with derivations along the lines of (22).

(22) [$_S$ Bill V into the restaurant [$_S$ PRO belch]] $\Rightarrow$
     [Bill belch his way into the restaurant]

(22) has an underlying syntactic structure that pretty well matches the manner paraphrases; through syntactic manipulation, it achieves the observed surface form. This treatment has the flavor of 1960s "abstract syntax" derivations (recall the pre–generative semantics treatment of inchoative and causative in Lakoff 1970, for example). Unfortunately, the sorts of arguments advanced in the 1960s against such derivations are just as appropriate now as then.

A first problem is that the derivation must not only raise the verb but also introduce *his way* (and somehow get its adjectival modifiers from some other position). Second, the movement rule has to be sensitive not only to the lower verb's being intransitive—which seems reasonable—but also to its being an action verb that can be construed as an internally articulated process—which does not seem reasonable in a theory of autonomous syntax. That is, the movement rule (or other autonomous syntactic principles) must prohibit derivations like those in (23).

(23) a.   [Bill V out of the room [PRO blush]] $\nRightarrow$
         *Bill blushed his way out of the room.
     b.   [Bill had to V through the low opening [PRO crouch]] $\nRightarrow$
         *Bill had to crouch his way through the low opening.

Third, the verbs *wend* and *worm*, and the special senses of *thread* and *make*, and *work* must be marked as obligatorily undergoing verb raising. This is doubly problematic, in that their interpretation as manner of motion rather than accompanying action does not follow from the proposed underlying structure.

Fourth, what is the verb indicated by *V* in (22)? It cannot just be an empty verb, since it must license the PP and produce the interpretation GO in conceptual structure. However, it can't always be the lexical verb *go*, because sometimes *get* is appropriate, as seen in (13). And in certain cases of "metaphorical" movement such as (24a) (= (10a)), neither *go* nor *get* is appropriate; instead the motion verb *enter* turns up as fairly acceptable.

(24) a.   Babe Ruth homered his way into the hearts of America.
     b.   ?*Babe Ruth went into the hearts of America homering.
     c.   ?*Babe Ruth got into the hearts of America (by) homering.
     d.   Babe Ruth entered (into) the hearts of America (by) homering.

Alternatively, a number of these difficulties might be solved by assuming (1) that the idioms with *worm*, *wend*, *thread*, *make*, and *work* are base-generated, (2) that V in (22) is *make one's way*, and (3) that the lower verb replaces *make*. (This possibility was suggested by J.-R. Vergnaud.) Still, this does not account for the semantic constraints seen in (23); these sentences should be acceptable, by derivations seen in (25a,b). Conversely, the putative underlying form for (8c) is out, so there is a problem with the derivation in (25c).

(25) a.   Bill made his way out of the room blushing $\nRightarrow$
          *Bill blushed his way out of the room.   (= (23a))
     b.   Bill had to make his way through the low opening crouching $\nRightarrow$
          *Bill had to crouch his way through the low opening.   (= (23b))
     c.   ??The barrel made its way up the alley rolling $\nRightarrow$
          The barrel rolled its way up the alley.   (= (8c))

In short, although it might be possible to devise a technically adequate solution along these lines, a syntactic approach to the *way*-construction does not on the face of it look too promising. In particular, because of the construction's complex mixture of syntactic and semantic properties, no solution that relies on autonomous syntax alone would appear to have the right characteristics.

Next, consider the possibility of using the Lexical Rule Strategy of section 8.1: suppose that the *way*-construction is due to a lexical rule that converts intransitive action verbs such as *belch* into idioms such as *belch one's way*. (26) might be an appropriate statement.

(26) Way-*Adjunct Rule* (version 2: word or idiom formation)

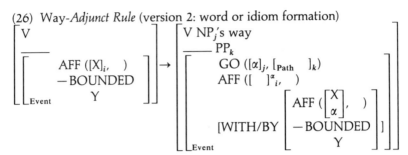

Under this approach, then, *belch NP's way* will be treated as a derived lexical item. It will be inserted into syntactic structure in exactly the same way as *crane NP's neck*, except that it will license a PP-complement. On this view, the creation of *V one's way* idioms from intransitive action verbs is about as productive as the creation of passive participles from transitive verbs; and *wend/worm/thread/make/work one's way* are complex lexical items that have no lexical base, rather like the passive participles *born* and *rumored*. The inability of the *way*-construction to undergo passive follows from more general constraints on passivizing idioms.

The interpretation of *way*-idioms is specified by lexical rule (26): it is identical to the conceptual structure specified by rule (15) in the earlier formulation. The reading of the base verb is substituted for

[AFF ([X],   ), −BOUNDED, Y];

the possessive NP is bound to the external argument, so it must be a pronoun. From this point, everything proceeds in normal fashion, using Argument Fusion.

At least some of the semantic subtleties of the *way*-construction are already accounted for in (26). In particular, the constancy of the function GO—independent of its particular lexical expression as *go*, *get*, or *enter* in the paraphrases—is encoded straightforwardly in (26). Likewise, the requirement that the base verb be an Action and process verb is encoded as the restriction to base verbs of the form

[AFF ([X],   ), −BOUNDED].

Further selectional restrictions on the base verb, if any, can be added to Y in the rule. Finally, the irregular interpretations of the purely idiomatic cases with verbs like *wend* follow from the fact that there is no base verb. These cases contain the GO-function found on the right-hand side of the rule but substitute an unpredictable manner modifier for the accompaniment/means modifier.

There remains the question of how the adjectives modifying *way* in (18) are interpreted. Actually, it looks as though a parallel problem arises with adjectives modifying other idiomatic nonargument NPs. For instance, *take unfair advantage of* NP approximately paraphrases *unfairly take advantage of* NP, so the adjective conceptually functions as a manner adverb on the sentence. As promised, I will not offer a solution to this aspect of the construction but will content myself with reducing it to a previously unsolved problem. What is important is that an approach using a lexical rule permits the case of (18) to fall in with parallel problems about other idioms.

Next let us return to the correspondence rule approach to the *way*-construction offered in the previous section, rule (15). This account local-izes the complexity of the construction in an extralexical correspondence rule. Here verbs are not "converted into idioms" prior to lexical insertion. Rather, an intransitive action verb is inserted into a VP of the form [V-NP's way-PP], and it and its complements are all licensed and interpreted "on the fly" by the correspondence rule. That is, rule (15), like the adjunct rules of the previous two chapters, is an alternative available for interpreting a VP, in place of normal Argument Fusion.

Rule (15) accounts for semantic properties of the *way*-construction in essentially the same way as the lexical rule (26). In particular, since the two rules contain the elements GO, AFF, and −BOUNDED in identical configurations, the accounts of these aspects of interpretation are the same. The previous section also dealt with the prohibition the construction places on the passive.

What this approach leaves somewhat unclear is the status of the idioms with verbs like *wend* and the interpretation of pre-*way* adjectives. In order to capture these cases a little better within this approach, it is useful to rethink the formalism for (15). In a sense, the *way*-construction can be thought of as a kind of "constructional idiom," a specialized syntactic form with an idiomatic meaning, marked by the noun *way*. To come closer to this fashion of understanding the construction, let us restate rule (15) as (27).

(27) Way-*Adjunct Rule* (version 3: constructional idiom)
      $[_{\text{VP}} V_h [_{\text{NP}} \text{NP}_j\text{'s way}] \text{PP}_k]$ may correspond to
$$
\left[
\begin{array}{l}
\text{GO}\,([\alpha]_j,\,[_{\text{Path}}\quad]_k) \\
\text{AFF}\,([\quad]^\alpha_i,\,) \\
[\text{WITH/BY}\,\begin{bmatrix}\text{AFF}\,([\alpha],\,) \\ -\text{BOUNDED}\end{bmatrix}_h]
\end{array}
\right]_{\text{Event}}.
$$

This version is a notational variant of (15), differing only in the way the conditions on the base verb are expressed. In (15), the conditions are expressed by line (i) in the structural description; in (27), they are expressed by means of a coindexing between the head verb in the syntax and the position it fills in conceptual structure, parallel to the coindexing of complements. (The index h is used to suggest "head.") The conventions on coindexing are as usual:

[AFF ([α],   ), − BOUNDED]

is fused with the reading of the verb, and hence it behaves as a selectional restriction on possible verbs participating in the construction.[6]

But now notice how close (27) is to the form of a lexical entry. It is a matching of partial syntactic and conceptual structures, in which corresponding substructures are identified by coindexing. The main difference between this and other lexical entries we have examined is the coindexing on the head: whereas other (normal) entries specify the syntactic head and leave the complements open, this one specifies one of the complements and leaves the head open.

Suppose then that we think of (27) as some odd kind of lexical item. (It is still a correspondence rule rather than a word formation rule, since, as stressed at the outset, *all* lexical items are correspondence rules.) This lexical item takes four conceptual arguments, indexed i, j, k, and h. The first of these is the external argument; the next two are expressed syntactically as the possessive NP and the PP respectively; the fourth is the verb of the sentence. The idea, then, is that in the *way*-construction, lexical item (27) rather than the verb functions as the conceptual head of the VP. (The verb however is still the *syntactic* head.) With appropriate caveats on the notion of "head," then, (27) can be thought of as preserving the Linking Condition (or Neo-θ-Criterion, (3.12)), albeit in a somewhat strange fashion.

Returning to the adjectives modifying *way*, it is now not so surprising that syntactic modifiers of *way* turn up as modifiers of the superordinate conceptual expression. Since (27) is conceptually the head of its VP, any of its direct modifiers should be modifiers of the superordinate Event, whether they are syntactically embedded or not. That is, the relative inversion of syntactic and conceptual embeddinrg in (27) should have the effect of carrying along the relative position of modifiers as well. Thus, although this account of the *way*-construction does not solve the problems posed by (18)−(20) either, it at least points to the possibility of a principled approach: we have an inkling of why the facts should be as they are.

Finally, consider again the verbs like *wend* that occur idiomatically in the *way*-construction. In this approach, they appear to be "cranberry morphemes." *Wend NP's way*, for example, can be regarded as a compound, the first of whose elements (*wend*) appears only in this compound, and whose interpretation incorporates the meaning of its second element (*V NP's way*) plus an idiosyncratic contribution. This approach to the *way*-construction, then, also has a comfortable niche for the idiomatic cases.

We have now considered four approaches to the syntax-semantics mismatch in the *way*-construction. The Syntactic Strategy (22) localizes the mismatch in the syntactic derivation from underlying to surface structure; this does not appear feasible. By contrast, the Lexical Rule Strategy (26)—treating the construction as due to a word or idiom formation rule—and both versions of the Correspondence Rule Strategy—localizing the mismatch in either an extralexical (15) or a lexical (27) correspondence rule—seem promising. At the moment I have little basis for deciding among the latter three approaches. The last of them, as the most unusual approach, strikes my fancy, although it raises complex problems concerning the proper definition of "head." In particular, how deeply embedded an inversion of headedness can be tolerated in a quasi-lexical entry such as (27)? (This question appears to be a counterpart to the issue of subjacency in syntactic movement, especially head-to-head movement, and I suspect it has a similar localistic answer.)[7]

To decide among the remaining three approaches and to refine them further, we must ask what natural class of linguistic phenomena the *way*-construction belongs to. By investigating a class of such constructions rather than a single example, we should be able to hone the parameters in Universal Grammar that license this sort of syntax-semantics mismatch. The rest of this chapter deals with two other constructions that appear to be of the same type.

10.3 *Willy Jumped into Harriet's Arms*

Section 5.2 introduced a single-argument conceptual function MOVE that encodes simple intransitive "manner-of-motion" verbs such as *wiggle, dance, spin, bounce,* and *jump.* These verbs need not imply that their subjects have traversed a Path:

(28) Willy wiggled/danced/spun/bounced/jumped for hours, without ever leaving the same spot.

However, they can occur with Path-expressions—in English but not in Spanish or Japanese:

(29) Willy wiggled/danced/spun/bounced/jumped into Harriet's arms.

A good paraphrase of (29) in English (and essentially the only way to express (29) in Spanish) is to use the verb *go* or *get* plus a gerundive means or accompaniment phrase:

(30) Willy went/got into Harriet's arms (by) wiggling/dancing/spinning/ bouncing/jumping.

The similarity of this to the *way*-construction suggests that a parallel adjunct rule is at work. Here is a version of the rule in the format of (15):

(31) *GO-Adjunct Rule* (version 1)

   If V corresponds to $\begin{bmatrix} \text{MOVE} ([\quad]_i) \\ Y \end{bmatrix}$,

   then [$_{VP}$ V...PP] may correspond to

   $$\begin{bmatrix} \text{GO} ([\alpha], [_{\text{Path}} \quad]) \\ \text{AFF} ([\quad]^{\alpha}_{i,} \quad) \\ [\text{WITH/BY} \begin{bmatrix} \text{MOVE} ([\alpha]) \\ Y \end{bmatrix}_1] \end{bmatrix}.$$

Alternatively, the rule can be stated in a form parallel to (27):

(32) *GO-Adjunct Rule* (version 2)

   [$_{VP}$ V$_h$...PP] may correspond to

   $$\begin{bmatrix} \text{GO} ([\alpha], [_{\text{Path}} \quad]) \\ \text{AFF} ([\quad]^{\alpha}_{i,} \quad) \\ [\text{WITH/BY} [\text{MOVE} ([\alpha])]_h] \end{bmatrix}$$

As in the case of the *Way*-Adjunct Rule, the choice of WITH or BY appears to be a function of the volitionality of MOVE. As suggested (but not implemented) for the *Way*-Adjunct Rule, the PP is not coindexed with the Path; the PP-Adjunct Rule (8.37) independently takes care of it.

(31)/(32), then, is an adjunct rule that adds a superordinate conceptual function to the structure of the sentence *without* using an overt grammatical marker such as *way*. The grammatical clue for the use of this rule in a sentence is a main verb of the MOVE class, which permits only a Theme argument, followed by a PP of Path. The rule creates a conceptual argument structure into which the PP argument can be fused, subordinating the MOVE-function to a modifying conceptual clause.

Interestingly, the verbs to which (31)/(32) applies are a subset of those to which (15)/(27) applies, so *his way* can be inserted into (29) without affecting grammaticality:

(33) Willy wiggled/danced/spun/bounced/jumped his way into Harriet's arms.

Notice, however, that the interpretations are not identical: *jump his way into Harriet's arms* suggests a series of jumps, whereas *jump into Harriet's arms* can consist of a single jump. The reason for this is that the *way*-construction requires the modifying Event to be a process (that is, −BOUNDED). As a result, *jump* in (33) must be interpreted as repeated jumps, just as in *jump for hours*. By contrast, the GO-adjunct construction lacks this restriction, so *jump into Harriet's arms* can be interpreted with the usual bounded reading of a single jump.

On the other hand, not all the verbs to which (15)/(27) applies are cases of MOVE, and hence sentences like (34) are ungrammatical.

(34) *Bill belched/sang/whistled/joked/moaned/ate right out of the restaurant.

Thus the two constructions overlap only partially in their choice of possible verbs and in their interpretations.

According to this account, the reason that sentences like (29) are grammatical in English but not in Spanish or Japanese is that the latter languages lack a counterpart of rule (31)/(32). The claim is that languages may differ not only in their syntactic patterns but also in their correspondence rules—their ways of mapping from syntax to conceptual structure. In the present case, Spanish has the syntactic pattern Verb + PP, but this pattern cannot be mapped into a conceptual structure if the verb is a MOVE-verb, since the language has no way to license the PP.

Is this a surprising conclusion? We certainly would not expect all languages to have a *way*-construction, which seems to be a rather peculiar idiomatic construction of English (though perhaps my imagination is deficient here). The GO-Adjunct Rule, though, is formally little different from the *Way*-Adjunct Rule, other than lacking a specific grammatical morpheme to mark the construction. So there seems no immediate reason to expect something like (31)/(32) necessarily to be more universal than something like (15)/(27).

On the other hand, if the GO-Adjunct Rule is not universal, it has to be learnable on the basis of universal principles and primary linguistic evidence. Is this plausible? Again consider the *Way*-Adjunct Rule: to the extent that this must be learnable, so must the GO-Adjunct Rule, inasmuch as they differ so little. In particular, if the GO-adjunct construction, like the *way*-adjunct construction, is regarded as a "constructional idiom," then learning it ought to be more like learning a new idiom than like learning some drastically different sort of rule. It only devolves on Universal Grammar to include a possible class of such idioms.

10.4   Charlie Laughed Himself Silly

Another construction of this class that has been noted in the literature (e.g. Rothstein 1983; Simpson 1983; Carrier and Randall, forthcoming) is *resultative predication*.[8] This construction superficially resembles the depictive predication construction discussed in section 9.6, in that there is an AP or PP at the end of the VP that is not subcategorized by the verb. However, as mentioned in section 9.6, the meanings of the two constructions differ: compare the most salient readings of (35a) and (35b).

(35) a. Charlie chewed the meat raw.   (depictive predication, object host)
    b. Charlie chewed his knuckles raw.   (resultative predication)

In depictive predication such as (35a), the meat *is* raw as Charlie chews it; in resultative predication such as (35b), Charlie's knuckles *become* raw as a result of his chewing them.

Another difference between depictive and resultative predication is that in the latter the direct object is always host of the predication; the subject can never be. For example, (36a) has a depictive reading in which Charlie ate the hot dogs while (or even though) he *was* full. But it cannot be understood as a resultative, in which Charlie *became* full as a result of eating the hot dogs, even if such a reading is pragmatically more plausible than the depictive reading. Similarly, if subject hosts were possible, (36b) would have a pragmatically plausible reading in which Amy and Beth went into a torpor from watching TV; but the sentence is ungrammatical. (However, see the next section for *intransitive* resultatives with subject host.)

(36) a. Charlie ate the hot dogs full.
    b. *Amy and Beth watched TV into a torpor.

Exploring the range of verbs that can enter into this construction, we discover that no matter what the subcategorization of the verb, the VP in the resultative construction has a fixed syntactic form: V-NP-AP/PP. (37) shows the most frequently cited case, in which the verb is transitive. ("Base forms" are shown in parentheses.)

(37) a. The gardener watered the tulips flat.
      (The gardener watered the tulips.)
    b. The machinist filed his chisels sharp.
      (The machinist filed his chisels.)
    c. The potter baked the clay hard.
      (The potter baked the clay.)
    d. The horses dragged the logs smooth.
      (The horses dragged the logs.)
    e. The cook scrubbed the pots shiny.
      (The cook scrubbed the pots.)
    f. Charlie cooked the food black.
      (Charlie cooked the food.)

In (38), the direct object of the resultative cannot be the object of the "base verb," but it may appear as an oblique complement in the "base form."

(38) a. Harry hammered/pounded the metal flat.
      (Harry hammered/pounded $\left\{ \begin{array}{l} \text{?the metal.} \\ \text{on the metal.} \end{array} \right\}$)

b. Fred cooked the stove black.

(Fred cooked $\left\{\begin{array}{l}\text{*the stove.}\\ \text{on the stove.}\end{array}\right\}$)

c. The professor talked us into a stupor.

(The professor talked $\left\{\begin{array}{l}\text{*us.}\\ \text{to us.}\end{array}\right\}$)

d. His friends laughed Bill out of town.

(His friends laughed $\left\{\begin{array}{l}\text{*Bill.}\\ \text{at Bill.}\end{array}\right\}$)

e. Bill shaved his razor dull.

(Bill shaved $\left\{\begin{array}{l}\text{*his razor.}\\ \text{with his razor.}\end{array}\right\}$)

In (39), the "base verb" is intransitive, and the object of the resultative is a reflexive or a body part.

(39) a. Charlie laughed himself silly/sick/into a stupor.
    (Charlie laughed (*himself).)
  b. Veronica sang herself crazy.
    (Veronica sang (*herself).)
  c. Amy walked her feet to pieces.
    (Amy walked (*her feet).)
    (or Amy walked on her feet.)
  d. Beth chewed her gums sore.
    (Beth chewed (*her gums).)
    (or Beth chewed with her gums.)

In (40), the base verb is intransitive, and the object of the resultative is an NP noncoreferential with the subject. (I find only (40a) reasonably acceptable, and the rest marginal. Carrier and Randall, however, accept them all, and I have encountered one other speaker who concurs with their judgments.)

(40) a. ?The rooster crowed the children awake.
    (The rooster crowed (??to/at the children).)
  b. ??The boxers fought their coaches into an anxious state.
    (on the desired reading: The boxers fought (*their coaches).)
    (possibly: The boxers fought for their coaches.)
  c. ?*In the movie's longest love scene, Troilus and Cressida kiss most audiences squirmy.
    (on the desired reading: Troilus and Cressida kiss (*most audiences).)
  d. ??John washed the facecloth dirty.
    (on the desired reading: John washed (*the facecloth).)
    (possibly: John washed with the facecloth.)

The fixed syntax of this construction suggests that, even in the transitive cases in (37), the direct object as well as the predicate AP is actually an adjunct—not part of the verb's argument structure.[9]

Four issues arise in accounting for the resultative construction: (1) What is its conceptual structure? (2) What is the rule that licenses the construction? In particular, is it a lexical rule or an extralexical rule? (3) What is the relation between the resulative construction and various verbs and idioms that apparently have the same basic conceptual structure? (4) How can various constraints on the construction be incorporated naturally into the analysis? I take up these issues in turn, in this section and the next.

The most consistent paraphrases of (37)–(40) are much like those of the adjunct constructions in the previous three sections: the main verb is causative *make* or *get*, and the verb of the original sentence appears in a means clause. (41) gives the paraphrases for the first examples in each of (37)–(40).

(41) a. The gardener made the tulips flat by watering them.
     b. Harry made the metal flat by pounding/hammering (on) it.
     c. Charlie made himself silly/sick by laughing.
        Charlie got himself into a stupor by laughing.
     d. The rooster got the children awake by crowing.

The choice between *make* and *get* here appears to be determined on syntactic grounds: *make* is best when the predicate is an AP, and *get* when it is a PP. The meaning in either case has one of the forms in (42), where F ([X]) is the reading of the verb in the means clause. (The next section will take up an alternative structure proposed by Dowty (1979) and defended by Carrier and Randall.)

(42) a. $\begin{bmatrix} \text{CAUSE ([X], [GO ([Y], [TO [Z]])])} \\ \text{[BY [F ([X])]]} \end{bmatrix}$
     b. $\begin{bmatrix} \text{CAUSE ([X], [INCH [BE ([Y], [AT [Z]])])])} \\ \text{[BY [F ([X])]]} \end{bmatrix}$

The causative of GO (42a) appears to be more appropriate for the paraphrases with *get*, where the Path-function is always TO or one of its elaborations. The causative of INCH BE (42b) appears to be more appropriate for the paraphrases with *make*, since *make* was argued in section 6.4 to be an INCH BE-verb (though with some hesitation).

Following the strategy adopted for the *way*- and GO-adjuncts, we will take the syntactic structure of the paraphrases as indicative of the organization of the conceptual structure. This conceptual structure will be related to the surface syntax by a rule parallel to the *Way*- and GO-Adjunct Rules.[10] For a first approximation, I will deal with the AP case only and assume the causative inchoative structure (42b). (43a) is a statement in the format of (15) and (31); (43b) is in the format of (27) and (32).

(43) a. *Resultative Adjunct Rule* (version 1: extralexical rule)

If V corresponds to $\begin{bmatrix} \text{AFF } ([X]_i, \ldots) \\ W \end{bmatrix}$,

NP corresponds to [Y],
and AP corresponds to [Z],

Then [$_{VP}$ V NP AP] may correspond to

$$\begin{bmatrix} \text{CAUSE } ([\alpha], [\text{INCH } [\text{BE}_{\text{Ident}} ([\beta], [\text{AT } [Z]])]]) \\ \text{AFF}^- ([\quad]^\alpha_i, [Y]^\beta) \\ [\text{BY} \begin{bmatrix} \text{AFF } (\begin{bmatrix} \alpha \\ X \end{bmatrix}, \ldots) \\ W \end{bmatrix}] \end{bmatrix}.$$

b. *Resultative Adjunct Rule* (version 2: constructional idiom)
[$_{VP}$ V$_h$ NP$_j$ AP$_k$] may correspond to

$$\begin{bmatrix} \text{CAUSE } ([\alpha], [\text{INCH } [\text{BE}_{\text{Ident}} ([\beta], [\text{AT } [\quad]_k])]]) \\ \text{AFF}^- ([\quad]^\alpha_i, [\quad]^\beta_j) \\ [\text{BY } [\text{AFF } ([\alpha], \ldots)]_h] \end{bmatrix}.$$

This rule creates a structure like (42b) from a main verb followed by an NP and an AP. The fact that the construction has a fixed syntax follows from the structural description of the rule, which like the *Way*-Adjunct Rule rigidly prescribes the VP's syntactic form.

Notice how the notation used in (43b) really comes into its own in stating this rule: the correspondence of the direct object with the Patient and the AP with the reference object follows the standard conventions for coindexing in lexical entries. That is, this version of the rule captures the fact that a verb in the resultative construction behaves exactly like an ordinary causative inchoative verb with respect to the positions of the Agent, Theme, and reference object. In effect, what is being licensed by this rule is again a calque: a verb that is not a causative inchoative is being jammed into the syntactic frame for causatives, with the result that the lexical meaning of the verb is combined with the "constructional meaning."

What happens to the arguments of the lexical verb, though? In (43), the Actor of the lexical verb is bound to the Actor of the causative. However, the rule says nothing about other arguments of the verb. This might be fine for intransitive cases like (39) and (40), where the verb has no arguments other than the subject, but it does not produce the correct interpretation for sentences where the lexical verb has further arguments. For example, in (37a), the rule as it stands produces a reading something like "The gardener made the tulips flat by watering (something)"; in (38a), it yields something like "Harry made the metal flat by hammering ((on) something)." That is, the rule does not tell us enough about the argument structure of the means clause—it does not say, as it should, "...by watering *the tulips*" and "...by hammering (on) *the metal*." The rule must therefore be elaborated, to bind the Patient of the main conceptual clause to some role in the means clause. What is this role?

It appears to me that the proper role is Patient. Notice that all the direct objects in (37)–(38) can be construed as Patients of their respective "base forms," as shown by the usual pseudocleft test for Patient:

(44) a. What the gardener did to the tulips was water them.
   b. What the machinist did to his chisels was file them.
   c. What the potter did to the clay was bake it.
   d. What the horses did to the logs was drag them.
   e. What the cook did to the pots was scrub them.
   f. What Charlie did to the food was cook it.

(45) a. What Harry did to the metal was hammer/pound (on) it.
   b. What Fred did to the stove was cook on it.
   c. What the professor did to us was talk to us.
   d. What Bill's friends did to him was laugh at him.
   e. What Bill did to his razor was shave with it.

In (45b–e), the Patients are probably not "grammatical Patients"—that is, Patienthood is not licensed by the verb itself. Rather, these NPs are Patients by virtue of discourse or pragmatics: a story is generated in which the Actor somehow adversely affects the Patient (see note 1 to chapter 7). Evidently, then, either grammatical or discourse Patienthood in the means clause is acceptable for a resultative.

In cases where Patienthood in the means clause is less plausible, the resultative is less plausible as well. (46) presents a range of cases less acceptable than (44)–(45), comparing the resultative construction to the pseudocleft test for Patienthood.

(46) a. ?The rooster crowed the children awake.   (=(40a))
         ??What the rooster did to the children was crow.
   b. ??The boxers fought their coaches into an anxious state. (=(40b))
         ??What the boxers did to their coaches was fight.
   c. ?*...Troilus and Cressida kiss most audiences squirmy.   (=(40c))
         ?*What Troilus and Cressida did to their audiences was kiss.
   d. ??John washed the facecloth dirty.   (=(40d))
         ?What John did to the facecloth was wash with it.
   e. *Max received the letter flat.   (*on resultative reading)
         *What Max did to the letter was receive it.

f. ?*Simmy slept the bed lumpy.

   ?What Simmy did to the bed was sleep on it.

g. ?Fred read the newspaper to tatters.

   ??What Fred did to the newspaper was read it.

h. ?Bob belched his mother crazy.

   ?What Bob did to his mother was belch (a lot).

i. *Harry liked Betty to desperation.

   *What Harry did to Betty was like her.

In short, the acceptability of the resultative construction correlates with the possibility of Patienthood in the means clause. (For speakers such as Carrier and Randall who are more liberal about resultatives, this condition is evidently relaxed.)

The main exception to this generalization is the reflexive resultative, where the person picked out by the reflexive need not also be Patient in the means clause:

(47) a. Charlie laughed himself silly. $(=(39a))$

         *What Charlie did to himself was laugh.

     b. Veronica sang herself crazy. $(=(39b))$

         *What Veronica did to herself was sing.

As a result, the reflexive resultative allows a somewhat freer choice of verbs than the nonreflexive version.

The overall condition on argument structure is therefore evidently disjunctive: either (1) the direct object of the resultative is construed as Patient of the means clause or (2) it is reflexive. (48) is a version of the rule that expresses this disjunction by using the disjunctive curly brackets notation. I state it only in terms of the latter of our two notations; the other alternative becomes cumbersome, and it is unclear how to adapt the curly brackets to it.

(48) *Resultative Adjunct Rule* (version 3: constructional idiom)

   $[_{\text{VP}} \, V_h \, \text{NP}_j \, \text{AP}_k]$ may correspond to

   $$\left[\begin{array}{l} \text{CAUSE} \, ([\alpha], \, [\text{INCH} \, [\text{BE}_{\text{Ident}} \, ([\beta], \, [\text{AT} \, [\quad]_k])]]) \\ \text{AFF}^- \, ([\quad]^\alpha_i, \, [\{\alpha\}]^\beta_j) \\ [\text{BY} \, [\text{AFF}^- \, ([\alpha], \, \{[\beta]\})]_h] \end{array} \right].$$

What does this rule say? The entire construction is mapped into a causative inchoative, whose Patient and Theme is the direct object and whose reference object is the predicate AP. The verb of the construction is mapped into a subordinate means constituent; the Actor of the main conceptual clause and the Actor of the lexical verb are jointly coindexed with the subject.

The tricky part is in the binding of α and β. There are two alternatives, encoded in the two expressions within curly brackets. (49) shows them separately.

(49) a.
$$\begin{bmatrix} \text{CAUSE} ([\alpha], [\text{INCH} [\text{BE}_{\text{Ident}} ([\beta], [\text{AT} [\quad]_k])]]) \\ \text{AFF}^- ([\quad]^{\alpha}{}_i, [\quad]^{\beta}{}_j) \\ [\text{BY} [\text{AFF}^- ([\alpha], [\beta])]_h] \end{bmatrix}$$

   b.
$$\begin{bmatrix} \text{CAUSE} ([\alpha], [\text{INCH} [\text{BE}_{\text{Ident}} ([\beta], [\text{AT} [\quad]_k])]]) \\ \text{AFF}^- ([\quad]^{\alpha}{}_i, [\alpha]^{\beta}{}_j) \\ [\text{BY} [\text{AFF}^- ([\alpha], \quad)]_h] \end{bmatrix}$$

(1) If the verb permits a Patient (either grammatical or discourse), this Patient is bound to the Patient of the main conceptual clause. This is case (49a), where $[\beta]$ is present in the means clause of (48) and α is absent in the Patient of the main clause. (2) If, as in (49b), α is present in the Patient of the main clause and $[\beta]$ is absent in the means clause, the Patient of the main clause must be bound to the Actor; the single-argument variant of AFF, without a Patient, must appear in the means clause. Since the Patient of the main clause must at the same time be lexically filled, it has to be expressed syntactically as a reflexive pronoun. Thus (37), (38), and—marginally—(40) fall under case (1) of the rule, and (39) falls under case (2).

Here is how the rule works out. First consider (37a), *The gardener watered the tulips flat*. The verb *water* assigns its direct object the role Patient on the action tier as well as reference object on the thematic tier; these positions are bound together. (50) gives its lexical entry.

(50)
$$\begin{bmatrix} \text{water} \\ [_V N] \\ \underline{\quad\quad} NP_j \\ \begin{bmatrix} \text{CAUSE} ([\alpha], [\text{INCH} [\text{BE} ([\text{WATER}], [\text{ON}_d [\beta]])]]) \\ \text{AFF}^- ([\quad]^{\alpha}{}_i, [\quad]^{\beta}{}_j) \end{bmatrix} \end{bmatrix}$$

Fusing this with V_h in (48) yields the following conceptual structure for (37a):

(51) The gardener watered the tulips flat.
$$\begin{bmatrix} \text{CAUSE} ([\alpha], [\text{INCH} [\text{BE} ([\beta], [\text{AT} [\text{FLAT}]])]]) \\ \text{AFF}^- ([\text{GARDENER}]^{\alpha}, [\text{TULIPS}]^{\beta}) \\ [\text{BY} \begin{bmatrix} \text{CAUSE} ([\gamma], [\text{INCH} [\text{BE} ([\text{WATER}], [\text{ON}_d [\delta]])]]) \\ \text{AFF}^- ([\alpha]^{\gamma}, [\beta]^{\delta}) \end{bmatrix}_h] \end{bmatrix}$$

Here there are two chains of binding. One links the Actor of the main clause to the Agent of the main clause and to the Actor and Agent of the means clause. The other links the Patient of the main clause to the Theme of the main clause and to the Patient and reference object of the means clause. Thus this representation answers the question of how we know it was the tulips that the gardener put water on.

Next consider a case where the Patient of the means clause is only a discourse Patient, for example (40a): *The rooster crowed the children awake.* The lexical entry of *crow* does not include a Patient role, so (48) simply inserts a Patient in the means clause that is not linked to anything on the thematic tier of the means clause:

(52) The rooster crowed the children awake.
$$\begin{bmatrix} \text{CAUSE} ([\alpha], [\text{INCH} [\text{BE} ([\beta], [\text{AT} [\text{AWAKE}]])])]) \\ \text{AFF}^- ([\text{ROOSTER}]^\alpha, [\text{CHILDREN}]^\beta) \\ [\text{BY} \begin{bmatrix} \text{CROW} ([\gamma]) \\ \text{AFF}^- ([\alpha]^\gamma, [\beta]) \end{bmatrix}] \end{bmatrix}$$

Finally consider a case with a reflexive. Here the Patient of the main conceptual clause is bound to the Actor, and AFF in the means clause has an Actor but no Patient:

(53) Charlie laughed himself silly.
$$\begin{bmatrix} \text{CAUSE} ([\alpha], [\text{INCH} [\text{BE} ([\beta], [\text{AT} [\text{SILLY}]])])]) \\ \text{AFF}^- ([\text{CHARLIE}]^\alpha, [\alpha]^\beta) \\ [\text{BY} \begin{bmatrix} \text{LAUGH} ([\gamma]) \\ \text{AFF} ([\alpha]^\gamma, \quad) \end{bmatrix}] \end{bmatrix}$$

Thus there are three cases of resultatives, differing in the status of the action tier in the means clause. Cases like (51) have a grammatical Patient, cases like (52) have a discourse Patient, and cases like (53) have no Patient at all.

The resultatives discussed so far have all been predicative; that is, the phrase describing the result has been an AP or an Identificational Path-PP. However, there are also resultatives where the final phrase is a spatial Path:

(54) a. Bill pushed the piano into the orchestra pit.
   b. Beth wiggled the tooth out of her mouth.
   c. The critics laughed the show out of town.
   d. Harry sneezed his handkerchief right across the room.

Again these have paraphrases with the main verb in a means clause:

(55) a. Bill made the piano go into the orchestra pit by pushing (on) it.
   b. Beth made the tooth come out of her mouth by wiggling it.
   c. The critics got the show out of town by laughing (at it).
   d. Harry made his handkerchief go right across the room by sneezing (on/into/it).

This construction can be derived by means of a rule very much like (48), differing primarily in that it has a spatial GO and a spatial Path instead of INCH BE_{Ident} plus a reference object. The rule seems somewhat freer than (48) in its application, though. For instance, I find the spatial examples in (56a) somewhat better than the parallel Identificational examples in (56b).

(56a) a.   Harry sneezed his handkerchief across the room.
             ?The Lorelei sang her victims to a watery grave.
      b. ??Harry sneezed his handkerchief soggy.
             ??The Lorelei sang her victims dead.

The rule for spatial resultatives seems to incorporate the same Patient constraint as (48), as can be seen from the test for Patients in the "base forms" of (54) and (56):

(57) a.   What Bill did to the piano was push (on) it.
     b.   What Beth did to her tooth was wiggle it.
     c. ?What the critics did to the show was laugh at it.
     d. ?What Harry did to his handkerchief was sneeze on/into it.
     e. ?What the Lorelei did to her victims was sing to them.

And similarly, the reflexive resultatives do not require Patients:

(58) a.   Harry rolled himself along the carpet.   (resultative)
     b.   *What Harry did to himself was roll (himself).

Thus it appears that spatial resultatives in most respects generalize with Identificational resultatives, although the differences in judgments in (56) remain to be explained. Leaving these aside, the rule can be stated as (59).

(59) *Spatial Resultative Adjunct Rule*
     $[_{VP}\ V_h\ NP_j\ PP_k]$ may correspond to
     $$\begin{bmatrix} \text{CAUSE } [\alpha],\ [\text{GO } ([\beta],\ [\ \ ]_k)]) \\ \text{AFF}^-\ ([\ \ ]^\alpha{}_i,\ [\{\alpha\}]^\beta{}_j) \\ [\text{BY } [\text{AFF}^-\ ([\alpha],\ \{[\beta]\})]_h] \end{bmatrix}.$$

Recall that the *way*-construction supports a number of lexical idioms such as *wend one's way.* Section 10.2 argued that these are to be viewed more or less as compounds constructed from the constructional idiom plus further information. Parallel examples exist for the resulative construction, in profusion. Here are a few, pointed out by Carrier and Randall (forthcoming):

(60) a.   work one's fingers to the bone
     b.   cry one's eyes red
     c.   eat someone out of house and home
     d.   drink someone under the table

In addition, there are of course words that *lexically* incorporate the causative inchoative structure found in the resultative, for instance *render* and *lull*, which have only resultative readings, plus *get* and *make*, which have a variety of readings.

It is worth mentioning that there is a syntactic difference between lexical resultatives and those derived by rule (48). Some of the lexical resultatives permit an NP predicate as well as an AP or PP:

(61) a. Bill painted the house a disgusting shade of red.
     b. MIT made me a linguist.

So far as I know, no resultatives derived by the adjunct rule permit an NP predicate; Carrier and Randall find them "rare." A minimal pair is their *He pounded the dough flat/*a pancake.* In the present approach, this is a simple fact of subcategorization: the Resultative Adjunct Rule does not allow NP predicates, but certain causative inchoatives do.[11]

10.5 An Alternative Treatment of Resultatives

Carrier and Randall (forthcoming) (henceforth C&R) propose a treatment of resultatives very much in the spirit of the one developed in the previous section, so in the interests of exploring closely related alternatives, let us briefly examine where their analysis differs from mine. (In turn, C&R discuss and reject other proposals in the literature. I have nothing to add to their discussion and therefore will concentrate on their treatment.)

There are two major differences. The first concerns what type of rule produces resultatives. In the present approach, it is a correspondence rule that applies to sentences "on the fly" to provide them with an interpretation. If there is a sense in which this rule belongs in the lexicon, it is as a lexical item that specifies a "constructional meaning." By contrast, C&R argue for the Lexical Rule Strategy, treating the formation of resultatives as a rule that derives new verbs from old *within* the lexicon. They give three arguments.

First, resultatives are subject to Middle Formation:

(62) a. New seedlings water flat easily.
     b. My running socks won't wash clean.

Following Keyser and Roeper (1984), C&R take Middle Formation to be a lexical rule that suppresses the verb's external argument, so that the object moves to subject position. Since Resultative Formation feeds Middle Formation, the former must be a lexical rule as well. If Keyser and Roeper's account is correct, this is a serious problem for the present approach.

However, an alternative that has not been explored in the literature is that Middle Formation is itself a kind of adjunct rule, a way of interpreting sentences "on the fly" when the argument structure of the verb does not match the syntax. Circumstantially, the English middle has the proper flavor: (1) it has a fixed syntax that does not match that of the verb; (2) it has curious semantic restrictions requiring an adverb such as *easily* or the volitional sense of *won't*; (3) roughly, it requires the derived subject to be a Patient of the verb. In illustration of this last point, contrast (63) and (64).

(63) a.   New seedlings water flat easily.
           What I did to the seedlings was water them.
      b.   The bread sliced easily.
           What I did to the bread was slice it.
      c.   The books sell easily.
           What I did to the books was sell them.

(64) a.   *The room enters easily.
           *What I did to the room was enter it.
      b.   *The letters receive easily.
           *What I did to the letters was receive them.
      c.   *The books buy easily.
           *What I did to the books was buy them.

(On the other hand, there are exceptions, for example *This book reads easily* but ?**What I did to the book was read it*.)

These characteristics—fixed syntactic form combined with idiosyncratic semantic restrictions—are typical of the adjunct rules investigated here. If indeed Middle Formation were an adjunct rule rather than a lexical rule, the argument in terms of ordering could be eliminated. It remains, however, for a satisfactory treatment of Middle Formation to be formulated in the present framework and compared with proposals in the literature.

C&R's next argument that Resultative Formation is a lexical rule is that they find adjectival passive forms like those in (65) acceptable.

(65) a.   swept-clean room
      b.   squashed-flat grapes
      c.   spun-dry clothes
      d.   smashed-open safe
      e.   jiggled-free tooth

Since adjectival passives are usually taken to be derived within the lexicon, and since resultatives must form the input to Adjectival Passive Formation in (65), Resultative Formation too must be a lexical derivation. My main response to this argument is that I find (65) at best marginal; other examples such as *washed-clean clothes*, *watered-flat tulips*, *hammered-round wire*, and *cooked-black stove* are totally out. Hence the evidence for Resultative Formation following Adjectival Passive Formation is at best weak.

A third argument concerns nominalizations of resultatives. Here are C&R's examples:

(66) a. The slicing of cheese into thin wedges is the current rage.
   b. The painting of fire engines the color of schoolbuses is strictly prohibited by state law.
   c. The surgeon general warns against the cooking of food black.

Again, since nominalization is a lexical process that must be fed by Resultative Formation, the latter must be a lexical process as well. However, I find the data again equivocal. *Slice NP into wedges* is not an adjunct resultative but a lexical one: *slice* is a verb of composition of the type discussed in section 6.4, and *into wedges* is its complement. Similarly, *paint NP the color of schoolbuses* is likely a lexical resultative, since the predicate is an NP; as pointed out above in connection with (61), adjunct resultatives only occur with APs and PPs. Finally, *the cooking of food black* is probably an adjunct resultative, but I find it distinctly less acceptable than the other two. The conclusion appears to be that in fact nominalizations of adjunct resultatives are ungrammatical, as the present approach would predict.

The second major difference between C&R's approach and the present one is in the conceptual structure proposed for resultatives. Their conceptual structure, translated into present notation, is (67). Essentially the same structure is proposed in Dowty 1979. Roughly, this conceptual structure says "The gardener's watering the tulips made them flat."

(67) The gardener watered the tulips flat.
   [CAUSE ([$_{\text{Event}}$ WATER (GARDENER, TULIPS)],
           [INCH [BE ([TULIPS], [AT [FLAT]])]])]

This structure preserves the sense of a resultative as a causative inchoative; but, instead of subordinating the lexical verb into a means clause, C&R place it in the Agent argument of the causative function.

A difficulty with C&R's "Agent" analysis is that it accords the surface subject no role in the main conceptual clause. By contrast, the "Means" analysis proposed here gives the surface subject the roles of Actor and Agent in the main conceptual clause. This appears to be correct. Compare a typical resultative in the pseudocleft test for Actor (68a) with its means paraphrase (68b) and its Agent paraphrase (68c,d).

(68) a. What the gardener did to the tulips was he watered them flat.
   b. What the gardener did to the tulips was he made them flat by watering them.   (Means paraphrase)
   c. ??What the gardener did to the tulips was his watering them made them flat.   (Agent paraphrase)
   d. What the gardener's watering the tulips did to them was it made them flat.   (Agent paraphrase)

In the resultative (68a), the surface subject *the gardener* is Actor. This is also true in the means paraphrase (68b). However, in the Agent paraphrase, *the gardener* can be construed as Actor awkwardly at best, as seen in (68c); rather, the entire Event *the gardener's watering the flowers* appears to fall into the Actor role, as seen in (68d). Thus, with respect to the assignment of the Actor role, the means paraphrase is more satisfactory. Since the paraphrases are taken to be a direct syntactic expression of the conceptual structure of the resultative, this argues that the Means analysis of the resultative is also more satisfactory.

A second argument for the Means analysis is based on its parallelism with the other constructions that introduce a superordinate conceptual function. For each such construction we have discussed, there is a good paraphrase with a subordinate accompaniment or means clause. However, particularly in the cases involving accompaniment, there is no suitable paraphrase (or conceptual structure) parallel in form to (67). For example, the sentences in (69) are not well paraphrased by those in (70).

(69) a. Harold belched his way out of the restaurant.
     b. Bill jumped into Harriet's arms.

(70) a. Harold's belching made him go out of the restaurant.   (wrong meaning)
     b. Bill's jumping made him go/got him into Harriet's arms.   (wrong meaning)

In other words, the structure induced by rule (48) forms a natural class with other constructions, whereas structure (67) does not. Therefore, on grounds of restricting the class of possible adjunct rules in Universal Grammar, we should prefer the Means analysis over the Agent analysis.

C&R give two arguments that they claim favor the Agent analysis over the Means analysis. One concerns sentences like (71), which they say at least some speakers find acceptable. I do not, nor do people I have asked.

(71) a. It snowed the roads slippery.
     b. It rained the seedlings flat.
     c. It thundered the children awake.
     d. It rained the golf course useless.
     e. It rained the animals nearly crazy.

There are no paraphrases for these such as "It made the roads slippery by snowing"; but "Its snowing made the roads slippery" is acceptable. Given C&R's judgments, they count this as an argument for their analysis; given my judgments, I count it as an argument against.[12]

C&R's major argument, however, concerns non-Agentive resultatives such as (72).

(72) a. The toast burned black/to a cinder.
    b. The lake froze solid/into a solid mass.
    c. The pitcher broke into a million little fragments.
    d. The candybar melted into a gooey mess.
    e. The corn grew as high as an elephant's eye.
    f. The pebbles rolled smooth.

C&R point out that these do not have the paraphrases required by the Means analysis: "X made the toast black by burning it," and so on. However, they do have paraphrases consistent with the Agent analysis: "The toast's burning made it black." Thus the Means analysis will need a different rule to derive the interpretations of (72), whereas the Agent analysis generalizes across the two cases.

In fact, for some of these cases, the present analysis requires no additional rule. *Freeze, break,* and *melt* all have an implicit Goal argument that encodes the final state of the Theme; *grow* has an implicit Path giving the direction of change of size. Thus the PP-adjuncts in (72b–e) can fall under the PP-Adjunct Rule (8.37), which provides additional information about an implicit argument. On the other hand, we have given no parallel rule for the AP-adjuncts in (72b,e). In addition, *burn* in (72a) has no implicit Path or Goal, and *roll* in (72f) does not allow a Property as its Goal. So there is at least a subset of these cases that are relevant to C&R's argument.

To deal with these remaining cases, let me state the rule required in the present analysis. (As in rule (48), for simplicity I restrict myself to the case of AP-complements.)

(73) *Noncausative AP Resultative Adjunct Rule*
    [$_{VP}$ V$_h$ AP$_k$] may correspond to

$$\begin{bmatrix} \text{INCH [BE}_{\text{Ident}} \, ([\alpha], \, [\text{AT} \, [_{\text{Property}} \quad]_k])] \\ \text{AFF ([\quad]}^\alpha_i, \quad) \\ [\text{BY [AFF}^- \, (\quad , [\alpha])]_h] \end{bmatrix}.$$

Using this rule, *The toast burned black* receives conceptual structure (74) ("The toast got black by burning").

(74)
$$\begin{bmatrix} \text{INCH [BE}_{\text{Ident}} \, ([\alpha], \, [\text{AT} \, [_{\text{Property}} \, \text{BLACK}]])] \\ \text{AFF ([TOAST]}^\alpha, \quad) \\ [\text{BY} \begin{bmatrix} \text{BURN} \, ([\beta]) \\ \text{AFF}^- \, (\quad , [\alpha]^\beta) \end{bmatrix}] \end{bmatrix}$$

Now let us consider the status of this additional rule. If we view (73), like (48), as a "constructional idiom," then it is related to (48) in much the same way as noncausative *break* and *roll* are related to their causative variants. In fact, (75) shows that this construction shares the property of intransitive *break* and *roll* (noted in section 7.1) of having an ambiguous action tier.

(The statement in (73) only accounts for the Actor reading. I leave open the proper emendation.)

(75) a. What the toast did was burn black.
   What happened to the toast was it burned black.
   b. What the lake did was freeze solid.
   What happened to the lake was it froze solid.
   etc.

That is, apart from its curious status as a constructional idiom, (73) is a typical intransitive verb that undergoes the causative alternation; its causative is the causative resultative (48). If this generalization is correct, it is not so objectionable after all to have a different rule for noncausative resultatives under the Means analysis; the two rules are related in a well-known way.

Next consider the action tier in the means clause of (73). It contains just a Patient (or Undergoer). This accounts for an interesting restriction on the intransitive resultative, pointed out by Levin and Rappaport (1989). It appears that no "unergative" verbs can appear in this construction: *Bill ate sick; *Bill walked woozy. Neither can point-event "unaccusatives": *Bill arrived sick (on resultative reading). The class of verbs that can appear in this construction, a subclass of "unaccusatives," turns out to be just those that have an Undergoer subject: What happened to X was it burned/froze/broke/melted/grew/rolled, but not *What happened to X was he ate/walked/arrived. This difference falls out from the selectional restriction on the verb's action tier in (73).

The "unergative" verbs, by contrast, appear in the "fake reflexive" resultative construction: Bill ate himself sick; Bill walked himself woozy. This follows from the fact that these verbs have only an Actor in their action tier; they therefore meet the selectional restriction for (49b), the "fake reflexive" case of the transitive resultative construction.

Finally, the point-event verbs are excluded by a general restriction on resultatives (not stated here) that parallels the process (or −BOUNDED) requirement on the way-construction. Since arriving cannot be construed as a process, it is excluded from the resultative construction. Similarly, the nonrepeatable point-event verb break is excluded from either transitive or intransitive AP resultatives: *Bill broke the vase worthless; *The vase broke worthless. And repeatable point-even verbs such as jump acquire the process reading of repetition: Bill jumped himself into a stupor conveys multiple jumps.

Turning to intransitive spatial resultatives, the evidence is equivocal. Manner-of-motion intransitives fall under the GO-Adjunct Rule: The ball rolled into the room. "Unergative" intransitives can fall under either the "fake reflexive" resultatives licensed by (59) (Harry sneezed himself across the room) or, with a slightly different meaning, the *way*-construction (*Harry sneezed his way across the room*). Some of the verbs in (72) are not so good in spatial resultatives (76); others are all right (77).

(76) a. *The rocket burned into the hotel.   (in sense "The rocket got into the hotel by burning")
 b. *The water froze out of the bottle.   (in sense "The water got out of the bottle by freezing")
 c. *The window broke into the room.
  The pitcher broke onto the floor.   (OK, but not in sense "*The pitcher got onto the floor by breaking")
(77) a. The chocolate melted out of the box.
 b. The corn grew over the top of the house.   (possible PP-adjunct)
 c. The pebbles rolled out of the box.   (GO-adjunct)

I do not want to pursue the relevant restrictions here. The main point is that the spatial causative resultatives do not generalize to the noncausative case in exactly the same way as the Identificational resultatives do.

I will not pursue the delicate and detailed work necessary to discover exactly which of the rules should be collapsed and how. I suspect, though, that one reason that work on resultatives has proven relatively inconclusive in the past is that people have expected there to be a single uniform rule of resultative formation that subsumes all cases. This is certainly the assumption that C&R use in the argument for the Agent analysis, for example. Without the formal machinery of conceptual structure to help tease various cases apart, the apparent exceptions have for the most part been treated by semantic handwaving. Here we have been more precise in our description, and, although a full explanation is still forthcoming, we have at least been able to avoid the error of an overly facile generalization. The actual explanation will have to be more complicated.

10.6 Final Remarks on Adjuncts

One of the more persistent assumptions in many brands of contemporary syntactic theory is that the syntactic complement structure of a phrase is determined (exclusively or nearly so) by the conceptual argument structure of the phrase's head. The last three chapters have given strong reason to temper these assumptions and regard them as only part of the picture. It has turned out that the syntactic structure of the complement results from the interaction of the lexical structure of the head with a wide variety of adjunct rules. Through these rules, implicit arguments can become explicit, new arguments can be added, and explicit arguments can be bound to new arguments. The result is that a complement structure may become a good deal more varied than the head's subcategorization alone would permit.

Viewed from a different angle, these rules permit drastic simplification of lexically marked argument structures, since much of the variation is due to the presence of adjuncts.

The class of adjunct rules has been developed under very conservative assumptions about phrase structure, and with only minimal enrichments of conceptual structure, for example the action tier and the subordinators BY, WITH, FROM, FOR, and EXCH—enrichments that are needed in any case for encoding the meanings of sentences. The major innovation has been rather in the correspondence rule component: the adjunct rules are a class of rules quite distinct from standard Argument Fusion and from the rules for interpreting restrictive modifiers such as prenominal adjectives and manner adverbs.

The adjunct rules introduce no new principles of syntactic or conceptual composition—just a new class of routes between old well-known syntactic forms and old well-known conceptual forms. Thus the traditional distinction between "arguments" and "adjuncts" is not a structural distinction in either syntax or semantics. It is rather a distinction in what kind of correspondence rule achieves the match between the two.

What about other possibilities for adjunct constructions? Levin and Rapoport (1988) discuss a number of constructions, including the resultative and the *way*-construction, that for them form a natural class. Among the other constructions they mention are *smile her thanks/snort her disgust/* etc.; *poke a hole in the screen; file the serial number off ⟨the terminal⟩*. For a different sort of example, one might want to investigate the possibility of treating *out*-prefixation (as in *Bill outran Harry*) as an adjunct rule whose effect is to embed the meaning of the base verb in a larger conceptual construction.

A more radical possibility concerns the "rules of construal" mentioned briefly in section 1.5. Consider an example like (78).

(78) (= (1.8a))
[One waitress says to another:]
The ham sandwich over in the corner wants some more coffee.

Section 1.5 suggested that (78) is interpreted by means of a rule of construal that maps [HAM SANDWICH] into [PERSON CONTEXTUALLY ASSOCIATED WITH HAM SANDWICH]. Such a rule has the property of creating a conceptual constituent in which the lexical head of the phrase, *ham sandwich*, serves not as head but as an argument of a modifier. But this is exactly what the "superordinate" adjunct rules of this chapter do—with the exception that, in the case of (78), neither the lexical noun *ham sandwich* nor the adjunct construction has any other argument structure. That is, the rule of construal responsible for (78) appears to be an extremely simple version of the class of rules we have been exploring here. It might therefore be worthwhile looking into the feasibility of assimilating the class of rules of construal (or some interesting subset) to adjunct rules.

If one wished to preserve the more standard assumption that the head completely determines its complement structure, one could restate the adjunct rules as lexical rules that add additional argument positions to lexical items. I have kept this possibility alive on and off throughout these chapters. I am not yet convinced that such an approach is totally wrong, but one should not adopt it solely in order to be able to beg the question. An empirically based decision will among other things depend on the interaction of the adjunct rules with other constructions such as causative, passive, dative, and middle and with derivational morphology. For instance, I have already suggested the possibility that the English middle construction might be due to an adjunct rule; certain cases of datives have already proven to be adjuncts (section 9.5). However, I have not explored these interactions here, because I have deemed it more important first to lay down a firm foundation for the new and relatively unfamiliar phenomena, which do not on the whole fit comfortably into more purely syntactic approaches to argument structure. At the same time, I have tried to show some of the riches that can be mined from a conception of semantic structure in which it is as highly articulated—and as susceptible to rigorous argumentation—as the syntactic component.

Chapter 11
Toward a Theory of Linking

11.1 The Notion of Linking Rules

I noted in section 2.3 a glaring deficiency in my formulation of lexical correspondence rules: the fact that the correspondence of conceptual arguments to syntactic positions is completely stipulated. As many people have observed, such stipulation grants too much expressive freedom to the correspondence rule component.

For example (to adapt an argument of Carter (1976)), what is to prevent the existence of the unlikely lexical items *benter and *succeive, identical to enter and receive except that subject and object are reversed?

(1) a. $\begin{bmatrix} \text{benter} \\ \text{V} \\ \underline{\quad} \text{NP}_j \\ [\text{GO} ([_{\text{Thing}} \quad]_j, [\text{TO} [\text{IN} [_{\text{Thing}} \quad]_i]])] \end{bmatrix}$

b. $\begin{bmatrix} \text{succeive} \\ \text{V} \\ \underline{\quad} \text{NP}_j \\ [\text{GO}_{\text{Poss}} ([_{\text{Thing}} \quad]_i, [\text{TO} [_{\text{Thing}} \quad]_j])] \end{bmatrix}$

If they existed, these items would appear in sentences like (2a, b), synonymous with (3a, b) respectively.

(2) a. The room bentered Bill.
    b. The package succeived Bill.

(3) a. Bill entered the room.
    b. Bill received the package.

Why aren't there such words? Another, better-known case: what accounts for the fact that explicit Actors are always in subject position? There is nothing in the present theory that says that Actor position always receives the external argument index i; it could just as well be coindexed with a postverbal position.[1]

There has been a longstanding intuition in the field that the relationship between syntactic and semantic roles is highly constrained—more constrained than the stipulative relationship assumed so far here. As mentioned in the Introduction, Chomsky (1957) noted a close relationship, though he explicitly denied that it is one-to-one. The theory of the relationship between syntactic and semantic arguments is now generally called *linking theory*; this chapter will lay out the preliminaries of a linking theory whose semantic roles are those of Conceptual Semantics.

Perhaps the strongest hypothesis of linking in recent literature is Baker's (1988, 46) *Uniformity of Theta Assignment Hypothesis* (UTAH), which claims that "Identical thematic relationships between items are represented by identical structural relationships between those items at the level of D-structure." As stated, this does not require a one-to-one mapping, since it leaves open the possibility of different thematic roles mapping into the same structural position. A parallel notion, the *Universal Alignment Hypothesis* (Rosen 1984; Perlmutter and Postal 1984), has been debated within Relational Grammar. Case Grammar (Fillmore 1968) is an earlier and still more constrained expression of the same idea: every semantic role is claimed to map into a unique "deep syntactic case." We have seen earlier and will recapitulate below that surface grammatical relations do not obey such a stringent correspondence. Hence any of these "rigid" theories entails various amounts of syntactic movement and deletion or insertion of prepositions in order to account for surface syntactic distribution.

A variety of less restrictive theories have also appeared in the literature (Carter 1976; Anderson 1977; Ostler 1979; Marantz 1984; Foley and Van Valin 1984; Carrier-Duncan 1985; Grimshaw 1987, 1990; Bresnan and Kanerva 1989). Instead of assigning each thematic role to a particular syntactic position, these theories invoke a mapping between an ordered list of θ-roles (a "thematic hierarchy") and an ordered list of syntactic roles. The general form of the mapping is given in (4).

(4) *Hierarchical Argument Linking* (version 1)
Following the thematic hierarchy, order the θ-roles in the lexical conceptual structure (LCS) of a verb V from first to nth. To derive the syntactic argument structure of V, map this ordering of θ-roles into the first through nth roles in the syntactic hierarchy.

A simple version of this appeared in section 8.1, where we discussed optionally causative verbs such as *open*:

(5) a. The door [*Theme*] opened.
   b. Bill [*Agent*] opened the door [*Theme*].

In a rigid theory such as UTAH, the Theme must appear in the same D-Structure position in (5a) and (5b), and the difference in surface position must, by hypothesis, be due to a syntactic movement. In a hierarchical approach, though, the surface position of NPs can be determined directly by the following skeletal theory:

(6) a. *Thematic hierarchy*
       Agent > Theme
    b. *Syntactic hierarchy*
       Subject > Object
    c. *Linking Principle*
       Map the ordered θ-roles from the LCS into the syntactic hierarchy from left to right.

The effect will be that of Anderson's (1977) Theme Rule: If the LCS contains only a Theme, this role is mapped into subject position; if the LCS contains an Agent and a Theme, the former is mapped to subject position and the latter to object position.

As it turns out, the system in (6) forms a subpart of all the hierarchical approaches cited above. Within this limited part of their respective domains, they differ primarily in how the syntactic hierarchy is specified. Marantz (1984) and Foley and Van Valin (1984) map directly into syntactic (phrase structure) configurations; Bresnan and Kanerva (1989) map into the LFG functional roles SUBJ and OBJ; Carrier-Duncan (1985) maps into the case-markers NOM and ACC (in Tagalog); Grimshaw (1990) maps into a hierarchical argument structure that in turn determines syntactic configuration. But the basic conception of the system from the point of view of the thematic-to-syntactic correspondence is the same.

11.2 What Conceptual Semantics Can Do for Linking Theory

I want to address two basic issues in this chapter. First, how can Conceptual Semantics sharpen the formulation of linking theory? Second, how can linking theory sharpen Conceptual Semantics, helping both to simplify lexical entries and to eliminate the possibility of such weird items as *benter* and *succeive*?

Let us start with the contribution of Conceptual Semantics to linking theory. As stressed in chapter 2, we are now in a position not to treat thematic roles just as names for intuitive semantic relations. Rather, thematic roles are now formally defined as particular argument positions in conceptual structure. Agent (Instigator) is defined formally as the first argument of CS, Effect as the second argument of CS. Theme is defined formally as the first argument of any of the class of Location and Motion functions (GO, BE, STAY, EXT, ORIENT, MOVE, CONF). Goal is defined as the argument of TO; Source as the argument of FROM. Actor is the first argument of AFF; Patient and Beneficiary are the second arguments of AFF$^-$ and AFF$^+$ respectively. Thus the terms in the thematic hierarchy can be specified in as formal a fashion as those in the syntactic hierarchy. Moreover, Conceptual Semantics has provided techniques for motivating and justifying thematic roles in some detail. Hence specification of a thematic hierarchy rests on a firmer foundation than it has previously.

Another advantage of the present approach emerged in chapters 8 through 10: a great number of phrases previously treated as arguments have turned out to be adjuncts. For instance, consider an alternation like (7), where the Theme appears either as direct object or as object of *with*.

(7) a. Harry loaded *dirt* on the truck.
    b. Harry loaded the truck *with dirt*.

Argument Linking is responsible for the Theme only in the first of these; in the other, the Theme is an adjunct, linked by its own extrinsic rule. In particular, there is no need to appeal to some principle of "argument demotion" to account for the Theme in (7b). Similarly, the complements in (8) are not licensed by the verb and therefore do not fall under Argument Linking; rather, they are adjuncts, licensed by the rules of chapter 10.

(8) a. Bill belched his way out of the restaurant.
    b. Sue hammered the metal flat.
    c. We laughed ourselves silly.

As a result, the task faced by Argument Linking per se is considerably simplified.

Chapter 3 discussed another potential problem for linking theory. All the theories mentioned above presume that a syntactic position can be linked with a unique θ-role. However, as seen there and illustrated abundantly in the examples since, a syntactic position is frequently linked with a multiplicity of θ-roles. Section 3.2 offered a solution: all the θ-roles expressed by a particular NP are linked together by binding in conceptual structure, and only one of them, the *dominant θ-role*, is directly linked to the syntax. In chapter 3 this linking was accomplished by stipulated indices, in accordance with our practice up to this point. But the approach is easily adapted to a linking theory: our linking theory can simply use the dominant θ-role where the cited theories speak of "the" θ-role of an argument. That is, we can replace (4) by (9) (difference italicized).

(9) *Hierarchical Argument Linking* (version 2)
    Following the thematic hierarchy, order the *dominant* θ-roles in the LCS of a verb V from first to nth. To derive the syntactic argument structure of V, map this ordering of θ-roles into the first through nth roles in the syntactic hierarchy.

This does raise a difficulty of its own, though. Consider a verb such as *buy*, whose NP arguments receive multiple θ-roles. If linking is stipulated, it doesn't matter very much which of the θ-roles is chosen as dominant. For instance, the subject of *buy* could be linked directly to Actor, or to Goal, or even to Source of the countertransfer. However, if linking is determined by a thematic hierarchy, it matters very much which of these roles is dominant. Depending on which role is chosen, this argument could fall either above or below another argument on the hierarchy, leading to indeterminate or ambiguous linkings.

In notating lexical forms up to this point, of course, I have had to make explicit choices about dominant θ-roles. Anticipating the present problem, I have tacitly assigned the dominant θ-role by the following principle:

(10) *Dominant θ-Role Principle*
      The dominant θ-role in a bound complex of θ-roles in the LCS of a verb is that role that is highest in the thematic hierarchy.

This cannot be illustrated in detail until section 11.5. For the moment, notice that it accounts for the fact that a combination of θ-roles consisting of Actor and anything else always behaves like an Actor. The reason is that Actor is the highest role on the thematic hierarchy and is therefore the dominant θ-role. So, for instance, the dominant θ-role of the subject of *buy* is Actor, and that is why this argument ends up in subject position.

Still another problem for linking theory is that, as argued in chapter 10, the verbs in constructions such as (8) do not head the conceptual structure of their respective sentences. Rather, the main conceptual clause of the sentence comes from the adjunct construction; the verb is "demoted" to an accompaniment or means modifier, and its arguments are bound by the adjunct. As a result, linking theory cannot speak of determining syntactic argument structure from the verb alone; the verb's LCS does not always determine the syntactic arguments of the sentence. We take up this problem in section 11.9; for the moment we conveniently ignore it.

11.3 What Linking Theory Can Do for Conceptual Semantics

As observed at the outset, the motive behind linking theory is to eliminate the stipulation of coindexing between conceptual arguments and syntactic arguments. The question is, How far can we go in simplifying lexical entries?

The absolute minimal theory of lexical entries requires a phonological structure, a syntactic category, and a lexical conceptual structure. Transitive *open*, for example, would look like this:

(11) $\begin{bmatrix} \text{open} \\ \text{V} \\ [\text{CAUSE} ([_{\text{Thing}} \quad], [\text{GO}_{\text{Ident}} ([_{\text{Thing}} \quad], [\text{TO [OPEN]}])])] \end{bmatrix}$

Unlike our previous entries, (11) has neither a subcategorization feature nor the indices in LCS that specify argument structure. The idea behind this "minimalist" approach is that, with no further information, the linking rules can identify the syntactically expressed open arguments of *open* as the two Thing-constituents. Since Things must be expressed by NPs, the syntactic argument structure must contain two NPs. In turn, since one of these Things is Agent and the other Theme, the Linking Principle specifies their syntactic positions: the Agent belongs in subject position and the Theme in object. In short, nothing need be said in the entry of *open* about which conceptual constituents are arguments, and nothing need be said about how these constituents are syntactically realized.

This theory immediately solves the problem raised in section 4.1 concerning the use of the dashed underline notation to abbreviate the two forms of optionally causative verbs like *open*. The difficulty is that the addition of the Agent argument changes the position of the Theme argument; hence it is impossible to unify the coindexing from arguments to syntactic positions in the two forms. The minimalist theory, however, permits a lexical entry like this:

(12) $\begin{bmatrix} \text{open} \\ \text{V} \\ [\text{CAUSE} ([_{\text{Thing}} \quad], [\text{GO} ([_{\text{Thing}} \quad], [\text{TO [OPEN]}])])] \end{bmatrix}$

This correctly leaves open whether the verb is transitive or intransitive; the choice depends on the number of conceptual arguments. In addition, though, it leaves open where the argument(s) end up in syntactic structure; this is determined by the Linking Principle. So this is already an improvement.

Unfortunately the minimalist theory is too much to hope for; it is not expressive enough. For one thing, it gives no way to express the difference between optional and obligatory arguments. Consider the well-known minimal pair *eat* and *devour*. They apparently have the very same LCS, except that *devour* has an additional manner modifier. Yet *eat* is optionally transitive and *devour* is obligatorily transitive. Similarly, *put*, *place*, and *set* require an NP-PP complement, but *insert*, which is conceptually identical except for a selectional restriction on the Goal (it must be an interior), allows either NP-PP or NP alone. *Try* and *attempt* are conceptually virtually identical, yet *I'll try* is all right and **I'll attempt* is not; likewise for *ask* versus *demand* (Grimshaw 1979).

These differences cannot be encoded in the minimalist theory; something must be added to the notation for lexical entries. Whatever this something is, though, it does not threaten linking theory: all the verb's arguments, *when they appear*, are in the right places. But the minimalist theory has cut back too far in search of simplification.

Let us look at a few more examples. Consider noncausative inchoative *fill*:

(13) a. Water (slowly) filled the tank.
     b. The tank (slowly) filled (with water).

Recall that (13a) and (13b) were analyzed in section 8.2 as having the same conceptual structure, (14).

(14) [INCH [BE ([WATER], [IN$_d$ [TANK]])]]

The syntactic difference was accounted for by claiming that in (13a), *fill* treats both Theme and Goal as arguments; but in (13b), the Theme is an adjunct and only the Goal is an argument. This difference was encoded in the stipulated coindexing for the two frames of *fill*:

(15) a. [INCH [BE ([ ]$_i$, [IN$_d$ [ ]$_j$])]]   (for (13a))
     b. [INCH [BE ([ ], [IN$_d$ [ ]$_i$])]]   (for (13b))

Collapsing these two presents the same problem of unmatched indices as the causative; we hope to solve this by means of the linking theory. But there is yet another problem: intransitive *fill*, unlike intransitive *open*, still has two open arguments. If we adopt the minimalist theory of linking, simply dropping all indices, (15a) and (15b) will no longer be distinct. Hence it should be impossible under minimalist assumptions to derive both forms in (13).

Suppose we try to escape this consequence by inventing an auxiliary principle P that somehow preserves the minimalist theory but succeeds in deriving both forms of (13) from the same LCS. Consider then (16).

(16) a.　Snow (slowly) covered the field.
     b.　*The field (slowly) covered (with snow).

Cover is conceptually exactly the same as *fill*, except that its Place-function is ON$_d$ instead of IN$_d$. Principle P thus would predict—incorrectly—that *cover* should appear in both forms in (16), completely parallel to *fill*. In short, the minimalist theory is deficient again: it is not expressive enough to sort out the syntactic differences between (13) and (16).

For a final case, consider a verb such as *pass*, which has multiple argument structures abbreviated by the curly bracket notation. Here is the entry of *pass* worked out in section 4.2.

(17)
$$
\begin{bmatrix}
\text{pass} \\
\text{V} \\
\underline{\quad\quad} \langle XP_j \rangle \\
[\text{GO} ([_{\text{Thing}}\quad]_i, [_{\text{Path}} \text{VIA} [_{\text{Place}} \{\text{NEAR} [_{\text{Thing}}\quad]_j\}]]_{\{j\}})]
\end{bmatrix}
$$

Recall that this entry encodes the alternate conceptual structures given in (18).

(18) a. $[_{\text{Path}} \text{VIA} [_{\text{Place}} \text{NEAR} [_{\text{Thing}}\quad]_j]]$
   (argument is Thing, as in *The train passed the station*)
   b. $[_{\text{Path}} \text{VIA} [_{\text{Place}}\quad]]_j$
   (argument is Path, as in *The train passed through the tunnel*)

Suppose we adopt the minimalist theory and drop all indices. There are at least two difficulties. First, how do we know that the second argument position in (18b) is a Path with VIA as a selectional restriction, rather than a Place argument of VIA? (The latter would give the form *The train passed in the tunnel* rather than *The train passed through the tunnel*, for instance.) Second, how can we collapse the two structures in (18) into the form in (17)? The curly bracket notation makes crucial use of the indices and therefore becomes incoherent when they are dropped.

The essential fact revealed by these examples is that lexical conceptual structure must distinguish those constituents that are arguments from those that are not. The coindexing notation does this by placing indices on the arguments. Eliminating these indices loses all differentiation among arguments, implicit arguments, selectional restrictions, and adjuncts. Given the variation among lexical items, a linking theory cannot unambiguously pick out the arguments without some help from the lexical items themselves.

A proper enrichment of the minimalist theory seems to be to indicate which constituents of the LCS are arguments, but to leave it for the linking rules to determine in what syntactic position each argument is to be expressed. Accordingly, we will introduce a marker of argumenthood, notated as a subscript A. This marker will appear in just those positions in LCS that previously contained a coindex to syntactic structure. So, for instance, the lexical entries of *open* and *pass* can be specified as in (19).

(19) a.
$$
\begin{bmatrix}
\text{open} \\
\text{V} \\
[\text{CAUSE} ([_{\text{Thing}}\quad]_A, [\text{GO} ([_{\text{Thing}}\quad]_A, [\text{TO} [\text{OPEN}]])])]
\end{bmatrix}
$$
   b.
$$
\begin{bmatrix}
\text{pass} \\
\text{V} \\
[\text{GO} ([_{\text{Thing}}\quad]_A, [_{\text{Path}} \text{VIA} [_{\text{Place}} \{\text{NEAR} [_{\text{Thing}}\quad]_A\}]]_{\{A\}})]
\end{bmatrix}
$$

In this approach, the Dominant θ-Role Principle (10) determines which position in a bound complex of conceptual constituents is marked A; the

Linking Principle determines which syntactic positions correspond to which A-marked conceptual constitutents.

Notice that (19a) still solves the problem of collapsing the causative alternation. The difficulty for the coindexing theory was that the two syntactic positions of the Theme could not be collapsed. But the A-marking theory, while it stipulates that the Theme is an argument, does not stipulate where the Theme is to be expressed syntactically. That responsibility is transferred to the Linking Principle. Hence collapsing the two argument structures does not present a difficulty.

Next notice that (19b) restores to the LCS of *pass* just the information necessary to find the possible choices of arguments. At the same time, it makes no commitment to the syntactic realizations of the arguments; that again is up to the Linking Principle. Thus the A-marking theory strikes a compromise between the coindexing theory and the minimalist theory that avoids the difficulties of either extreme.

Consider next the problem of optional arguments. A simple way to encode optionality is to permit optional A-marking. For instance, the difference between *eat* and *devour* can be encoded as in (20) (using a tentative conceptual analysis parallel to that of *drink* in chapter 2).

$$(20)\ a.\ \begin{bmatrix} \text{eat} \\ V \\ [\text{CAUSE} ([_{\text{Thing}}\ ]^{\alpha}_{A}, [\text{GO} ([_{\text{Thing}}\ ]_{\langle A \rangle}, \\ \qquad\qquad\qquad [\text{TO} [\text{IN} [\text{MOUTH-OF} [\alpha]]]])])] \end{bmatrix}$$

$$b.\ \begin{bmatrix} \text{devour} \\ V \\ [\text{CAUSE} ([_{\text{Thing}}\ ]^{\alpha}_{A}, [\text{GO} ([_{\text{Thing}}\ ]_{A}, \\ \qquad\qquad\qquad [\text{TO} [\text{IN} [\text{MOUTH-OF} [\alpha]]]])])] \end{bmatrix}$$

The difference is only that *eat* encloses the second A-mark in brackets, indicating its optionality. The number of arguments, hence the transitivity of the verb, depends on whether A is chosen or not. By contrast, *devour* has an obligatory A-mark on the second argument, so it is always transitive.

The case of *fill* and *cover* is more interesting. Here are the lexical entries for these verbs:

$$(21)\ a.\ \begin{bmatrix} \text{fill} \\ V \\ [\text{INCH} [\text{BE} ([_{\text{Thing}}\ ]_{\langle A \rangle}, [\text{IN}_d [_{\text{Thing}}\ ]_A])]] \end{bmatrix}$$

$$b.\ \begin{bmatrix} \text{cover} \\ V \\ [\text{INCH} [\text{BE} ([_{\text{Thing}}\ ]_A, [\text{ON}_d [_{\text{Thing}}\ ]_A])]] \end{bmatrix}$$

Cover comes out as straightforwardly transitive, with two arguments. Assuming a thematic hierarchy in which Theme precedes Goal (to be justified in section 11.5), the Theme comes out in subject position and the Goal in object position, as in (16a). *Fill*, however, marks the Theme as an optional argument. If the Theme is an argument, the syntactic frame comes out the same as *cover*, as seen in (13a). On the other hand, if the Theme is not an argument, the only remaining argument is the Goal, which therefore is mapped into subject position. At the same time, the Theme now is not A-marked and is therefore available to the *With*-Theme Adjunct Rule, yielding the form seen in (13b). Thus the A-marking theory again avoids the pitfalls of both the stipulative theory and the minimalist theory.

Finally, the A-marking theory explains why there could not be such lexical items as *benter* and *succeive*. These items, by assumption, have the same LCS as *enter* and *receive* respectively but reversed linking to syntax. The problem with the coindexing theory is that this reversed linkage was all too easily expressed. In the A-marking theory, though, there is no way to differentiate *benter* from *enter*: both have two A-marked arguments, the Theme and the Goal. Thus, assuming linking theory provides the correct syntactic realization for the arguments of *enter* (in fact paralleling *cover*), *benter* could not help but have the same syntax. Similarly for *receive* and *succeive*.

To summarize the theory up to this point, the claim is that lexical entries stipulate their conceptual arguments (A-marking) but do not stipulate the syntactic positions to which the arguments link. This preserves all the elements of θ-theory worked out in part I, but leaves the way open for a linking-theoretic account of the syntactic position of arguments.

This theory bears a strong resemblance to approaches such as those of Rappaport and Levin (1985, 1988) and Grimshaw (1987, 1990), in that it specifies arguments but not their syntactic positions. The major difference is that these other approaches posit a level of representation separate from LCS for this purpose—Predicate Argument Structure for Rappaport and Levin, Argument Structure for Grimshaw. In the present approach, this information is carried simply as annotations on the LCS—the A-markings.[2]

The theory so far makes no provision for explicit recognition of an external argument—the argument that maps to subject position. Rather, following Grimshaw (1987), the external argument is a derived role: it is just the most prominent of the A-marked positions. Should it prove of interest to stipulate the external argument in LCS, one could reserve a special mark, say A', for one of the arguments. However, notice that this would reintroduce one of the problems raised by the stipulative theory, namely the proper collapsing of the multiple argument structures in causatives and in *fill*. Similar remarks pertain to the stipulation of a postverbal "direct argument," as in Marantz 1984 and Tenny 1987. The possibility of such stipulations defeats the purpose of a linking theory. So let's try to do without them. The role of the notion "external argument" in the theory will emerge more clearly in section 11.8.

11.4 Digression: What Is Left of Subcategorization?

In backtracking from the minimalist theory to the A-marking theory, we have not yet addressed the issue of subcategorization features. Before continuing to work out the linking theory, let me insert a few words on this matter.

From what has been said so far, it looks as if we might be able to predict subcategorization from argument structure alone. However, this conclusion conflicts with the treatment of "obligatory adjuncts" in section 8.7. Recall the following minimal pairs:

(22) a. Bill emptied/rid the room of insects.
          Bill emptied/*rid the room.
      b. The dwarves decorated/encrusted the throne with jewels.
          The dwarves decorated/*encrusted the throne.
      c. Bill supplied/provided the students with some books.
          Bill supplied/*provided the students.   (on Goal reading of *students*)
      d. Bill robbed/deprived Harry of his money.
          Bill robbed/*deprived Harry.

These involve contrasts of obligatory versus optional expression of conceptual arguments, just like *eat/devour* or *put/insert*. Unfortunately, optional A-marking, which worked for *eat* versus *devour* (20), cannot be applied to the cases in (22). The reason is that our treatment of the *of-* and *with-*phrases in (22) depends specifically on their being adjuncts; that is, the requisite conceptual arguments in (22) are not A-marked at all in the LCS of the verb. As a consequence, the distinctions in (22) cannot be expressed with optional A-marking, and another treatment is necessary.

The solution proposed in section 8.7 was to include the obligatory constituents in the verb's subcategorization feature but to indicate their adjunct status by not coindexing them to the LCS. Translated into the A-marking notation, here is *rid*:

(23) $\begin{bmatrix} \text{rid} \\ \text{V} \\ \underline{\hspace{1em}} \text{NP } [_{PP} \text{ of NP}] \\ [\text{CAUSE } ([\ \ ]_A, [\text{INCH } [\text{NOT BE } ([\ \ ], [\text{IN}_d [\ \ ]_A])]])] \end{bmatrix}$

The Theme is unindexed, hence susceptible to the *Of*-Theme Adjunct Rule, which provides an interpretation for the *of-*phrase.

Entry (23) reintroduces subcategorization, which we had hoped to eliminate (though it does still do without stipulated linking between LCS and
subcategorization). On the other hand, maybe this isn't such a disaster.
Further consideration suggests that despite our success in simplifying subcategorization up to this point, there still remain some residual cases where
syntactic subcategorization is necessary.

One case is where a verb stipulates an idiosyncratic preposition, for
instance *believe in NP, convince NP of NP, depend/rely/count on NP*. One
might also include here the idiosyncratic differences in use of preposition in
the verbs of contact and attachment (sections 6.2, 6.3); *touch/contact NP* but
attach/stick to NP. These appear to be purely syntactic facts about these
verbs; even granted the semantic generalizations concerning which verbs
are liable to take which prepositions, the prepositions themselves seem to
play no discernible semantic role. Thus these verbs must stipulate their
syntactic context in a fashion not unlike (23).

For a case that illuminates the situation further, consider idiomatic verb-
particle combinations such as *throw up* ("vomit"). In syntactic structure,
these are indistinguishable from productive verb-particle combinations
where the choice of particle is fairly free (24a) and the particle alternates
with a full PP (24b).

(24) a. send the books out/away/up/down
     b. send the books to Bill/down the chute

In particular, both kinds of particles alternate in order with the object: *throw
up his lunch/throw his lunch up, send out the books/send the books out*. How are
idiomatic verb-particle combinations lexically listed? Given the approach
for *rid*, we could say there is a special entry for *throw* that (1) means
"vomit" and (2) obligatorily subcategorizes an intransitive PP *up*. This
seems somewhat forced, though. What we really want to say is something
like this:

$$(25) \left[\begin{array}{l} [_{VP} \, [_V \, \text{throw}] \, [_{PP} \, [_P \, \text{up}]]] \\ [_{Event} \, \text{CAUSE} \, ([\quad]^z_A, \, [\text{GO} \, ([\quad]_A, \\ \qquad\qquad\qquad\qquad [\text{FROM} \, [\text{IN} \, [\text{STOMACH-OF} \, [\alpha]]]])])] \end{array} \right]$$

This entry is a partially specified VP rather than a V, whose meaning is
something like "eject stuff from one's stomach." Similarly, the idiom *take
NP to task* would be a lexical VP with an unspecified object but a specified
PP. Under a parallel treatment, the syntactic part of *rid* would substitute the
expression (26) for the category feature V and the subcategorization feature.

(26) $[_{VP} \, [_V \, \text{rid}] \, \text{NP} \, [_{PP} \, [_P \, \text{of}] \, \text{NP}]]$

(Perhaps this could be simplified a little by eliminating the direct object.) In short, the treatment of specified prepositions and "obligatory adjuncts" falls in with that of idiomatic verb-particle combinations.[3]

Another sort of argument for subcategorization concerns semantically unpredictable restrictions on the syntactic category of a complement. Here is a possible minimal triplet:

(27) a. Harry became/went/got crazy.
    b. Harry became/*went/*got a raving maniac.
    c. Harry ??became/went/*got out of his mind.

The three verbs are pretty much synonymous when they have an AP-complement (27a), yet *become* allows an NP alternant, *go* allows a PP alternant, and *get* in the relevant sense allows neither. These look at least in part, then, like syntactic restrictions.

Parallel cases are adduced by Grimshaw (1979). Consider the contrast in (28).

(28) a. Sue asked/wondered what time it was.
    b. Sue asked/*wondered the time.

The NP object in (28b) has the same interpretation as the indirect question complement in (28a); that is, with the application of a rule of construal that Grimshaw calls the Concealed Question Rule, *the time* fills the same conceptual argument position as *what time it was*. Grimshaw asks why the use of concealed questions is not totally free—why *wonder* cannot occur with one. She shows that the possibility is conditioned by whether or not the verb independently has NP-complements—for example, *ask the question* is all right but *wonder the question* is not. She concludes, then, that ability to occur with an NP object is in part a syntactic fact about a verb that is independent of the semantics of the complement in question. In short, some lexical syntactic specification is again necessary, in order to constrain the mapping of LCS into syntactic structure.

There appears therefore to be some balance yet to be struck between conceptual A-marking and syntactic subcategorization in determining the syntactic argument structure that appears with a verb. We have managed to eliminate much of the superficial complexity of subcategorization, but at the moment I would hesitate to endorse without more careful research the claim that *all* syntactic argument structure is determined by conceptual structure plus A-marking.

11.5 Refining the Thematic Hierarchy

We now must work out some of the technical details involved in switching from a stipulative coindexing theory of linking to the A-marking theory.

The first item on our agenda is to specify somewhat more precisely the actual content of the linking rules.

The basic principle of the thematic hierarchy appears to be the following:

(29) *Thematic hierarchy*
       Order the A-marked arguments in the action tier from left to right, followed by the A-marked arguments in the main conceptual clause of the thematic tier, from least embedded to most deeply embedded.

That is, in the present configurational theory of θ-roles, the thematic hierarchy emerges as a semiprincipled ordering. (To repeat the admonition once again, this result cannot be stated in a taxonomic theory of θ-roles as diacritics.)

More precisely, the hierarchy can be listed as follows; the relevant constituents are marked with *:

(30) *Thematic hierarchy*
       a. $[\text{AFF}\ (X^*, \langle Y \rangle)]$ (Actor)
       b. $[\text{AFF}\ (\langle X \rangle, Y^*)]$ (Patient (AFF$^-$) or Beneficiary (AFF$^+$))
       c. $[_{\text{Event/State}}\ F\ (X^*, \langle Y \rangle)]$ (Theme)
       d. $[_{\text{Path/Place}}\ F\ (X^*)]$ (Location, Source, Goal)

(31) is a minimal syntactic hierarchy for English.

(31) *Syntactic hierarchy*
       a. $[_S \text{NP}^* \ldots]$
       b. $[_{VP}\ V\ \text{NP}^* \ldots]$
       c. $[_{VP}\ V \ldots \text{NP}^* \ldots]$

Some notes:

1. (30) and (31) give no special recognition to the syntactic position subject, nor, as mentioned previously, to the external argument. These are nothing but the highest positions on their respective hierarchies. Section 11.8 will briefly motivate a modification that restores to these notions some of the prominence they have in most current theory.

2. The syntactic hierarchy pertains only to NP arguments. PP-, AP-, and S'-complements are not included. Section 11.7 takes up the linking of these complements.

3. The role Agent (first argument of CS) does not appear on the thematic hierarchy, because it is always bound either to Actor or, in the case of verbs of reaction (section 7.3.3), to Patient.

4. As a result, the various functions that define Theme need not be named: Theme is the first argument of all Event- and State-functions other than CS. This is the formulation in (30c); it is clearly simpler than an enumeration of GO/BE/STAY/etc.

5. There is no mention of a role Instrument in (30). Instrumental PPs (*with a key*), being adjuncts, do not appear in the hierarchy. For the most part, instrumental subjects (*The key opened the door*) are grammatically just inanimate Agents. The only verbs I have encountered that might be said specifically to select an Instrument role are *use*, whose object is an Instrument, and *serve*, as in *The key serves to open the door*, whose subject is an Instrument (this case pointed out by Joan Bresnan and given this analysis by Jane Grimshaw). These verbs still await conceptual analysis, so I leave their account in terms of the hierarchy open. Meanwhile, it should be recalled from section 7.6 that the role Instrument can be structurally decomposed into a particular configuration of Actor and Patient roles, so the omission of Instrument from the hierarchy is not particularly serious.

6. With the caveats above, (30) is pretty close to all the hierarchies I have encountered in the literature. The main remaining disparities involve the lack of a role Experiencer in (30) and the relative ordering of Theme and Goal, which differs among theories. I return to these questions shortly.

For the moment, let us take the linking rule to be (9), which links the dominant θ-roles of the verb in the order specified by (30) with the syntactic roles in the order specified by (31).

Here are the combinations of thematic roles and NP argument structures encountered in previous chapters, plus a few extras. Dominant θ-roles are italicized.

(32) *Intransitives*

    a. *Actor*/Theme: Sarah walked (for hours).

    b. *Actor*/Source: The chimney smoked. The whistle shrieked.

    c. *Actor* or *Patient*/Theme: The ball rolled/spun (for hours).

    d. *Patient*/Goal: The tank filled.

    e. *Beneficiary*/?: Only Harry benefited (from X).

(33) *Transitives*

    a. *Actor*/Agent, *Patient*/Theme: Emily threw the ball.

    b. *Actor*/Agent, *Patient*/Goal: Pete hit the ball (with the bat).

    c. *Actor*/Agent, *Patient*/Source: Sam skinned the rabbit. Emma emptied the sink. Jayne robbed Phil.

    d. *Actor*/Agent, *Beneficiary*: The girls helped the boys.

    e. *Actor*/Agent, *Beneficiary*/Goal: The store supplies students (with books).

    f. *Actor*/Theme, *Patient*/Goal: The car hit the tree. Snow covered the field.

    g. *Actor*/Theme, *Source*: Bill left the room.

    h. *Actor*/Theme, *Goal*: The smoke entered the room.

    i. *Actor*/Theme, *Reference Object*: The train climbed the mountain.

The plane approached the house. The car passed the house. Abe avoided the beach.
j. *Actor*/Source, *Theme*: The sodium emitted electrons.
k. *Beneficiary*/Goal, *Theme*: Laurie received a present.
l. *Actor* or *Beneficiary*/Goal, *Theme*: Laurie got a book.
m. *Patient*/Source, *Theme*: Amy lost the money.
n. *Theme, Location*: Kangaroos inhabit Australia.
o. *Theme, Identificational Reference Object*: Ortcutt is a spy.
p. *Patient*/?,?: Max underwent an operation.

The tentative analyses of "psych-verbs" in section 7.3.3 as verbs of reaction add the following possibilities:

q. *Actor*/Agent, *Patient*/Goal: Louise/The news frightened Fred.
r. *(Re)actor*/?, *Stimulus*/?: Fred dislikes Milton.

(We never named the second argument of REACT; I'll call it *Stimulus* here.)

(34) *Ditransitives*
a. *Actor*/Agent, *Patient*/Source, *Theme*: Bill lost Harry his job.
b. *Actor*/Agent/Source, *Beneficiary*/Goal, *Theme*: Jane gave Alan a book.
c. *Actor*/Agent, *Patient*/Theme, *Identificational Goal*: MIT made Peter a linguist.
d. ??: The book will cost you $5. The job took Harry 3 days.
e. ??: I envy you your even disposition.

These are just about all the combinations possible. There would seem to be enough of them to make life extremely difficult for a rigid linking theory like UTAH. I therefore abandon the possibility of a rigid linking theory at this point without regret, leaving (32)–(34) as a challenge to its proponents.

A notable gap in this list is ditransitive causative verbs of motion. A pattern like (35) does not exist, though the hierarchy does not rule it out.

(35) **Actor*/Agent, *Patient*/Theme, *Goal*: *Harry entered the car the tunnel. ("Harry made the car enter the tunnel.")

(35) is awful enough to seem a principled gap. The best solution I can offer within the minimal syntactic theory is to restrict the choices for top-to-bottom matching to a stipulated class of possible linkages. This class is given in (36), which differentiates spatial from identificational reference objects; only the latter are permitted to link to 2nd object.

(36) Actor

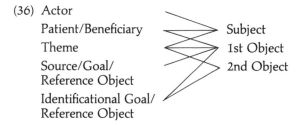

Patient/Beneficiary   Subject

Theme   1st Object

Source/Goal/   2nd Object
Reference Object

Identificational Goal/
Reference Object

(36) lists possible linkings; top-to-bottom matching is carried out just among these possibilities.

One of the conflicts among previous hierarchical theories has been the relative status of Theme and Goal; some (e.g. Carrier-Duncan 1985; Bresnan and Kanerva 1989) place Theme above Goal, some (e.g. Grimshaw 1986) below it. The empirical basis for this conflict is seen in the initial examples of this chapter: *enter* and *receive* both have a Theme and a Goal, but they have opposite mappings to the syntax: *Bill* (Theme) *entered the room* (Goal) but *Bill* (Goal) *received the letter* (Theme).

As it turns out, the Goals that turn up *before* Theme are all possessional Goals, such as the subject of *receive* and the indirect object of *give*. Those that appear *after* Theme are spatial Goals, such as the object of *enter*. To account for this, one could split Goal further in the hierarchy. However, the present theory, incorporating the action tier, provides a more principled solution. In verbs of possession, the dominant θ-role of the possessional Goal is Beneficiary, which puts it ahead of Theme. By contrast, in a spatial verb, either the Goal is itself the dominant θ-role, putting it below Theme (e.g. *enter*), or else the Theme is also Actor and the Goal is also Patient (e.g. *hit*). In either case the Theme comes first. Hence the apparent conflict is resolved.

Turning to counterexamples to this linking theory, the most prominent one, I think, is the verb *have*. Following the standard analysis of Gruber 1965 and Jackendoff 1972, the subject of *have* is a possessional Location and the object is Theme, violating the hierarchy. Noting (a version of) this problem, Falk (1985) and Pinker (1989) independently suggest an alternative analysis in which having something is, in a sense, controlling it. In present terms, this would amount to the subject being a sort of stative Actor and the object a stative Patient, restoring the order of the thematic hierarchy. Alternatively, *have* could be a stative version of *receive*, its subject being a stative Beneficiary, again restoring the hierarchy. Though theory urges me in one of these directions, I am not yet altogether convinced.

Another problem concerns application of the hierarchy to a language like Icelandic, which is much richer in ditransitives than English, or like French, which lacks a second object position altogether. Where are the parameters of variation to be located? Is the thematic hierarchy different, or are the linking principles different, or some combination of the two? Or some other as yet unforeseen possibility?

Still another problem is the analysis of psych-verbs, which has been only minimally justified here. Specifically, the role standardly called Experiencer is treated here as a Location or Goal on the thematic tier: the Experiencer is the location of the fear, pleasure, and so forth. The two main classes of psych-verbs, the *fear/like* class and the *frighten/please* class, differ in the action tier, accounting for their differences in syntactic configuration. A potential difficulty with this treatment is that there seems to be nothing especially out of the ordinary about the *frighten/please* class, which is rife with problems in English and in other languages as well (Postal 1971; Jackendoff 1972; Belletti and Rizzi 1987; Grimshaw 1987; Pesetsky, forthcoming). All of these analyses ascribe the problems to an exceptional property somewhere in the mapping from thematic roles to S-Structure. So far we have not located a cognate exceptional property here, from which the peculiarities of these verbs could be deduced. So something has been missed.[4]

From this list of problems, it should be clear that all I intend here is a preliminary exposition of how a hierarchical linking theory would interface with the present theory of thematic roles. This is only the beginning of the enterprise of putting the semantic end of linking theory on as firm a basis as the syntactic end. But for now, and not without regret, I will have to leave these puzzles as is.

11.6 Factoring Argument Fusion

Given this first approximation to the thematic hierarchy, the next task is to get the linking rules to interact properly with the rest of the correspondence rule. In particular, we need to integrate linking theory with the rule of Argument Fusion (2.13), which is the locus of interaction.

(2.13) *Argument Fusion*
   To form the conceptual structure for a syntactic phrase XP headed by a lexical item H:
   a. Into each indexed constituent in H's LCS, fuse the conceptual structure of that phrase YP that satisfies the coindexed position in H's subcategorization feature.
   b. If H is a verb, fuse the conceptual structure of the subject into the constituent indexed *i* in H's LCS.

The output of this rule undergoes the Restrictive Modifier Rule (2.18), which integrates the interpretation of the head and its arguments with the readings of restrictive modifiers.

(2.13) is now incorrect in two respects. First, in the case of "super-ordinate" adjuncts of the sort discussed in chapter 10, the linking is specified by the adjunct rather than the verb; we return to this problem in section 11.9. Second, the head's LCS does not provide coindexing to syntax any more. It only provides A-marking that serves as input to the linking rules, which in turn determine the linking. Thus we have to factor Argument Fusion into two independent parts: (1) establishing the linking of arguments, and (2) fusing the readings of arguments with argument positions.

To work through a concrete example, suppose that the syntactic structure whose interpretation we are constructing is (37). Then (19a), the lexical entry for the verb *open*, provides the two possibilities given in (38a, b).

(37) $[_S [_{NP}$ Bill] $[_{VP}$ opened [NP the door]]]

(38) a. $[CAUSE ([_{Thing}\ ]_A, [GO ([_{Thing}\ ]_A, [TO [OPEN]])])]$
     b. $[GO ([_{Thing}\ ]_A, [TO [OPEN]])]$

The rule of Argument Linking (9) now determines the proper matching of syntactic arguments to A-marked conceptual arguments. However, (9) leaves inexplicit how the matching is to be encoded. As it happens, nothing could be more convenient than our previous coindexing notation: the A-marking theory can retain the coindexing notation, but it uses Argument Linking to *derive* the coindexing that we previously *stipulated*. (39) incorporates this refinement.

(39) *Argument Linking* (version 3)
     a. Order the A-marked constituents in the verb's LCS according to the thematic hierarchy (30).
     b. Order the NP-constituents in the syntactic structure according to the syntactic hierarchy (31).
     c. Coindex the first through nth NPs with the first through nth A-marked constituents respectively, choosing coindexations from among the possibilities in the network (36).

Given this rule, syntactic structure (37) is matched with (38a) in the manner shown in (40a); it is matched with (38b) as in (40b).

(40) a. $[[Bill]_i$ [opened [the door]$_j$]] corresponds to
        $[CAUSE ([_{Thing}\ ]_i, [GO ([_{Thing}\ ]_j, [TO [OPEN]])])]$
     b. $[[Bill]_i$ [opened [the door]]] corresponds to
        $[GO ([_{Thing}\ ]_i, [TO [OPEN]])]$

In (40b), of course, *the door* is not coindexed with a conceptual position. This means that it cannot be integrated into the interpretation. As a result, this derivation is ill formed; (37) must be matched with the causative interpretation of *open*.

Consider, alternatively, the case in which Argument Linking applies to *The door opened*. Here, if it attempts to link *The door opened* with (38a), the result will be ill formed, because the second of the A-marked conceptual arguments will remain unlinked. Rather, *The door opened* can properly link only with the single-argument structure (38b). In other words, Argument Linking guarantees the proper number of arguments as well as their proper position.

Once Argument Linking has established the matching of arguments, it remains to combine the readings of the arguments with the LCS. This function still falls to Argument Fusion, whose residue can now be simply restated as (41).

(41) *Argument Fusion* (final version)

To form the conceptual structure of a syntactic phrase that has been linked with an LCS, fuse the conceptual structure of each indexed syntactic position into the coindexed conceptual constituent in the LCS.

This rule applies to the coindexed syntactic and conceptual structures in (40a) to produce the full conceptual structure for the sentence, (42).

(42) [[Bill]$_i$ [opened [the door]$_j$]] corresponds to

[CAUSE ([$_{Thing}$ BILL]$_i$, [GO ([$_{Thing}$ DOOR]$_j$, [TO [OPEN]])])]

11.7 Linking Non-NP Arguments

As it stands, Argument Linking pertains only to A-marked conceptual constituents that are syntactically expressed as NPs. It does not permit A-marked constituents to be linked with APs, PPs, or complement S's. This is obviously a mistake: there undeniably are syntactic arguments that belong to these categories, and in particular they often alternate with NP arguments:

(43) a. Bill considers Harry $\begin{Bmatrix} \text{a fool.} \\ \text{crazy.} \end{Bmatrix}$ (NP/AP alternation)

b. The train climbed $\begin{Bmatrix} \text{the hill.} \\ \text{up the hill.} \end{Bmatrix}$ (NP/PP alternation)

c. Sandy told us $\begin{Bmatrix} \text{a story.} \\ \text{that it snowed.} \end{Bmatrix}$ (NP/S' alternation)

The simplest approach seems to be to permit completely free coindexation between conceptual arguments and non-NP syntactic arguments. In contrast to the problem of determining the order of NP arguments, which motivated linking theory in the first place, there is no problem with the relative order of AP, PP, and S' arguments. Rather, their relative order is predicted by principles of phrase structure: NPs in V' are followed in succession by APs, PPs, and S's. Moreover, within-category ordering does not present a problem either. Consider APs, PPs, and S's in turn.

1. *APs.* There is never more than one complement AP, so the issue of relative ordering of multiple AP arguments never arises.

2. *PPs.* When there is more than one complement PP (if indeed such cases are arguments rather than adjuncts), the relative order is usually free, with no particular evidence that one is derived from the other:

(44) a. Did you hear from Lila about Henry?
     Did you hear about Henry from Lila?
   b. We don't usually speak of/about such matters to/with our children.
     We don't usually speak to/with our children of/about such matters.

(An exception is *think of Harry as a genius/ *think as a genius of Harry.*)

3. *S's.* When there is more than one complement S', the first is the object complement (i.e. under V'); but the second is an "extraposed" subject complement and therefore under V" rather than V' (see section 9.6 for explanation of the scare quotes):

(45) It would [$_{V'}$ prove that Charley isn't guilty] for him to arrive so soon.   (from Jackendoff 1977, 96)

So the issue of relative ordering of S'-complements does not arise either. In short, the thematic hierarchy need not play any role in determining the position of non-NP arguments.

What about the relation between NP arguments and non-NP arguments? It appears that linking of non-NP arguments can in principle be freely interspersed with that of NP arguments. Nothing in Argument Linking per se has to check if arguments are of the right type, since, if a linking is established between an argument position and a semantically incompatible argument, Argument Fusion will simply produce a selectional restriction violation. Furthermore, all linking can be optional, since anything that remains unlinked by either Argument Linking, an adjunct rule, or the Restrictive Modifier Rule will lead to an ill-formed derivation.

Accordingly, let us restate Argument Linking to accommodate these possibilities:

(46) *Argument Linking* (version 4)
   a. Order the A-marked constituents in the verb's LCS according to the thematic hierarchy (30).
   b. Order the NP-constituents in the syntactic structure according to the syntactic hierarchy (31).
   c. Optionally coindex APs, PPs, and S's freely to A-marked constituents in the LCS.
   d. Coindex the first through nth NPs with the remaining A-marked

constituents in thematic order, choosing coindexations from among the possibilities in the network (36).

A virtue of this arrangement is that it permits a simple account of alternations between NP- and S'-complements. Consider (47).

(47) a.   Ben said some strange things to Hilary.
      b.   Ben said to Hilary that the sky was red.
      c.   *Ben said to Hilary.

The Theme argument of *say* is of the category Information, and so it can be expressed either by an NP as in (47a) or by an S' as in (47b). (47c) shows that this argument is obligatorily expressed in the syntax. If we were restricted to a rigid linking theory, we would have to account for this alternation by generating the NP and the S' in the same D-Structure position, then moving one of them to its surface position. But this would miss the generalization of English phrase structure that NPs precede PPs but S's follow PPs.

Using rule (46), though, there is no difficulty. The phrase structure rules generate the surface order directly. If there is an S'-complement, it links to Theme by rule (46c); any other linkages produce anomaly. If there is an NP-complement, it takes its place in the syntactic hierarchy behind the subject and thus is linked to Theme, which falls behind Actor in the thematic hierarchy. If both NP and S' were present (*Ben said some strange things to Hilary that the sky was red*), one would have to remain unlinked, again resulting in anomaly.

This formulation of Argument Linking also permits a reasonably elegant solution to "dative shift" in the "true *to*-dative" verbs such as *give*. (See Section 9.5 for the distinction between "true *to*-datives" and "*to*-dative adjuncts.") Recall (sections 7.3 and 9.5) that in the ditransitive form of a *to*-dative verb, the Goal is also Beneficiary, but in the NP-PP form this is not so clearly the case:

(48) (= (7.29))
      a.   What Harry did for Sam was give him a book.
      b.   ?What Harry did for Sam was give a book to him.

This suggests that the difference between the two forms is whether the verb grammatically specifies the Goal as a Beneficiary; whatever Beneficiary character it has in (48b) can be regarded as a weaker discourse function (see note 1 to chapter 7).

Accordingly, here is a lexical entry for *give*:

$$(49) \begin{bmatrix} \text{give} \\ \text{V} \\ \begin{bmatrix} \text{CAUSE } ([\alpha], [\text{GO}_{\text{Poss}} ([\quad]_A, [\text{TO } [\beta]]_{\{A\}})]) \\ \text{AFF}^+ ([\quad]^{\alpha}_A, \{[\quad]^{\beta}_A\}) \end{bmatrix} \end{bmatrix}$$

The curly brackets abbreviate the two forms in (50).

(50) a. $\begin{bmatrix} \text{CAUSE} ([\alpha], [\text{GO}_{\text{Poss}} ([\quad]_A, [\text{TO} [\quad]]_A)]) \\ \text{AFF}^+ ([\quad]^{\alpha}_A, \quad) \end{bmatrix}$

   b. $\begin{bmatrix} \text{CAUSE} ([\alpha], [\text{GO}_{\text{Poss}} ([\quad]_A, [\text{TO} [\beta]])]) \\ \text{AFF}^+ ([\quad]^{\alpha}_A, [\quad]^{\beta}_A) \end{bmatrix}$

(50a) has as dominant θ-roles an Actor, a Theme, and a Path. The first two of these map into subject and object respectively, following the thematic hierarchy. The third maps into a PP, which, because of the phrase structure rules of English, automatically follows the object. In turn, because of the selectional restriction on the Path argument, the only possible realization of the Path-function is with the preposition *to*. On the other hand, the dominant θ-roles of (50b) are Actor, Beneficiary, and Theme in that order, mapping into subject, object, and second object respectively. In other words, the syntactic reordering of arguments in the dative alternation follows automatically from the alternation in argument structure.

A further aspect of this analysis is that *non*–dative shift verbs of possessional transfer like *donate* must differ in their LCS from *give*. This is easily arranged: the LCS of *donate* is just (50a), the form that produces the NP-PP syntax. Insofar as *donate* patterns like (48b) in the test for Beneficiary, this seems like a correct analysis.[5]

Summing up the results of this section, we might see the basic principle of linking as "Link freely," with one particular subsystem—the NP arguments—being subject to a further constraint, the thematic hierarchy. That is, the constraints on NP linking are more properly seen as specializations within a basically much looser system. One can imagine why such constraints might be there: the NP arguments, unlike the others, give no intrinsic hints as to their roles, so they have to be positionally differentiated. But such speculation awaits further research before it can be advocated responsibly.

11.8 The Subject and the External Argument

We turn next to another refinement of Argument Linking, concerning the roles of the subject position in the syntactic hierarchy and of the "external argument" position in the LCS. There are various reasons why one might want to accord these slightly different treatment. First, of course, the subject is not governed by the verb, as are the other syntactic arguments. Second, one may (depending on one's syntactic theory—see section 9.7) want to admit the possibility of bare VP-complements that lack even a PRO subject, for example in the complement of *try*. In such a treatment, the removal of the top position on the syntactic hierarchy certainly does not have the effect of moving all the conceptual arguments one step down the ladder—it is just to remove the external argument, and leave all other arguments in their usual places.

Third, Grimshaw (1986) shows that in nominals—even those that take arguments—the possessive NP is always an adjunct, not a true subject. Among her evidence is the fact that the possessive NP is always optional, and it is often replaceable by a determiner, as in *that destruction of the city* or *such examinations of the students*. She also points out that the "subject" argument of an NP can be satisfied by an adjective, as in *the American destruction of Nicaragua's economy*.

Such phenomena suggest factoring the subject out of the linking hierarchy, replacing it in (36) with the intermediary term *External Argument*, as in (51).

(51) *Linking hierarchy*

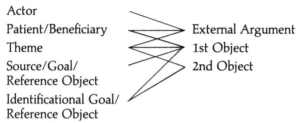

The External Argument can then be treated in a variety of ways, say those in (52).

(52) *External Argument Linking*
 a. If the head is a V, and there is a subject, coindex the External Argument with the subject.
 b. If the head is a V, and there is no subject, satisfy the External Argument with a bound variable ξ. (see rule (9.72))
 c. If the head is an N, suppress the A-marking on the External Argument.

We might even be able to include here an "interpretive" account of the subject in the imperative construction:

 d. In a subjectless main clause with a tenseless V, satisfy the External Argument with [YOU].

In short, this modification of the linking hierarchy permits us to perform a variety of manipulations on the External Argument before settling on the necessity of linking it to a subject.

This treatment accords subject and External Argument the special status they have in most current theory. But it still makes external argument a derived rather than a stipulated property of an LCS, in accordance with

Grimshaw's treatment: the External Argument is simply the highest dominant θ-role of the verb's LCS.

Incorporating this approach into Argument Linking yields (53).

(53) *Argument Linking* (version 5)
   a. Order the A-marked constituents in the verb's LCS according to the thematic hierarchy (30).
   b. Order the NP-constituents in V′ according to the syntactic hierarchy (31).
   c. Link the first A-marked constituent with the External Argument.
   d. Optionally coindex APs, PPs, and S's freely to A-marked constituents in the LCS.
   e. Coindex the NPs in V′ with the remaining A-marked constituents in thematic order, choosing coindexations from among the possibilities in the network (51).

The intermediate term External Argument then comes to be realized by (52), the rule of External Argument Linking; finally, the result is submitted to Argument Fusion to derive the full interpretation for the sentence or phrase in question.

11.9 Incorporating Most of the Adjunct Rules

We now return to the problem raised by the linking of adjuncts. The fundamental difficulty is that the verbs in constructions such as (8) do not head the conceptual structures of their sentences; rather, the LCS of the verb appears as part of a subordinate means or accompaniment modifier.

(8) a. Bill belched his way out of the restaurant.
   b. Sue hammered the metal flat.
   c. We laughed ourselves silly.

Nor does the verb's LCS determine the syntactic structure of the sentence. Rather, the structure of the VP is established by the adjunct construction.

Interestingly, though, the adjunct constructions themselves obey the thematic hierarchy. (8a) has only one argument (I assume *his way* is not an argument), so it does not reveal any generalization. But (8b, c) have two NP arguments each. Following the analysis in section 10.4, the conceptual structures of these sentences are essentially the same as *Sue made the metal flat by hammering on it* and *We made ourselves silly by laughing* respectively. In other words, the subject is linked to the Actor in the main conceptual clause of the sentence, and the object to the Patient—even though the main conceptual clause is not determined by the verb.

This leads to a reformulation of Argument Linking that refers not to the LCS of the verb but to the main conceptual clause of the sentence. In ordinary cases, the main conceptual clause is indeed provided directly by the LCS of the verb. But in other cases, such as (8), the LCS of the verb must be combined with the conceptual structure of an adjunct to determine the main conceptual clause. That is, the adjunct rules will now be conceived of as combining with the LCS of the verb prior to Argument Linking; as a result, they have effects on syntactic argument structure.

This section will apply this approach to three representative adjunct rules from chapters 8, 9, and 10. With one exception, to be treated in the next section, the remaining rules present no different problems; they are all restated, for completeness, in the Appendix to this chapter.

11.9.1 The *With*-Theme Adjunct Rule

The *With*-Theme Adjunct Rule is responsible for the final PPs in *The tank filled with water, We buttered the bread with cheap margarine*, and *They loaded the truck with dirt*. Here is the final version arrived at in section 8.4 (rule (8.32)):

(54) With-*Theme Adjunct Rule* (version 4)
  If V corresponds to [... [BE ([X], [F ([$_{\text{Thing}}$])])] ...],
  with [X] unindexed, and NP corresponds to [Y],
  then [$_S$ ... [$_{VP}$ ... [$_{PP}$ with NP] ...] ...] may correspond to
  [... [BE ($\begin{bmatrix} X \\ Y \end{bmatrix}$, [F ([$_{\text{Thing}}$])])] ...], where $\begin{bmatrix} X \\ Y \end{bmatrix}$ is distinct from [X].

Chapter 10 developed an alternative formalism for adjunct rules, in which the verb is treated as an argument of the adjunct construction. Here is a translation of (54) into that formalism:

(55) With-*Theme Adjunct* (version 5)
  [$_{VP}$ V$_h$ ... [$_{PP}$ with NP$_k$] ...] may correspond to   (i)
  [... [BE ([   ]$_k$, [F ([$_{\text{Thing}}$])])] ...]$_h$.   (ii)

Let me decode this. The coindexing *h* between the verb in line (i) and the conceptual expression in line (ii) means that the LCS of the verb is to be fused with line (ii). This is possible only if the verb is of the requisite form, namely if it has a main conceptual clause whose innermost functions are of the form shown in line (ii). In addition, the coindexing between the object of *with* and the Theme of BE stipulates a linking extrinsic to those provided by the LCS of the verb and implemented by Argument Linking. Argument Fusion does not care which rule has established the coindexing, so it fuses the reading of the object of *with* into the Theme argument in the standard way. (This formulation thus differs from (54), which itself performs the fusion. Here we have factored this step out.)

In order to use (55) in a derivation, we need a rule that combines it with a verb. Here it is, essentially a variant of Argument Fusion:

(56) *Adjunct Fusion* (version 1)

To determine the conceptual structure of a VP containing a verb and an adjunct, fuse the LCS of the verb into the constituent indexed h in the adjunct.

In short, we have now factored apart the syntax-semantics correspondence established by the *With*-Theme Adjunct from Adjunct Fusion, which combines the adjunct with a verb, and from Argument Fusion, which incorporates the object of *with* into the reading. (Accordingly, (55) is now named "*With*-Theme Adjunct" rather than "*With*-Theme Adjunct Rule.")

For an example of the use of these rules, let us derive the reading of *The tank filled with water*. The LCS of *fill* shown in (21a) abbreviates two alternative argument structures, shown in (57).

(57) a. [INCH [BE ([$_{\text{Thing}}$], [IN$_d$ [$_{\text{Thing}}$]$_A$])]]

b. [INCH [BE ([$_{\text{Thing}}$]$_A$, [IN$_d$ [$_{\text{Thing}}$]$_A$])]]

Adjunct Fusion combines (57a) with (55) to form (58).

(58) [$_{\text{VP}}$ [$_V$ fill] ... [$_{\text{PP}}$ with NP$_k$] ...] may correspond to
[INCH [BE ([$_{\text{Thing}}$]$_k$, [IN$_d$ [$_{\text{Thing}}$]$_A$])]].

This is the derived main conceptual clause, including a slot for the object of *with*. Applying to this configuration, Argument Linking assigns the single A-marked argument to the External Argument (thence to subject). Finally, Argument Fusion fuses the readings of *tank* and *water* into the two linked argument places.

Consider instead what happens if we try to combine (55) with the alternative LCS (57b), the one responsible for *Water filled the tank*. The result of Adjunct Fusion is two independent indices on the Theme—the k from the adjunct rule plus the A from the LCS. Presumably this is ill formed by convention. This violation is what rules out **Water filled the tank with hot soup;*[6] it corresponds to (and supplants) the stipulation "[X] unindexed" in the previous version of the rule, (54).

(54) contains a further stipulation: that the fusion of [X] (the verb's selectional restriction on the Theme) and [Y] (the reading of the object of *with*) is distinct from [X]. Section 8.3 proposed this condition in order to rule out *??He buttered the bread with butter* but permit *He buttered the bread with cheap margarine/with smooth, creamy butter*. This stipulation too is absent from (55). One can think of various ways to incorporate it: stipulation again, conventions on Adjunct Fusion, conventions on explicit linking. Having no evidence bearing on this issue, I leave it open.

A couple of things to notice about version (55) of the *With*-Theme Adjunct, in part pulling together points made earlier. First, its syntactic part, line (i), is easily adapted to constructions in which an adjunct is marked by case-marking instead of a preposition. Thus this formalism ought to be well suited to at least some phenomena of "semantic case-marking."

Second, there is a very fine line between the pair (55)–(56) and a lexical rule with a similar effect. As they stand, (55)–(56) set up a correspondence between an extralexical syntactic configuration *V ... with NP* and a conceptual structure that incorporates the LCS of the verb. One could just as easily construe this pair of rules as a lexical process that adds an argument to the verb's LCS, linking it with the object of the lexically specified preposition *with*. This potential parallelism has been noted sporadically throughout chapters 8 to 10. In light of the construal of adjunct rules now being adopted, the parallelism is if anything closer than before.

One reason for keeping adjunct rules separate from lexical rules, as mentioned earlier, concerns the conception of the lexicon as a repository of things one must learn about words. The standard cases of lexical rules, say those of derivational morphology for English deverbal nouns, provide *possibilities* for lexical items, but one must still learn which of the possibilities are *actual* words of the language. By contrast, this is not the case with adjuncts: if a verb satisfies the structural conditions of an adjunct, it can always occur with the adjunct. One does not have to learn that the adjunct is an actual realization of the verb's argument structure. The adjunct rules are therefore conceived of as extrinsic to the verb's lexical entry, as principles active in the derivation of the syntax-semantics correspondence of sentences.

To recapitulate a point of section 11.2, adjunct rules now enable us to keep linking theory maximally simple. On the present construal of adjunct rules, the rule of Argument Linking has to provide only one way to link a Theme, for example: through A-marking and the thematic hierarchy. The linking of Theme to the object of *with* is *never* encoded in a lexical entry in terms of an A-marked conceptual argument. This is another reason to keep adjunct rules independent from lexical rules: it permits significant constraints on A-marking and linking theory.

In light of the treatment of subcategorization in section 11.4, a different interpretation of the adjunct rules, advocated especially in chapter 10, comes to the fore. Section 11.4 suggested that idioms like *throw up* and *take NP to task* are lexical VPs; the latter has a syntactic argument that must be satisfied by Argument Linking. Notice now that the formal distinction between the *With*-Theme Adjunct (55) and such idiomatic cases is minimal. (55) in effect amounts to a lexical VP whose only stipulated phonological content is *with*; this VP leaves open two arguments, the verb and the NP. That is, the *with*-Theme adjunct can be regarded as a kind of idiom, having a specialized meaning and learned not too differently from other idioms. (Extending this construal to "semantic case-marking," the proposal is that "semantic case" is a kind of idiom too.) This view of adjunct constructions as complex lexical items makes it more plausible (1) that there should be so many of them, (2) that many of them (such as the *For*-Exchange Adjunct Rule) should have such complex meanings, and (3) that some of them (such as the resultative) should combine with verbs to form still more idiomatic expressions, just as verbs and particles do.

This reformulation of the *With*-Theme Adjunct Rule can be generalized straightforwardly to the *Of*-Theme Adjunct Rule (section 8.4), the PP-Adjunct Rule (section 8.5), the Passive *By*-Adjunct Rule (section 8.8), the *For*-Adjunct Rules of beneficiary (section 9.2), benefit (section 9.2), and exchange (section 9.4), and the Instrumental Adjunct Rule (section 9.2); see the Appendix to this chapter for complete statements.

11.9.2 The Recipient NP Adjunct

Consider next the Recipient NP Adjunct Rule, which is responsible for the indirect objects in *Bill threw Harry the ball, Fran sent Sue some money*, and so forth. As observed in section 9.5, this adjunct occurs with causative verbs of spatial motion and adds a sense of intended possession; it can be clearly distinguished from the "true *to*-dative" indirect objects, which occur with verbs of possession like *give* and *sell*. Here is a translation of the previous form of the rule, (9.44), into the new format:

(59) *Recipient NP Adjunct*

$[_{VP} V_h NP_k \ldots]$ may correspond to

$$\begin{bmatrix} \text{CAUSE}_{\text{launch}} \left([\ \ ], [\text{GO} ([\ \ ]^\alpha, [\text{TO} [\ \ ]^\beta_k])]) \right) \\ [\text{FOR} [\text{GO}_{\text{Poss}} ([\alpha], [\text{TO} [\beta]])]] \end{bmatrix}_h .$$

Let us use (59) to derive the conceptual structure of *Bill threw Harry the ball*. The LCS of *throw* is (60).

(60) $\begin{bmatrix} \text{CAUSE}_{\text{launch}} ([_{\text{Thing}} \alpha], [\text{GO} ([_{\text{Thing}} \beta], [_{\text{Path}} \ \ ])]) \\ \text{AFF}^- ([\ \ ]^\alpha_A, [\ \ ]^\beta_A) \end{bmatrix}$

Note that *throw* has two A-marked arguments, the Actor/Agent and the Patient/Theme. Combining (60) with (59) by Adjunct Fusion yields (61).

(61) $[_{VP} [_V \text{throw}] NP_k \ldots]$ may correspond to

$$\begin{bmatrix} \text{CAUSE}_{\text{launch}} ([_{\text{Thing}} \alpha], [\text{GO} ([_{\text{Thing}} \beta]^\gamma, [_{\text{Path}} \text{TO} [\ \ ]^\delta_k])]) \\ \text{AFF}^- ([\ \ ]^\alpha_A, [\ \ ]^\beta_A) \\ [\text{FOR} [\text{GO}_{\text{Poss}} ([\gamma], [\text{TO} [\delta]])]] \end{bmatrix} .$$

(61) then undergoes Argument Linking. The Actor position links as usual to subject position. The next argument on the thematic hierarchy is Patient, which normally would link to first object position. However, in (61) the first object is prelinked, so the Patient goes one step down the syntactic hierarchy to second object. The result is (62).

(62) $[_S \text{NP}_i [_{VP} [_V \text{throw}] \text{NP}_k \text{NP}_j]]$ may correspond to

$$\begin{bmatrix} \text{CAUSE}_{\text{launch}} ([_{\text{Thing}} \alpha], [\text{GO} ([_{\text{Thing}} \beta]^\gamma, [_{\text{Path}} \text{TO} [\quad]^\delta_k])]) \\ \text{AFF}^- ([\quad]^\alpha_i, [\quad]^\beta_j) \\ [\text{FOR} [\text{GO}_{\text{Poss}} ([\gamma], [\text{TO} [\delta]])]] \end{bmatrix}.$$

This straightforwardly undergoes Argument Fusion, substituting the readings of *Bill*, *Harry*, and *the ball* into the i, k, and j arguments respectively.

As observed in chapter 9, this adjunct construction does not differ significantly from other adjuncts such as the *for*-beneficiary in terms of the conceptual structure it induces. The major difference is in the syntactic side of the rule, which marks the construction positionally instead of with a specified preposition. The extra innovation added here is that the "demotion" of the normal object of the verb to second object position follows automatically from the hierarchical linking theory.[7]

11.9.3 Superordinate Adjuncts

The most complex cases are the superordinate adjuncts of chapter 10. These have already been stated in the quasi-lexical form suggested in this section, in which the verb is treated as an argument coindexed with some part of the adjunct's conceptual structure. To convert these to the linking-theoretic approach, we only need to make two rather minor modifications. Let us look at the simplest case, the GO-adjunct (10.32), which is responsible for the use of verbs of body-internal motion in motion sentences, for instance *Willy wiggled into Harriet's arms*. Here is the previous version:

(63) *GO-Adjunct Rule* (version 2)

$[_{VP} V_h \ldots \text{PP} \ldots]$ may correspond to

$$\begin{bmatrix} \text{GO} ([\alpha], [_{\text{Path}} \quad]) \\ \text{AFF} ([\quad]^\alpha_{i'}) \\ [\text{WITH/BY} [\text{MOVE} ([\alpha])]_h] \end{bmatrix}.$$

The first change is fairly clear: the Actor need no longer be indexed by stipulation to subject position. Rather, the index i can be replaced by A; from the point of view of linking this is an ordinary argument position.

The second change corrects a defect left unresolved in the formulation of these rules in chapter 10. Consider what happens when the LCS of the verb *wiggle*, (64a), is fused with the conceptual structure of the adjunct. The result is shown in (64b).

(64) a. $\begin{bmatrix} \text{MOVE} ([\quad]_A) \\ [_{\text{Manner}} X] \end{bmatrix}$

b. $\begin{bmatrix} \text{GO} ([\alpha], [_{\text{Path}} \quad]) \\ \text{AFF} ([\quad]^\alpha_{A'}) \\ [\text{WITH/BY} \begin{bmatrix} \text{MOVE} ([\alpha]_A) \\ [_{\text{Manner}} X] \end{bmatrix}_h] \end{bmatrix}$

The problem with (64b) is that it has A-marking in two positions, one bound to the other. We obviously want only one; the other must be suppressed. The one that must be retained in order to get the desired form is the one from the adjunct: it is the one in the main conceptual clause. The one from the verb, being within a modifier, has to be suppressed. Not feeling too imaginative by this point in the book, I propose to accomplish this suppression by a flat stipulation in the rule of Adjunct Fusion; no doubt there are cleverer solutions.

(65) *Adjunct Fusion* (version 2)
To determine the conceptual structure of a VP containing a verb and an adjunct, fuse the LCS of the verb into the constituent indexed h in the adjunct; delete any A-markings from the LCS that mark conceptual constituents bound by the adjunct.

The result of applying (65) to fuse (63) with (64a) is the desired form (66).

(66) $[_{VP} [_V$ wiggle$] \dots$ PP $\dots]$ may correspond to

$$\begin{bmatrix} \text{GO } ([\alpha], [_{Path} \quad]) \\ \text{AFF } ([\quad]^{\alpha}_{A'} \quad) \\ [\text{WITH/BY} \begin{bmatrix} \text{MOVE } ([\alpha]) \\ [_{Manner} X] \end{bmatrix}] \end{bmatrix}.$$

The Path-constituent is then linked with the PP by the PP-Adjunct Rule; Argument Linking and the External Argument Rule coindex the Actor with the subject; and Argument Fusion fills in the readings of the single linked argument.

Similar considerations apply to the other superordinate adjuncts, the *way*-adjunct and the resultative adjuncts. They are treated in the Appendix.

11.10 Depictive Predication Again

Finally, let us reexamine depictive adjuncts, for example the AP in *Bill read the book drunk*. Here is the version from section 9.6, (9.60):

(67) *Depictive Predicate Adjunct Rule* (version 2)
If NP corresponds to [X] and AP corresponds to [Y],   (i)
then $[_S \dots NP^1 \dots AP^1 \dots]$ may correspond to   (ii)
$$\begin{bmatrix} \text{F } (\dots [X]^{\alpha} \dots) \\ _{Event} [\text{WITH } [\text{BE}_{Ident} ([\alpha], [\text{AT } [Y]])]] \end{bmatrix}.$$ (iii)

In this rule, the syntactic superscripts identify the NP as the "host" of the AP; this host-to-dependent relationship appears in a number of rules with different semantic effects. One other case briefly discussed was the relationship between an expletive *it* and an "extraposed" complement clause;

other possibilities are the relationship of an "extraposed" relative clause to the NP it modifies and the relationship of a degree phrase such as *for us to eat* to a degree word such as *too* in a phrase like *too big for us to eat*. That is, there seems to be some point in factoring out the syntactic relation between host and predicate in (67) from the conceptual relation. (67) therefore assumes the host-to-predicate relation is marked extrinsically, and based on this marking it imposes the appropriate semantic relation for the construction.

(67) differs in an important respect from the other adjuncts discussed here. All the other adjuncts make essential reference to the conceptual structure of the main conceptual clause: for instance, the *With*-Theme Adjunct refers to the Theme in a particular configuration; the *For*-Benefit and *For*-Beneficiary Adjuncts refer to the Actor; the Recipient NP Adjunct refers to the Path of a causative motion; the GO-Adjunct and Resultative Adjunct create a whole new main conceptual clause. By contrast, depictive predication does not care at all about the structure of the main conceptual clause, beyond the condition that the host NP is somewhere in it. This is reflected in the fact that the main conceptual clause in line (iii) of (67) is the totally vague expression [F (... [X] ...)].

This difference creates a formal difficulty for restating (67) in the format worked out in the previous section. The closest we can get is (68).

(68) *Depictive Predicate Adjunct* (version 3)
$[_S \ldots NP^1{}_j \ldots AP^1{}_k \ldots]$ may correspond to
$$\left[\begin{array}{l} F (\ldots [\quad]^{\alpha}{}_j \ldots) \\ _{Event} [WITH [BE_{Ident} ([\alpha], [AT [\quad]_k])]] \end{array} \right].$$

The problem with (68) is that it establishes a linking between the NP host and some indefinite position in the main conceptual clause. In other cases where an adjunct establishes a linking, either the phrase is not otherwise linked (as in the *With*-Theme Adjunct), or the previous linking is suppressed (as in the GO-Adjunct). In (68), though, neither of these is the case. Rather, this time we want the rule to *superimpose* the linking due to the adjunct on the linking established independently by the verb. Thus some distinction must be introduced in the linking theory to permit this difference in behavior.

Here is one possibility. We already have in the theory two ways to mark linking. The first, which might be called *constant linking*, is the simple coindexation of a syntactic constituent with a conceptual constituent. The second is *A-marking*, where a conceptual constituent is linked, but the choice of which syntactic constituent it links to is determined by the rule of Argument Linking. In effect, Argument Linking converts A-marking to constant linking. Let us now introduce a third kind of marking, to be called *variable linking*. This will be notated also as coindexation of a syntactic constituent and a conceptual constituent, but we will use indices v/w/etc. instead of i/j/etc. (More formally, the two kinds of coindexation could be treated as differing by a feature on the index.) The idea is that variable linking in a rule, instead of *establishing* a linking, is treated formally as a *condition* that a constant linking exists. This is just what we need to make an appropriate modification to depictive predication:

(69) *Depictive Predicate Adjunct* (version 4)

$[_S \ldots NP^1_v \ldots AP^1_k \ldots]$ may correspond to (i)

$$\begin{bmatrix} F(\ldots[\quad]^\alpha_v \ldots) \\ _{\text{Event}} [\text{WITH} [\text{BE}_{\text{Ident}} ([\alpha], [\text{AT} [\quad]_k])]] \end{bmatrix}.$$ (ii)

The only difference between this and (68) is the way the host NP is linked—using variable linking, with coindex v, instead of constant linking, with coindex j.

The variable linking in (69) requires that a constant linking be preestablished. Hence this rule must apply after Argument Linking, which converts A-marking into constant linking. (This contrasts with the other adjunct rules, which are intrinsically ordered *before* Argument Linking.)

To see how this works, let us derive the conceptual structures for the two readings of *Bill left Harry drunk*. (70a) is the syntactic structure; (70b) and (70c) have undergone application of the rule marking potential predicate-to-host relationships for the two possibilities.

(70) a. $[_S [_{NP} \text{Bill}] [_{VP} \text{left} [_{NP} \text{Harry}] [_{AP} \text{drunk}]]]$

  b. $[_S [_{NP} \text{Bill}]^1 [_{VP} \text{left} [_{NP} \text{Harry}] [_{AP} \text{drunk}]^1]]$ (subject host)

  c. $[_S [_{NP} \text{Bill}] [_{VP} \text{left} [_{NP} \text{Harry}]^1 [_{AP} \text{drunk}]^1]]$ (object host)

Argument Linking applies to (70a) to give the partial correspondence shown in (71).

(71) $[_S [_{NP} \text{Bill}]_i [_{VP} \text{left} [_{NP} \text{Harry}]_j [_{AP} \text{drunk}]]]$

corresponds to

$[_{\text{Event}} \text{GO} ([\quad]_i, [_{\text{Path}} \text{FROM} [\quad]_j])]$.

Now (69) can apply. It has two effects. First, it establishes a constant linking for the AP, which is as yet unlinked in (71). Second, it looks in the syntactic structure to see what NP has been superscripted 1. Through the variable linking, it traces the correspondence of this NP to a constituent in conceptual structure and binds this constituent to the Theme of the predication. Applied to (70b), the result is (72a); applied to (70c), the result is (72b).

(72) a. $[_S [_{NP} \text{Bill}]^1_i [_{VP} \text{left} [_{NP} \text{Harry}]_j [_{AP} \text{drunk}]^1_k]]$

corresponds to

$$\begin{bmatrix} \text{GO} ([\quad]^\alpha_i, [_{\text{Path}} \text{FROM} [\quad]_j]) \\ _{\text{Event}} [\text{WITH} [\text{BE}_{\text{Ident}} ([\alpha], [\text{AT} [\quad]_k])]] \end{bmatrix}.$$

b. $[_S [_{NP} \text{Bill}]_i [_{VP} \text{left} [_{NP} \text{Harry}]^1_j [_{AP} \text{drunk}]^1_k]]$
corresponds to

$$\begin{bmatrix} \text{GO} ([\ ]_i, [_{\text{Path}} \text{FROM} [\ ]^\alpha_j]) \\ _{\text{Event}} [\text{WITH} [\text{BE}_{\text{Ident}} ([\alpha], [\text{AT} [\ ]_k])]] \end{bmatrix}.$$

Argument Fusion then applies in the usual way to fill in the readings of *Bill*, *Harry*, and *drunk*. The resulting two readings are precisely as desired.

The claim, then, is that the Depictive Predicate Adjunct is typologically a different kind of rule than the other adjunct rules we have discussed—or more generally, that the correspondence rule component contains a variety of different classes of rules. All the previous adjunct rules have contained essential reference to the verb heading the phrase in which the adjunct occurs; (69) does not. All the previous adjunct rules have depended on a particular conceptual configuration in the main conceptual clause; (69) does not. Moreover, (69) is the only rule we have encountered that makes use of variable linking and the syntactic host-to-predicate relationship.

On the other hand, the other rules that appear to form a natural class with depictive predication share these characteristics. For instance, in the present format, the rule interpreting "extraposed" S'-complements looks something like (73).

(73) *Extraposed S'-Complement Interpretation*
$[_S \dots [_{NP} \text{it}]^1_v \dots S'^1_k \dots]$ may correspond to
$[F (\dots [[\ ]_k]_v \dots)]$.

Here the host is expletive *it*, which lacks semantic content; it is syntactic host for the complement S'. (73) does not care what argument position the host *it* is linked to in conceptual structure. But, thanks to the variable linking, whatever position it is linked to, the reading of the S'-complement is plugged in as the content of this position. In this rule, then, a syntactic configuration very similar to that for depictive predication is linked to a quite different conceptual structure.

11.11 Summary

To sum up the overall shape of the theory of linking: There are a variety of ways in which linking can be specified in lexical items and adjunct rules. These specifications interact with the rules for establishing linking to yield a correspondence satisfying the following conditions:

(74) *Linking Principle*
  a. Every major syntactic constituent (NP, PP, AP, S') is uniquely linked to a conceptual constituent that holds the dominant θ-role in a bound complex of one or more θ-roles.

b. Every conceptual constituent that is required to link is in fact linked.

This is the present theory's counterpart of the θ-Criterion.
The various kinds of linking are listed in (75).

(75) a. Elements that contain A-marking:
lexical items, "superordinate" adjuncts

   b. Elements that contain constant linking:
adjuncts

   c. Elements that contain constant linking to syntactic head
(V_h in our rules): most adjuncts

   d. Elements that contain variable linking:
depictive adjunct construction, "extraposed" S'-complement

The roles played by these kinds of linking in establishing full correspondence are summarized in (76).

(76) a. Apply Adjunct Fusion to combine LCS of head with elements containing V_h-type linking.

   b. Convert A-linking into constant linking: Apply Argument Linking and External Argument Linking to output of (a) (using thematic and syntactic hierarchy for NP arguments).

   c. Apply rules containing variable linking, depending on constant linkings established in (a), (b).

   d. Integrate readings of linked arguments into overall reading: Apply Argument Fusion, following constant linkings established in (a), (b), (c).

   e. Integrate readings of modifiers: Apply Restrictive Modifier Rule.

The general implications of a theory of this form involve one's overall conception of the theory of semantics and its place in the theory of language as a whole. I therefore leave further discussion to the Epilogue, where I place things back in a larger framework of discussion.

11.12 Appendix: Restatement of the Rest of the Adjunct Rules

For completeness, this section restates all the adjunct rules of chapters 8 through 10 that were not reformulated earlier in the chapter. I will keep commentary to a minimum.

(77) Of-*Theme Adjunct*
Responsible for *He emptied the sink **of dishes***.
Previously stated in (8.31)

$[_{VP} V_h \dots [_{PP}$ of $NP_k] \dots]$ may correspond to

$[\dots$ NOT BE $([\quad]_k, \dots) \dots]_h.$

(78) *PP-Adjunct*

Responsible for *She bottled the wine **in tall green bottles**, He threw the ball **in the air**.*

Previously stated in (8.37)

$[_{VP} V_h \dots PP_k \dots]$ may correspond to

$[\dots$ GO/BE $(\dots, [\quad]_k) \dots]_h.$

(79) *Passive By-Adjunct*

Responsible for *Bill was attacked **by Harry**.*

Previously stated in (8.65)–(8.66)

$[_{VP} V_h\text{-en} \dots [_{PP}$ by $NP_k] \dots]$ may correspond to

$[AFF (\langle, \rangle [\quad]_k \dots)]_h.$

(80) *For-Beneficiary Adjunct*

Responsible for *Bill sang a song **for Mary**.*

Previously stated in (9.10)

$[_{VP} V_h \dots [_{PP}$ for $NP_k] \dots]$ may correspond to

$$\begin{bmatrix} AFF ([\quad]^\alpha, \dots) \\ [FOR [AFF^+ ([\alpha], [\quad]_k)]] \end{bmatrix}_h.$$

(81) *For-Benefit Adjunct*

Responsible for *Bill sang a song **for fun**.*

Previously stated in (9.12)

$[_{VP} V_h \dots [_{PP}$ for $NP_k] \dots]$ may correspond to

$$\begin{bmatrix} AFF ([\quad]^\alpha, \dots) \\ [FOR \begin{bmatrix} INCH [BE_{Poss} ([\quad]_k, [AT [\alpha]])] \\ AFF^+ (\quad, [\alpha]) \end{bmatrix}] \end{bmatrix}_h.$$

(82) *On-Adversative Adjunct*

Responsible for *My car broke down **on me**.*

Discussed but not stated in section 9.2

$[_{PP}$ on $NP_k]$ may correspond to

$[WITH [AFF^- (\quad, [\quad]_k)]].$

Note: This rule contains no linking of the head verb. It therefore does not affect the main conceptual clause. Rather, it is treated as a simple restrictive modifier, parallel to time, location, and manner expressions. Thus, instead of undergoing Adjunct Fusion, which depends on V_h linking, it is integrated into the reading by the Restrictive Modifier Rule.

(83) *Instrumental Adjunct*

Responsible for *Phil opened the door **with a key**.*
Previously stated in (9.16)

$[_{VP} V_h \ldots [_{PP}$ with $NP_k] \ldots]$ may correspond to

$$\begin{bmatrix} \text{AFF}^- ([\;\;]^\alpha, [\;\;]^\beta) \\ [\text{BY} \begin{bmatrix} \text{CS}^+ ([\alpha], [\text{AFF}^- ([\gamma], [\beta])]) \\ \text{AFF}^- ([\alpha], [\;\;]^\gamma_k) \end{bmatrix}] \end{bmatrix}_h$$

(84) For-*Exchange Adjunct*

Responsible for *Bill obtained a book **for \$5**.*
Previously stated in (9.22)

$[_{VP} V_h \ldots [_{PP}$ for $NP_k] \ldots]$ may correspond to

$$\begin{bmatrix} \ldots \text{GO}_{\text{Poss}} (\ldots, \begin{bmatrix} \text{FROM} [\;\;]^\alpha \\ \text{TO} [\;\;]^\beta \end{bmatrix}) \ldots \\ [\text{EXCH} [\text{GO}_{\text{Poss}} ([\;\;]_{k'} \begin{bmatrix} \text{FROM} [\beta] \\ \text{TO} [\alpha] \end{bmatrix})]] \end{bmatrix}_h$$

(85) *Beneficiary NP Adjunct*

Responsible for *Bill made **Harry** a soda.*
Previously stated in (9.35)

$[_{VP} V_h NP_k \ldots]$ may correspond to

$$\begin{bmatrix} \text{CREATE/PREPARE} ([\;\;], [\;\;]^\alpha) \\ [\text{FOR} [\text{AFF}^+ ([\alpha], [\;\;]_k)]] \end{bmatrix}_h$$

Note: CREATE/PREPARE here is a vague specification of the selectional restriction on verbs that permit the *"for*-dative" construction. The CREATE part has been formalized in section 6.4 as

$[\text{CAUSE} ([\;\;], [_{\text{Event}} \text{GO}_{\text{Comp}^+} ([\;\;], [\;\;])])]$

The PREPARE part, and its relation to CREATE, has been left as yet unexplored.

(86) Way-*Adjunct*

Responsible for *Bill belched **his way out of the restaurant**.*
Previously stated in (10.27)

$[_{VP} V_h [_{NP} NP_j's$ way] PP $\ldots]$ may correspond to

$$\begin{bmatrix} \text{GO} ([\alpha]_j, [_{\text{Path}} \;\;]) \\ \text{AFF} ([\;\;]^\alpha_{A'} \;) \\ [\text{WITH/BY} \begin{bmatrix} \text{AFF} ([\alpha], \;) \\ -\text{BOUNDED} \end{bmatrix}_h] \end{bmatrix}$$

(87) *AP Resultative Adjunct*

Responsible for *Charlie laughed **himself silly**, Sue hammered **the metal flat***.

Previously stated in (10.48)

$[_{VP} V_h$ NP AP] may correspond to

$$
\begin{bmatrix}
\text{CAUSE ([}\alpha\text{], [INCH [BE}_{\text{Ident}} \text{([}\beta\text{], [AT [}_{\text{Property}} \quad]_A\text{])])])} \\
\text{AFF}^- \text{([\quad]}^\alpha_A, [\{\alpha\}]^\beta_A) \\
\text{[BY [AFF}^- \text{([}\alpha\text{], }\{[\beta]\}\text{)]}_h]
\end{bmatrix}.
$$

Note: As shown in section 10.4, the case with α in the upper action tier and no β in the lower action tier corresponds to the resultatives with "fake reflexives," in which the main verb is lexically intransitive. The case with β in the lower action tier and no α in the upper action tier corresponds to the resultatives in which the object is a Patient (grammatical or discourse) of the main verb.

(88) *Spatial Resultative*

Responsible for *Harry sneezed **his handkerchief across the room***.

Previously stated in (10.59)

$[_{VP} V_h$ NP PP] may correspond to

$$
\begin{bmatrix}
\text{CAUSE ([}\alpha\text{], [GO ([}\beta\text{], [\quad]}_A\text{)])])} \\
\text{AFF}^- \text{([\quad]}^\alpha_A, [\{\alpha\}]^\beta_A) \\
\text{[BY [AFF}^- \text{([}\alpha\text{], }\{[\beta]\}\text{)]}_h]
\end{bmatrix}.
$$

(89) *Noncausative AP Resultative*

Responsible for *The toast burned **black***.

Previously stated in (10.73)

$[_{VP} V_h$ AP] may correspond to

$$
\begin{bmatrix}
\text{INCH [BE}_{\text{Ident}} \text{([}\alpha\text{], [AT [}_{\text{Property}} \quad]_A\text{])]} \\
\text{AFF ([\quad]}^\alpha_A, \text{)} \\
\text{[BY [AFF}^- \text{(\quad , [}\alpha\text{])]}_h]
\end{bmatrix}.
$$

Epilogue
Compositionality, Autonomy, Modularity

The preceding chapters have developed a substantial body of analysis in pursuit of Chomsky's (1957) vision of a "general theory of language concerned with syntax and semantics and their points of connection." As stressed in chapter 1, I have taken it as criterial for such a theory that the treatment of semantics be foundationally compatible with generative syntax. This requires that it be a theory of I-semantics or the "syntax of thought"—the formal structure of those mental representations that encode humans' grasp of the concepts expressed by language.

The first principles of I-semantics, paralleling the first principles of generative grammar, lead to the conclusion that lexical and sentential concepts must both have compositional structure. We have seen extensively that such compositional structure can be discovered and formalized, and that there are numerous theoretical advantages to doing so, in both the lexical and the extralexical domains. For example, the relationships among multiple syntactic uses of the same lexical item have over and over again been explicated in terms of (1) the addition of simple operators in conceptual structure such as the causative, the inchoative, and various subordinating operators (WITH, BY, etc.), and (2) alternations concerning which part of a lexical conceptual structure corresponds to a syntactic argument. Without the machinery of lexical decomposition, these relationships could not be given a formal status. Moreover, the conditions on many syntactic configurations such as *with*-Theme adjuncts, recipient-NP adjuncts, and the resultative prove to be not only semantic, but readily formulated in terms of units of conceptual structure that have been independently motivated for the purpose of explicating lexical items. A theory that denies the possibility or utility of lexical decomposition simply cannot make such explanations available.

The fact that almost every word meaning has fuzzy boundaries and various sorts of indeterminacies does not threaten a theory of lexical decomposition, despite frequent claims to the contrary. It is however necessary to develop a theory of decomposition in which such indeterminacies are part of the fabric of conceptual structure. The descriptive innovations suggested in section 1.7 go a long way toward accounting for the variety of these phenomena.

On the other hand, such conceptual indeterminacies seem to play a relatively minor role in the relation between conceptual structure and syntax. That is, the correspondence rules between these two levels of representation make reference primarily (and perhaps exclusively) to those aspects of conceptual structure that are more or less discrete and digital. This is why the present work, concerned most directly with the syntax-semantics correspondence, has not made much reference to formal devices such as preference rules, graded conditions, and 3D model stereotypes. By contrast, S&C and C&CM, which sought to establish the overall texture of conceptual structure, had to discuss and motivate these innovations extensively.

It should be further emphasized that, whatever one's view on conceptual decomposition, a satisfactory theory of human language understanding must somehow or another encode all the distinctions that have been treated here as part of lexical conceptual structure. These distinctions are necessary not only to account for lexical relations and syntactic argument structure but also for a formal treatment of inference and of the relation of language to the perceived world. Hence, if the complexity is not encoded as part of lexical items, it must be somewhere else in the theory of language understanding and/or reasoning. It is hard for me to imagine an alternative that is not essentially a notational variant of lexical decomposition, though this may just reflect my own lack of imagination. It would seem, though, that the theory of lexical decomposition is by now well enough established, with enough significant results, that the burden of proof falls on those who advocate a different approach.

At the same time, the formalization of conceptual structure helps us see more clearly the true status of various appurtenances in the theory of grammar such as lexical predicate argument structure or the θ-grid. These turn out essentially to be filtered versions of lexical conceptual structure, encoding just that part of conceptual structure that is "visible" to the syntax. Similarly, the notions of selectional restrictions and implicit arguments turn out not to be primitives of lexical organization but rather epiphenomena arising from the way lexical conceptual structure interfaces with syntactic expression. Moreover, as has been shown, many descriptive generalizations fall out under the present approach that cannot be expressed with previous devices.

As stressed throughout, the theory of the syntax-semantics correspondence worked out here has relied on a fairly rudimentary theory of syntax—basically little more than a mid-1970s version of phrase structure. In particular, I have not employed anything like LFG's intermediate level of f-structure, nor such GB Theory subtleties as unaccusative movement, small clauses, abstract Case, and head-to-head movement. The reasons for this have been twofold. On one hand, I have not had particular need for these devices and, wishing to develop the theory in a context independent of sectarian syntactic disputes, have therefore simply done without them. Advocates of more specialized brands of syntax should be able to translate the present results into their own frameworks. On the other hand, the present results lead one to ask in various cases whether the phenomena that are taken as motivation for one syntactic framework over another are genuinely syntactic phenomena, or whether these phenomena are artifacts of the correspondence rules—in which case the syntactic innovations in question may not be justified at all. Notable cases raised here have included (1) aspects of binding theory and control theory, which are no longer syntactic (or purely syntactic) but part of the correspondence rules and of conceptual structure; (2) the status of predication, which is no longer a syntactic phenomenon at all but a conceptual one; (3) alternation of NPs between argument and adjunct position (a major preoccupation of Relational Grammar), which now appears to be part not of syntactic theory but of the theory of linking.

The work developed here has important implications for the issue of the autonomy of syntax, or more broadly, the modularity of mentally instantiated rules and representations. I think the issue of autonomy of syntax has been somewhat misconstrued by both its advocates and its opponents. Roughly, common practice seems to argue that if a linguistic phenomenon has syntactic reflexes (e.g. differences in word order, or differences in use of grammatical formatives such as reflexives), then the rules conditioning this phenomenon must be purely syntactic in nature. Should it turn out that some phenomenon apparently has semantic conditions on its occurrence, an advocate of autonomy along these lines must try to show that in fact the semantic conditions have a precise syntactic counterpart. On the other hand, an opponent of autonomy will attempt to drive a deeper and deeper semantic wedge into the phenomenon (Lakoff's (1987) treatment of *There*-Insertion is a good contemporary example).

But in fact, the logical structure of the problem of language understanding leads to a somewhat different form of the autonomy thesis:

Autonomy of Syntax: There is a set of purely syntactic primitives (the features defining lexical and phrasal categories, categories of anaphoric elements, inflectional morphology, etc.) and principles of combination (domination, linear order, X-bar theory, theory of movement, etc.) that collectively define a set of possible syntactic structures. Particular languages further constrain the set of possible structures through language-particular rules or parameters.

Autonomy of Semantics: There is a set of purely conceptual primitives (the ontological category features, the thematic and action tiers, the basic spatial functions, the semantic field features, etc.) and principles of combination (function-argument structure, restrictive modification, binding, etc.) that collectively define a set of possible conceptual structures, independent of linguistic realization.

Since language understanding by necessity involves correlating syntactic structures with conceptual structures, these two components cannot be enough. Rather, a third component is *logically* necessary—the correspondence rule component. Correspondence rules, in order to do their job, have to have structural descriptions of the general form "Syntactic Structure S corresponds to Conceptual Structure C"; that is, they must crucially involve the vocabularies of both autonomous components. In other words, although (or perhaps *because*) syntactic and conceptual primitives are strictly segregated in mental representations, there have to be rules that cross the boundaries.

Once one acknowledges the necessity of correspondence rules, a great deal of the apparent conflict between advocates and opponents of autonomy can be dissolved. Suppose one finds a syntactic alternation that appears to carry secondary semantic consequences—the dative alternation might be a good example. One is not now faced with a choice between (1) ignoring the phenomenon, (2) finding a more abstruse syntactic difference underlying it, or (3) abandoning syntactic autonomy. Rather, there is now a kind of rule in the grammar in which a conjunction of syntactic and semantic conditions is expected, namely the correspondence rules. Thus the debate is not about autonomous versus nonautonomous syntax, but rather about the relative expressive power of the syntactic rules and the correspondence rules.

The work developed here leads to a position that might be termed "autonomy of correspondence rules," the idea that the correspondence rules have their own properties and typology, to a considerable degree independent of the syntactic structures and conceptual structures that they relate. For one thing, much of lexical theory is now subsumed under the correspondence rules; the whole treatment of how lexical items can encode multiple conceptual argument structures, with or without corresponding multiple syntactic argument structures, is part of correspondence rule theory, not part of pure syntax or semantics. For another, linking theory accomplishes a many-to-many mapping of syntactic to conceptual structure, so that, for instance, constant NP-V-NP syntax corresponds to myriad distinct configurations of thematic relations. The richness of linking theory permits us to keep the syntax simple.

For a more complex case, let us look at the typology of adjunct rules. Consider depictive predication in the variant with object host, as in *Bill likes his sandwiches soggy*. The syntactic configuration here is identical to that for resultative predication (*Bill pounded the sandwich flat*) and for predicative argument structure (*Bill considers the sandwich soggy*), so the syntactic configuration is autonomous of the rule. The conceptual configuration in this construction forms a natural class with other "subordinate" adjuncts such as beneficiary *for* (*Bill sang a song for Harry*), exchange *for* (*Bill obtained a book for $5*), and absolutives (*With Bill sick, we had to stay home*), so the conceptual configuration too is autonomous of the rule. Finally, the formal character of the correspondence rule that licenses the construction falls into a natural class with the rule interpreting "extraposed" complement clauses (*We took it for granted that you would come*), which syntactically and conceptually seems quite distant from depictive predication. In other words, the means for relating various syntactic and conceptual structures are to a degree formally independent of the structures they relate.

The present work has been concerned with establishing a fairly robust set of cases in terms of which the theory of correspondence rules can be developed and defended. I have therefore shied away from well-known trouble spots such as the passive, the middle, reflexivization, and so forth; other cases such as control, unaccusativity, and psych-verbs have received passing mention but hardly systematic treatment. One has to hone one's tools on relatively easy cases first. So perhaps I will not have solved the problems of argument structure that many take to be the real nuts for grammatical theory to crack. However, given that these are phenomena whose difficulties stem in large part from the subtle intrusion of semantics into the syntax, the work done here has opened a road on which one can approach them from a different and perhaps more productive angle, and I take this to be progress of a sort.

Returning to first principles, the theory presented here has also opened a new vein for learnability theory. There is a growing body of work on the learning of lexical argument structure (e.g. Pinker 1989); such work can now be seen in a broader context of the learnability of the correspondence rule component in general. How does the child learn that "such-and-such a construction can be used to express such-and-such a concept in language L"? Having a better idea of the formal nature of principles of this sort sharpens the issues posed for learnability.

But it comes time to stop and admire the view before pushing on again.

Notes

Chapter 1

1. Chomsky has suggested (personal communication) that his notion of E-language is somewhat different from the sense taken here. For my purposes, though, it does not prove too important precisely how one construes the term, beyond the crucial stipulation that "the construct is understood independently of the properties of the mind/brain" (Chomsky 1986, 20).

2. A historical note: These issues were discussed vigorously in the literature of the late 1960s (for example Chomsky 1965, 160; Katz 1966; Postal 1966b; Weinreich 1966; Bierwisch 1967, 1969; McCawley 1968c). However, they dropped out of sight for the most part during the successive ascendancies of generative semantics and model-theoretic semantics as the leading paradigms among linguists who continued to pursue semantic analysis. Interestingly, these issues are not addressed at all in more recent work of Katz, who has abandoned a psychological interpretation of semantic theory for a Platonist variant of E-semantics (see Katz 1981, for example).

3. My interpretation here is confirmed by Dennett's (1987, 288) anecdote about Fodor's remarks on Searle.

4. In previous work, I mistakenly identified conceptual structure with Fodor's Language of Thought. In part I was misled by an ambiguity in the term *language*. In the technical sense adopted by Chomsky (1957), a language is a set of expressions generated by a set of rules. In this sense, conceptual structure is indeed a language, and Fodor's term is appropriate. However, it has become clearer through Fodor's more recent work that he has always intended the term in the sense "set of *semantically interpreted* expressions," in which case conceptual structure is *not* a Language of Thought.

5. Generative Semantics used this observation as motivation for assimilating semantics to syntactic principles. The central program of the theory was to reduce *all* semantic compositionality to syntax. As more and more was discovered about semantic structure, it became clear that this program was not feasible. For at least some generative semanticists, the conclusion was that syntax should be abandoned altogether. As seen in figure (1), the approach here is to retain syntax for its proper traditional purposes but to invest semantic expressivity in a different component with appropriate expressive power: conceptual structure.

6. It has been suggested by various people, including Grimshaw (1981), Macnamara (1982), and Pinker (1984), that such markedness conditions are crucial in children's initial acquisition of syntactic categories.

7. A notational point: I will consistently use angle brackets ⟨ ⟩ to enclose an optional constituent in a formal expression, the traditional parentheses being reserved to notate arguments of a function.

8. See *S&C*, sections 10.3–5, for further discussion of the Thematic Relations Hypothesis, in particular how it differs from a theory of "metaphor" of the type proposed by Lakoff and Johnson (1980), and why it justifies the approach of Conceptual Semantics as opposed to model-theoretic (E-) semantics. These sections also implicitly answer Dowty's (1988) charge that the "metaphorical extension" of thematic relations to nonspatial fields is incoherent; basically, Dowty is looking for an explication of thematic relations based on E-semantics, but the generalization of thematic relations probably only makes sense in terms of I-semantics.

9. This analysis of *climb* was to my knowledge first proposed by Fillmore (1982); a formal treatment in terms of preference rules appears in Jackendoff 1985. Other aspects of *climb* appear in section 4.2.

10. This analysis of *see* is adapted from Miller and Johnson-Laird 1976 and appears in more detail in *S&C*, chapter 8.

11. Actually, he finds evidence and disregards it: see *S&C*, pages 125–127 and 256, note 8.

Chapter 2

1. Examples from other chapters are identified by a chapter prefix. The reference here is to example (16) in chapter 1. Within-chapter examples omit the chapter prefix.

2. This entry for *run* is of course only approximate, since at this level of detail it is not differentiated from other verbs of locomotion such as *walk, swim,* or *fly*. I assume, following section 1.7.1, that much of this further differentiation is localized in the associated 3D model representation and plays no role in the level of conceptual structure. See however sections 5.2 and 10.3 for possible further refinements of the conceptual structure of *run*. Similar caveats apply to many of the decompositions throughout the text: I have usually provided only as much detail as is necessary for the analysis at hand, without precluding the possibility of further elaboration in a complete analysis.

   The formalism in these entries differs slightly from that in *S&C*, where the indices for conceptual arguments are inside the brackets, for example, $[_{\text{Thing}}\ i]$ for the first argument of *run* and *enter*. The change in notation has two advantages: first, it parallels the notated indexation in the syntactic structure, which is outside the NP; second, it facilitates the representation of selectional restrictions to be presented in section 2.3. It is otherwise of no significance.

3. McCawley (1988) suggests that *enter* is actually a bit more complicated than this, meaning something like "go across boundary of X into X." If so, this only amplifies the need for lexical incorporation of Path-functions advocated here.

4. This is a major difference between the *S&C* theory and that of Jackendoff 1972, 1976, where Source and Goal were direct arguments of the GO-function. The difficulty with the earlier formalism was that it could not express the semantic contribution of any prepositions other than *from* and *to*. The innovation of a Path-constituent corresponding to PP permits all prepositions of Path to be handled uniformly, an important descriptive advance.

5. It should be mentioned that this position on thematic roles is implicit in Gruber 1965 and explicit in Jackendoff 1972: see especially pages 37–41, where it is compared in examples (2.56) and (2.58) with the view of thematic roles as diacritics.

6. Something formally similar to fusion appears in Kaplan and Bresnan's (1982, 274) "Merge" operator, which fuses f-structures instead of conceptual structures. Fusion is a variety of the "unification" operation developed by Shieber (1986). However, it differs from Shieber's formulation in that it does not itself reject anomalous combinations; that is, the derivation of anomalous sentences must not self-destruct. Rather, anomalous phrases must still receive conceptual structures, since there are predicates that select for

anomaly, for instance *There couldn't be such a thing as a . . .* and *It's crazy to speak of . . . .* That is, judgment of anomaly is separate from the principles like (13) that construct phrasal concepts. (I am grateful to Eloise Jelinek, Ann Farmer, and Dick Oehrle for reminding me in the present context of the importance of this difference, which in fact was noted in McCawley 1968b and Jackendoff 1972, page 18.)

7. A historical note: A similar conclusion, based on similar evidence, is reached by Weinreich (1966), who uses the term *transfer features* for features that a verb stipulates for its arguments. McCawley (1968c) attributes to Fillmore (personal communication) the view that selectional restrictions are presuppositions that verbs place on their arguments, yet another way of stating the same position. Katz, who criticizes Weinreich 1966 at length in Katz 1967, arrives at a similar conclusion in Katz 1972, page 107, without mentioning Weinreich. Although he nearly states an equivalent of Argument Fusion, his analysis is not quite so general as Weinreich's, in that he keeps separate the use of selectional restrictions to predict anomalies from their use to fill in readings of proforms; the latter is his rule (3.77).

8. It is worth noting here that the conceptual structure of restrictive modification must be formally distinguished from that of nonrestrictive modification (or apposition), which has different inferential properties. As I have no strong proposals at present and we currently have no need for appositive structures, I leave the problem open.

Chapter 3

1. This is the θ-Criterion as generally understood. It is stated in essentially this form on page 36 of Chomsky 1981 and repeated in various places throughout the book (e.g. on page 112) and also on page 6 of Chomsky 1982. However, Chomsky's initial statement of the θ-Criterion is immediately hedged by note 14, page 139, where he refers to precisely the sorts of examples we are about to examine. This note makes clear that the objective of the θ-Criterion for Chomsky is to make sure that NPs do not acquire additional θ-roles in the course of a derivation. His formal statement of the θ-Criterion (1981, 335) makes this insight explicit but otherwise little resembles the original statement. On the other hand, subsequent literature has often made use of the θ-Criterion as though its primary insight is biuniqueness between θ-roles and NPs in argument positions; it is this aspect of the θ-Criterion I shall be addressing, not the one Chomsky regards as most significant for GB Theory.

2. Readers versed in the history of the theory of control will find this argument familiar. In early approaches (e.g. Rosenbaum 1967; Ross 1967), the absence of an overt subject in an infinitive was accomplished by a transformation of Equi-NP Deletion. For instance, (ia) was derived from the underlying structure (ib).

(i) a. Bill wanted to leave.
   b. Bill wanted [for Bill to leave]

One of the difficulties with this was that (iia) and (iib) had to be derived from the same underlying structure, (iic).

(ii) a. A funny old man wanted to leave.
    b. A funny old man wanted a funny old man to leave.
    c. A funny old man wanted [for a funny old man to leave]

The solution adopted, which persists in current theory, was to eliminate Equi-NP Deletion and to claim that (ia) and (iia) have the structures in (iii), while (iib) retains (iic) as its structure.

(iii) a. Bill$_i$ wanted [PRO$_i$ leave]
  b. A funny old man$_i$ wanted [PRO$_i$ leave]

Much of current binding theory grew out of exploring this solution.

The relevance of this historical parallel is that now the same problem is occurring *within a lexical entry*, where syntactic structure plays no role. The use of a bound conceptual argument, however, solves the problem in the same way as the use of a bound NP PRO: it expresses the fact that a constituent performs multiple functions, without actually duplicating that constituent in the representation.

3. It may or may not be possible to further constrain an index from appearing more than once in the *syntactic* structure. This depends on the disposition of the examples given in the previous section such as *The box has books in it*.

4. I couch the discussion in this section in terms of the GB Theory formulation of binding. However, it applies equally to the "control equations" of LFG (Kaplan and Bresnan 1982), where the arrow from an anaphoric element in f-structure to a fully specified element is considered part of the syntax, just as the binding relation is in GB Theory. A full translation into LFG terms is left to the interested reader.

5. Williams (1987) has proposed a similar reconception of binding theory in terms of θ-roles rather than syntactic positions, for rather similar reasons. However, given his taxonomic rather than structural account of θ-roles, Williams's approach must necessarily be less specific in various respects than the present account. Also, Williams does not extend the binding theory to within lexical entries, the case that provides primary motivation here.

6. Two remarks on this representation beyond those immediately relevant here. (1) I assume the verb means "cause someone to go into clothing." An alternative possibility, "put clothing onto someone," does not mesh properly with the PP-complement. This is still not quite right; a somewhat better analysis, "cause someone to come to be in clothing," can be formulated in terms of the Inchoative function to be developed in section 5.3. (2) The PP-complement is coindexed with the Place-constituent, which carries a selectional restriction that the Place be of the form IN CLOTHING. When the PP is absent, IN CLOTHING acts as an implicit argument, as in the cases discussed in chapter 2.

7. See also the treatment of Romance reflexives in Grimshaw 1990 and Rosen 1989, generalizing Grimshaw's 1982 treatment to the use of reflexives in Romance for middles and anticausatives.

8. Růžička (1983) offers a solution to (23) in terms of thematic roles, rejecting any purely syntactic solution. His solution—namely that *promise* requires identity of thematic roles between matrix and complement subjects—is not restricted enough, in that it should allow *Bill was promised to receive the letter, where both subjects are Goals. At the same time, it does not account for the evident oblique object control in (25b). His study is nevertheless valuable for its illustration of cross-linguistic variation in control conditions. Farkas's (1988) approach to (23) in terms of a relationship of responsibility strikes me as having the right flavor, in that it deepens the conceptual basis of control relations.

Chapter 4

1. *S&C*, section 9.1, points out these alternations but does not show how to combine them in the lexicon. The same is true of Talmy 1983 and also of Brugman 1981 and its re-exposition in Lakoff 1987 (where prepositional senses are expressed as informal "image schemas" rather than algebraic expressions).

2. The AT-END-OF alternation is also discussed in Brugman 1981, Talmy 1983, Lakoff 1987, and *S&C*. Further senses of transitive *over* discussed by Brugman and Lakoff concern whether the Theme does or does not make contact with the reference object (*Bill*

climbed over the wall vs. *The plane flew over the city*). If these are further senses, they concern an alternation within what I have called "core" *over*. As Lakoff points out, this alternation is projected into the Path senses as well. On the other hand, I am inclined to wonder whether these are genuinely distinct senses as opposed to a simple nonspecificity in core *over*. Brugman and Lakoff observe that *over* also has a number of intransitive senses, as in *The wall fell over* and *The meeting is over*. These senses do not seem as systematically related as those discussed in the text, even if one can motivate some similarities along the lines Brugman and Lakoff suggest.

3. This looks slightly different from the version in Jackendoff 1985, because of the change in notation for indices described in note 2 to chapter 2. The present notation is somewhat more perspicuous for the cases to follow.

4. This case was brought to my attention by my daughter Beth, who at the ages of 3 and 4 regularly used the relatively unusual PP-complement form *pass by NP* instead of the transitive form *pass NP*.

5. I am grateful to Dick Carter (personal communication) for pointing this problem out to me.

6. The case is clouded by the numerous prepositions such as *under* and *between* that can express either (1) a Place-function, or (2) the Path-function TO plus a Place-function, or (3) the Path-function VIA plus a Place-function (see the previous section). The PPs in (32a), however, seem never to be expressions of Path. If one *runs at the corner of the bed*, one is presumably running more or less in place, not traversing a path. If one *runs with the telephone*, one is carrying the telephone, not approaching it, leaving it, or traversing its extent.

7. *Put a gun to his head* and *put his ear to the telephone* are acceptable. However, these *to*'s may be a different preposition *to*, since they can be paraphrased by *against*. The usual *to* of Goal cannot: *John ran to the wall* does not equal *John ran against the wall*.

8. One would, however, expect **Joe put the book to its place* to be acceptable if, as seems reasonable, *place* is a noun that expresses a Place. I have no solution at the moment; perhaps a division of Places into finer classes is involved.

9. As is now generally accepted, the *by*-phrase in the passive is not an argument of the passive participle. In the present theory, this means it is not coindexed with the verb's conceptual structure. It receives its interpretation by means of one of a class of "adjunct rules" whose function is to integrate the interpretation of adjuncts into *non*indexed arguments of the verb. See section 8.8.

Chapter 5

1. The extent readings are sometimes said to be "metaphorical" and "imply a journey over time" and therefore are claimed not to be relevant to a proper semantic theory. I reject this line of argument, for reasons detailed in *S&C*, section 10.5; I will not repeat the arguments here.

2. It should be mentioned that *Bill and Harry came together* combines the effects of conjunction and accompaniment. It is therefore symmetrical, like conjunction, but it also expresses a mutual dependence between Bill's coming and Harry's coming, like accompaniment. *Together*, in this context at least, evidently is interpreted roughly as "with each other." See Landau and Gleitman 1985, note 3, pages 216–222.

3. The form "Bill had a smile on his face" is indicated rather than the simpler "a smile was on Bill's face" because of the required binding of the possessive to the subject. Note that (i) is ungrammatical in the same way as (ii), whereas (iii) is perfectly all right.

(i)   *Bill entered the room with a smile on Harry's face.

(ii)   *When Bill entered the room, he had a smile on Harry's face.

(iii)   When Bill entered the room, a smile was on Harry's face.

Chapter 6

1. Note that the bare mass and plural subjects here are not taken generically, as they are in *Dogs are animals*: these are not sentences about what *water* and *people* characteristically do. Notice also that the definite article is impossible with plural generics: *The dogs are (the) animals*.

2. This use of *stick* is not to be confused with the GO-verb *stick*, as in *stick one's head out the window*.

3. I am indebted to unpublished work by Karen Pasternack for an inventory of these verbs.

4. Possession too breaks down into various subcategories, for instance alienable versus inalienable possession, ownership versus temporary possession, possession of objects versus possession of information. Each of these has its own subtleties within the overall logic and grammar of possession, just as has been seen with the subcategories within Location and Character.

Chapter 7

1. As seen in (8b), the test for Patients is sometimes clouded by the possibility of *discourse Patients*—elements that are considered "affected" by virtue of some surrounding context. So, for example:

   (i)   What happened to Bill? He looks terrible!
   What happened to Bill was he received this letter that said his girlfriend was breaking up with him, and so he got depressed.

   (ii)   What happened to the room? It's a mess!
   What happened to the room was a herd of elephants entered it and, well, you can guess the rest.

   By contrast, what I will call *grammatical Patients*, whose Patient role is assigned by the verb of the sentence itself, require no surrounding story in order to be acceptable. Admittedly, the line is sometimes hard to draw; I will be as sensitive as I can.

2. It might be of interest to note that the verbs that have ambiguous action tiers like *roll* are often characterized as unaccusative, for instance *slide, skid,* and *bounce.* (These constitute one of the two major classes of spatial unaccusatives identified by Levin and Rappaport (1989); the other class is achievement verbs such as *arrive.*) It should also be noted that the unaccusative analysis is often supposed to account for the possibility of a homophonous causative, as suggested in section 4.1. However, there exist potentially causative verbs such as *march* with an unambiguous action tier (12), and verbs such as *fall* with an ambiguous action tier but no homophonous causative. As is becoming clearer from the literature (e.g. Rosen 1984; Levin and Rappaport 1989; Napoli 1988a; Van Valin 1987; Zaenen 1988), each so-called criterion for unaccusativity has its own semantic and syntactic peculiarities; the syntax and the semantics do not fully explain each other. For the moment, therefore, I remain agnostic on the Unaccusative Hypothesis.

3. Dowty takes this dissection as casting doubt on the notion of thematic roles rather than increasing our understanding of them. His attitude, I believe, is a result of his wanting thematic roles to function like case-markers rather than in the manner proposed here.

4. I have been aided in this reanalysis of Talmy by unpublished work by David Gow. Pinker (1989) independently develops a formalization not dissimilar to mine.

5. This analysis and those to follow differ from those in S&C. Note 10 in section 7.7 discusses the differences briefly.

6. The information conveyed this way is equivalent to Talmy's formulation: the opposition between agonist and antagonist is expressed on the action tier, so the agonist's tendency or desire can be inferred—namely *not to leave*.

7. A potentially more sophisticated account of the entraining versus launching distinction would involve a direct correlation of the parts of the causative Event with a temporal representation. One possible notation is suggested in the "temporal tier" of Jackendoff 1987c, a part of that paper omitted from the present work in favor of more immediately relevant matters.

8. This is not the only possible analysis for instrumentals one can imagine in the present framework. However, it is sufficient to demonstrate the general approach of treating thematic roles as structural positions. Limitations of space and patience preclude working through other alternatives.

It is worth mentioning that so-called Instrumental subjects such as *the key* in *The key opened the door* probably do not fall under this analysis. I am inclined rather to regard them as inanimate Instigators—that is, not as grammatical Instruments at all.

9. A difficulty in adapting the dashed underline notation will be the treatment of the default Instrument HAND, which appears in the intermediate elaboration (50) but not in the largest, (51). This is not possible in the dashed underline notation, which does not permit one to leave out material in the course of successive elaboration. I have no suggestions on how to deal with this notational problem.

10. This analysis of *force* differs from that in S&C, section 10.2, where the S-complement version is given the conceptual structure (i) (translated into present notation).

(i) $[\text{CAUSE} ([\quad]_i, [\text{GO}_{\text{Circ}} ([\quad]_j, [\text{TO} ([\quad]_k)])])]$

This is identical to the spatial version except for the change in the semantic field variable to Circumstantial. In this field, Events and States appear as reference objects, and a Theme is "located" at an Event or State if it is a character or participant in that Event or State. The field is motivated in S&C on the basis of aspectual verbs like *begin, stop,* and *keep,* then extended to causative verbs like *force*. The extension is motivated by the fact that it provides a way to combine the two frames of *force*. The curly bracket notation, which was not yet developed at the time of S&C, provides a combination of frames that I find superior. I am inclined now to retain the Circumstantial analysis only for the aspectual verbs. See section 9.7 for another use of the Circumstantial field.

Chapter 8

1. I must confess not to be completely convinced of the analyses of the "negative" verbs proposed here. The point is, though, that if one can differentiate the analyses of the various classes, one can state adjunct rules sensitive to those differences. I would feel that an explanation had been achieved if one could state a theoretical reason why *empty* takes *of*-adjuncts and *uncover* does not. At the moment it is only a matter of stipulation in the rule—but at least the stipulation can be formalized, which I consider an advance.

2. This class apparently admits of innovation: my children use the verb *roof,* "to throw/kick/ etc. a ball/frisbee/etc. onto a roof," in sentences like *Sean roofed the tennis ball.* They were surprised I didn't know what they meant.

3. This account predicts that *?Bill sprayed the wall with some paint* ought to be better than *?*Bill loaded the truck with some books.* I don't find it as good as it ought to be, though. On

the other hand, *Spray me with some water* does sound a good deal better than *?Load that truck with some books*, as predicted.

4. Rappaport and Levin (1985) observe that *wipe* resembles *clear*, with the exception that the *of*-adjunct is not permitted:

(i) a. Bill wiped crumbs off the table.
   b. Bill wiped the table (*of crumbs).

I believe the reason for this difference is that (ib) does not have a conceptual structure with an incorporated Theme: one can wipe a table even if there is nothing on it that one thereby removes. By contrast, one cannot clear a table without there having been something on the table to remove. That is, *wipe* in (ib) is simply a verb of moving contact like *rub* and *scratch*, and its conceptual structure therefore bears little resemblance to that of *clear* in (48). Under this account, there is no reason to expect an *of*-adjunct: the similarity of syntactic patterns masks a difference in conceptual structure, and it is over the latter that the ability to take an *of*-adjunct is defined. Sentence (ia) is then a resultative; see section 10.4.

5. In fact, a case almost like *shmid* really exists. Notice that the adjective *full* should be conceptually related to *fill* in the same way that the adjective *covered* is related to the verb *cover*. However, the relation is not preserved in the syntax:

(i) a. The storm covered the field with/*of snow.
   b. the field covered with/*of snow
   c. The tank filled with/*of water.
   d. the tank full of/*with water

For syntactic parallelism, the Theme of *full* ought to be a *with*-adjunct just like the others; instead it occurs with an *of*-phrase. This is probably not the *of*-adjunct that goes with verbs of removal, but rather the argument *of* that is the AP's closest counterpart to a direct object, as in *afraid of Bill*, *proud of his kids*. Thus the lexical entry of *full* has to treat this phrase as an optional coindexed argument rather than as an adjunct. (On the other hand, under fairly standard assumptions, the *of* does not have to be specified in the lexical entry, being filled in as a case-marker or the like. So *full* is still not as bad as the hypothetical *shmid*.)

6. This discussion presumes that *present, provide, furnish, supply, rob, cheat,* and *deprive* are all INCH BE- rather than GO-verbs, whereas most of my discussion of possessional verbs has assumed the GO analysis. There are two alternatives: (1) generalize the adjunct rules to GO-verbs, or (2) find arguments that these particular verbs are in fact inchoative rather than motion. The latter alternative might be indicated by the fact that we have ruled out *of*-adjuncts for GO-verbs such as *smoke* and *steam* (section 8.4). I leave the issue open.

7. Actually, it is not so clear that the sense of the *with*-phrase in (63d) is an incorporated Theme—it seems more like a Source or Cause: "the room buzzed *from* excitement." This case shades off into others still less Theme-like, such as *The tree drooped with fruit* and even *The hills are alive with the sound of music.* Perhaps we are therefore dealing with a different *with*-adjunct here.

8. This assumes that the direct object, indexed *j*, then moves to subject position—alternatively, in a no-movement treatment, it would be reindexed *i*.

Chapter 9

1. An alternative structure for adversative *on* is roughly "The car's breaking down caused an adverse effect on me," more formally (i).

(i) [CS⁺ ([BREAK-DOWN ([CAR])], [AFF⁻ (, [ME])])]

I reject this possibility because it does not respect the primacy of the main conceptual clause *my car broke down*, which shows up as a Cause in (i). The cases to be discussed in the next chapter that *do* violate the primacy of the main conceptual clause have a different syntax and highly uniform conceptual structure, so (i) does not form a natural class with them. Although we are for the moment concerned mostly with just achieving a description, our structures should be selected with an eye for eventual explanation of their properties, which requires us to try to group constructions into natural classes.

2. I ignore subtleties of the subcategorization frame with *pay*, in particular the possibility of a dative alternation and consequent optional omission of the Theme, as in *pay Bill for the lawnmower*—and I leave altogether open the structure of *pay the bill*. I also omit the action tier.

3. Larson (1988, 350), proposing a syntactic "neo-dative shift" relation, cites references for some of these differences but not the facts themselves. He then proceeds quite pointedly to disregard them, on the grounds (1) that there are other languages that lack these irregularities and (2) that a movement theory permits uniform assignment of θ-roles to D-Structure. On the other hand, he never accounts for the irregularities of English, and, as far as I can tell, he abandons uniform θ-assignment (except in some attenuated sense) in the final section of his paper. See Jackendoff (1990) for more detailed commentary.

4. The information transfer verbs *show* and *teach* belong in this class along with *tell*. Evidently perceiving something and learning something count as kinds of possession, as argued early on by Gruber (1965).

   Some sources cite a difference in meaning between *teach French to the students* and *teach the students French*; allegedly the students are more liable to have learned French in the latter case. I have been laughed off the podium when I tried to present this claim in public; the distinction is extremely tenuous. Whatever slight difference there is between the two probably resides in the stronger Beneficiary status of the students in the latter case: the way they could be more "affected" by learning more.

5. Notice that this contrast does not obtain with the construction *with/without NP PP*; both permit object hosts. For instance, *Harry* can be the antecedent of *his* with either choice of preposition in (i).

   (i) Bill encountered Harry with/without a smile on his face.

   This suggests that the analogy drawn between this construction and the gerundive is not as close as was assumed in section 5.4. I have no explanation to offer.

6. In comparable structures, Williams (1980) asserts that it is sufficient to coindex PRO with its sister VP and coindex the S dominating them both with the matrix subject:

   (i) [Bill_i [[encountered Harry]_i [PRO_j [leaving the room]_j]_i]]

   This does not however say that *Bill* and PRO are coreferential, except with a number of additional unstated assumptions. Thus it does not solve the problem at hand.

Chapter 10

1. Oddly, *Bill went/walked/ran his way down the hallway* is out as well, as if these verbs don't add enough to the meaning of the construction. I don't know how to characterize this constraint (pointed out by Donna Jo Napoli).

2. A couple of people have suggested to me that the process requirement on the verb in the *way*-construction is present only in the accompaniment reading and that it is not necessary on the means reading. For example, *Bill* can be said to have *lied his way into*

the meeting even if Bill tells only a single lie, provided the lie is his means for entry. If correct, this complicates the rule still further, but it does not materially affect the points I am concerned with here.

3. Ann Farmer has pointed out (personal communication) this constraint on bound pronouns. In the idiom *gnash one's teeth, teeth* is passivizable if the bound pronoun is omitted, for instance in *Many teeth were gnashed as the home team went down to defeat.*

4. I have a small preference for the latter interpretation, though my judgments are not totally secure. The reason for my preference is that some adverbs that are acceptable in the manner paraphrase form, such as (ia), cannot appear as parallel adjectives with *way*, as seen in (ib). The absolute construction (ic), like the *way*-construction, is out in this case.

    (i) a.   Bill went rapidly out of the restaurant belching.
        b.   *Bill belched his rapid way out of the restaurant.
        c.   ?*Bill, rapid (as ever), went out of the restaurant belching.

    One might wonder if instead the adjective preceding *way* might be treated conceptually as a modifier of the lexical verb itself. However, this would predict that *Bill belched his loud way out of the restaurant* would be all right, since it would mean *Bill went out the restaurant, belching loudly.*

5. In addition, there are a few transitive verbs that occur idiomatically in the *way*-construction, for example *force, push, elbow*, and so on, plus *find* and perhaps *lose*. *See one's way* might be a further case, meaning roughly "GO_{Circ} in an aware fashion" (where GO_{Circ} is Circumstantial motion in the sense of *S&C*, section 10.2). However, its relation to the other idiomatic cases is not completely obvious, in that its complement must be an Event. The expression *on one's way ⟨PP⟩* may also be related, though still more distantly.

6. The variables X and Y of (15) are no longer necessary in (27) because the selectional restrictions on the subject, represented by X, and the rest of the verb's meaning, represented by Y, simply come in by virtue of the fusion operation. This rule itself does not have to copy over the verb, as (15) did.

7. The treatment in terms of the Lexical Rule Strategy raises questions of productivity. The *way*-construction seems more regular in its interpretation than, say, the causative in English: other than the small number of truly idiomatic cases, there do not seem to be any examples comparable to the numerous causatives with specialized meanings in English such as *jump (a horse/*a goat)* or *smoke (a cigar/*a chimney)*. That is, once its semantic conditions are stated properly, the *way*-construction appears to be more productive than most rules of English derivational morphology. It is more like the verbal passive than the adjectival passive. Whether this is grounds for deriving it by a different type of rule than the causative remains to be seen, but it is food for thought.

8. My discussion here owes a great deal to Carrier and Randall (forthcoming). In particular, most of my examples are taken from their work. My debt to them may be masked by the fact that I take exception to many of their points in section 10.5; but the value of their work to me is that it reveals the richness and complexity of the construction in a way altogether congenial with the present approach. In fact, there are many interesting aspects of their work that I have not been able to incorporate here, either for reasons of space or simply because I cannot provide a sufficiently explicit analysis of the phenomena.

9. On Sato's (1987) classification of resultatives, (37) is Type C, (38) is Type E, (39a,b) are Type A, and (39c,d) are Type D. His Type B appears in section 10.5. On Yamada's (1987) classification, the examples in (37) are "true resultatives"; (39) and (40) are "fake resultatives"; I am uncertain how he would classify (38).

10. I leave it to the interested reader to construct a purely syntactic alternative, along the lines of that rejected for the *way*-construction in section 10.2, and to find independent arguments for rejecting it here. A solution in terms of a lexical rule is also possible; see the discussion of Carrier and Randall's treatment in the next section.

11. Carrier and Randall account for this difference by stipulating that the secondary predicate must be a State, and *a pancake* is not a State. In the present theory, *flat* is not a State either—it is a Property. It would presumably be possible to change Carrier and Randall's stipulation to Property rather than State and thereby give the difference a semantic rather than syntactic explanation. The fact remains, though, that this stipulation concerns resultative *adjuncts* and not resultatives in general.

12. I suspect that these examples are somewhat acceptable just to the extent that the "weather *it*" can be construed as a kind of nonspecific Agent. Such Agentivity is seen in examples like *Even though the temperature had dipped down, it still wouldn't snow; Despite the wind, it's managing to get foggy.* On this reading of the weather *it*, it can serve as Actor in the Means analysis, as required. See Napoli (1988b) for some arguments that weather *it* can have such status.

Chapter 11

1. Note that this problem occurs in *any* theory that stipulates external arguments in lexical entries; the subscript *i* in the present theory is just a notational variant of the bracketing or underlining used to designate external arguments in other theories such as those of Williams (1984), Marantz (1984), or Rappaport, Levin, and Laughren (1988). Why couldn't these theories mark the Goal of *benter* or the Theme of *succeive* as external argument?

2. The main burden of Grimshaw 1986 is to demonstrate a difference in argument structure between two types of nominals. Grimshaw shows that *process* nominals such as *the frequent examination of the students* have an argument structure parallel to that of verbs, with the exception of the treatment of the external argument. By contrast, in *result* nominals such as *the linguistics examination on Tuesday*, all syntactic complements are adjuncts rather than arguments; that is, these nominals do not have argument structure in Grimshaw's sense. See Grimshaw's work and the references therein for details of the distinction. The point of raising the distinction here is that it can be captured nicely in the present system: process nominals A-mark arguments in conceptual structure, but result nominals do not. As a result, process nominals treat their complements in the same way as verbs do, but all arguments of result nominals are implicit and therefore can be satisfied by adjuncts.

3. Moving a little more deeply into idioms, we can provide a lexical difference between those verb-object idioms that passivize, such as *let the cat out of the bag*, and those that do not, such as *kick the bucket*. As has been frequently observed, the object in the former type of idiom has some sort of independent interpretation. For instance, *the cat* in *let the cat out of the bag* can be interpreted roughly as "secret information." By contrast, *the bucket* in *kick the bucket* is a purely syntactic excrescence. This difference can be specified in the way the LCS of the idiom is A-marked. Very approximately, the LCS of *let the cat out of the bag* is (i) and that of *kick the bucket* is (ii).

(i) [LET ([   ]$_A$, [GO ([SECRET INFORMATION]$_A$, [TO [OUT OF INNER CIRCLE]])])]

(ii) [DIE ([   ]$_A$)]

The linking rules will map [SECRET INFORMATION] onto the direct object, providing an idiosyncratic interpretation for *the cat*; but *the bucket* will remain unlinked. It remains to be seen how this will account for the difference in passivization—but at least it can be stated instead of merely stipulated with a wave of the hand.

I should, I suppose, explicitly inveigh against analyses of the verb-particle construction which presume that it must be a constituent, in particular a V, in D-Structure:

[$_V$ [$_V$ throw] [$_{Prt}$ up]]

or the like. There is no motivation for this other than a dogma that lexical items must belong to so-called lexical categories. As shown by Emonds (1976), idioms like *take to task* (of which there are many) are little different from verb-particle idioms, except that they contain a full PP instead of a particle; the price of insisting that these are D-Structure verbs is high. So much more so for *let the cat out of the bag*. If, on the other hand, we admit that idioms may be lexical VPs, then nothing in the theory stands in the way of giving idiomatic verb-particle constructions parallel treatment.

4. Perhaps there is some promise in Pesetsky's (forthcoming) semantic analysis. Translated into present terms, Pesetsky analyzes the Themes of *frighten* and *please* as the emotional affects FEAR and PLEASURE. These affects are directed toward something; that is, they can take an argument. Following Pesetsky, then, *x frighten y* means

[CS$^+$ ([X]^z, [INCH [BE ([FEAR ([α])], [AT [Y]])]])],

that is, "X causes fear of X to come to be in Y." As suggested in section 7.3, this constituent may be a State or an Event, accounting for one of the alternations in meaning. The unusual property here is the binding of the Agent to the argument of the Theme, which with luck might turn out to yield the proper strange results.

5. Larson (1988) makes just the opposite claim: that *give* assigns to the indirect object both Beneficiary and Goal roles, but *donate* assigns only Beneficiary. He gives no evidence for this claim; he adopts it on purely theory-internal grounds. See Jackendoff 1990 for comments.

It is worth asking why the syntactic alternation of the "dative-shift" is the way it is. Why couldn't there be another verb just like *give* except that instead of A-marking the Path, as in (50a), it A-marked the Goal? This would yield a "dative alternation" like this:

(i)   Bill smoofed Harry the book.   (Beneficiary A-marked)
(ii) Bill smoofed the book Harry.   (Goal A-marked)

The reason is, evidently, that a linkage of Goal to second object is not possible in English, unless it is an Identificational Goal (see (36)). Thus the only choice is to A-mark the larger Path-constituent, with the preposition in effect being lexically specified by the resulting selectional restriction.

This analysis however leaves open the possibility of there being a verb just like *give* except that it has only the ditransitive form:

(iii) Bill glibbed Harry the book.
(iv) *Bill glibbed the book to Harry.

Such verbs, the converse of the *donate* class, don't seem to exist. I don't know why.

6. Actually, the story is not quite that simple. We have unfortunately not excluded the possibility that the Theme, rather than being A-marked in the LCS, is bound to some other A-marked argument, say Patient. Combining (55) with such an LCS would result in a configuration like (i) for the Theme-constituent.

(i) [$_{Thing}$ α]$_k$

This configuration has previously been associated with bound pronouns, PRO, and reflexives (section 3.3 for *dress himself*, section 7.7 for obligatory control with *try*, section 10.1 for *belch his way out of the room*), so it cannot be ruled out in principle. Thus something like **Bill threw the ball with itself*, where *the ball* is Patient bound to Theme, and *itself* is a *with*-Theme adjunct, ought to be all right instead of repulsive. One could add to (55) a stipulation that the Theme is free (not bound), or (preferably) make this a general condition on Adjunct Fusion. I leave open the best way to state such a stipulation.

7. This form of the rule, even more than that in section 9.5, appears to be adaptable to the Bantu applicative constructions discussed by Baker (1988) (in the UTAH theory of linking) and Bresnan and Kanerva (1989) and Bresnan and Moshi (1988) (in a hierarchical theory of linking). The only difference in the syntactic part of the rule would be that the Bantu rules are sensitive to the presence of a verbal affix that marks the construction. As stressed in section 9.5, I have not yet investigated whether the similarity of this approach to that of Bresnan, Kanerva, and Moshi permits a complete translation of their analysis into the present framework.

References

Anderson, S. (1971). "On the Role of Deep Structure in Semantic Interpretation." *Foundations of Language* 6, 387–396.

Anderson, S. (1977). "Comments on the Paper by Wasow." In P. Culicover, T. Wasow, and A. Akmajian, eds., *Formal Syntax*, 361–377. Academic Press, New York.

Bach, E. (1986a). "Natural Language Metaphysics." In R. Barcan-Marcus, G. Dorn, and P. Weingartner, eds., *Logic, Methodology, and Philosophy of Science*, 573–595. North-Holland, Amsterdam.

Bach, E. (1986b). "The Algebra of Events." *Linguistics and Philosophy* 9, 5–16.

Baker, M. (1988). *Incorporation: A Theory of Grammatical Function Changing*. University of Chicago Press, Chicago. [Doctoral dissertation, 1985, MIT, Cambridge, MA]

Belletti, A., and L. Rizzi (1988). "Psych-Verbs and θ-Theory." *Natural Language and Linguistic Theory* 6, 291–352.

Berlin, B., and P. Kay (1969). *Basic Color Terms: Their Universality and Evolution*. University of California Press, Berkeley.

Biederman, I. (1987). "Recognition-by-Components: A Theory of Human Image Understanding." *Psychological Review* 94, 115–147.

Bierwisch, M. (1967). "Some Semantic Universals of German Adjectivals." *Foundations of Language* 3, 1–36.

Bierwisch, M. (1969). "On Certain Problems of Semantic Representation." *Foundations of Language* 5, 153–184.

Bolinger, D. (1965). "The Atomization of Meaning." *Language* 41, 555–573.

Bresnan, J., ed. (1982a). *The Mental Representation of Grammatical Relations*. MIT Press, Cambridge, MA.

Bresnan, J. (1982b). "The Passive in Lexical Theory." In Bresnan 1982a, 3–86.

Bresnan, J. (1982c). "Polyadicity." In Bresnan 1982a, 149–172.

Bresnan, J. (1982d). "Control and Complementation." In Bresnan 1982a, 282–390.

Bresnan, J., and J. Kanerva (1989). "Locative Inversion in Chicheŵa: A Case Study of Factorization in Grammar." *Linguistic Inquiry* 20, 1–50.

Bresnan, J., and L. Moshi (1988). "Applicatives in Kivunjo (Chaga): Implications for Argument Structure and Syntax." Manuscript, Stanford University, Stanford, CA.

Brugman, C. (1981). "Story of Over." Indiana University Linguistics Club, Bloomington, IN. [M.A. thesis, University of California, Berkeley]

Burzio, L. (1986). *Italian Syntax: A Government Binding Approach*. Reidel, Dordrecht.

Carrier, J., and J. Randall (forthcoming). *From Conceptual Structure to Syntax: Projecting from Resultatives*. Foris, Dordrecht.

Carrier-Duncan, J. (1985). "Linking of Thematic Roles in Derivational Word Formation." *Linguistic Inquiry* 16, 1–34.

Carter, R. (1976). "Some Linking Regularities." In Carter 1988, 1–92.

Carter, R. (1984). "On Movement." In Carter 1988, 231–252.

Carter, R. (1988). *On Linking: Papers by Richard Carter*, edited by B. Levin and C. Tenny. Center for Cognitive Science Lexicon Project, MIT, Cambridge, MA.

Cattell, R. (1984). *Composite Predicates in English*. Academic Press, New York.

Chierchia, G. (1988). "Structured Meanings, Thematic Roles, and Control." In G. Chierchia, B. Partee, and R. Turner, eds., *Properties, Types, and Meaning*. Vol. 2: *Semantic Issues*, 131–166. Kluwer, Dordrecht.

Chomsky, N. (1957). *Syntactic Structures*. Mouton, The Hague.

Chomsky, N. (1965). *Aspects of the Theory of Syntax*. MIT Press, Cambridge, MA.

Chomsky, N. (1970). "Remarks on Nominalization." In R. Jacobs and P. Rosenbaum, eds., *Readings in English Transformational Grammar*, 184–221. Ginn, Waltham, MA. Also in Chomsky 1972, 11–61.

Chomsky, N. (1972). *Studies on Semantics in Generative Grammar*. Mouton, The Hague.

Chomsky, N. (1981). *Lectures on Government and Binding*. Foris, Dordrecht.

Chomsky, N. (1982). *Some Concepts and Consequences of the Theory of Government and Binding*. MIT Press, Cambridge, MA.

Chomsky, N. (1986). *Knowledge of Language: Its Nature, Origin, and Use*. Praeger, New York.

Chomsky, N., and M. Halle (1968). *The Sound Pattern of English*. Harper & Row, New York.

Clark, E. V., and H. H. Clark (1979). "When Nouns Surface as Verbs." *Language* 55, 767–811.

Comrie, B. (1975). Review of Jackendoff 1972. *Linguistics* 160, 71–86.

Comrie, B. (1985). "Causative Verb Formation and Other Verb-Deriving Morphology." In T. Shopen, ed., *Language Typology and Syntactic Description*, vol. 3. Cambridge University Press, New York.

Culicover, P., and W. Wilkins (1984). *Locality and Linguistic Theory*. Academic Press, New York.

Culicover, P., and W. Wilkins (1986). "Control, PRO, and the Projection Principle." *Language* 62, 120–153.

Declerck, R. (1979). "Aspect and the Bounded/Unbounded (Telic/Atelic) Distinction." *Linguistics* 17, 761–794.

Dennett, D. C. (1987). *The Intentional Stance*. MIT Press, Cambridge, MA.

Dowty, D. (1979). *Word Meaning and Montague Grammar*. Reidel, Dordrecht.

Dowty, D. (1988). "On the Semantic Content of the Notion 'Thematic Role'." In G. Chierchia, B. Partee, and R. Turner, eds., *Properties, Types, and Meaning*: Vol. 2: *Semantic Issues*, 69–130. Kluwer, Dordrecht.

Emonds, J. (1976). *A Transformational Approach to English Syntax*. Academic Press, New York.

Falk, Y. (1985). "Semantic Representation and the Dative Alternation." Paper presented at The First Israeli Conference on Theoretical Linguistics, Tel Aviv.

Faraci, R. (1974). *Aspects of the Grammar of Infinitives and For-Phrases*. Doctoral dissertation, MIT, Cambridge, MA.

Farkas, D. (1988). "On Obligatory Control." *Linguistics and Philosophy* 11, 27–58.

Farmer, A. (1984). *Modularity in Syntax*. MIT Press, Cambridge, MA.

Fauconnier, G. (1984). *Mental Spaces: Aspects of Meaning Construction in Natural Language*. MIT Press, Cambridge, MA.

Fillmore, C. (1968). "The Case for Case." In E. Bach and R. Harms, eds., *Universals in Linguistic Theory*, 1–90. Holt, Rinehart and Winston, New York.

Fillmore, C. (1982). "Towards a Descriptive Framework for Deixis." In R. Jarvella and W. Klein, eds., *Speech, Place, and Action*, 31–52. Wiley, New York.

Fodor, J. A. (1970). "Three Reasons for Not Deriving 'Kill' from 'Cause to Die'." *Linguistic Inquiry* 1, 429–438.

Fodor, J. A. (1975). *The Language of Thought*. Harvard University Press, Cambridge, MA.

Fodor, J. A. (1980). "Methodological Solipsism Considered as a Research Strategy in Cognitive Psychology." *Behavioral and Brain Sciences* 3, 63–73.

Fodor, J. A. (1981). "The Present Status of the Innateness Controversy." In *Representations*, 257–316. MIT Press, Cambridge, MA.

Fodor, J. A. (1983). *The Modularity of Mind*. MIT Press, Cambridge, MA.

Fodor, J. A. (1987). *Psychosemantics*. MIT Press, Cambridge, MA.

Fodor, J. A., M. Garrett, E. Walker, and C. Parkes (1980). "Against Definitions." *Cognition* 8, 263–367.

Fodor, J. D., J. A. Fodor, and M. Garrett (1975). "The Psychological Unreality of Semantic Representations." *Linguistic Inquiry* 6, 515–532.

Foley, W., and R. D. Van Valin (1984). *Functional Syntax and Universal Grammar*. Cambridge University Press, Cambridge.

Frege, G. (1892). "On Sense and Reference." Reprinted in D. Davidson and G. Harman, eds., *The Logic of Grammar*. Dickenson, Encino, CA.

Gee, J., and F. Grosjean (1983). "Performance Structures: A Psycholinguistic and Linguistic Appraisal." *Cognitive Psychology* 15, 411–458.

Gergely, G., and T. Bever (1986). "Relatedness Intuitions and the Mental Representations of Causative Verbs." *Cognition* 23, 211–277.

Green, G. (1974). *Semantics and Syntactic Irregularity*. Indiana University Press, Bloomington, IN.

Grimshaw, J. (1979). "Complement Selection and the Lexicon." *Linguistic Inquiry* 10, 279–325.

Grimshaw, J. (1981). "Form, Function, and the Language Acquisition Device." In C. L. Baker and J. J. McCarthy, eds., *The Logical Problem of Language Acquisition*. MIT Press, Cambridge, MA.

Grimshaw, J. (1982). "On the Lexical Representation of Romance Reflexive Clitics." In Bresnan 1982a, 87–148.

Grimshaw, J. (1986). "Nouns, Arguments, and Adjuncts." Manuscript, Brandeis University, Waltham, MA.

Grimshaw, J. (1987). "Psych Verbs and the Structure of Argument Structure." Manuscript, Brandeis University, Waltham, MA.

Grimshaw, J. (1988). "Adjuncts and Argument Structure." Center for Cognitive Science Occasional Paper 36, MIT, Cambridge, MA.

Grimshaw, J. (1990). *Argument Structure*. MIT Press, Cambridge, MA.

Gruber, J. S. (1965). "Studies in Lexical Relations." Doctoral dissertation, MIT, Cambridge, MA. Reprinted by Indiana University Linguistics Club, Bloomington, IN. Reprinted 1976 as part of *Lexical Structures in Syntax and Semantics*. North-Holland, Amsterdam.

Herskovits, A. (1986). *Language and Spatial Cognition*. Cambridge University Press, New York.

Higginbotham, J. (1985). "On Semantics." *Linguistic Inquiry* 16, 547–594.

Hinrichs, E. (1985). "A Compositional Semantics for Aktionsarten and NP Reference in English." Doctoral dissertation, The Ohio State University, Columbus.

Hust, J., and M. Brame (1976). "Jackendoff on Interpretive Semantics" [review of Jackendoff 1972]. *Linguistic Analysis* 2, 243–277.

Jackendoff, R. (1972). *Semantic Interpretation in Generative Grammar*. MIT Press, Cambridge, MA.

Jackendoff, R. (1974). "A Deep Structure Projection Rule." *Linguistic Inquiry* 5, 481–506.

Jackendoff, R. (1975). "Morphological and Semantic Regularities in the Lexicon." *Language* 51, 639–671.

Jackendoff, R. (1976). "Toward an Explanatory Semantic Representation." *Linguistic Inquiry* 7, 89–150.

Jackendoff, R. (1977). $\bar{X}$ Syntax: A Study of Phrase Structure. MIT Press, Cambridge, MA.

Jackendoff, R. (1983). Semantics and Cognition. MIT Press, Cambridge, MA.

Jackendoff, R. (1985). "Multiple Subcategorizations and the θ-Criterion: The Case of Climb." Natural Language and Linguistic Theory 3, 271–295.

Jackendoff, R. (1986). "Distributive Location." Sophia Linguistica 20/21, 15–24.

Jackendoff, R. (1987a). Consciousness and the Computational Mind. MIT Press, Cambridge, MA.

Jackendoff, R. (1987b). "X-Bar Semantics." In Berkeley Linguistics Society: Proceedings of the Thirteenth Annual Meeting, 355–365. University of California, Berkeley.

Jackendoff, R. (1987c). "The Status of Thematic Relations in Linguistic Theory." Linguistic Inquiry 18, 369–411.

Jackendoff, R. (1989). "What Is a Concept, That a Person Can Grasp IT?" Mind and Language 4, 68–102.

Jackendoff, R. (1990). "On Larson's Account of the Double Object Construction." Linguistic Inquiry 21.

Jackendoff, R. (in press). "Babe Ruth Homered His Way into the Hearts of America." In T. Stowell and E. Wehrli, eds., Syntax and Semantics, vol. 24. Academic Press, New York.

Jackendoff, R. (in preparation). "Parts and Boundaries."

Kac, M. (1975). Review of Jackendoff 1972. Language Sciences 36, 23–31.

Kaplan, R., and J. Bresnan (1982). "Lexical-Functional Grammar: A Formal System for Grammatical Representation." In Bresnan 1982a, 173–281.

Katz, J. (1966). The Philosophy of Language. Harper & Row, New York.

Katz, J. (1967). "Recent Issues in Semantic Theory." Foundations of Language 3, 124–194.

Katz, J. (1972). Semantic Theory. Harper & Row, New York.

Katz, J. (1981). Language and Other Abstract Objects. Rowman and Littlefield, Totowa, NJ.

Katz, J., and J. A. Fodor (1963). "The Structure of a Semantic Theory." Language 39, 170–210.

Katz, J., and P. Postal (1964). An Integrated Theory of Linguistic Descriptions. MIT Press, Cambridge, MA.

Keyser, S. J., and T. Roeper (1984). "On the Middle and Ergative Constructions in English." Linguistic Inquiry 15, 381–416.

Klima, E. S. (1964). "Negation in English." In J. A. Fodor and J. Katz, eds., The Structure of Language, 246–323. Prentice-Hall, Englewood Cliffs, NJ.

Lakoff, G. (1970). Irregularity in Syntax. Holt, Rinehart and Winston, New York.

Lakoff, G. (1971). "On Generative Semantics." In Steinberg and Jakobovits 1971, 232–296.

Lakoff, G. (1987). Women, Fire, and Dangerous Things. University of Chicago Press, Chicago.

Lakoff, G., and M. Johnson (1980). Metaphors We Live By. University of Chicago Press, Chicago.

Landau, B., and L. Gleitman (1985). Language and Experience: Evidence from the Blind Child. Harvard University Press, Cambridge, MA.

Langacker, R. (1986). Foundations of Cognitive Grammar, Vol. 1. Stanford University Press, Stanford, CA.

Larson, R. (1988). "On the Double Object Construction." Linguistic Inquiry 19, 335–392.

Lees, R. B. (1960). The Grammar of English Nominalizations. Mouton, The Hague.

Lerdahl, F., and R. Jackendoff (1983). A Generative Theory of Tonal Music. MIT Press, Cambridge, MA.

Levin, B., and T. Rapoport (1988). "Lexical Subordination." In Papers from the Twenty-fourth Regional Meeting of the Chicago Linguistics Society, 275–289. Department of Linguistics. University of Chicago, Chicago.

Levin, B., and M. Rappaport (1986). "The Formation of Adjectival Passives." Linguistic Inquiry 17, 623–661.

Levin, B., and M. Rappaport (1989). "An Approach to Unaccusative Mismatches." In *Proceedings of the Nineteenth Annual Meeting of the North-Eastern Linguistic Society*. GLSA, University of Massachusetts, Amherst.

Lewis, D. (1972). "General Semantics." In D. Davidson and G. Harman, eds., *Semantics of Natural Language*, 169–218. Reidel, Dordrecht.

Link, G. (1983). "The Logical Analysis of Plurals and Mass Terms: A Lattice-Theoretic Approach." In R. Bauerle, C. Schwarze, and A. von Stechow, eds., *Meaning, Use, and Interpretation of Language*, 302–323. Walter de Gruyter, Berlin.

McCawley, J. D. (1968a). "Lexical Insertion in a Transformational Grammar without Deep Structure." In B. Darden, C.-J. N. Bailey, and A. Davison, eds., *Papers from the Fourth Regional Meeting of the Chicago Linguistic Society*. Department of Linguistics, University of Chicago, Chicago.

McCawley, J. D. (1968b). "The Role of Semantics in a Grammar." In E. Bach and R. Harms, eds., *Universals in Linguistic Theory*, 125–170. Holt, Rinehart and Winston, New York.

McCawley, J. D. (1968c). "Concerning the Base Component of a Transformational Grammar." *Foundations of Language* 4, 243–269.

McCawley, J. D. (1978). "Conversational Implicature and the Lexicon." In P. Cole, ed., *Syntax and Semantics*, vol. 9, 245–259. Academic Press, New York.

McCawley, J. D. (1981). "Notes on the English Present Perfect." *Australian Journal of Linguistics* 1, 81–90.

McCawley, J. D. (1988). *In, Into, and Enter*. Manuscript, University of Chicago, Chicago.

Macnamara, J. (1982). *Names for Things*. MIT Press, Cambridge, MA.

Marantz, A. (1984). *On the Nature of Grammatical Relations*. MIT Press, Cambridge, MA.

Marr, D. (1982). *Vision*. W. H. Freeman, San Francisco.

Marr, D., and L. Vaina (1982). "Representation and Recognition of the Movements of Shapes." *Proceedings of the Royal Society of London B* 214, 501–524.

Michotte, A. (1954). *La perception de la causalité*. 2nd ed. Publications Universitaires de Louvain, Louvain.

Miller, G., and P. Johnson-Laird (1976). *Language and Perception*. Harvard University Press, Cambridge, MA.

Mourelatos, A. P. D. (1981). "Events, Processes, and States." In P. J. Tedeschi and A. Zaenen, eds., *Syntax and Semantics*, vol. 14, 191–212. Academic Press, New York.

Napoli, D. J. (1988a). Review Article on Burzio 1986. *Language* 64, 130–142.

Napoli, D. J. (1988b). "Subjects and External Arguments: Clauses and Non-Clauses." *Linguistics and Philosophy* 11, 323–354.

Napoli, D. J. (1989). *Predication Theory: A Case Study for Indexing Theory*. Cambridge University Press, New York.

Nunberg, G. (1979). "The Nonuniqueness of Semantic Solutions: Polysemy." *Linguistics and Philosophy* 3, 143–184.

Oehrle, R. (1975). "The Grammatical Status of the English Dative Alternation." Doctoral dissertation, MIT, Cambridge, MA.

Oehrle, R. (forthcoming). *The English Dative Constructions: Form and Interpretation*. Reidel, Dordrecht.

Ostler, N. (1979). "Case Linking: A Theory of Case and Verb Diathesis Applied to Classical Sanskrit." Doctoral dissertation, MIT, Cambridge, MA.

Perlmutter, D. (1978). "Impersonal Passives and the Unaccusative Hypothesis." In *Proceedings of the Fourth Annual Meeting of the Berkeley Linguistics Society*. University of California, Berkeley.

Perlmutter, D., and P. Postal (1984). "The 1-Advancement Exclusiveness Law." In D. Perlmutter and C. Rosen, eds., *Studies in Relational Grammar 2*, 81–125. University of Chicago Press, Chicago.

Pesetsky, D. (forthcoming). "Experiencer Verbs, Lexical Decomposition, and Universal Alignment."

Peterson, P. (1985). "Causation, Agency, and Natural Actions." In Chicago Linguistic Society, *Proceedings of 21st Regional Meeting and Parasession on Causatives and Agentivity*. Department of Linguistics, University of Chicago, Chicago.

Piaget, J. (1970). *Genetic Epistemology*. Columbia University Press, New York.

Pinker, S. (1984). *Language Learnability and Language Development*. Harvard University Press, Cambridge, MA.

Pinker, S. (1989). *Learnability and Cognition: The Acquisition of Argument Structure*. MIT Press, Cambridge, MA.

Platzack, C. (1979). *The Semantic Interpretation of Aspect and Aktionsarten*. Foris, Dordrecht.

Postal, P. (1966a). "On So-Called 'Pronouns' in English." In F. Dinneen, ed., *19th Monograph on Languages and Linguistics*. Georgetown University Press, Washington, DC. Also in Reibel and Schane 1969, 201–224.

Postal, P. (1966b). Review Article of Martinet, *Elements of General Linguistics*. *Foundations of Language* 2, 151–186.

Postal, P. (1970). "On the Surface Verb 'Remind'." *Linguistic Inquiry* 1, 37–120.

Postal, P. (1971). *Crossover Phenomena*. Holt, Rinehart and Winston, New York.

Postal, P., and G. K. Pullum (1988). "Expletive Noun Phrases in Subcategorized Positions." *Linguistic Inquiry* 19, 635–670.

Rappaport, M. (1983). "On the Nature of Derived Nominals." In L. Levin, M. Rappaport, and A. Zaenen, eds., *Papers in Lexical-Functional Grammar*, 113–142. Indiana University Linguistics Club, Bloomington, IN.

Rappaport, M., and B. Levin (1985). "The Locative Alternation: A Case Study in Lexical Analysis." Manuscript, Center for Cognitive Science, MIT, Cambridge, MA.

Rappaport, M., and B. Levin (1988). "What to Do with Theta-Roles." In Wilkins 1988a, 7–36.

Rappaport, M., B. Levin, and M. Laughren (1988). "Levels of Lexical Representation." Lexicon Project Working Papers 20, Center for Cognitive Science, MIT, Cambridge, MA.

Reibel, D., and S. Schane, eds. (1969). *Modern Studies in English*. Prentice-Hall, Englewood Cliffs, NJ.

Rosch, E. (1978). "Principles of Categorization." In E. Rosch and B. Lloyd, eds., *Cognition and Categorization*, 27–48. L. Erlbaum Associates, Hillsdale, NJ.

Rosen, C. (1984). "The Interface between Semantic Roles and Initial Grammatical Relations." In D. Perlmutter and C. Rosen, eds., *Studies in Relational Grammar 2*, 38–77. University of Chicago Press, Chicago.

Rosen, S. (1989). "Argument Structure and Complex Predicates." Doctoral dissertation, Brandeis University, Waltham, MA.

Rosenbaum, P. (1967). *The Grammar of English Predicate Complement Constructions*. MIT Press, Cambridge, MA.

Rosenberg, M. S. (1975). "Generative vs. Interpretive Semantics" (Review of Jackendoff 1972). *Foundations of Language* 12, 561–582.

Ross, J. R. (1967). "Constraints on Variables in Syntax." Doctoral dissertation, MIT, Cambridge, MA.

Ross, J. R. (1969). "Adjectives as Noun Phrases." In Reibel and Schane 1969, 352–360.

Rothstein, S. (1983). "The Syntactic Forms of Predication." Doctoral dissertation, MIT, Cambridge, MA.

Růžička, R. (1983). "Remarks on Control." *Linguistic Inquiry* 14, 309–324.

Sato, H. (1987). "Resultative Attributes and GB Principles." *English Linguistics* 4, 91–106.

Schachter, P. (1976). "A Nontransformational Account of Gerundive Nominals in English." *Linguistic Inquiry* 7, 205–241.

Schank, R. (1973). "Identification of Conceptualizations Underlying Natural Language." In R. Schank and K. Colby, eds., *Computer Models of Thought and Language*, 187–248. W. H. Freeman, San Francisco.

Selkirk, E. (1982). *The Syntax of Words*. MIT Press, Cambridge, MA.

Selkirk, E. (1984). *Phonology and Syntax: The Relation between Sound and Structure*. MIT Press, Cambridge, MA.

Shibatani, M. (1976). "The Grammar of Causative Constructions: A Conspectus." In M. Shibatani, ed., *Syntax and Semantics*, vol. 6. Academic Press, New York.

Shieber, S. (1986). *An Introduction to Unification-Based Approaches to Grammar*. Center for the Study of Language and Information, Stanford University, Stanford, CA.

Simpson, J. (1983). "Resultatives." In L. Levin, M. Rappaport, and A. Zaenen, eds., *Papers in Lexical-Functional Grammar*, 143–157. Indiana University Linguistics Club, Bloomington, IN.

Steinberg, D., and L. Jakobovits, eds. (1971). *Semantics: An Interdisciplinary Reader*. Cambridge University Press, New York.

Stowell, T. (1981). "Origins of Phrase Structure." Doctoral dissertation, MIT, Cambridge, MA.

Talmy, L. (1978). "The Relation of Grammar to Cognition—A Synopsis." In D. Waltz, ed., *Theoretical Issues in Natural Language Processing 2*. Association for Computing Machinery, New York.

Talmy, L. (1980). "Lexicalization Patterns: Semantic Structure in Lexical Forms." In T. Shopen et al., eds., *Language Typology and Syntactic Description*, vol. 3. Cambridge University Press, New York.

Talmy, L. (1983). "How Language Structures Space." In H. Pick and L. Acredolo, eds., *Spatial Orientation: Theory, Research, and Application*. Plenum, New York.

Talmy, L. (1985). "Force Dynamics in Language and Thought." In *Papers from the Twenty-first Regional Meeting of the Chicago Linguistic Society*. Department of Linguistics, University of Chicago, Chicago. IL Also in *Cognitive Science* 12, 49–100 (1988).

Tenny, C. (1987). "Grammaticalizing Aspect and Affectedness." Doctoral dissertation, MIT, Cambridge, MA.

Van Valin, R. D. (1987). "The Unaccusative Hypothesis vs. Lexical Semantics: Syntactic vs. Semantic Approaches to Verb Classification." In *Proceedings of the Seventeenth Annual Meeting of the North East Linguistic Society*. GLSA, University of Massachusetts, Amherst.

Vendler, Z. (1957). "Verbs and Times." *Philosophical Review* 56, 143–160. Reprinted in Z. Vendler (1967). *Linguistics in Philosophy*, 97–121. Cornell University Press, Ithaca, NY.

Verkuyl, H. (1972). *On the Compositional Nature of the Aspects*. Reidel, Dordrecht.

Verkuyl, H. (1989). "Aspectual Classes and Aspectual Composition." *Linguistics and Philosophy* 12, 39–94.

Weinreich, U. (1966). "Explorations in Semantic Theory." In T. Sebeok, ed., *Current Trends in Linguistics*, vol. 3. Mouton, The Hague. Reprinted in U. Weinreich (1980). *On Semantics*, 99–201. University of Pennsylvania Press, Philadelphia, PA.

Wertheimer, M. (1923). "Laws of Organization in Perceptual Forms." In W. D. Ellis, ed. (1938). *A Source Book of Gestalt Psychology*, 71–88. Routledge & Kegan Paul, London.

Wilkins, W., ed. (1988a). *Syntax and Semantics*, vol. 21. Academic Press, New York.

Wilkins, W. (1988b). "Thematic Structure and Reflexivization." In Wilkins 1988a, 191–214.

Williams, E. (1980). "Predication." *Linguistic Inquiry* 11, 203–238.

Williams, E. (1983). "Against Small Clauses." *Linguistic Inquiry* 14, 287–308.

Williams, E. (1984). "Grammatical Relations." *Linguistic Inquiry* 15, 639–674.

Williams, E. (1985). "PRO and Subject of NP." *Natural Language and Linguistic Theory* 3, 297–315.

Williams, E. (1987). "Implicit Arguments, the Binding Theory, and Control." *Natural Language and Linguistic Theory* 5, 151–180.

Wittgenstein, L. (1953). *Philosophical Investigations*. Basil Blackwell, Oxford.

Yamada, Y. (1987). "Two Types of Resultative Construction." *English Linguistics* 4, 73–90.

Yoneyama, M. (1986). "Motion Verbs in Conceptual Semantics." *Bulletin of the Faculty of Humanities* No. 22, 1–15. Seikei University, Tokyo.

Zaenen, A. (1988). "Unaccusative Verbs in Dutch and the Syntax-Semantics Interface." CSLI Report 123, CSLI, Stanford University, Stanford, CA.

Index of Words Discussed

Pages on which an LCS is proposed are noted in boldface.

Index